A Cultural History of Finance

The world of finance is again undergoing crisis and transformation. This book provides a new perspective on finance through the prism of popular and formal culture and examines fascination and repulsion toward money, the role of governments and individuals in financial crises and how the crisis of 2008, like others since 1720, repeat the same patterns of enthusiasm, greed, culpability, revulsion, reform and recovery.

A Cultural History of Finance explores the political and socio-economic factors which determine fallibility and resilience in financial cultures, periods of crisis, transition and recovery based on cyclical rather than linear progression. Examining the roots of financial capitalism, in Europe and the United States and its corollary development in Asia, Russia and emerging markets proves that cultural and psychosocial reactions to financial success, endeavor and calamity transcend specific periods or events. The book allows the reader to discover parallel and intersecting reactions, controversies and resolutions in the cultural history of financial markets and institutions. It explains why capitalism is still alive and dynamic, what factors can and cannot assure its survival and recovery, as well providing a new interpretation on the complex 25-year trajectory toward deregulation, privatization and trading culture which incited and accelerated the crisis of 2008.

Covering topics such as the historical and cultural antecedents of financial panics and bank crises and the public–private financial sector relationship, this book will be of particular interest to higher level postgraduate students, and finance specialists including bankers, traders, and finance executives.

Irene Finel-Honigman is Adjunct Professor of International Affairs at the School of International and Public Affairs, Columbia University, USA.

Routledge explorations in economic history
Edited by Lars Magnusson
Uppsala University, Sweden

A Cultural History of Finance

Irene Finel-Honigman

LONDON AND NEW YORK

First published 2010
by Routledge
2 Park Square, Milton Park, Abingdon, Oxon OX14 4RN

Simultaneously published in the USA and Canada
by Routledge
711 Third Avenue, New York, NY 10017

Routledge is an imprint of the Taylor & Francis Group, an informa business

First issued in paperback 2013

© 2010 Irene Finel-Honigman

Typeset in Times by Wearset Ltd, Boldon, Tyne and Wear

British Library Cataloguing in Publication Data
A catalogue record for this book is available from the British Library

Library of Congress Cataloging in Publication Data
Finel-Honigman, Irene.
A cultural history of finance/Irene Finel-Honigman.
p. cm.
Includes bibliographical references and index.
ISBN 978-0-203-86661-0 (eb) – ISBN 978-0-415-77102-3 (hb) 1.
Finance–History. 2. Capitalism–History. I. Title.

HG171.F57 2009
332.09–dc22

2009018030

ISBN13: 978-0-415-77102-3 (hbk)
ISBN13: 978-0-415-74517-8 (pbk)
ISBN13: 978-0-203-86661-0 (ebk)

Contents

Preface

The day the music died.

(Don MacLean, American Pie, 1971)

We must change the culture of greed.
(President Obama, Speech, White House, March 18, 2009)

Culture is for yoghurt.

(Sandy Weill, former CEO Citibank, 2004)

The second Gilded Age of American capitalism came to a brutal and abrupt end on September 15, 2008. The day that Lehman Brothers failed, followed in rapid succession by the need for the United States (US) government to re-nationalize the largest mortgage lenders, Freddie Mac and Fannie Mae, and to extend the first of many lifeline bridge loans to AIG, the largest global insurer, will go down in history as the new Black Monday. The New York Stock market plunged over 900 points by mid-week, a loss overall of almost 9 percent in value, only to rebound dramatically within two days, regaining almost 800 points by September 19, on the news that the Treasury, the Federal Reserve and Congress would prepare a Resolution Trust Corporation solution, entitled TARP, the Troubled Asset Relief Program. This program would essentially strip primarily non performing mortgage loans off the balance sheets of banks and Freddie–Fannie. This good bank–bad bank style solution, established in 1989 in the aftermath of the catastrophic losses incurred by the Savings and Loans in the mid-1980s, was subsequently adapted for the Swedish banking sector in 1991 to 1992, and the EU Commission-mandated restructuring of Crédit Lyonnais, the largest state owned corporate French bank, after its bailout in 1995. Within a few months, and under the administration of President Obama, TARP morphed into TALF, Term Asset-Backed Securities Loan Facility, part of the Emergency Economic Stabilization Act of 2008. By 2009, the original amount of US$700 billion in government aid had increased to US$1.5 trillion. The dramatic loss of share value at Citibank, the world's largest bank by market capitalization, required, in November 2008, a US$20 billion rescue package, and an additional US$306 billion in asset guarantees. It was followed by seemingly endless revelations:

toxic assets on the balance sheets of Bank of America and Merrill Lynch; the fraud in excess of US$60 billion by fund manager, Bernard Madoff; similar, lesser frauds and schemes in India and the Bahamas; and abuses in compensation, disclosure, and the use of government funds in AIG. All served to create a picture of unmitigated corruption and confusion in global financial markets.

The entire financial system of retail, corporate and investment banks, private equity and hedge funds, insurance and mortgage firms, heavily invested in esoteric derivative instruments and operations based on the assumption of permanently rising property valuations, apparently turned out to be a humungous, global version of the "Emperor's New Clothes." Within less than a year, it became evident that the entire regulatory system in the US and Europe would require total restructuring and that the government–financial sector relationship would have to be reformulated, a process which had not been substantively addressed since the 1930s.

In a fully interdependent global economy, the disarray and piecemeal solutions in the United States worsened a worldwide crisis of confidence, forecasting scenarios of 1929 redux. In the fall of 2008 and winter of 2008–2009, the "meltdown" in Iceland, the need for International Monetary Fund (IMF) intervention in Hungary, the dramatic collapse of the Irish economy, the need for unprecedented government intervention in the United Kingdom, in an attempt to salvage some of the world's oldest financial institutions, revealed the extent to which Europe, both European Union (EU) and non-EU members, and Russia, were impacted, leading into a worldwide recession and prognosis of negative growth for 2009–2010. A sharp reduction in investment and a near freeze on consumer spending in the United States and Europe provoked rapid downturns in wealthy export economies in Asia and Latin America, and a total breakdown in emerging markets across the EU. The "financial supermarket" megabank era ended as US and EU banks declared that they would return to core business: retail, wholesale, and advisory functions, and dramatically reduce expansion and investment services.

However long and deep this global recession lasts, it is clear that, once again, an era of unbridled US capitalism has come to an end, and a new group of scapegoats, heroes and villains will be examined, deconstructed and offered up for analysis. Responding with outrage and fury at compensation packages, perceived misuses of government aid and lack of disclosure, the public, politicians and pundits rail against Wall Street and its abuse of Main Street, as they did in the crises of 1873, 1907, 1929, 1982, 1987 and 2002. However, in 2008, the real danger lurks in the depth of the damage across a broader swath of the population, as it affects home owners, lenders, borrowers and small business owners across the economic spectrum. Evoking the Great Depression is the theme of the day, although the analogy is structurally flawed, since checking, savings and pension accounts are fully protected, unemployment is peaking at 10 percent versus 20 to 30 percent in 1932, and credit, despite tightening and restrictions, remains available.

In this age of global markets, there is fear of global contagion. The immediate downturn in emerging markets, especially in the former East Central European countries of the EU, showed the fragility of their economic progress, and the risk of political repercussions. However it is important to recall that long before tech-nology, when the market went through a panic in New York, there were reper-cussions in London, Paris and later Berlin and Moscow since the mid-nineteenth century. As in other crises, and especially in 1987, the responsibility was placed on the United States and its philosophy of "cowboy capitalism," based on the twin culprits of reckless speculation and greed. Immediately the French, British and German press began accusing the United States of having dumped "toxic waste" on its unwitting European counterparts. In truth, since 2006 in, a highly integrated and global financial environment, European banks decided in varying degrees to enter the same markets and trade the same instruments, allowing an overvalued property market and the attractiveness of new high yield, high risk instruments to affect their inherent sense of caution and supervision. A small prudent nation, Iceland, having entered the global casino by mid-October, had to declare the bankruptcy of its three state banks, and the depletion of its pension and savings accounts, urgently calling for an IMF rescue.

Although it became clear by October 1, 2008, that European banks had suffered far greater losses than anticipated or reported, and that European governments and treasuries, led by Chancellor Brown and President Sarkozy, had to rapidly and cohesively intervene with guarantees of liabilities, increased deposit insurance, and major capital injections, the crisis is blamed on Anglo-American financial culture.

Belief in the market and in the basic ethos of the free hand, laissez faire philo-sophy of the market will be seriously affected, and even eroded in the short-term. As in the 1973 oil crisis, and the major financial crisis of 1987, initially the role of government will not only be expanded but welcomed. The need to turn to the US government as lender of last resort, and as the caretaker of a delinquent and run away market, will have a deeper psychological impact than the immediate financial crisis. As in 1929, and in the rescue package of the New Deal, announced in Roosevelt's inaugural fireside chat of March 1933, a massive gov-ernment rescue is critical in restoring confidence. However, this throws into question the entire premise of American capitalism as antithetical to large scale government intervention, control and regulation.

The immediate response will be a re-evaluation of values, accusations of greed and fraud, calls for changes in the compensation of wealthy chief execu-tive officers and boards, versus the small shareholder or employee who have become the real victims. A populist message will again resound, as it has since the 1850s in every Wall Street versus Main Street scenario. In each financial crisis there is an immediate populist response of outrage at the excesses of the rich. The attacks take on apocalyptic proportions from so called "Main Street," often aggravated by the indifference, ignorance or venality of politicians. Yet, within a few years the public becomes more complacent and accepting as markets recover, and new shiny bright, equally tenuous and equally hazardous instruments and transactions appear.

Once calm returns and politicians, the media and academics take stock of this changed environment, it will be necessary to inform the public that effective capit-alism, as Adam Smith already understood in 1776, requires effective government to offer basic protections. Washington and Wall Street cannot function as adversaries, as well as this may play in political rhetoric. They must strike a balance of interests, tactics and philosophy.

The major challenge will be in the overhaul of the regulatory agencies and rules, largely in place since the New Deal. They will have to be changed to meet the needs of a far more diffuse and diverse group of financial institutions, including investment banks and private equity firms, and bring some order to the state regulated insurance sector. The public will demand stricter oversight and greater transparency in the types of operations, instruments, risk management, and compensation structures of financial firms. However, in this process there is the concern that in the name of risk aversion overregulation, stifling bureaucracy and weak cooperation between the financial marketplace and regulatory bodies will instill a fear of innovation. As Charles Kindleberger and John K. Galbraith in their analysis of the Great Crash so cogently demonstrated, the basics of overvaluation, over-optimism in an instrument or asset, from tulips to junk bonds to securitized mortgage instruments, will always recur. There is the element of greed but also the element of temptation and hope as individuals allow themselves to be persuaded that get rich schemes in Florida swamps and stock deals on Wall Street in 1927–1929, oil and gas concessions in 1849 or 1982, dotcom deals on virtual products in 2000, or mortgage and real estate speculation in 2006 would be the "real deal."

As technology mechanized trading operations, since 2000, the financial industry has prided itself on its increased efficiency and profitability in an era of "24/7" markets, instantaneous communication and post space-time technology. However, in the process, thought, reflection, analysis, and reasoned response have disappeared. Each new set of esoteric instruments, derivatives and subprime mortgage structured investment vehicles (SIVS) in the crisis of 2008, understood by few, become the domain of those chosen few.

Will the scope and depth of this crisis and the antagonism against speculative activity effect real change in a culture of profit and "bottom line' in place since the mid-1980s? The question of how to assure that educated, rather than wild emotional bets are placed, that rules in place actually assess the true value of assets and make this information available, that investors can access credit, but will also have to be held accountable for their decisions, and how to guarantee that the average citizen can continue to have absolute faith in the workings of a market economy, will be among the challenges faced by central banks and governments across the world.

Americans are optimists and gamblers at heart. Historically and psychologically far more tolerant of financial failure, bankruptcy or default, Americans are essentially cheerful winners and good losers, willing to start again, and capable of quickly regaining dynamic initiative after any crisis. Charles Dickens often described American capitalism as coarse and brutal, yet like Tocqueville a generation before, appreciated the strength and vitality of American initiative and its ability to rebound. In *American Notes* in 1842 he expressed this admiration for "love of smart dealing which gilds over many a swindle and gross breach of trust; many a defalcation, public and private and enables many a knave to hold his head up with the best" (Dickens 1842: 242). American capitalism and the culture of profit and money is unique because it is fundamentally devoid of moral content, self perpetuating, renewable, deemed essential rather than existential in the collective psyche.

We are told that time heals all loss, yet the one element missing in this financial crisis is time. Over a few months the world financial markets went from shock to seizure to near death with no respite. Markets can collapse in a week but require months and years to recover. Since the crises of 1873, 1893, 1907, 1929, 1987, 2002 and 2008, the sums risked and lost have increased but the basic causes remain the same. Greed, competitive fervor, and new, poorly understood instruments flourish in an environment which encourages, stimulates and hugely rewards ever greater risk. In each case the casino analogy reappears, but as both the house and the losses get bigger, the repercussions expand from the national to the regional to the global level.

In 1929 it took almost two years for Europe to flail, in 1987 it took over two days for Tokyo to become infected. On the morning of September 18, 2008, in the age of instantaneous communication, the drop in the New York Stock Exchange, provoked by the US$85 billion AIG bridge loan from the Federal on September 17, provoked panic in Tokyo.

Politicians in each and every case attack Wall Street as having betrayed Main Street; the paradigm is politically convenient, simplistic and effective. Shareholders feel abandoned and at a loss for clear, precise explanations, so a scapegoat must be found. However, in each crisis, all the way back to the Mississippi Bubble, there has to be a counterparty: the public, or segments of the public, willing and eager to participate, to buy the shares, to sign the mortgage, to invest in junk bonds, to buy into dotcom nonexistent assets: the perennial "sucker" or perennial optimist, hoping that this time there will be a free lunch or El Dorado. In 2008, the public at large may not have been responsible, but a large swathe of financial specialists, traders, market makers, auditors, accountants, lawyers, and managers knew of the risks and of the vulnerability of their assets and institutions.

A semi-hysterical press added to the carnage by allowing endless rumors to swirl in cyberspace, as damaging and confusing as the rumors in the Rue de Quincampoix in 1720, as valets, merchants and dukes vied to buy overpriced shares in the John Law's Mississippi scheme.

The real challenge will be how quickly, how deeply, and how efficiently systems, in place since the Great Depression, can be updated, integrating insurance, investment, private equity, and even the nefarious hedge funds into a comprehensive regulatory framework. A huge amount of wealth has been generated, unevenly distributed, with little or no supervision, oversight, disclosure requirements or actual equivalence between performance and profit.

As in each previous crisis, is capitalism to blame, is the market to blame, or are specific individuals to blame for having misled, over extended, defrauded or merely taken advantage of collusion between lax government supervision, enthusiastic clients, customers and shareholders and overly-ambitious managers, traders and financial institutions?

The second Gilded Age may be over, but as Leonard Silk wrote in the *New York Times* on the literary and cultural response to the Crash of 1987, "But first will come the works of repentance and rediscovery of other values. And eventually the works of rising spirit and capital. For unless capitalism is dead, which it isn't, Wall Street and the City will rise again" (Silk 1988).

It is on this note that this book begins, as it will try to explore the historical, psychological and political determinants which affect and direct financial culture.

Acknowledgments

This book project benefited from a seed grant from the Institute for Social and Economic Research and Policy (ISERP) at Columbia University.

I would like to pay homage to Charles Kindleberger who inspired this book, and to Sidney Zion who inspired me to write it.

Among the many friends and colleagues at Columbia University who provided invaluable advice and encouragement I am especially grateful to Volker Berghahn who helped initiate this project and offered steadfast support and to Hans Decker, Tanya Domi, Pierre Force, Joan Helpern, Rebecca Kobrin, Katherine Morgan, Seamus O'Cleireacain, Richard Robb, Glenda Rosenthal, Vanessa Scherer, Fernando Sotelino and Fritz Stern.

For providing economic and banking insights, sharing their expertise and giving me the opportunity to speak on these topics at many conferences and seminars, my sincere appreciation to Mordechai Kreinin, Bernard Shull, Alfred Eckes, Hugo Kaufmann, Serge Bellanger and Francoise Soares- Kemp.

For comments, information and interest in this project I would like to thank David Askren, Jon Benjamin, Bernard Brown, Walter Brenner, Marc Chandler, Luc de Clapiers, Theresa Collins, Francois Delattre, Niall Ferguson, Maria Findrik, Raymond Finel, Gerhard Fink, Jean-Louis Galliot, Charles Gasparino, Edward Giacomelli, Peter Gray, Gerard Grunberg, John Gutfreund, John Heimann, Beverly Schreiber Jacoby, David Jestaz, Alain Kaspereit, Alfred Kingon, Christopher Kobrak, Roger Kubarych, Isabelle Lescent-Giles, Philippe Mathe, Frederic Mortimer, Elizabeth Platt, Robert Paxton, John Quinn, Roy Smith, Georges Ugeux, Pili Verzariu and Norbert Walter.

My great appreciation to Geraldine McAllister at Columbia University, whose knowledge and skill proved invaluable in formatting and editing the manuscript.

I am deeply grateful to Robert Langham, my editor at Routledge for his help, encouragement and patience and to my superb copy-editor Philippa Mulberry who helped transform the manuscript into the book.

To Steven and Ana, thank you as always for everything.

Introduction

Living in a material world, And I am a material girl.
(Material Girl, Madonna, 1985)

The moral is: money, money, money, it pays to pray: Jupiter is money in the bank.
(Satyricon)

For money represents pure interaction in its purest form ... it is an individual thing whose essential significance is to reach beyond individualities.
(Simmel 1978: 129)

From pre-capitalist societies to modern financial centers, psycho-historical determinants have influenced economic evolution, destruction and renewal in Europe, Russia and the Americas. As new economic powers and new political financial paradigms emerge in Asia, the progression and regression of financial activity, agents, instruments and centers continue to be guided by political, societal and cultural forces.

This work will focus on Europe and subsequently on the United States as "the breeding ground" of modern world financial history, with references to cultural and commercial exchanges between former Ottoman, Asian, and Western nations and empires. Despite the sophistication of new quantitative methods and instruments, and the transformational impact of technology, financial decision makers and institutions are defined by what Niall Ferguson called the "cash nexus," the forces at work in the interstices of power and money. Moving beyond the confines of economic history and quantitative analysis, while respecting the rigors of the discipline, this study will follow what Fernand Braudel called "the elusive set of principles which define material life or civilization."

By interpreting structures and mentalities which in turn reflect and explain not the how but the why of economic phenomenology, the "tropisms" of a collective consciousness, it will examine the origins and psychology of financial behavior, institutional development and societal and political responses. Georg Simmel, Fernand Braudel, Jacques LeGoff, Pierre Vilar, Jean Bouvier, Alain Plessis, Charles Kindleberger, David Landes, Niall Fergusson, and Harold

James, among others, defined modern capitalism as an evolutionary process of gradual reconfiguration, described by Simmel as the transition from Naturalwirtschaft to Weltwirtschaft. But in his seminal work, "The Philosophy of Money" Simmel also specified that the most neutral of objects elicits the most conflicted and charged emotional responses. In *La dynamique du capitalisme* (1985), Braudel described long-term equilibrium and disequilibrium, simultaneously propelling and propelled by the development of systems of value (currencies) and geo-financial urban centers, as economic evolution is accompanied by geographic shifts: "in about 1590 the center of gravity of Europe swung over to the Protestant north" (Braudel 1982: 569).

Although the public, press, media, graduate and business school programs are fascinated by finance, financial instruments, operations and crisis, financial history and the culture of finance are too often relegated to an introductory chapter in a finance textbook or an elective course deemed "soft science." There are excellent new studies in economic and business history (Mirati, Fear, Galambos), but few works specifically devoted to the cultural dimension of contemporary finance, banking and investment: the interplay between history, economics and culture. For Wai Chee Dimock, cultural historian, cultural history involves appropriation of literary and historical genres which transcend specific historical periods, beyond an interdisciplinary approach, while respecting the theoretical definitions of each discipline or science. In her Hegelian analysis, literary studies take on empirical dimensions,

> Not segregated by periods of time or by nations, the fields of knowledge would feature long backgrounds as well as minute evidence, with texts both ancient and modern and groupings both large and small, understood to be prenational in their evolutionary past and transnational in their geographic spread.
>
> (Dimock 2007: 1377)

Examining the role of bankers in nineteenth-century France involves looking at Balzac, Flaubert, Zola, Maupassant, Valles' business bankers anti-heroes, Daumier's caricatures, Prudhon's utopist essays, as well as the economic and political framework which inspired these characters and images. Novels in eighteenth- and nineteenth-century France and England are topologies of economic norms and mores. Literature and art reflect, transform, distort and recreate political, economic and social phenomenon. Attitudes toward borrowing, lending, profit, investment, speculation, and acquired versus inherited wealth reveal atavistic responses which underscore how governments and individuals view their financial institutions and systems.

Contemporary cultural theorists such as Shell, Taylor, Dimock, and Apter integrate language theory and economic theory, as language becomes a medium of exchange. Karl Marx's daughter, Eleanor Marx's translation of *Madame Bovary* integrated "a glimpse of a language of labor released from a transcendental, capitalist logic of equivalence, exchange, project and credit" (Apter

2007); Marc Shell in *Money, Language and Thought* (1982), attributes to Shylock and Antonio use of biblical imagery as the meta text of economic exchange.

Does culture – defined as art, literature, philosophy – influence economic development, or does economic activity – momentum, market forces, cross-border trade, social mobility, commerce, and finance – influence culture? Is there a point of convergence based on a constant point–counterpoint, a perpetual attraction–repulsion between culture and finance, a constructive tension, which Landes (2003) describes as specific social, geographic, and psycho-historical determinants, which provide certain societies with the necessary conditions to develop a flourishing economic and financial culture? When Manet painted the train station, Verlaine and Hugo wrote about industry and railroads, and Tolstoy sent Ana Karenina to her death under the train; when multimedia, technology, and commercial symbols become the basis of art, Warhol's soup cans to Basquiat's graffiti to Jeff Koons and Damien Hirst's transformational objects sold at exorbitant prices in an art market rather than an art world; has a new symbiosis been attained, are they exalting and validating economic progress, or has economic progress inspired them to translate industry, money and commerce into art?

As guilt and redemption are always inherent in the relationship between money and society, there is an endless need in Western culture to justify economic activity in the name of a higher goal, in the name of the state, in the name of the individual's right to a better future. The relationship of power to money and money to power dominates the development of modern society, whether in its negation under Marxism, in its transcendence under the aegis of the Church, or in its functionality in the name of the state. Enrichment, profit, and gain are acceptable only within the context of specific moral strictures. Since Aristotle defined the essential character of the state as moral rather than material, and happiness as having an intellectual and virtuous component, money and accumulation of wealth for its own sake is condemned in all religious traditions, as is the generation of interest for its own reward. Under the name of usury, hoarding, and miserliness, the individual who does not allow money to circulate or to achieve a higher goal, is universally condemned. Georg Simmel, in *The Philosophy of Money*, specifies that money in and of itself has no intrinsic value, but once the concept is granted value by authority or the market it acquires mythical, legendary and even death defying dimensions, using the example of Croesus, last king of Lydia (560–546 BC) who, according to legend, was saved at his own funeral pyre by Apollo in gratitude for his lavish gifts to the Delphic shrine.

As financial transactions and instruments become more abstract, and the future value of objects or instruments are substituted for actual specie or tangible value, transactions self perpetuate and multiply based on the promise of potential future gains, and original instruments and valuation are no longer priced according to real value. Charles Kindleberger explains in *Manias, Panics and Crashes: A History of Financial Crisis* (2005) that within a period of two to ten years, "manias" become unable to fulfill their promise of consistently increased valuation and profitability, provoking a crash and panic until the next bubble occurs.

Charles Mackay in *Extraordinary Popular Delusions and the Madness of Crowds* (1852 [1841]) describing the Tulip Mania for the British public, explained how, during the early years of the Amsterdam Stock Exchange, an active arbitrage market, propelled by the raising costs of the wars, encouraged speculation in currencies and commodities such as tulip bulbs, first introduced by the emissary of the Ottoman Emperor, Suleiman the Magnificent, in the mid-sixteenth century. A sign of wealth and snobbism, the bulbs are bought and sold at ever higher prices. By 1625 a bulb titled "Semper Augustus is sold for the sum of 3000 florins" (Mackay 1852). De Jaucourt, author of most of the economic articles in Diderot's Encyclopedia (1760) wrote an article entitled "Tulip":

> For a single bulb, called the Viceroy, the buyer not having cash, provided 36 bushels of wheat, 72 of rice, 4 fattened steers, 8 pigs 2 casks of wine, 4 barrels of beer, 2 tubs of butter, 1,000 pounds of cheese, a bed, garments, and a large silver cup all estimated at 2,500 florins for one bulb.

By 1637, the mania reached absurd proportions and the Dutch Parliament set curbs, lowering the price, leading to a crash, the loss of fortunes, and the end of the mania. The significance of such excesses became the stuff of legend, folklore and literature, coining the phrase "windhandel" (air business), "luft geschaft" in nineteenth-century German and Yiddish, emphasizing the illusory nature of these speculative ventures. From the Tulip Mania to the Mississippi and South Sea Bubbles, based on fraudulent land and commodity futures, annuities sold in Geneva on the life span of French royalty in the 1780s, these schemes are similar to Charles Ponzi's schemes, Florida land deals in the 1920s, fraudulent stock transactions in Russia and Albania in the early 1990s, junk bonds, derivatives and the subprime mortgage debacle in 2008, based on "poor credit, no credit, no problem" advertising, prevalent for credit cards and low rate mortgages in America since the late 1990s. The lure is the same: quick, easy riches, large gains, low risk and long-term profits.

As money has progressed from tangible to intangible to virtual, there should be greater harmonization, transparency and technological models established for all types of transactions, however each crisis in the first decade of the twenty-first century has proven that the elements of greed, risk as well as adaptability, flexibility and ingenuity, remain as prevalent as they were in the past 400 years of financial innovation, over-valuation, loss of confidence, panic and recovery. In fact, it can be argued that the more sophisticated the models, the greater the losses, as seen in the Merton and Scholes Long-term Capital Management fiasco of 1998, and the subprime mortgage exposure and losses in 2008. Semantically and ideologically, banking and financial operations have an intrinsic lack of transparency and accessibility which feed into stereotypes, biases and mythologies. From Goethe to Balzac, Zola to Dreiser, Dos Passos, Faulkner to Martin Ames to Tom Wolfe's "Masters of the Universe," there is an element of alchemy, mystery and power which, when successful, yields vast profits.

However, once they fail or are perceived as the primary cause of large scale losses, they are accused of being obtuse, esoteric, and dangerous to the health of the individual, institution and nation.

The basic definition of a stock is relatively simple: "A stock is a legal claim to a share in a company's current and future profits" (Cassidy 2003). Yet since World War II, economists have established numerous hypothesis, theories and models about how this definition can best be interpreted. Benjamin Graham's analysis of financial statements in *The Intelligent Investor* (2003), Burton Malkiel in *A Random Walk Down Wall Street* (1973, reissued 2003), contradicted by Andrew Lo and Craig Mackinlay's "A Non Random Walk Down Wall Street" (2002), Victor Niederhoffer's *The Education of a Speculator*, basing decisions on past movements, and Andre Shleifer's precepts of behavioral finance all present theoretical interpretations of how to beat the dealer.

Alan Greenspan, Chairman of the Federal Reserve was not only known, but also admired and feared for his esoteric, obtuse, almost Delphic pronouncements. In his memoirs, *The Age of Turbulence* (2007), in a chapter entitled "The Delphic Future" he refers to his famous statement: "How do we know when irrational exuberance has unduly escalated asset values which then become subject to unexpected and prolonged contractions?" (Greenspan 2007: 466). Greenspan exposes the question which is as relevant to the market conditions of 1996 as they are to the conditions of 1720, 1857, 1929, 2000 or 2008. In each subsequent financial crisis, panic and loss of confidence, young, innocent knights venture forth into the dark forest of financial mystery and speculation, to be seduced, almost destroyed, and redeemed, as Nick Leeson and Jerome Kerviel or not…

David Landes defines geography as determinant of economic destiny or evolution: "such terms as 'values' and 'culture' are not popular with economists, who prefer to deal with quantifiable (more precisely definable) factors" (Landes 2003). Looking for clues to America's psycho-historical fascination with money, profit, and wealth requires sifting through the American landscape, from Dreiser and Norris' Chicago, Marquand, Auchincloss, Bromfield's, Wolfe's New York, Fitzgerald's North Shore and Wall Street, from Dos Passos' America, to Jon Shayne (i.e. Merle Hazzard's) Elvis Presley spoof "Hedge in the Hamptons," in search of attitudes toward bankruptcy, credit worthiness, moral and political evolution and renewal.

Reprising the paradigm set up in *L'Argent des Autres* (1890), the protagonist in the 1990 movie *Other People's Money*, Larry the Liquidator (played by Danny de Vito), is the New York banker and merger and acquisition magnate, who acquires losing businesses, coming up against the tall, noble, and courteous small community company owner in New England (played by Gregory Peck). Simplistically, but effectively, it sets up the dichotomy between populism and capitalism, shareholders and stakeholders, heroes and antiheroes, urban and rural American value systems. The shareholders choose Larry the Liquidator, short, megalomaniacal, vicious, smart, and potent, as the next step in economic evolution. Like Daddy Warbucks, the industrialist, philanthropist worth "ten zillion dollars" in the *Little Orphan Annie* comics (ranked number one on the *Forbes* list of 50 fictional financiers), he is paternal, protective of widows and orphans, yet a domineering and brutal speculator. In 2005, Deborah Solomon, in an interview with the tycoon, Carl Icahn (Solomon 2005) asked, "Are you concerned that so many of the deals you're involved in just move money around and don't build value?" Carl Icahn responded "That's the PR, but it isn't true. I am not closing the company down; I am making it more productive. I am not taking money out, but bringing money in by buying stock."

American capitalism is also a study in contradictions. It is the freest market, too often accused of practicing "cowboy capitalism," yet it is has been the most tightly regulated and legalistic market since the regulatory reforms of the Great Depression. When the Canadian media mogul, Conrad Black, was convicted of white-collar financial crimes in Chicago in 2007, Geoffrey Wheatcroft best expressed the paradox, "What Black never understood is that the Americans really do take capitalism seriously which is why they police it so stringently" (Wheatcroft 2007).

Merchants, moneychangers, bankers, traders, and financiers, from usurer to hedge fund operators, function as subversive yet dynamic, risk taking forces in societal evolution. Since antiquity, never allowed to be heroes, they have been relegated to anti-heroes, comical, practical, farcical, and vulgar counterpoints to the aristocrats, warriors, scholars or clergy, from the Merchant of Venice, Le Roman Bourgeois, the Jew of Malta, l'Avare, le Bourgeouis Gentilhomme, Moll Flanders, Candide to Frank Copperworth, Frank Newman, and Sherman McCoy. Within this framework there is a "human comedy" side of finance and banking; the dramas, crises, power plays and elements of greed and altruism that move the actors forward. Yet why in large parts of Europe, Latin America, the Muslim world and emerging markets does there continue to be a pervasive discomfort with money? Why must it be justified? Why must the pro-business Sarkozy presidency in France explain itself as much as did the regime of Napoleon III? Why does it have to be defined within a larger national agenda rather than justifiable on its own merit?

Official culture, "hoch culture" as well as participatory culture, theater, art, the popular novel, and the press both codify and debunk political and economic mythology. From classical antiquity through the eighteenth century, money, profit, gain, speculation and loss are represented in popular art, literature and theater. However, judged to be unworthy and perfidious to the health of society at large, they remain marginalized from classical drama, literature and art. The Catholic Church's refutation and condemnation of monetary activities, coupled with equating poverty with virtue, only allowed those excluded or on the margins of society, Semites (Jews and Arabs), and later Protestants, to engage in commercial and financial activity.

Economic historians of the medieval period and the Renaissance, including Pirenne, Braudel, Tawney, and LeGoff demonstrated that the reality was more complex, as successful, and even respected economic activity, co-existed with the end of feudalism. There was greater fluidity in the social hierarchy than often presupposed, while Church-dictated cultural norms continued to perpetuate fundamental prejudices. Braudel, in his seminal study on capitalism, refutes the myth of Jewish usury: "But whenever we have evidence of usury being practiced by Jews, their activities run side by side with those of Christian moneylenders" (Braudel 1982: 563).

As nations become wealthy through trade and commerce, monetary professions become more easily assimilated. In times of economic shift and transition from demand to market economy, and from a rural to an urban economy, the image of the banker, merchant, and even moneylender improved. By the seventeenth century in the Low Countries, the profession of moneychangers was still marginalized, yet Rembrandt in *The Money Changer* (1627) and Christian Van Donck in *The Money Changers* (1653) depict the faces of the elderly money handlers as kindly and studious, concentrating on the coins, surrounded by books, their expressions devoid of malice or specific Semitic traits. By the 1730s, Voltaire, in *Lettre Sur le Commerce*, and Lessing, in *Nathan the Wise* (based on his friend and mentor Mendelssohn), portray merchants and even moneylenders as sympathetic, concerned good citizens.

Marcel Proust, the most elitist of French novelists, defined the paradox of nineteenth-century French aristocracy, where money was never mentioned in polite society but breeding and style required the lowest of common denominators – solid investments and good brokers. The Princess of Parma's sense of worth and self confidence was attributed as follows: "After all, she owned most of the shares in the Suez Canal and three times as many Royal Dutch as any single Rothschild" (Proust 1989 vol. II: 427).

Royal Dutch invested in the oil fields of Oklahoma, and Proust's personal fortune derived in part from large investments in American stocks, including Union Pacific, Pennsylvania and Southern Pacific railroad bonds.

Tensions between profit and exploitation, the greedy and the profligate, tangible and intangible, national and international, and material versus immaterial are illustrated in the James Bond film *Goldfinger* (1964). In the conspiratorial post-Kennedy era, Goldfinger's diabolical scheme is not to rob Fort Knox (as Ian Fleming's 1959 novel), but rather, with Chinese aid, to render the gold radioactive, through a dirty bomb, therefore inaccessible, astronomically raising the price of gold reserves and thus making the eponymously named Auric Goldfinger's supply essential and existential. He would indeed rule the world, not through possession of wealth but through manipulation of the market, creating an artificial need and dependency. In the real world of 2008, the concern was that, in times of economic volatility, the price of gold continue to rise, passing US$1,000 an ounce, as central banks in emerging economies, which held small gold reserves, would start to shift away from the US dollar and into gold or other currencies such as the euro.

From Jacques Coeur to Thomas Gresham, from Fugger to Samuel Bernard to Mires, the Rothschilds, the Rockefellers, J.P. Morgan, and from Lazard to Sandy Weill, do certain characteristics define the "money man," the banker, the financier? Do these traits make him a scapegoat, a savior to society, or both? John Law, Charles Ponzi, Ivan Kreuger, Michael Milliken, Nick Leeson, and Jerome Kerviel: each attempted to beat the system, reconstruct, salvage or invent financial transactions beyond all existent valuation. They all crashed and burned, only to encourage the next scam artist or financial genius. As Daphne Merkin puts it, "The rich are different, not only because they have more money but also because they elicit such an oxymoronic barrage of responses. They're worse and they're better, reviled and adulated. They stir up envy and invite respect" (Merkin 2007).

This work will be divided into the following sections:

Chapter 1 Dead gages, naked debentures

Etymology: the Anglo-American roots of financial terminology and its impact on financial semantics

Instruments, agents, institutions and financial centers: biblical, classical, and medieval to Renaissance references

Currency: silver, gold, sterling, ducats, florins, guilders, ecus, bills of acceptance, letters of credit, bank notes to paper money, stocks

Agents: usurers, moneychangers, speculators, merchant bankers, financiers, bankers, jobbers to brokers

Institutions: fairs, money markets, exchanges, deposit, banks, central banks

Financial centers: Rome, Athens, Constantinople, Florence, Bruges, Amsterdam, London

Chapter 2 Myths, stigmas and morality of "dirty sexy money"

"Morality and Mammon": societal, political and moral marginalization

Anti-Semitism to Anti-Capitalism

Financial women: banker's wives, lady speculators, whores

Paper money: lure of the devil

Dante's seventh circle of inferno: counterfeiting, financial fraud

Financial bubbles, manias and crises: South Sea Bubble, Mississippi Bubble, Crash of 1929

Chapter 3 Metamorphosis: materialism to capitalism

Secularization, science, literacy, literature: reading the market

Wealth distribution and societal mobility: merchants, banking dynasties, financiers, tax collectors, bankers

Amsterdam, London, Paris: the market and society

Consumerism to luxury

Moral and legal regulation

Market concepts, mores and beliefs: Jean Bodin to Adam Smith, Rousseau to Voltaire The individual and the states' economic impulses: stock exchanges, central banks

The Bank of England

Chapter 4 World bankers: ambivalences of modernity

British financial universalism: Dickens to Bagehot
Political–Financial matrix: capitalism in the name of the nation
British and French bankers to the universe: Barings, Rothschild, International and colonial banking
Forging banking and market institutional identity, culture, philosophy
Monetary bipolarity: Saint-Simon to Marx
French financial exceptionalism: hate the banker, revere the bank
The middle class: ascension, ambivalence, nostalgia
Traders, speculators, brokers: the rise of the market
Prussian to German financial power: institutions and culture

Chapter 5 Capitalism is dead, long live capitalism

First and second Gilded Ages: "dynamic of capitalism and its relationship to the state"
The last waltz of the empires
Marxism and post-Marxist societies: deconstructing and reconstructing financial culture in former Soviet Union, China and emerging markets
Post WWI cultural manifestations of financial chaos, inflation, depression
WWII wartime finances
Bretton Woods: the Americanization of financial culture and global finance
International finance and economic security: the good, the bad and the ugly from Ambrosiano, BCCI to terrorism funding
Rogues on the trading floor, knaves in the boardroom
European Monetary Union: inventing Europe, ECB, Euro, banking harmonization
Benign neglect to intervention, deregulation, privatization: French, German, British, Japanese banking
Anti-globalization to Anti-Americanism
Art, money, financial art

Chapter 6 American financial culture: myths and model of American capitalism

Land of opportunities: American old and new money
The New York stock exchange
Wall Street–Main Street myths and dichotomies
Debt to creditor nation: new banker to the world, American banks and bankers in international finance, J.P. Morgan to the Federal Reserve
Crash of 1929 and the Great Depression: how do you regulate American finance
"Cowboy capitalism" from the Civil War to 2001: gold and silver standards, tariffs, monopolies, the "Almighty dollar"
Transformation of American financial culture: banks and bankers 1933–1983

American financial technology and innovation: FOREX, NASDAQ, futures, derivatives

Great American financial scandals: Penn Square, S&L, junk bonds, Enron, crisis of 2008

Traders take charge: Lehman Brothers, road to deregulation, masters of the universe

Too big to fail to the end of Glass-Steagall, LTC to irrational exuberance

The second Gilded Age: American wealth distribution

American financial market places: Philadelphia, Chicago, New York

The Great Depression, Glass-Steagall Act and US regulatory structures

1 Dead gages, naked debentures

> Pox on these bonds! I must persuade him to take another L1000 and hedge all
> into one good mortgage.
>
> (Quote from 1664, compact edition of *OED* vol. 1 1971: 1281)

From the seventeenth century to contemporary subprime mortgage schemes, the etymology of financial semantics is rich in political, cultural, sexual, and theological signifiers. The language of finance, rife with moral innuendo, often associated with physical activity, hedging, hiding, manipulating and transacting, reflects the dynamism and the ambivalence toward all financial activity. The terminology derived from expressions connoting mutual trust, faith in repayment, and long-term commitment, also reveals its antithesis, the lack of moral rectitude and violation of trust. In the financial crisis of 2008, the root cause has been attributed to one of the oldest known contractual agreements, the pledge and repayment of land and property – mortgage, derived from old French "mort" and "gage," implying payment completed and the pledge rendered dead (OED 1971: 1854). Used in England since 1390, and in common usage in legal writs by the late fifteenth century, in France the French term was replaced by the Greek derivative "hypotheque" by the eighteenth century. Intrinsically, financial transactions are based on credit and debit, derived from ethical concepts of mutuality and communality. The root of credit, "credere," to have faith, connotes a fundamental sense of trust; the root of debt "debere" to owe, an obligation, implies the need to honor the obligation.

Financial terminology followed the evolution and geo-economic shifts of commerce, money exchange, and banking operations, from Italy to the Low Countries to its permanent home in England after 1600. The largest number of transactional terms were translated from old English into French, German and Nordic languages, while certain terms reversed course from old French to English: broker from "brochier," the act of selling wine from the cask, balance from "balancer."

The term to speculate, "speculare" in Latin, meant to look out for trouble. Speculation, described in Edward Chancellor's *Devil Take the Hindmost: A History of Financial Speculation* (1999), had always carried an element of risk and slightly "shady" implications. Adam Smith defined a "speculative merchant" as one who "exercises no one regular, established or well known branch of business" (Chancellor 1999: x).

Speculators, also called "questor" in ancient Rome, deal makers, or seekers of profit, trafficked in land shares, cash and credit transactions. Moneychangers, often referred to as "metikoui," foreigner, many of Greek origin, congregated in the Forum where they mingled with moneylenders and merchants looking for a good deal in goods, slaves, cattle, and prostitutes. All hawked any wares worthy of a price or exchange, similar to London's Change Alley in 1680, Paris' Place Royale, or the masses congregating in the Rue de Quincampoix in 1720.

Investment derives from "investare," meaning to don or to put on, which first appeared in a modern financial context, *circa* 1783, in relation to monies placed in the East India Trading Company: "a portion of revenues of Bengali has been set apart to be employed in purchase of goods for exportation to England and this is called the Investment" (*OED* vol. I 1971: 1478). The investment of "capital" separately from "goods" appears in early nineteenth-century British tracts, taxation documents, and stock subscriptions, but the actual concept was already described in Renaissance exchange contracts that were used in silver markets to distinguish fixed versus circulating capital.

Juno Moneta was one of the names attributed to the goddess Juno, wife of Jupiter, whose temple on Capitolene Hill, was consecrated in 345 BC, and replaced an older shrine where sacred geese had been kept – the possible origin of the term "golden goose." Adjoining the Roman mint, her shrine and name was the derivation for the French term monnaie and English money.

Bank derived from the Italian "banco," which referred to the tradesman and moneychanger's bench or stall, a variation of the moneychanger's table in Rome, "mensa argentaria." Translated as baunche or baunck in Middle English charts and wills, as bancour in Old French, and as banhvere in Old German-Nordic, it appears in legal documents since the mid-twelfth century (*OED* 1971: 163). References are found in estate wills and charts by the fifteenth century: "There was a changeour, a man came to hym and sayd and affermyd he had delyveryd to his banke five hundred floryins of gold to kepe" (Caxton 1474 quoted in *OED* 1974: 163). Shakespeare makes mention of bills of exchange, which appear in 1485 in the *Taming of the Shrew* (Act IV, Scene ii, 80). De Roover and LeGoff emphasize how "banchi" were distinguished from moneychangers, "cambio," which became the root of the French term for currency traders, "cambistes." However, in fourteenth-century Florence cambio was synonymous with "banchi grossi," or important bankers.

After the failure of the Royal Bank under John Law and Philip d'Orleans, in 1720, "French experience with John Law was such that there was hesitation in even pronouncing the word bank for 150 years hereafter – a classic case of collective financial memory" (Kindleberger 1993: 100). Other than the Bank of France, created in 1800, "banking institutions were typically called caisse, credit, societe or comptoir and not banque until the banque d'affaires in the last quarter of the nineteenth century" (Kindleberger 1993: 100).

Bankruptcy's etymology, banka rota (bankrout or banqueroute), referred to Italian moneychangers who, when declared insolvent, had their benches broken.

By 1536, in France "faire banqueroute" meant to desert one's place of business without paying one's liabilities. Adam Smith in *Wealth of Nations* (1776), and Steele in the *Spectator* (Steele and Addison 1712), refer to the social ignominy of having to declare bankruptcy.

"Finance," derived from the Old French, finance, finer, to settle, end dispute, procure, or render payment in metals, is used as early as 1160. Medieval English defined "fynaunce" as tax collection. In France between 1549 and 1789, "financier" specifically designated an agent of public finances or a landowner who reported on fiscal matters to the king. The English teller or exchequer is named a "financier" in *Blount's Dictionary* in 1656. By 1656, financier is an exchequer receiver, under treasurer or teller in the exchequer. Mentioned in *Johnson's Dictionary* (1755), as one who collects and farms the public revenue, in the far less sophisticated French financial system, the financier is a collector of taxes. Edmund Burke, in *The French Revolution* (1790), writes that "the objects of a financier are … to secure ample revenue, to impose it with judgment … to employ it economically" (*OED* vol. I 1974: 1000). By 1866, "financial combination of London financiers and financial houses" (*OED* vol. I 1974: 1000), referred to firms and individuals who had access to capital. After the publication of *Das Kapital* in 1867, the term "financier" became analogous to Marx's usage of capitalist or industrial capitalist. Capital, pertaining to funds of a trader, company or corporation, the basis for financial operations, was already in use in 1709, "An Act for Enlarging the Capital Stock of the Bank of England" (*OED* vol. 1 1974: 334). Disraeli, in his romantic novel *Sybil* (1863), writes disparagingly that "The capitalist flourishes, he amasses great wealth, and we sink lower, lower than the beasts of burden" (quoted in *OED* vol. I 1974: 334).

The *Oxford English Dictionary* (*OED* vol. II 1974: 3576–3577) provides the following derivations for usury and usurer: Usury, derived from the Latin "usura," connoted money lent at interest in Old French, around 1170. The *OED* makes reference to Old English south English legends (1290), Brunne (1303), Wycliffe (1380): "no Christian is a usurer," and Dekker's *Seven Sins* (1606) which refers to usuries as a means of defrauding goods and land: "there are usurers who for a little money bring young novices in a fool's paradise till they have sealed the mortgage of their lands." A rare usage is in Brathwait (1641) of "a usuress or woman usurer." Money lending is defined as "usury" by 1440. But by 1649, "how odious usury contracts have been in all times," distinctions begin to appear between different types of loans: "every increase by loan of money is not usurance".

Semantic and historical confusion between usurer, moneylender, and banker continued through the end of the Renaissance. English sermons in the sixteenth century translated Jesus' words in Luke as the bankers' or moneylenders tables.

Loan can be traced to Old High German, "lehan" and ledger from "legden," to lie down, which was required in order to read or transcribe in the Grand Livre, the huge tome of accounts. During and after the crusades, merchants and knights brought back Arabic currency and terminology: "douane," customs in French; "magazine," from mohartra, a basic form of forward selling and resale.

"Arbitrage" from French, became the universal term for bills of exchange bought or sold on sight of daily quotations of rates. By 1880, in the British press, the term defined an operation which took advantage of different prices among categories of stocks.

By the eighteenth century, moral and political characteristics were attributed to financial agents and operations. Daniel Defoe, who had lost large sums in speculative activity in Spain in the 1690s, became one of the most virulent critics of speculative activities and especially stock jobbing. Stock jobbers, originally described as speculators undervaluing a company's prospects and overvaluing the shares, are castigated by Defoe in *The Villainy of Stock Jobbers Detected* (1701), *Anatomy of Exchange Alley* (1719) and *The Complete English Tradesman* (1726), accused of being "born of Deceit and nourished by Trick, Cheat, Wheedle, Forgeries, Falsehoods and all sorts of Delusions."

"Agiotage" in eighteenth-century France carried political and social stigma. From its creation in 1704, through the Revolution, it was considered synonymous with the most unscrupulous type of speculation. Derived from the Italian "agio," it indicated profit realized in gold to paper speculation. An agioteur was a new kind of speculator who bet gold against the newly printed paper money, benefiting from monetary instability due to gold shortage. Dancourt's popular comedy of manners *Les Agioteurs* (1710) combined the nefarious activity of usury with agiotage. In describing John Law's Mississippi Bubble, Saint-Simon, in his memoirs, talks of agiotage as the paper notes on futures in Louisiana, bought in gold in the initial frenzy where shares worth 500 pounds were bought up as high as 20,000. Mirabeau, in a speech to the French National Assembly in 1790, raged against agioteurs who speculated, accusing them of leading France into bankruptcy.

Since the 1990s, it has become fashionable in times of crisis, to write and speak of "moral hazard," dating back to the insurance industry in 1875, which described the impact of "the ascending scale of life insurance premiums" which encouraged the healthy to drop out and the sick to stay in. The term, which appeared in the *Quarterly Journal of Economics* in 1895, attributed the "lack of moral character [which] gives rise to a class of risks known by insurance men as moral hazards" (Safire 2008).

In English, words for money abound in each generation's slang: greenback, moola, chump change, scratch, sawback, dinero, fiver, geld, a grand, lucre, loot, and cash. These terms derive from outlaw, immigrant and gangster culture popularized by dime novels, traveling salesmen, prison literature, and by the 1920s, movies, comics, radio and television. Barbara Guilder Quint in *Wall Street Talk* (1983), traced the new set of terms which were popularized on Wall Street from the late 1970s, tracing the trajectory of changes in market procedures, operations and instruments: boiler room, bucket shop, cyanide capsules, shark repellent, golden parachutes, naked options, sleeping beauty, tombstone ads, white knight and vestal virgin. This was followed, in the mid-1980s, by hostile bid, green mail and raiders. Tom Wolfe, in *Bonfire of the Vanities* (1987), created the expression "Masters of the Universe" (Wolfe 1987: 12), attributed to high risk, high reward traders, from a series of superhero plastic toys.

Martin Mayer, the American banking scholar, in 1997, provided a definition for the product blamed in the latest financial crisis, "Derivatives: The conventional definition says that it is a financial instrument that 'derives' its value from changes in the price of other financial instruments" (Mayer 1997: 289). But Mayer presciently warned that

> A derivative is a bet, not an instrument – a bet on the direction, dimension, duration and speed of changes in the value of another financial instrument. And like any bet, its value is entirely a function of the creditworthiness of the man who wrote it.
>
> (Mayer 1997: 291)

The market for derivatives began in 1991 with an instrument called a "credit-default swap," at Bankers Trust in New York. In 1998, two J.P. Morgan bankers, an American, Bill Demchak, and a British woman, Blythe Masters (a rare women in this type of financial transaction), introduced "broad indexed secured trust offering," to offset corporate credit risk after the 1998 Asian crisis. By 2003, Warren Buffet called derivatives "financial weapons of mass destruction" as the instruments under the rubrique of derivatives become more and more complex and less transparent (*Portfolio*, October 15, 2008).

In 2006, hedge funds dominated the press and media. Hedge funds describes firms created by speculators who practice speculative hedging, a term with one of the most colorful etymologies. From plying trade under a hedge, "engaging in illegal activity as hedge curate, parson, doctor, lawyer, poet, wench, whore, clandestine since the 1530s, to hedge as to secure a debt by including it into a larger one for which there is better security" (*OED* vol. I 1974: 1281). By the early nineteenth century, hedging implied securing against loss by making transactions on both sides "hedge your bets." American hedge funds in the last decade have adopted mythological, medieval names: Renaissance, Highbridge, Citadel, Maverick, and Lone Pine, and their charities include names such as the Robin Hood Foundation.

The public outcry against the perpetrators of the financial schemes, frauds, misleading testimony, and potential bank failures has been fraught with terms of moral condemnation. Chief executive officers of banks, hedge fund managers, and individuals such as Bernard Madoff and Allen Stanford have been labeled as "pure evil," and their crimes compared to acts of sacrilege and violation of public trust. Financial terminology integrates sex, violence, and prostitution with terms of medieval quest, as these functions remain locked in a primal moral battle between evil action and potentially noble consequences.

Each crisis and scandal adds to the financial semantic field: Securitization is "the stuff of what are called securities – the safe sounding word for stocks and bonds – with often insecure, risky loans which brought about the sub prime mortgage crisis by offering cheap mortgages to non credit worthy buyers" (Safire 2007). All this is part of the "bubble" economy, a term already used by Steele, Shadwell, and Defoe. One culprit in this crisis is "naked short selling," a semantic combination of " 'selling short' in which the investor sells securities he does not own in the hope of buying them back later at a lower price" (Quint 1983:102) and "naked option" also popularized in the 1980s Wall Street boom. Naked short selling is not necessarily illegal, unless done to manipulate securities prices.

The most commonly used, and often misused word, in the ongoing financial crisis, introduced in the United States, is "bailout," which has appeared in all languages as the crisis spread to Europe and Asia, requiring governments to step in with various rescue plans, including nationalization, capital injections, and buyouts. The term, which in the Oxford English Dictionary only appears as "make emergency parachute descent" (1974), became part of popular financial terminology in the 1970s during the rescue of Penn Central Railroad (1970) and Chrysler (1979).

By the nineteenth century, French, Spanish, German, Italian and later Japanese banking and market participants and press, either used Anglo-American terms or reverted to more precise, less colorful verbiage. As financial principles grew increasingly complex, computational, and as technology compressed time and human contact, language increasingly integrated mathematical computer terminology. Creating, incorporating, or merely translating financial and commercial terminology is an intrinsic part of economic evolution, as language needs to express new activities, and as larger parts of a population begin to understand, use or take part in these activities. A novel by Ma Jian, exiled Chinese writer, *Beijing Coma* (2008), expresses this new found linguistic hodgepodge: "As society changes new words and terms keep popping up, such as sauna, private car ownership, property developer, mortgage and personal installment loan" (quoted in Row 2008). In one fell swoop, China absorbed and appropriated over 200 years of Western financial, consumer and luxury vocabulary.

1.1 Coinage to currency, silver and gold to paper

"Money makes the world go round," is a modern rendition of Ecclesiastes 10:19 "money answereth all things," emphasizing the symbiotic relationship between money and power, but also the symbolic role of money in defining national and individual identity. Although references to coinage, silver, gold, copper, and later paper, appear in documents, legal contracts, testaments and popular literature, drama and comedy after the end of the Roman Empire, for thousands of years actual usage and knowledge of these instruments was restricted to a small fraction of the population in urban centers. In largely rural societies, economic activity functioned on a barter basis, what Simmel called "Natural Wirtschaft." By the eleventh century, the evolution of market, fairs and the greater concentration of early urban centers helped to propagate the concept and acceptance of coins and specie, but across Europe through the eighteenth century millions lived and died on their farms and in their villages, having never seen or held a silver or gold coin. Money, its mutable value, weight, and convertibility into goods or other types of coinage or currency, was always seen as mysterious, only available to a chosen few. From the moneychangers in the temple to medieval usurers, Wall Street speculators, the latest evil doers, and oil futures speculators, financial transactions needed an esoteric set of skills, numerical at best, alchemic at worst, in order to be able to understand and profit from the complexities of price differentials, fees, commissions and changing valuations. A purview of how money was viewed through the ages illustrates the universality and the immutability of these perceptions.

Coinage is imbued with psycho-historical atavistic symbolism. When Israel reinstated the shekel as legal currency in 1948, it was as profound a symbolic gesture as the recreation of Hebrew as a living language. The discovery of the Dead Sea Scrolls in 1947, also later revealed at Qumran a stash of over 500 silver shekels from AD 1, according to the texts, to be used for community purposes (Jewish Museum, Dead Sea Scroll exhibit, New York, fall 2008).

In the early 1990s, after the fall of the Soviet Union, each country reinstated its currency, flag and national anthem as symbols of nationhood. These currencies such as the Rumanian lei, Bulgarian lev, and Latvian lats were not convertible currencies and actual transactions continued in Deutschmarks. The charming suggestion in the *Financial Times* ("The Florin in your Pocket" 1995), to name the new European Union currency the "florin or ducat" was facetious, but also profoundly aware of the impact of a coin's cultural history and prestige. Creating and naming a new, untested, borderless regional currency was an integral part of creating European Monetary Union. The decision was made by the European Commission and various committees, to create a currency which, for the first time in history would bypass all socio-historical and cultural connotations, opting instead for a neutralized and neutered semantic form: euro. In order to avoid any specific reference to the original eleven Economic and Monetary Union member states, the notes would have imaginary architectural arches, portals and monuments on one side and specific national references on the other. Margaret Thatcher's decision to demand an opt-out clause and to refuse to join a single currency union underlined the position of sterling as Europe's oldest currency, in continuous use since 1266.

Although Germany welcomed full integration into Europe and monetary unification, with the European Central Bank located in Frankfurt, replacing the Deutschmark with the euro was a profoundly wrenching and complex transition. On June 20, 1948, when Erhard announced the creation of the Deutschmark, Germany did not exist as a state. In the rubble of the Third Reich, Germany had been stripped of all national identity. The Deutschmark became its first post-war symbol, its first step toward economic recovery and stability, and post-1957, with the creation of the Bundesbank, the symbol of its economic success, power and influence. In order to be viable, a currency must establish trust, and guaranty that the government can safeguard its value and protect its citizens savings, hence the fear of inflation, devaluation and disappearance of specific national currencies.

Forgery was always seen as a serious sin and crime against the state, punishable by death in thirteenth-century Florence, as it sought to circumvent the basic relationship between the state, commerce, and the consumer. Despite the advent of electronic money and the perpetual movement of global currencies in a nearly US$2 trillion a day foreign exchange market, the psycho-historical relationship between money and power remains in place. There are lead currencies: the US dollar and the euro; powerful independent currencies, sterling, yen and the Swiss franc, and aggressive new currencies that seek to rival, or surpass in value, prestige and eventual global convertibility, such as the Chinese renminbi (RB).

In 1971, Pierre Vilar wrote on the supremacy of the US dollar and decoupling from gold:

> Every country has given up distinguishing between its internal currency and the currency or precious metal necessary for foreign exchange (in Catalan, moneda corrent (monnaie courante), and moneda corrible). A single currency has now been imposed on most of the world: but is it any more a universal phenomenon than the Spanish piaster was or more recently the pound sterling?
>
> (Vilar 1976: 15)

As long as currencies have been in existence, they have been revalued and devalued against one another and against commodities, of which gold remains the key money-commodity. Since ancient Rome, during periods of war, instability, and prosperity the value of gold and silver changed according to availability. Gold had ten times its weight in silver during the Peloponnesian War, twelve times in Rome under the long reign of Augustus, while silver had from 50 to 100 times the value of bronze from the fifth to the third century in Greece (value of coinage was 6 obols (one of the oldest forms of coinage) = 1 drachma, 100 drachma = 1 mina, 60 mina = 1 talent). Under Philippe of Macedonia and his son, Alexander the Great (356–323 BC), the drachma became a global currency. Documents from the fifth century BC, mention Antisthenes and Archestratos, who engaged in currency exchange between Athens and Middle Eastern merchants. Demosthenes and Isocrates mention Pasion, a former slave, and Phormion (394 BC), who deal in monetary transactions known for the trust they engender. The operations are commercial in nature, the rate of interest is between 10–18 percent on large loans for maritime commerce, based on the safe arrival in port of the merchandise, and the collateral is either the ship or the freight. Pasion died in 370 BC, leaving his widow a vast fortune valued at 60 talents. The French banking historian Petit Dutaillis, referencing the 1875 translation of Demosthenes, valued the equivalent to be over FF330,000.

The earliest treatment of banking from Mesopotamia is procedural. Hammurabi's Code (1728–1686 BC) depicted in cuneiform, payments in weighted amounts of silver, rules governing interest, guarantees, loans, and other transactions. Earlier codes from northern Mesopotamia, the Eshnunna code (c. 2000 BC) already identified the king as the authority for establishing standard weights. The interest rate on loans in silver was 20 percent, although grain was used for the value of food, and commodities such as wool, oil, and lard, metals were valued in silver. Hoards of gold and silver were found in excavations in Egypt and the word "hedj"for silver was often interchangeable for money. As this standard depended on supply, both commodities were intrinsically of value. Thus, throughout the ancient world, areas rich in metals had political power such as the kingdom of Lydia in Asia Minor and its last king, Croesus, defeated by the Persians in 547 BC. Lydia had mines and natural sources of electrum, a natural alloy of gold and silver, prevalent in Greek coinage (since 700 BC). The ancient Greek world used and transacted in coinage throughout all strata of society. In the sixth century, each city state of the extended Hellenic empire minted coins. Coin designs symbolized the authority of the state and in turn the state's authority guaranteed the quality and value of the coins, protecting them against forgery. The fourth-century Darius vase depicts a royal treasurer recording large amounts of silver shekels using an abacus.

References to money and transactions, including Abraham buying the Cave of Machpelah for 400 shekels (Gen: 23:15), and the enslavement of Joseph sold to the Ishmaelite for 20 pieces of silver (Gen. 37:28) occur throughout the Old Testament. Shekels were used in ancient Palestine, Mesopotamia, and Egypt. Exodus (30:13–15) specifies that a half shekel, called a beak was paid into the Treasury by all participants in the national census. Jews paid an annual levy for the maintenance of the sanctuary during the Second Temple period, and were taxed for restoration of the Second Temple, as described in the Mishna, which transcribed oral law in the Talmud. The tract Shekalim told before reading the Megillah at Purim described these procedures. Shekels, the ancient Hebrew monetary unit, resurfaced in Poland in the 1890s, in the Zionist movement, as the name of the small annual contribution. In Ezra, money is put into the Treasury for the house of God, and in First Chronicles (22:7) there is reference to "1000 talents of gold, thousand and thousand talents of silver to build the house of the Lord" (Werblowsky and Wigoder 1966: 354). Interdictions and rules on financial transactions were laid out for practical purposes in the Old Testament. Certain practices, usury based on exorbitant or unjust interest fees, types of loans, term limits and conditions for repayment follow a trajectory from ancient Egypt, to Israel to Greece and Rome, incorporating moral and religious connotations and establishing sharp dichotomies between accepted and non-accepted practices.

The Talmud recommends that a wealthy man should divide his fortune into three parts, real estate, business and specie, advice reiterated by Jacob Fugger in his correspondence (c. 1518) on investments in the Orient. Excerpts from Jewish literature, read in morning services of the New Year include,

> The wealthy man who trusts in God will not find his wealth a hindrance to his faith; for he does not place his reliance upon his wealth.... Instead he will render thanks to the Creator who has made him the agent of His beneficence.
>
> (Bachya Ibn Pakuda, eleventh century, quoted in the *Union Prayerbook for Jewish Worship* 1960: 118)

In the Old Testament there are two words for interest: neshekh (biting) and tarbit (increase). But in the Mishnah there are interpretations, first the prohibition against interest applies only among Jews, so that a non-Jew can be an intermediary in a loan transaction. In a basic agricultural economy, loans are only proffered in times of crisis, crop failure, and famine. Slowly the practice evolved into "hetter iska" loan in the form of a partnership. Loans between individuals should remain free of interest, "gemilut hesed," with average loan periods of 30 days and property as collateral.

The prohibition "Thou shalt not lend upon interest," reiterated in Exodus (22:24), Leviticus (25:36–37), Deuteronomy (23:20–21), and Luke (6:34–35), specifies that money lending is a sterile activity that does not involve productive labor but instead reaps a profit through the mere passage of time, therefore contradicting the principles that advocate direct causality between an individual's efforts and the reward of his labors, a correlation which defines work, profit and worldly reward from Jesus to Marx.

Greek gods did not engage in commercial activity. However, Hermes, son of Zeus and Maia (daughter of the Titan, Atlas), became known as the "patron of merchants and thieves," roads, herdsman, commerce, negotiations, as well as literature and interpretation. Aristotle was only willing to justify money as a medium of exchange, a means of facilitating reciprocity between sellers and buyers. He condemned interest bearing transactions, stating in *Politika* (fourth century BC) that "The profession of handling money is justly hated" (1938). Herodotus portrayed moneylenders as so avaricious that they devised methods of enforcing debts by forbidding the most basic of human impulses, the burial of the dead.

> In the reign of this king, money being scarce and commercial dealings straitened, a law was passed that the borrower might pledge his father's body to raise the sum whereof he has need. A proviso was appended to this law, giving the lender authority over the entire sepulcher of the borrower, so that a man who took up money under this pledge, if he died without paying the debt, could not obtain burial either in his own ancestral tomb, or in any other, nor could he during his lifetime bury in his own tomb any member of his family.
>
> (Herodotus 1960).

Plutos "in Greek myth, the personification of wealth ... whom Homer regarded as a mortal was originally connected with abundance of crops and became a figure of popular rather than literary mythology" (Howatson 1989: 449) His name becomes the root of plutocracy and plutocrat, terms of derision and sarcasm to describe leaders of wealth, and leadership through wealth. Plutocrats are also "fat cats," the American slang expression for the rich, long synonymous with well fed and overweight predators from Hogarth to Phillipon, to Thomas Nast's caricatures of Tammany Hall politicians, Mr. Moneybags of Monopoly, to the sculptures of Tom Otterness where the fat gold colored bronze plutocrat sitting on his bag of dollars is also the ultimate consumer (Marlborough Chelsea Gallery, New York).

The son of Demeter and Iasion (brother of Dardanus, related to Zeus), Plutos is first associated with good harvests, and then blinded by Zeus to make him indiscriminate in the distribution of riches, formulating the concept that both justice and wealth are blind. Aristophanes (388 BC), in an early musical with lyrics and chorus, describes a poor honest man, Chremylus, who is so outraged at the injustice of wealth that he asks the Delphic oracle for advice. Meeting Plutos, god of wealth he persuades him to risk the wrath of Zeus to regain his sight which he does, against the advice of Poverty (who explains that virtue and effort are essential). For his advice, Chremylus is made rich, the righteous are rewarded, the wicked discredited, and Chremylus suggests that Plutos be installed in the Treasury. But the god, Hermes, complains for he is destitute as no one gives to the gods anymore. The play emphasizes all the sins of money: greed, venality, corruption: "But no man has ever enough of thee, for give a man a sum of thirteen talents. And all the more he hungers for sixteen, give him sixteen and he must have forty" (Aristophanes 1931).

Coinage of the Roman republic was uniform throughout the territories. Under the Republic, "argentarii" (silver smiths) were of the administrative rank "viri mensarii," they received and kept in deposit the money of citizens and could invest in further loans. Cicero makes mention of trapezitai (banks in ancient Greece, trapeze), nummularii (coin dealers) and collectarii (collectors). Roman currency, "pecunia" (the term derived from pigs and livestock) appears as early as 600 BC. In Rome, tresviri, mint masters are mentioned by 289 BC, when silver coinage is introduced. The silver denarius was roughly the equivalent of the silver drachma. Gold first appeared during the Second Punic War. The emperor had exclusive minting rights over gold and silver, while bronze coinage was granted by the Senate. By the end of the Roman Empire, political instability accompanied economic instability as weak and corrupt emperors were unable to control inflation. Diocletian's *Price Edict* (AD 301) condemned the practices of profiteers "who prey on soldiers charging exorbitant prices for basic necessities" (Howatson 1989: 190). Diocletian tried to restore order by a basic form of price control for wine, beef, bread, and barber and scribe services. Although gold and base metal coins were prevalent in the entire empire, and coins had uniform dimensions, metallic quality and inscriptions of the emperor, the value of money fluctuated as power and wealth moved from Rome to the East and the Byzantine Empire. The fall of Rome in AD 453 was the end of a long decline as urban structures declined, civil society deteriorated under weak leaders, and Rome became fragmented economically between new churches, military campaigns and large sums paid in gold to the Huns at the outer edges of the empire. Jean Andreau's definitive study *Banking and Business in the Roman World* (1999) analyses a three tier system: the imperial elite, knights, and senators who made loans to finance their own life style, tax obligations and some trade operations.

In Athens and Rome, satirical and comical literature derided individuals who dealt or handled money as a profession. During the empire, references to bankers and moneychangers appear in Cicero's letters to Atticus (*Ad Atticum* 199 [68–44 BC]), Petronius and Juvenal. In *Satyricon* (AD 60, attributed to Petronius) Trimalcheo, obese, grotesque, enormously wealthy, observes that money changing is the most difficult profession after literature and medicine because its practitioners must detect true value among falsehood and illusion. In all societal strata money and corruption are linked. Money is anti-art, philistine, anti-intellectual, but like the hatred of money in nineteenth-century literature, the artist, writer, and poet depend on the generosity of the wealthy to survive.

Juvenal's *Satires* (1958) make scornful references to fraudulent lending, embezzlement, payment of interest, and the supposed propensity of Jewish merchants to hoard money (*Satires* 7, 9, 13). *Satire 14* "On Education in Avarice," specifies Jews as money handlers and misers (lines 93–115).

Virgil, in recreating the Homeric epic and extolling the golden age of Augustus, makes few references to money or commerce, but the passage in *Aeneid* (Book 6, *The Kingdom of the Dead*, lines 702–710) inspires Dante's description of the damned in *Inferno*, and serves as model for the negative imagery in medieval literature. Aneas crosses past Tartarus' River of Fire into the nether regions where the worst sinners suffer eternal afflictions:

> Here those who hated their brothers while alive or struck their fathers down or embroiled clients in fraud, or brooded alone over troves of gold they gained and never put aside some share for their own kin – a great multitude these – followed by adulterers, inciters of civil war, traitors to their masters, they trundle enormous boulders, others dangle, racked to the breaking point on the spokes of rolling wheels, ... Here's one who bartered his native land for gold.
>
> (Virgil 2006: 202)

Dante categorized financial sins and sinners: the miser; those who neglect their children's inheritance, and those who sell their country for gold. In *Inferno*, Canto XVII, the serpent monster Geryon tortures the usurers who carry money pouches around their neck for all eternity. In Canto XI, usury is designated as against nature: "but since the usurer takes a different way, he condemns Nature" (Dante 1994: 115), but the most atrocious physical punishments are reserved in the eighth circle for sins of fraud, the falsifiers, counterfeiters in Canto XXX: "where I falsely coined the currency that bears the Baptist's face, for which on earth, I left my body, burned" (Dante 1961: 321). In Florence counterfeiting was punishable by death. In *Purgatorio* (Cantos XIX, XX ,XXII) reside the seven sins, and in the fifth level occurs the purgation of avarice and prodigality (Dante 1961).

In tenth- and eleventh-century feudal hierarchy, bankers, merchants, often interchangeable with moneylenders, were politically and socially marginalized. In pre-urban societies, moneylenders, often of Semitic, Jewish, or Arab origin, were outsiders, dealing often in stealth in order to avoid moral censure. Saint Jerome and Aquinas judge the merchant as unworthy. The Merovingian dynasties in France, as well as the Visigoths and Germanic peoples, functioned as barter societies adopting coinage and minting primarily to pay armies. As society regressed toward rural economies, the Church began to play a key role in the use of coinage for alms, charity, as well as the conversion of gold into plates and ornaments, a practice which lasted well into the eighteenth century in Portugal, Spain, and Austria. *Historia Francorum* by Gregory, Bishop of Tours (c. 570–585), used as primary source by the French historian Augustin Thierry in his *Recits des Temps Merovingiens* (1840), describes dowries in riches and not only in land and alliances: Chilperic I, of Neustrie (561–584) and Galeswinthe, daughter of the king of the Visigoths "whom he loves solely for her large sums of money and rare precious objects" (Thierry 1961: 35).

Under Charlemagne, as France secured its borders from the Moors (Chanson de Roland), Pepin the Short restored silver coinage. Under fear of Viking invasions, Carolinginean mints continued to issue silver. Under Charlemagne, and through the ninth and tenth centuries, the silver penny dominated. The rich silver mines in the Harz region of Germany, provided silver coinage throughout Bohemia, Hungary, and Poland, part of the Germanic Empire, and Scandinavia. Gold coinage, solidus of Constantine the Great, taxation in gold on land and property, dominated the Byzantine Empire from the fifth to the eighth centuries. In Western Europe gold was mainly used as ceremonial (bezants) and church objects.

The creation of Islam encompassed both religious and political systems, creating tension between earthly demands and religious requirements. There are repeated warnings about the nature of money in the Koran, specifically against accumulating wealth, "Money puts my community to the test" (Ibn Hanbal, Book 4). Therefore the giving of alms, the alms tax (zakat), is one of the five main obligations in Islam and usury (riba) is strictly banned. Islamic coins, the silver dirha, with specific religious inscriptions, seek to reconcile commerce and religious adherence, as do functionaries who oversee financial activities conducted according to sharia law. In Damascus, some of the first minting under the caliphate included elaborate Islamic verses honoring the Prophet, and crosses were removed from any residual Byzantine coins. By 813–833, under the Abbasid al Ma'mun, uniformity of coinage was established. With access to the gold mines of Africa, Ghana Sudan and Egypt, gold dinars became dominant in the Mediterranean area.

The crusaders brought gold dinars back to Barcelona, Italy, Sicily, Portugal and England. Henri III (1216–1272) preparing for a crusade accumulated foreign gold, including "denari de musc." But sociologically, money in Islam carries social more than economic functions, distributed by the rich for special holidays, weddings, women's jewelry and ornamentation. During the Middle Ages there was a sophisticated system of taxation, trade, and financial operations in promissory notes, bills of exchange, and letters of credit. Two bankers were allowed to operate in Isfahan in 1052; Baghdad had banking streets and moneychangers in souks. However many of the banking families were Jews or Christians, or Coptics in Egypt, as interdictions and stigma against finance was immutable and codified in society at large.

The Sunni Ottoman dynasty (1281–1924) captured Constantinople in 1453, and under Suleiman the Magnificent (1520–1566), expanded the empire through Egypt, the Balkans, North Africa, and Iran to the doors of Vienna in 1528. The dirham circulated with the ashrafi, but slowly by the seventeenth century the Austrian thaler became dominant. Ottoman coins, unlike Arab coins, did not carry religious inscriptions or symbols. In Europe capitalist activity began to evolve outside of the church and eventually outside of the monarchy, creating its system of rules, regulations, and requirements, allowing individuals a broader range of activities within secular and legal norms. In Muslim countries there occurred little evolution, aside from the very wealthy who dealt in international transactions. Validation and valorization of financial activity: banking, speculating, stock markets, capital markets, and large scale credit institutions did not become part of the social tapestry. Women, with few exceptions among the elite, remain largely ostracized from commercial and economic activity by theological dictates. When all economic transactions must adhere to religious specifications, every aspect of daily economic life is affected. The very wealthy can circumvent or modulate these conditions, but the development of a civil society or a broader economic consensus remains conscribed when transactional exchanges outside of family, mosque, and government cannot flourish.

As Voltaire and his contemporaries underscored, when theology prevails, it is much more difficult to condemn, criticize, satirize or discuss government, commerce or beliefs without the risk of being accused of heresy or worse. In order to conduct business, theological and theocratic exigencies required special instruments, such as the "sukuk," a precursor of checks and certificate of debt, but as Mahmoud El-Gamal, chair of Islamic finance at Rice University wrote, "As the name suggests, Islamic finance is first and foremost about religious identity," but he refutes the "simplistic" explanation of rejection of all interest in that traditional religious scholarship is far more sophisticated and solves the paradox, "to use legal devices to restructure interest bearing debt, collecting interest in the form of rent or price mark-up." One such instrument is the sale/lease-back bond "sukuk al-ijara." As the Koran bans "gharar," derivatives and hedge funds are technically forbidden ("Middle East Banking and Finance Survey" 2007). Every aspect of financial activity, from operational to regulatory, still has to pass a religious-moral set of obstacles which can create obstacles similar to those encountered by medieval finance in Western Europe. However in the crisis of 2008, the conservative nature of these operations, under religious interdiction, has greatly limited the exposure and risk of Sharia compliant institutions in home and host countries: "These products instead pay profits from an underlying business or rent from a building used as collateral to raise money" ("Middle East Banking and Finance Survey" 2008).

China, unlike other non-European empires, followed a unique trajectory from specie to paper and back to specie from the eleventh to the thirteenth century. Having mastered highly sophisticated printing techniques in the Sung dynasty, paper money, introduced to complement the shortage of metal, "produced a government supervised system for issuing printed sheets of paper currency, four million in a single year" (Boorstin 1983: 502). Used to pay the military, the paper currency was prone to devaluation, setting off a cycle of inflation in basic commodities. Marco Polo was astonished by the China of Kublai Khan where, after 1260, paper could replace gold and silver:

> Of this money the Khan has such a quantity made that with it he could buy all the treasures in the world. With this currency he orders all payments to be made throughout every province and kingdom and region of his empire.
>
> (Boorstin 1983: 502)

What Marco Polo found even more striking was that a man "goes to the Khan's mint with some of these papers and gives them in payment for the gold and silver which he buys from the mint-master" (Boorstin 1983: 502). However by the end of the Mongol's Yuan dynasty (1260–1368), and the start of the Ming dynasty (1368–1644), fear of inflation began to reduce paper money in circulation.

As long distance travel increased, monetary transactions in Europe through the thirteenth century included Byzantine as well as Arab dinars, bezant, and hyperpere which circulated freely. Since Charlemagne, silver coinage from the mines of northern Germany was predominant, but by the mid-thirteenth century gold minting spread throughout the major cities and states. Genoa, with deniers d'or (1252); Florence mints the florin; (1250s); France mints its first ecus d'or (1266); Venice its ducats (1284), by the early 1300s Flanders, Castile, Bohemia and England are minting and using gold coins. Bimetallism, which dominates Europe for the next five centuries, created an active foreign exchange market dictated by weather, seasons and the price of commodities.

> In Genoa, silver is expensive in September, January and April because of the departure of ships, in Rome where resides the Pope… and the travels of the Pope who raises the price of silver everywhere he locates, in Valencia, it is expensive in July because of the price of rice, in Montpellier there are three fairs which greatly increase the value of silver.
>
> (LeGoff 1972: 30)

The cost of specie dependent on location, political stability and the price of grain extends into the late Middle Ages. On April 26, 1399, Francesco Datini's correspondent in Bruges advised the Florentine banking house to place its funds in the following fashion:

> It appears that there is an abundance of specie in Genoa, so do not send our money to Genoa, or only if you can get a very good price for it; put it rather in Venice or Florence or here in Bruges, or in Paris, or Montpellier, or wherever seems best to you.
>
> (Braudel 1982)

Cross-border and intra-regional transactions necessitated the use of monetary instruments and a new found sense of trust and confidence in a community of merchants, bankers and moneychangers. Raymond de Roover, in his seminal studies on Bruges and the Low Countries, described how bills of acceptance, endorsed checks, bank notes, promissory notes, paper money, and new coinage were all part of a gradual transformation from tangible to intangible forms of commercial transaction. As the process become more impersonal and paper began to replace specie, the issue of trust, security and stability of the issuing authority became fundamental in the relationship between the state (authority), individual and currency (the transactional medium). Mobility was essential for financial activity, in order to develop and to earn rather than depend upon profits; merchants had to be free to conduct trade year round, to travel without penalties and restrictions, therefore, at the risk of freedom of new ideas and new influences. This led to organized trade within leagues, guilds and fairs, but also to piracy, smuggling and circumvention of often very restrictive laws, which even Adam Smith, understood to be counterproductive to transactional activity. Sir Francis Drake who produced vast profits of almost 300,000 pounds in his 1577 to 1580 voyages for Elizabeth I, was considered a hero in England, but a notorious pirate in Spain. The growth of commerce brought in its wake not only vast improvements in infrastructure, but also preventive measures, insured in the principles of maritime law and the industry of insurance in place since the twelfth century in Italy, but essential to commerce by the sixteenth century.

Greater accountability, through the introduction of double entry bookkeeping, by 1394 in Italy, commercial codes and courts to settle commercial disputes enforced moral codes of behavior, extolling the virtues of honesty, punctuality, fidelity, credibility, diligence applied to the commercial realm. The development of monopolies to protect specific sectors, leading to state protectionism to protect national industries and merchants at its origins, guaranteed more control over freewheeling trade, encouraging in England, the Low Countries and even in France under Colbert, closer interdependency between monarchs, governors and merchants.

The concept of public debt did not exist in ancient Greece or Rome. It originated in medieval Italy in the twelfth century, "secured on the state salt monopoly, the revenues of which were earmarked for debt service and redemption" (Ferguson 2001: 107). Whereas medieval monarchs depended on large private loans to fund wars and military expeditions, by the sixteenth century, following the more sophisticated model of the Italian city states, France, under Henri IV, issued in Paris annuities known as rentes. The Spanish crown created the "asientos," short-term, high interest loan contracts, and longer term, lower interest bonds assigned on ordinary revenues, "juros" (Ferguson 2001: 109). Basically these instruments invented the concept of state bonds or Treasury bonds. International loans were actually direct personal loans between monarchs and hugely wealthy families.

In the fourteenth century, Edward II was indebted to the Frescobaldis of Florence and Edward III to the Bardi and Perruzzi until the bankruptcy of 1347.

Genoa, a center of finance based on lending to the Spanish Crown in the 1550s, dealt in negotiable bills of exchange, combining paper and specie for long-term transactions. The concept of public banks as deposit banks for wealthy creditors, Casa di San Giorgio in Genoa in 1407, and Banco di Rialto in Venice in 1587, preceded the Bank of Amsterdam in 1609 and the Bank of England.

Spain borrowed vast sums, offering as guarantee gold and silver. However, between 1520–1556 the amounts borrowed rose till total payments, owed largely to German, Flemish, and Italian bankers, reached over 38 million ducats, of which 33 million was owed to foreigners. This debt exceeded by "roughly two million more than the amount of precious metals reaching Seville and belonging to the Crown" (Vilar 1976: 149). The problem was that while international financiers greatly benefited due to increase in taxes and price volatility, Spanish landowners and aristocrats, unable and unwilling to adjust to the new economic environment were often relegated to heavy indebtedness and near beggary. The peasant boy hero of the picaresque novel *The Life of Lazarillo de Tormes and His Fortunes and Adversities*, and Cervantes' impoverished delusional aristocrat *Don Quixote* personified broader instability and ruptures in social hierarchy. Tomas de Mercado's *Summa de tratos et contratos*, published in Salamanca in 1569, focused on the purchasing power of money, discussing in great detail price fluctuations in money and commodities within Spain, where: "a thousand ducats are esteemed much higher in Castile than in Andalusia" (Vilar 1976: 165). By the 1580s Spain was in the throes of surging inflation worsened by the outflow of precious commodities to the rest of the continent and increased dependency on promissory notes, bonds, bad currency (low grade foreign coin) and heavy taxation. In Spain, as the Holy Roman Empire disintegrated, there was fear of the illusory impact and dangers of gold in opposition to land.

The development of the printing press in Germany coincided with the creation of minting and coining presses across Europe. By the mid-fifteenth century French and English currency was standardized, at least nominally, public banks were established in Italy, and real estate speculation expanded in the form of land bonds. In consequence, relationships between money in its function as a medium of exchange and the commodities that it purchased became increasingly indirect.

1.2 Agents, institutions and transactions

History proves that it was not the Jews, but rather the Italians, Lombards, Cahorsieans, and Arabs who set in motion the concept of loans, accounts receivable and usurious loans. This evolution coincided with the first three crusades (1096, 1146, 1189) and the creation of the first banks in Genoa and Venice (1171, 1177). The crusades required complex financial dealings between the Germans, French knights, French kings, and Italian merchants and city state rulers. The chronicles of the crusades specify transactions on armament and supplies for the trip. It also revived active commodity and currency markets which flourished in Italy, transforming the monometallic and limited consumer markets across northern Europe. The crusades in the name of theology broke the barriers of transactional operations as necessity required "solidarity between Christian and Muslim merchants." In 1074, Pope Gregory VII intervened with Philippe I to gain restitution of goods seized from Italian merchants in France. The Second Lateran Council in 1139 condemned usury calling for excommunication, refusal of inhumation in Christian cemeteries and refusal of their offerings, reinforced by the interdictions of the Council of Vienna in 1311. The Church remained steadfast in its condemnation, however the merchant began to be acknowledged as a powerful and necessary part of society.

Gilles le Muisit, in his poem, *C'est des Marchands*, states that,

> No country can govern itself apart from others.
> For these do merchants work and labor
> For they are needed in all countries and under all regimes
> [Nul pays ne se peot de li seus gouvrener
> Pour chou vont marcheant travillier et pener....
> Chou que marcheant vont delà mer, decha mer
> Pour pourvir les pays, che les font entr'amer].
>
> (Le Muisit 1350)

The conquest and pillage of Constantinople in the fourth crusade, inspired two extraordinary first hand accounts detailing the costs, transactions and financial problems the crusaders encountered. In *La Conquete de Constantinople* by Robert de Clari, a poor member of minor nobility who followed his liege on the crusade, describes how he had to struggle to acquire supplies and ships from the doge of Venice in the amount of "cent mile marcs for armes and cinquante gallies [a hundred thousand marcs for armies and fifty galleys]" (*Historiens et Chroniqueurs du Moyen Age* (1952: 32). The doge charged four marcs per knight and four per horse, once in Genoa "costs ran so high in the city [la chertes fu si grans en la ville]" they could pay for neither meat nor grain long-term (1952: 32). Clari writes with wonderment of the markets, palaces and the opulence "richesse" of Saint Sophia. (1952: 64). Geoffroy de Villehardouin, a powerful noble and royal emissary wrote a far more sophisticated political and diplomatic account of the crusade, also entitled *La Conquete de Constantinople* (c. 1207) which corroborates the problems of negotiating and transacting with the Venetians. The French were only able to pay half the price demanded of 34,000 marcs outstanding and had to arrange for reimbursement from the king of Hungary and Slovenia while the barons complained that they have already paid for their passage. Jean de Joinville, who lived to the extraordinary age of 92, in his biography of Louis IX, *Histoire de Saint Louis*, completed in 1309, described the crusade of 1248 in which he participated, and an account of the last crusade in which Louis IX died in 1270. In the Egyptian crusade of 1248 he detailed the limitations placed upon the knights:

> As I did not have 1,000 pounds income from my land ... once arrived in Cyprus I had only 140 livres tournois, once my vessel paid, which caused a

number of my knights to let me know that if I did not find the necessary funds, they would have to leave me. And God, who has never failed me, had me called by the king who put me on salary and placed 800 pounds in my safebox. I had more money than I had need for.

(Joinville 1952: 232)

From these accounts it is clear that the crusaders depended on the will of God to guarantee not only victory, but the basic necessities which required money, exchange, commerce and solid business skills. By the twelfth century, images of money, both neutral and condemnatory, appeared in medieval texts and manuscript illumination. Horned and winged griffons accompany the hoarder, as the miser becomes the symbol of avarice among the seven deadly sins. As the papacy in Rome and higher clergy became wealthy, the distinctions between the lower clergy's vows of poverty and the power of the institution bifurcated.

In Gratien's (twelfth-century) work on canon law the phrase, "Homo mercatur nunquam aut vix potest Deo placer" (the merchant can never be pleasing to God), seemed to define the general environment against transactional activity. In the list of "forbidden professions," "illicita negocia," or dishonorable activities "inhonesta mercimonia," commerce or money professions are listed (LeGoff 1956: 71). However, Pope Gregory I and Thomas of Aquinas rank merchants alongside prostitutes, jugglers, butchers, and inn keepers. Yet, simultaneously those who engage in commercial and monetary activity are also often categorized with doctors, lawyers, notaries, and judges – part of a new class of urban civil professions, the result of the rebirth of urban communities, denser demographics, better roads, ports, new market neighborhoods, and fairs. The fairs of Champagne by the thirteenth century required a new set of regulations and above all official protection.

1.3 Instruments

New instruments, such as bills of exchange, appear in the archives of the Datini family by 1399, specifying exchanges between Bruges and Barcelona for the account of an Italian banker, Barberi. The bill of exchange, the first paper instrument in Europe, became a means of transferring funds, commercial payment, a source of credit, and established the basis for profit by fees collected on various operations.

Although the precept "nummus non parit nummos [money must not self perpetuate]" is prevalent, even Thomas Aquinas and Gilbert de Lessines understood that money was necessary in order to facilitate exchanges. LeGoff emphasizes that locking economic concepts within a "theological-moral bind" (LeGoff 1972: 75), leaves commercial and financial operations in limbo. Venice is a reluctant intermediary in the first three crusades, however this became counterproductive as interdictions against commerce with the enemy set up barriers against trade in lumber, arms, and ships, without which the crusaders would remain stranded in Italy. As early as the Council of Latran in 1179, dispensations begin to appear: "la treve de Dieu reclame la securite pour les pretres, moines ... pelerins, marchands, paysans" (LeGoff 1986: 76). The courtly novel, *Galeran de Bretagne*, attributed to Renault (c. 1210–1220), dedicates a passage to moneychangers in Metz who deal in silver, gold and precious metals. By 1250, documents in Lombardy, Genoa, and Venice discuss transactions with instruments such as bills of exchange, overdrafts, loans with concealed interest called "nutuum gratis et amore [free and loving notes]," and lettres de change, often involving parties in different countries. A hierarchy is established between usurers, Lombards or Jews, who dealt in short-term loans; "cambio," moneychangers, and deposit bankers, who received and lent in ordinary business contexts; and the great merchant bankers who lent long-term to monarchs, the church or the papacy. Because Christians were not allowed to practice these trades on the lower echelons, the image of the moneylender and the usurer melded into the image of the foreigner, subject to hatred and scorn. The moneylender takes on traits of physical deformity, ugliness, or moral perversity. Jehan de Meung's addition to *Roman de la Rose* (c. 1275), *Faux Semblant*, indicts usurers for hoarding reserves of gold. The "Prioress' Tale," in Chaucer's *Canterbury Tales* (1380–1400) condemns a Jewish quarter "for foul usury and love of villainy." The functions of bankers, money handlers, and merchants often overlapped. Raymond De Roover documented that the Lombards in Italy, the Cahorsians in Bruges, and Jewish money handlers in Italy and England, mentioned in Boccaccio's *Decameron* and Chaucer's *Canterbury Tales* were associated with short-term "usurious" transactions while the "banchi grossi" of Florence dealt in international trade, and coordinated government and papal loans. In Dante's *Divinia Commedia* (1320), usurers are placed in the seventh circle of *Inferno* with wealthy popes and cardinals. Usury is represented by the Gerydon, a griffin clawed, half-human monster, and the money pouches hang around the usurer's necks for all eternity.

Nicolas Oresme (1320–1382), who wrote *Treatise on the Origins, Nature, Law and Alterations of Money*, explained that profit can come from money changing, banking or exchange. Ranking financial activity in moral terms he specified that usury, which alters the value of the currency is contemptible and bad but that forgery is even worse than usury. Fundamentally the moral attack on finance derived from notions of charity rooted in spiritual belief. Bonaventure de Périers' *Nouvelles récréations et joyeux devis* (1965 [1558]) makes references to misuse of funds, poor investments, or poor debts, always in the context of negative themes of fraud or self-deception. In Pierre de Larivey's play, *Les esprits* (1579), the protagonist is the greedy usurer, Severin. In Jacques Grevin's *La Tresoriere* (1561), the young greedy wife of the treasurer needs the help of the wealthy merchants to bail her out. In *La Nouvelle* by Lasphrise, a tax collector and his valet are sent to collect 6,000 francs from a farmer, the money is stolen, and the shrewd servants get their share. Themes of an unscrupulous middle class, naïve nobility, and a conniving servant class, which dominated seventeenth- and eighteenth-century comedy farce and novellas, are already in place.

In England the theme of usury as a vice became a popular subject in the Elizabethan theater, with Marlowe's *The Jew of Malta* (c. 1589), Shakespeare's *The Merchant of Venice* (c. 1595), Thomas Middleton's *A Trick to Catch The Old One* (c. 1605 see Taylor and Lavagnino 2008), and the portrayal of shady dealings, greedy creditors, and the superstitious voluptuary financier, Sir Epicure Mammon, in Ben Jonson's *Alchemist* (1610). Shakespeare dealt with economic conflicts and transactions in *A Comedy of Errors* (c. 1594). In *The Merchant of Venice*, Shylock represents the anti-Semitic archetype of the Jewish usurer, a societal pariah whose venality, avarice, and desire for the humiliation of Christians, justify his downfall. Yet, he is also endowed with positive qualities, such as commercial acumen and love for his family, which make him function as a tragic figure rather than merely an object of contempt. On a more representational level, his clients, the Christian merchants Bassanio and Antonio, personify the developing merchant class embroiled in speculation and long-term borrowing based upon risky and unpredictable maritime ventures.

As early as 1163, in Genoa, commercial contracts are drawn up, as well as company contracts in Venice, to protect a given group of investors. Prominent Florentine families, the Peruzzi, Bardi, and Medici developed cross-border business ventures with home offices in Florence, and independent subsidiaries in London, Bruges, Geneva, Lyon, Avignon, Milan, Venice, and Rome. Consolidating power by inheritance and marriage, they gained a stronghold in government and finance with monopolies in minting and silver mining. During the years of the papal schism between French and Italian popes, there were shortages of money, and the link between merchants and the papacy increased.

Benedetto Cotrugli in his treatise "Le commerce et le marchand ideal" (c. mid-fifteenth century), stresses that international commerce is a necessity accepted by divine power, as it is understood that money and fortune is the merchant's ultimate goal. Cotrugli stresses that merchants need to overcome financial ruin, start again as courtiers, inn keepers or artisans,

> For no artisan ever knew, in no kingdom nor Nation how to handle money – which is at the core of human conditions – as can an honest and experienced merchant [car aucun homme de métier n'a jamais su, en aucun royaume ni en aucun Etat, manier l'argent – qui est la base de les états humains – comme le fait un marchand honnête et expérimente].
>
> (quoted in LeGoff 1986: 81)

By the early fourteenth century, the Church found that reconciling wealth and piety was highly advantageous and self serving. It began requiring works of charity, large contributions and donations, such as hospitals in Antioch and Sienna, and monasteries in Jerusalem, all in return for salvation. The best solution for final penitence was to renounce wealth by giving it to the Church and to join orders. Baude Crespin, famous banker of Arras becomes a monk of Saint-

Vaast, Bernardo Tolomei, great banker of Sienna, creates the order of Olivetains. Earlier, Goderic de Finchale, canonized by Pope Innocent III in 1197, was a great merchant of Cremona. Between the thirteenth and fifteenth centuries

> Cathedral chapters lend money at high rates of interest. The profits of usury, like those of simony, should have been refused by churchmen as hateful to God, but a Bishop in Paris, when consulted by a usurer as to the salvation of his soul, instead of urging restitution, recommended him to dedicate his ill gotten wealth to the building of Notre Dame.
>
> (Tawney 1953: 35)

There is also a weakening of the papacy in the Great Schism (1373–1417) with the double papacy in Rome and Avignon. Under the succession of French popes, France gained in stature and prestige, but there was an erosion in papal authority, and vast corruption within the Church. The papacy had to be obeyed, but it no longer had the same moral authority over the wealthy merchant and aristocratic urban elite. Simultaneously the relationship between nobility and finance began to shift. Philippe le Bel forced the dissolution of the Knights of Malta, as they had become the defacto bankers of Europe. Accusing the head of the order of Templars of sorcery and subsequently beheading him in 1314, the French king reclaimed control over the order's wealth. By the end of the twelfth century, "the social position of Italian bankers and merchants brought them so closely in touch with the nobility they were often confounded with it" (Pirenne 1963: 23). Like today's super-wealthy, who are imposed upon to pledge large sums for good works against disease, poverty, environmental causes, including Clinton's Global Initiative, they put celebrity in the service and patronage of righteous, worthy causes. During the Middle Ages, the Renaissance merchant bankers' patronage of art, sculpture, painting, iconography, as well as portraiture, granted earthly prestige and promises of divine redemption.

Wealth became more ostentatious as the rich attended to their appearance, clothing, accessories, and luxury in furnishings and household goods. In 1314, Philippe le Bel of France imposed an edict against bourgeoisie in furs. Sienna and Florence attempted to curb the excess of conspicuous consumption, as the newly wealthy merchants combined vast opulence with immense acts of generosity in the support of local armies. Much of the magnificent architecture of Italian and Flemish cities was originally the home or site of business of great fortunes: Hales de Bruges, Loggia della Mercanzia de Sienna, Medici palaces in Florence.

Wealth and power also required presence outside of home regions and cities. By the 1290s, the Bardi, Peruzzi, and Datini families had branches in England, lending to the Crown until the massive debts incurred by Edward III, at the start of the Hundred Years War, provoked the first city state bankruptcy in 1347. By 1338, there were more than 80 banking houses in Florence. In the mid-thirteenth century, banking dynasties in Italy conducted highly complex operations. The Leccacorvo bank in Genoa dealt in long distance transfers, overdrafts, as well as loans for merchants, bankers and officials, investing in the French silk industry. In Bruges, moneychangers, hostellers, brokers, and foreign merchants functioned in a tightly structured fashion. An active foreign exchange market flourished in thirteenth- and fourteenth-century Venice, Florence and Genoa, whose ruling doges and princes encouraged currency exports, and generated large loans to support England's military expeditions against France. The functions of bankers, money handlers, and merchants often overlapped. In the late thirteenth century, De Roover documented that the Lombards in Italy, the Cahorsians in Bruges, and Jewish money handlers in Italy and England (referred to in Boccaccio's *Decameron* and Chaucer's *Canterbury Tales*) were associated with short-term "usurious" transactions, while the "Banchi grossi" of Florence dealt in international trade, and coordinated government and papal loans. In 1470, the House of Medici had branches with banking functions outside of Italy in Lyon, Bruges, Avignon, and London. Account books were kept in florins, the official gold coin minted in Florence and convertible throughout Europe.

By the end of the fifteenth century, Louis XI had established four major fairs, and within a century Lyons, a major textile center, ranked with the large commercial centers of Seville, Medino de Campo, Lucca, Genoa, Nuremberg, and Augsburg. Bankers in Lyons included a roster of names as diverse as Medici, Bonvisi, Salvaiti, Martelli, Welzers, Obrechts and Kleberger as the city became a main center for public credit. By 1572, 224 merchants met in Paris to free up foreign exchange regulations that could not be imposed on "foreign countries of every nationality with different customs" (Braudel vol. 1 1979: 91). Bodin understood a century before Colbert that France needed trade and production to attract foreign capital, and bring in coin in circulation. Montaigne in his Essays (1580) reiterated the argument that the mere collection of metal, without the ability to dispense it and put it into circulation, ruined Spain, where gold was put into temples, palaces and ornamentation, while France allowed its gold to circulate and expand in trade. Yet within a century these precepts would no longer be applicable.

1.4 Investments and social mobility

Who were the first international investors and from where did they originate? Political and religious unrest in the late Middle Ages and during the war-ridden Renaissance forced a wealthy urban merchant class into political exile. The "fuorisciti," exiled old noble families in Italian city states, reestablished themselves in other Italian and French cities and continued to trade and to transact currency deals with their former colleagues (Braudel 1982: 167). Yet for Pirenne, although "they undoubtedly betray a tendency toward the development

of capitalism ... one of its most obvious characteristics was its hostility to capitalism" (Pirenne 1963: 98). For Pirenne, Italy alone represented economic life in
the fourteenth century,

> The only persons who engaged in affairs of any magnitude were those who
> had interests in the Italian companies and brokers. There was no such thing
> as a great commercial house or a great bank to the north of the Alps ... even
> Flanders ... was almost exclusively Italian.
>
> (Pirenne 1963: 236)

A new group of capitalists appeared in Flanders, France, and England, consisting
of men who did not necessarily come from old money. Lyon, Bruges, and Frankfurt, as well as the great Italian city states of Venice, Genoa, and Florence, and
finally London created real competition between old nobility tied to their lands
and immensely wealthy burghers with mobility and cross-border connections
and holdings. By the thirteenth century, through marriage, the middle class
began to penetrate the ranks of the nobility, acquiring titles in exchange for
wealth. LeGoff describes how in Florence, "Every day one sees a very wealthy
common man who seeks a poor but titled wife [On voit chaque jour un roturier
tres riche qui veut se marier a une femme pauvre mais noble]" (LeGoff 1972:
75). A moneychanger in Bruges, Evard Goederic, is called "Sire," his wife
"Madame." The shift from "noblesse de sang" to "noblesse de robe" across
Europe occurs through a symbiotic relationship between land rich but impoverished nobility, and wealthy merchants seeking prestige, titles and name recognition. This leads to political power and social responsibility on the part of
merchants in the welfare of their cities and communities. During the corrupt
period of the dual papacy in the thirteenth century, the popes depended on the
wealth of merchants. During the Avignon years, Italian bankers became responsible for the taxes sent to the Vatican, as bankers served the papacy as political
and economic advisors.

Henri Pirenne points out that major political and banking dynasties – Balbi in
Venice, Buonsignori in Sienna, Bardi, Peruzzi and the Medicis in Florence,
Fieschi and Grimaldi in Genoa, as well as in Gand and Arras – tended to follow
a pattern of first generation accumulation of wealth and the attempt to achieve a
higher social rank. The second generation focused more on wealth acquisition
and prestige, associated with socially recognized activities in the professions and
the arts. Cosimo de Medici (1389–1464), the patriarch of the family, was a merchant as well as a "banchierei" or "tavolieri" who dealt in commerce and bills of
exchange. Allied to the Bardi through marriage, one of Florence's wealthiest
families until the bankruptcy of 1347, he established what can rightly be called
diversified holdings with branches in over 16 European cities, and by 1447 he
became banker to Pope Nicolas V. His great grandson Jean became Pope Leon
X (1513–1521), followed by Jules, who became pope Clement VII (1523–1534).
Two descendants become queens of France, Catherine of Medici, the wife of
Henri II, and Marie de Medici, the wife of Henri IV. The dynasty was unique in

attaining the highest levels of commerce, political, and religious power across Europe. Their establishments took in account deposits and Cosimo and his brother had in deposit 10,000 florins in Florence and 10,000 in Venice. Term deposits were for three or six months and instead of direct interest payments, forbidden by the Church, fees were based on the "partage des benfices." Once designated bankers to the Vatican, all transactions to the Holy See went through the Medici's bills of exchange. By 1460, Cosimo de Medici's fortune was about 400,000 florins. His son, Lorenzo the Magnificent, spent close to 663,755 florins in commissioning buildings, artwork, charity, and taxes. In his study, *Dynasties*, David Landes describes a dynasty as "three successive generations of family control." Banking is a key industry as "success in banking historically draws on personal connections – which do you know, whom do you trust and who trusts you? Banking relies primarily on a single homogeneous commodity: legal tender. Banking is outgrowth of trade. Banking is "other people's money" (Landes 2006: xiv). Italian bankers provided funds to the English crown. Edward I had Ricciardi and Frescobaldi, and Edward III (1327–1377) Bardi and Peruzi, who lent them money. However, kings were notorious for not repaying loans and as Edward II defaulted so went the Italian economy.

In Bourges, Jacques Coeur (1397–1456), a furrier of modest background, became "maitre de la monnaie," in 1435, as well as silversmith to the king a few years later. As banker to the Crown, he lent money to the nobles at 10–20 percent interest, with representatives in Bruges, England, and Italy. He also linked up with merchant bankers in Lyons, and by 1441–1451 his functions included being in charge of tax collection in Languedoc. He became indispensable to the impoverished and mad King Charles VII. France used the livre tournois (about 31 grams of silver which was subdivided into 20 sous). In 1450, a gardener earned one sou a day, a sheep cost four sous. The tutor to the king's son earned 2,300 livres a year and the funeral of Charles VII, in 1461 cost 18,300 livres. When Jacques Coeur was accused of trafficking in bad money and commerce with infidels, he was condemned to pay a fine of 300,000 ecus, restitution of 100,000 ecus, and permanent banishment from the court in 1453. Jacques Coeur, mentioned in the Grand Testament of Villion as emblem of vast wealth, was efficient and corrupt, and made himself indispensable to the court. Montaigne wrote: "No man divulges his revenue, or at least which way it comes in; but everyone publishes his acquisitions" (Montaigne, Essays (1580); Oxford Book of Aphorisms (1983).

By the mid-1550s, the merchant banker had to have cross-border interests. His money could be generated and reinvested in different regions or countries, no longer limited or beholden to his community. Between 1450 and 1550, Europe saw an increase in strong monarchies under Louis XI and Francois I in France, Henry VIII in England, Ferdinand and Isabelle in Spain, Charles V, head of the Holy Roman Empire, Corvinus in Hungary, and Gustavus Vasa in Sweden.

Those countries in which capitalism was developing we see that the princes lavished upon it the proofs of their benevolence, … in England the Crown

supported the enterprises of the merchant adventurers … Francois I introduced Italian industries, encouraged commerce and capital … [In turn] the
bankers liberated them from the embarrassing control of their subjects.

(Pirenne 1963: 333)

1.5 Fairs and market places

Large seasonal markets, in Champagne and Flanders, and religious fairs and
trading houses became the forums which generated and put into circulation many
of the negotiable instruments and transactional networks which still dominate
modern investment. They acted as embryonic clearing houses where bills of
exchange, discount notes, letters of credit, and short- and medium-term exchange
contracts were instituted between merchant bankers in France, Spain, Italy and
the Low Countries. Long before the advent of the influential role of London and
New York's international financial centers, Genoa, Venice, Amsterdam, Bruges
and Antwerp dominated commerce and finance with active currency dealings,
short-term gold and silver contracts, and futures markets in commodities.

Braudel's study of markets from the twelfth to the seventeenth century in
Toulouse, Les Halles in Paris, Plaza Mayor in Madrid, in Bruges, and in Lisbon
demonstrated their role in the proliferation of financial activity in all aspects of
social interaction. Within the market took place "land sale agreements, emphy-
teutic leases (perpetual rent contracts), donations, marriage contracts and dowry
settlements" (Braudel vol. II 1979: 30). There were about 800 market towns in
England and Wales between 1500 and 1640. Money was rarely used in a rural
economy where it was hoarded and kept within the physical confines of the
household. Markets in urban centers brought together merchants, farmers, peddlers, and moneychangers from different areas, forcing them to develop long-
distance and long-term arrangements. "What was universal was the emergence
of people willing to advance funds and of networks of moneylenders, whether
Jews or Lombards, natives of Cahors or as in Bavaria, convents which specialized in loans to peasants" (Braudel vol. II 1979: 321). There began to be a
forward market in money, letters of exchange, and bills of acceptance. The fairs
of Besancon, Lyon, Genoa, Medina del Campo in Castile, and
Frankfurt-am-Maine functioned as clearing houses for large bills of exchange.
By the eighteenth century the same phenomenon would occur across Poland in
Lublin, Gdansk, and Poznan and across Russia in the nineteenth century.

Fairs transmuted into exchanges, or "bourses," across Europe. These buildings, often constructed near the old fair areas, become the centers of financial
life, a meeting place of bankers, merchants, currency dealers, bankers' agents,
and brokers, as described in Samuel Ricard, *Le Nouveau Negociant* (1686).

In Germany, the Low Countries, Italy, and England the trade routes created in
the fairs of the 1400s also perfected exchange and credit instruments, creating
account money, also introducing principles of installment payments; purchases
on credit and the start of commercial litigation which would help stimulate as
well as corrupt trading practices and long-term transactions. In *La Farce de*

Maitre Pierre Parthelin, one of the most popular plays performed in France, and later in Germany, first published in 1464 and reprinted in 1480 and 1490, the lawyer Pathelin, the draper Guillaume Joceaulme, and the shepherd are all equally dishonest and greedy. Alternating between expressions of piety and terms of commerce, "Before all, how much the first bale will cost me. The Lord must be paid first, that is the right thing to do. Here is one denier; let us do nothing without evoking the name of the Lord" (*La Farce de Maitre Pathelin*, in folio). There are references to deniers, francs as well as ecus, and silver pieces. The shrewd but impoverished lawyer, Pathelin, wants to purchase cloth without payment; defending the shepherd he tries in turn to cheat the merchant who wants to deprive the shepherd of his due. These types of plays, performed near the church, attracted nobles, bourgeois and common folk. The dynamics of the merchant class willing to extend credit, the needs of manufacturers, farmers and workers to be paid on time, and the interplay of law and commerce are already part of the social discourse.

Records of the Besancon fairs in 1596 describe the proceedings of wealthy merchants, government emissaries, brokers and important moneychangers (banchieri de canto, exchange rate bankers) that came from Genoa, Spain and Florence to establish a club that regulated the rates of exchange by decree (decretudos). Between 60–200 men paid a hefty membership fee of 3,000 gold ecus for the privilege of deciding rates and closing deals worth 30 million to 40 million ecus: "Four times a year it was the scene of decisive but discreet meetings, something like the International Bank of Basle in our day" (Braudel vol. 1 1979: 91).

These transactions in large sums required strict codes of behavior. Merchants developed networks not only as business contacts but as social structures based on trust, creditworthiness, reputation and effectiveness. Braudel elegantly debunked the premise that Jews were the only closed business community as laid forth by Werner Sombart (*Die Juden and das Wirtschaftleben*, 1922). Although wealthy merchants who controlled trade routes and networks were often foreigners, there were networks of Italian, Armenian, Greeks, Turks and Russians. Homogeneous groups, based on ethnic or religious community, offered a greater guarantee of trustworthiness, of community and of the ability to guarantee payment.

Boorstin's subtitle *A History of Man's Search to Know His World and Himself* (Boorstin 1983) perfectly elucidates the extraordinary quest for knowledge from cosmology to cartography, printing to optical sciences that occurred during the late Middle Ages and Renaissance. It was also a period of monetary evolution, in theory and practice. The newly found wealth in the Americas fueled an influx of gold and precious metal into Spain and Portugal, generating vast wealth. But, lack of government and legal structures in the fragmented Iberian Peninsula could not control the ensuing flooding of world markets, massive currency smuggling, inflation and economic chaos. Huge increases in circulation of gold and silver provoked devaluation, deflation and inflation as currencies, dependent on supply and demand, overextended the market. Where gold from

Africa had incited the first wave of gold minting in the 1250s in Italy and England, by the 1400s Spain and Portugal begin minting escudos rivaling the ducat and florin. Gold coming in through Lisbon and then Seville in the boom years of 1520–1540 began to decline due to excess of silver in the wake of the discovery of the Potosi mines in Peru.

During the reign of Francois I in France (1517–1547), and the unification of Europe under the Holy Roman Empire (1519), large merchant investment houses emerged, led by powerful, energetic men whose demeanor, luxurious lifestyle and keen business sense were similar to the Rothschilds, Schlumbergers, and Rockefellers. The two most representative banker-trader-investors were Jacob Fugger of Augsburg and Thomas Gresham of London. Fugger dominated the entire European currency, silver and copper market from the 1520s to the 1550s. His influence extended throughout Europe and the Ottoman Empire, with representative offices in Budapest, Cracow, Breslau, Dazing, Nuremburg, Mainz, Cologne, Antwerp, Venice, Rome, Naples, Lisbon and Madrid. Painted by Durer, known and respected by kings, advisor to Charles V, Holy Roman Emperor, Fugger ruled his own vast commercial empire involved in banking, underwriting maritime and government loans, land, mining and business holdings. He had a monopoly on copper and silver mining with exclusive rights to control prices. In 1523, in one of the first recorded antitrust suits, the High Council of Cologne accused Fugger of monopolizing the industry and trade of Augsburg. He invoked the help of the emperor and won back his rights to continue control of traffic in metals and currency. Fugger's advice to those seeking to invest in the Orient was "the principle is to invest one's capital into three parts: one third in land, one third in precious commodities and one third in business" (Petit-Dutaillis 1982: 94)

By the start of the sixteenth century, German bankers were as important as the Italians in cross-border dealings going through Lyons and other major commercial centers. Major bankers of Nuremberg, Augsburg, and Ulm had correspondents in Lyon, conducting transactions between Spain and German principalities and city states. Hans Kleberg, with offices in Lyon in 1515, and Berne in 1521, was instrumental in some the first reimbursements of Francois I to Lorenzo II de Medici. A skilled intermediary, he "was able to seduce and persuade others to lend money to the French king, thereby avoiding to commit directly to such loans" (Petit-Dutaillis 1982: 111).

Sir Thomas Gresham, financial advisor to Elizabeth I, began his career as negotiator of bills of exchange in London's Change Alley, and dealer in Spanish short-term gold contracts His father, having been designated by Henry VIII as merchant banker, Thomas became a goldsmith banker. In his Day Book in 1546 he wrote: "May God grant me profit and prosperity to defend myself against bad fortune, loss and damages, Amen" (Petit-Dutaillis 1982: 120). Titled by Elizabeth I in 1559, and sent as ambassador to the Netherlands, he speculated between the florin and sterling on the Antwerp Exchange. He also began an active traffic in Spanish state bonds, "juros" issued by Philippe II of Spain. Returning to England in 1566, Gresham created the Royal Exchange, based on the Amsterdam bourse. In honor of his father, who wanted to provide a place of shelter on Lombard Street for the merchants of Change Alley, he built a bourse modeled on the bourse of Antwerp. The building opened in 1568 with a bell tower to ring in the start and end of trading sessions. The building, renamed the Royal Exchange in honor of Queen Elizabeth I's visit in 1570, burned in the Great Fire of 1666, was rebuilt and burnt down in 1838, and again rebuilt in 1844, a few steps from the Bank of England and inaugurated by Queen Victoria. In the original building, Gresham set up a college where professors taught theology, jurisprudence, medicine, astronomy, geometry, music and rhetoric until 1596. A full classic curriculum was taught within the temple of money, without one course ever devoted to knowledge of economics, monetary activity or policy.

The Age of Discovery transformed economic thought and cultural perceptions of the influence of money and cross-border interdependency of financial flows. Exports of copper, coral, and lead augmented the seemingly endless flow of silver from the Americas as Spanish reals and Portuguese crusados dominated global trade. "In 1580, a five-ship fleet left Lisbon with 1,300,000 cruzados worth of reals or pieces of eight" (Vilar 1976: 101). The silver mines of Mexico and Peru, Huancavelica and Potosi, discovered in 1545–1546, became a "synonym for fabulous wealth" (Vilar 1976: 118). The conditions of extraction, and life in the mine fields were atrocious, requiring Indian forced labor. Friar Domingo de Santo Thomas wrote in a famous letter: "What is being sent to Spain is not silver, but blood and sweat of the Indians" (Vilar 1976: 126). These conditions in the indigenous city of Potosi, and the hyperinflation of commodities (similar to the Gold Rush in California in 1849–1851), began to reveal the adverse effects of unregulated free trade and movement of capital. The image of dirty money imposed itself on the collective conscience, from Potosi to the "blood diamonds" of Africa to Damien Hirst having to affirm that the diamond encrusted skull, uber symbol of twenty-first-century greed and fetishistic valuation of art and commodity, was ethically clean. Karl Marx's imagery of "capital comes dripping from head to foot, from every pore with blood and dirt" (*Das Kapital* quoted in Vilar 1976: 126) referring to the first industrial revolution's conditions in the mines and sweatshops of Germany and England, has its roots in the money tainted by the sweat, abuse, and destruction of indigenous populations in Latin American history.

By the 1560s, extraction from the mines of Peru caused hyper inflation in Peru, as the price of cloth, horses (1,000 ducats), and wine (200 ducats), skyrocketed before reaching Spain, Italy and then France. As wages rose in Spain, workers from France moved to Spain while wealth flowed to France, causing demographic and monetary shifts of balance. Vilar attributes basic exchange theory to a Spanish cleric, Tomas de Mercado, who observed in 1558 the difference in price for an ingot of silver and therefore the difference in purchasing power in Seville, Mexico, France and Italy. In 1566, at the court of France, de Malestroict, the king's counselor and master of the accounts, postulated how prices had consistently risen and inflation was rampant, the livre had less silver and the currency was being debased – 17.96 grams in 1513, to 14.27 grams in 1561 (Vilar 1976: 89). Jean Bodin, prominent historian, jurist and chief economic advisor, published the *Response of Jean Bodin to the Paradoxes of Malestroit*, in 1568, refuting this argument on the grounds that land prices had increased three times in 50 years, but the currency had not fallen in the same proportions. He traced the rise in prices to the increase in trade and the quantity of gold and silver in circulation as well as the interdependency of Spain on French imports, and the geopolitical shift from Italy to Portugal as main trading power. Following Bodin's precepts, in 1570 Henri III, concerned with the rising prices of grain and inflation, created the first account money, ecus de marc and ecus de soleil. He also established the first monetary tribunal in France, the equivalent of an embryonic regulatory agency.

Bodin's political treatise, *Six Livres de la Republique [Six Books on the Commonwealth]* (1576), called for rigorous analysis and historical methodology, but this was part of an opus which included one of the most important books on witchcraft dealing with its potential harm to society, remedies and commensurate punishments, including death at the stake (*La demonomanie des sorciers* 1581). This juxtaposition of beliefs was considered perfectly acceptable within the intellectual elite. The rapid internationalization of trade, finance, urban centers, the influx of new products, and the improvement in living conditions, coupled with the ravages of the wars of religion (the St Bartholomew Massacre, August 1572), and the destabilization of established social and theological norms, created fascination and fear with this wonderful new world. While plagued by associations with usury and anti-Semitic traits, the financier also represented new internationalism and prosperity. Christopher Marlowe in *The Jew of Malta* (1591–1592) and Shakespeare in *The Merchant of Venice* (1609) were responding to the English public's curiosity and wariness about finance and financiers able to muster fleets and capital around the world:

> But yesterday two ships went from the town. Their voyage will be worth ten thousand crowns. In Florence, Venice, Antwerp, London, Seville, Frankfurt, Lubech, Moscow and where not, have I debts owning, and in most of these, great sums of money.
>
> (Marlowe 1950: Act 1, Scene 1)

1.6 Urban financial centers

In 1111, in Lucca, "money changers were already in the habit of meeting near St Martin's Church" surrounded by merchants and notaries (Braudel 1982: 99).

As markets helped congregate and organize rural communities, international fairs helped create urban financial centers. Major fairs in the twelfth and thirteenth centuries occurred twice or four times a year with set rules and procedures for different types of merchants, goods and transactions, such as "nine days for trading cloth (six for showing and three for sales) ... and then fixed days for settlement" (Usher 1943: 118). "In due course all kinds of financial transactions came to be handled at fairs, not only foreign exchange but real estate, banking, early forms of insurance, and lotteries" (Kindleberger 1993: 29).

Braudel and De Roover stress the role of the city as an essential component in the transformation of economic life and culture. The city became a liberating force, "Stadluft macht frei" (Old German proverb from the late Middle Ages). Cities sharpened the interrelationship between political and economic life, as political autonomy was granted to towns in return for remission of specific taxes, as burghers gained far greater say in the governance of the town and its economic life than had the vassals. City states, Venice, Genoa, and Florence through the mid-fourteenth century, followed by the fifteenth-century Hansa towns and Dutch cities, became centers of commercial activity, but even more importantly, centers of movement for goods and capital. From Genoa to Lyons by the 1540s, to Besancon, and later to Bruges, where the bourse started, to Antwerp, and Amsterdam, fairs evolved into financial centers.

Across Europe "the catchment area of town or city" such as Nuremberg, leading commercial and financial powerhouse in the sixteenth century, with linkages as far as Warsaw, Poznan, Breslau, and Cracow in the East, and Medina del Campo, Lisbon, Venice and Antwerp, became "virtually the geometric center of the economic life of Europe during the early sixteenth century" (Braudel vol. III 1979: 188). Wealthy merchants not only congregated in these centers, but set up residences and places of business.

From the mid-sixteenth to the eighteenth century, exchanges, forerunners of stock markets, sprang up across Europe, and in New York in 1772. Bruges (1409), Antwerp (1460), Lyons (1462), Toulouse (1469), Amsterdam (1530), London (1556), Hamburg (1558), Paris (1563), Bordeaux (1564), Cologne (1566), Danzig (1593), Leipzig (1635), Berlin (1716), and Vienna (1771) offer a timeline of economic history across Europe, as well as a picture of the physical presence of financial agents, and operations and flow of monies in urban centers.

The symbiosis between financial activity and towns and cities was at the heart of early capitalism in city states and principalities across Germany, Poland and through the Iberian peninsula. Italian city states were centers of financial activity, but also sources of immense wealth which could serve regional and international bankers. Local small scale commerce, trade in local goods and commodities evolved from rural to urban and then returned to isolated and rural areas. Poor peddlers, often Jews ostracized from formal shop ownership within cities, were instrumental in distributing and introducing new products. Amos Elon describes how iterant Jews in Poland handled 40–50 percent of the trade crossing over from Germany.

By the 1690s, London, financial heart of Europe, would be unrivaled until the 1840s, by Paris, and in the 1890s, by Berlin, and only post-World War I would the mantle pass to New York until the resurgence of London by the early 1990s. However, in the 1980s, based on the rise of Japan, Braudel extrapolated a gradual geo-economic shift from the West to the Pacific Asian nations. This trend, witnessed by the growing importance of Tokyo, Hong Kong and Singapore, the leading roles of the dollar and the yen, subsided by the early 1990s. In his final work *La dynamique du capitalisme* (1984), Braudel predicted a long-term cyclical return to the originators of Western capitalism, Italy and Spain.

In 1999, Charles Kindleberger asked the following question:

> Will the European Monetary Union develop a single leading financial center as did its constituent countries in the eighteenth and nineteenth centuries? Frankfurt-am-Main has a long lead in the race for the position ... In nineteenth century Berlin as the capital of the German Empire won over Frankfurt, Dresden and Hamburg and moving the German capital from Bonn to Berlin may exert pressure on the banks to follow.
>
> (Finel-Honigman 1999: x)

He foresaw London "as a world, perhaps more than European financial center" when and if Britain joins the EMU (Finel-Honigman 1999: xi). A decade later, despite, or perhaps thanks to, not having joined the EMU, London, up to 2008 again assumed that position. Kindleberger mentioned Frances Cairncross' theory that distance is dead ("The Death of Distance," Harvard Business School Press, 1997), a thesis popular in the age of telecommuting and permanent telecommunication (as head of Deutsche Bank asset management expounded in a conference on GeoEconomic centers in New York, January, 2008). However, Kindleberger wisely added, "Nevertheless, I have strong reservations" (Kindleberger, Remarks on European Monetary Union Banking Issues 1999: xi).

2   Myths, stigmas and morality of "dirty sexy money"

A *Financial Times* sardonic editorial derides *Forbes*'s yearly "rich list" as undependable and narcissistic, as the wealthiest may reduce charitable giving in order not to lose their place on the list and yet, "despite all the above reservations, listing the wealthy still exerts a hideous and powerful fascination" ("Rich and Famous" 2008). Fear, myth, fantasy and revulsion toward money, its actors, transactions, and institutions are an integral part of financial and economic culture, defined by Helga Schultz "as the whole of the cognitive, affective and evaluative orientation, i.e. as the values, mentalities and attitudes toward economic structures" (Schultz 2003: 7).

Evolving from rural to urban, barter to monetary economy, specie to paper, and coinage to bills of exchange, letters of credit, financial operations, instruments, agents and institutions have required far more fluid sets of moral and theological criteria. As LeGoff so wittily opined, purgatory offered the Church's financiers a half way house between eternal damnation and heaven. In the interstices between what Ferguson named "morality and Mammon" are found the atavistic prejudices and stereotypes unique to these themes.

Earning rather than inheriting money is at the heart of the transition from serf to small landowner, to small businessman, but it is also at the core of dissolving social hierarchy and the sense of entitlement to wealth and its corollary power. This paradigmatic shift in social hierarchy and system of values remains subliminally unresolved in the collective European conscience. Are the wealthy worthy of their wealth? Can one be a businessman, yet retain intellectual, spiritual, and moral integrity? In the nineteenth and early twentieth century, European right-wing intellectual, Maurice Barres, in his tirade against speculative "agiotage" as antithetical to the destiny of France, and politicians and intellectuals such as Disraeli and Trollope, took pride in expressing contempt for monetary professions and their vulgar practitioners. The ability to achieve gain, "lucre," to profit, through manipulation and knowledge of non tangible entities, always fascinated and horrified, as it exemplifies the moral dilemma between society and religion's claim to prosperity and possessions.

Societies which accepted preordained class distinctions, lacked integration between rural and urban communities, and were strongly influenced by religious authority, tended to politically marginalize the middle class and to maintain cultural, historical, and theological prejudices and stereotypes against financial professions and disdained earned rather than inherited money. French anti-capitalism, closely associated to political anti-Semitism in the 1870s and 1880s in the works of Taine, Drumont, Bourget, Barres and Zola prior to the Dreyfus Affair, established clear distinctions between a moral code based on traditional French values versus cosmopolitanism, codeword for lack of national loyalty, based solely on money and personal gain.

Braudel's seminal exposition of medieval and Renaissance financial culture disproved that only Jews practiced usury:

> The truth was that usury was practiced by the whole of society: princes, the rich, merchants, the humble and even the Church – by a society that tried to conceal the forbidden practice, frowned on it, but resorted to it, disapproved of those who handled it, but tolerated them.
>
> (1982c: 563)

In the 1430s, Jews in Florence set up money lending offices in the same banks as Christians, using the same methods of "fictional sales, false fair bills, invented figures on notarial documents" (Braudel 1982b: 563). Yet throughout European literature the usurer, from Chaucer to Shakespeare, is described as a Jew; the stigma creates the prototype. The Reformation would accept and justify business practices as a means of betterment of society, yet interdictions against usury remained in place, including refusal of absolution or sacraments. "There was no intention, among either Lutherans or Calvinists or Anglicans of relaxing the rules of good conscience which were supposed to control economic transactional and social relations" (Tawney 1953: 77). Martin Luther wrote "money is the word of the devil [Gelt est verbum Diaboli]" versus the word of God and "the greatest misfortunes of the German nation are easily the traffic in interest" (cited in Shell 1982: 85). In Geneva and Zurich, for Zwingli and Calvin there was a complex dialectic between "full blooded denunciations of capitalism and practical life" (Tawney 1953: 100). But Calvinism was an urban movement, appealing to business men in Geneva and later Antwerp: "It was on this practical basis of urban industry and commercial enterprise that the structures of Calvinistic social ethics are erected" (Tawney 1953: 97). By 1525, Zwingli addressed pauperism, forbidding mendicancy and issuing edicts for provisions for sick and aged. In Elizabethan England, Sir Thomas Gresham condemned usury on economic rather than moral grounds: "usurious interest appeared not bad morals but bad business" (Tawney 1953: 151).

In periods of economic distress provoked by outside aggression, sudden loss of confidence in the currency, followed by a surge of inflation, bank failures or cross-border market crashes, quantitative logic no longer prevails. Victims of disruption, fearful for their livelihood, homes, assets, and savings, lose faith in institutions and governments. They demand not only reassurance and guarantees, but seek to identify and target specific scapegoats. Since the early 1700s, in each major financial downturn, foreigners, Jews, and ethnic minorities are sought out and held responsible, as collective fears resurface.

In American stock market crashes from 1857 to 2008, blaming Wall Street versus Main Street establishes a neat moral dichotomy between evil speculators and good, hard working people. Moneylenders, bankers, stockbrokers, and traders are identified as the initiated, versed in the intricacies and secret methods of their transactions, like the medieval alchemist who alone can conjure up money. Their jargon is a series of signs and symbols which remain unknown to others. The banker or stockbroker, like today's trader, international business "entrepreneur" or "raider," is an adventurer who has chosen a new field of endeavor and exploit. The Icelandic bankers, blamed for Iceland's collapse in October 2008, were named the new Vikings. In his description of the bankers who sold out French Indochina to protect French banking interests in *La Condition Humaine* (1933), Malraux termed "language chiffre" (numerical language) their skill, not to clarify, but rather to manipulate through obfuscation. In the Wall Street crisis of 2008, one recurring theme has been the inability to understand the instruments involved in the subprime mortgage crisis, such as structured investment vehicles; to decipher what a derivative actually was, and what it did. Pundits and practitioners, from Hank Greenberg to Henry Paulson, admitted that, too often, managers did not thoroughly understand the nature of their own instruments. This only reinforces the assumption and revives the old myth that banking is an esoteric science, whether alchemic, mathematical or just the luck of the draw. Clearly, as Ferguson charmingly put it, "as evolutionary biologists have demonstrated, homo sapiens is not homo economicus" (2001: 11).

2.1 Morality and Mammon

In Christian Europe since the twelfth century, the rich man must justify his wealth within the church, society, and the state. Fundamental to Judeo Christian and Islamic beliefs is the role of charity within the community, direct contribution to the Church from the twelfth to sixteenth centuries, or philanthropy in modern times, deemed necessary for redemption. Those who make money must justify their activity in the name of a higher goal, be it to better society, to protect or help the state, or to offer their family and community specific benefits. Kenneth Griffin, chairman of Citadel Investment Group, a hedge fund (which earned US$1 billion in 2006) explained: "The money is a byproduct of a passionate endeavor. We have helped to create real wealth in the US economy" (Uchitelle 2007). From the building of Chartres to Clinton's Global Initiative, the ubiquity of "it is easier for a camel to pass through the eye of a needle, than for a rich man to enter into the kingdom of heaven," remains in play (Matt. 19: 24).

At the base of these conundrums is the primary interrelationship between power and finance. Wealth is antithetical to the ideal condition of man, but without it man cannot achieve any ideal condition, not as individual, state or nation. Bernard Shaw reversed the biblical admonition: "The lack of money is the root of all evil" (1908), a declaration prescient of Ayn Rand as he expounded against the Victorian glorification of poverty. In *Major Barbara*, he claimed profits entirely justifiable, even by Undershaft, a capitalist manufacturer of gunpowder, as all social entities, even the Salvation Army, must solicit money in order to survive.

In pre-Revolutionary France, the aristocrat was not entitled to engage in commerce and banking, and in the 1820s it became fashionable for writers, artists, and academics to erect their own barriers by refusing to apply their creative talents, energies or skills to any commercial endeavor. For the Romantics in France and Germany, art and commerce were inexorably adversarial. Art had to be pure and untainted by any commercial or vulgar activity. Goethe's *Werner* and Vigny's *Chatterton* became the symbols of the distraught, suicidal, and impoverished true artist or poet.

Poverty, as characteristic of the starving artist hero or virtuous heroine, was idealized as the epitome of anti-monetary, Christian values. Victorian England, fascinated by money, refused to give it any moral validation, coining the phrase "genteel poverty." This was imitated in post-Civil War American literature, including Louisa May Alcott's *Little Women*, and in images of impoverished Southern gentry, deprived of their lands and possessions. The underlying message is that "others" have money, either duly inherited or somewhat shadily earned in commerce and finance. The image of the genteel, poor, often pious, chaste women that suffer in dignity suffuses English, French, German, and Russian literature in the works of Balzac, Zola, Maupassant, Dickens, Trollope, Chekhov, Turgenev and Dostoevsky.

In post-Revolutionary France and pre-Revolutionary Russia, the impoverished aristocrat, living off depleted estates, victim of poor investments, and loss of inherited income, represents an unspoken affront to the newly wealthy and active business, merchant or financial class. The schools of Realism and Naturalism in literature and painting illustrated the dichotomy between the growing deprivation of the working classes and the displays of consumption of the rich. By the 1850s, poverty extended to the overeducated, urban intellectuals: teachers, governesses, journalists, academics, scientists, and artists, unable to earn a living wage, without additional support from mentors, sponsors or inherited money. Disdainful of commerce, sympathetic to but unwilling to take on manual work, they develop a hatred and contempt tinged with envy toward the newly enriched commercial and financial middle class. Wanting to be heroes, they revel in the myth of Napoleon, like Stendhal's hero, Julien Sorel, in *Le Rouge et le Noir* (1830), but at best they are romantic protagonists, at worst they end up as revolutionaries and bourgeois manqué, like Flaubert's Frederic Moreau in *L'Education Sentimentale* (1869). Bitterly opposed to Napoleon III, whom they accuse of betraying heroism in the name of progress and profit, their disdain for money, tinged with anti-Semitism, extends to all bankers and businessmen, and especially the Rothschilds, Jules Mires, and other whom they associate with international financial interests.

Jules Valles, well known journalist, rabble rouser, and member of the Paris Commune, called his first work *L'Argent* (1857), a pamphlet harshly satirizing the power of the Stock Exchange. In subsequent novels and articles, he coined the words "déclassé," "refractaires," and "proletariat des Bacheliers," for this generation of young men who judged themselves to be too educated and sensitive for crass commercialism, yet too poor and marginalized to be given their due. In Chekhov's *The Sea Gull* and the *Cherry Orchard* in the 1890s, when Russia was beginning to emulate the Western Europe of the 1860s, the social discrepancies are more striking, as decrepit estates of landowners host bitter intellectuals, surrounded by silent servants, laborers, and young women desperately seeking emancipation. Society remains passive, steeped in feudal structures, a new generation enamored of progress, yet averse to modernization and capitalist endeavor.

In the 1930s and again in the 1950s, British intellectuals cultivate an anti-business, anti materialist outlook: "The teachers, poets, men and women of letters, and intellectuals – the people who set the tone and orchestrated the value – nurtured a sense of scorn for the shop and the office" (Landes 1999: 459). From Huxley to Orwell, only the very rich or the very poor merit any consideration. The middle classes are boring, pretentious, and mediocre, yet in every capitalist society, growth and progress depend on the small and medium enterprises, the small businessman, shopkeeper, and factory owner.

In the United States, during periods of financial shock, major losses, and social unrest, following the crashes of 1873, 1893, 1929, and 1987, literature, art and academia revive the corporate–intellectual adversarial relationship. Walter Goodman wrote, "As John Gardner observed, the poet who looks at a businessman today tends to see him as vulgar, spiritually debased, viciously uncharitable," or, as a "sadly unfulfilled creature deserving of the wise man's pity" (*New York Times*, March 1987). Post-2008, as all aspects of the financial system have been tainted by fraud, corruption, lack of oversight, and political laxity, there will be a deeper reaction against the excesses of the marketplace. America will not negate, nor deny the dynamism and fundamental belief in capitalism, but it will demand far greater accountability in order to restore loss of trust and faith.

Poverty is virtue, but poverty cannot function as sole moral, political or economic guideline. Catholic Europe and Latin America never fully resolve the paradox; America best succeeds at bypassing or ignoring it; Asia integrates it in parallel systems; for nearly a century, Marxism attempted to transform it and eliminate it, only to fail in the wake of global capitalism or in the case of China to attempt "the one state two systems solution."

Simmel and Freud, sociologists, psychoanalysts, and cultural theoreticians, Shell, Umberto Eco, Lacan, and Taylor have tried to define how and why money is conceptualized, its ephemeral nature, its intrinsic non-value outside of attributed or legalistic valuation, which creates an irresolvable conflict between the real and the assumed. Money demands an inherent sense of trust in order to transform inert valueless metal, paper, plastic or electronic blips into objects of exchange, societal prestige and guarantee. At its core, the financial crisis, from inflation to bank runs, is a breach of trust between owner and custodian of financial assets, be it the market, the bank or the government. As Gillian Tett wrote on the Bear Stearns crisis:

> It stems from a loss of trust in the whole style of modern finance, with its complex slicing and dicing of risk into ever more opaque forms… The credit world in other words now lacks "credit" – in the original meaning of "he/she trusts."

> (Tett 2008)

The immensity of Bernard Madoff's fraud was not only in the amount involved, nor in the number of individuals who lost savings, homes, and pensions, but in the ultimate breach of trust between the financier and the community.

> Now every stock broker and money manager and hedge fund operator and insurance rep who already had a tough time convincing prospective clients that what they are selling is good and honest must now also convince them that they are not like you.

> (Gellman 2008)

Within the complex mathematical, yet often illogical and erratic, domain of market trends and stock movements the banker or trader is always viewed as culprit and instigator in times of financial instability. However, in 2008, because the culprits, overpaid and unapologetic, cover the entire spectrum of financial activities, the level and scope of loss of confidence is far greater. The market will recover, but the ability of the financial profession to be seen as honorable or trustworthy will be a much slower and more complex process.

Unlike other professional or commercial activities, credit, at the heart of financial transactions, requires credibility, the act of believing in the value of the object as well as the subject. From Plato to Socrates, in Jewish as well as Islamic texts, the process of exchange is a process of intellectual as well as material debate. The quest for gold or the quest for the Holy Grail depends on its elusiveness which enhances its value. The act of giving money away, charity, is defined as a virtue; the act of hoarding, avarice, is a vice, but they are both components of economic transactions defined by moral coda. Marc Bloch, Braudel, Vilar, and LeGoff emphasize that, by the end of the thirteenth century, the difference between the intrinsic value of money and money of account begins to appear. The reconciliation between economic and moral demands and justification of transactional activity in its own right has still not been resolved. The offsetting of carbon footprints (the latest jargon of the environmentally conscious), is just as corrupt as the indulgences of the Middle Ages, one sins, but one can use earthly wealth to redeem one's soul or one's ecological conscience. There is a bargain struck between the corporeal and the spiritual, between the economic and the moral.

In the eighteenth and nineteenth century, philosophers and economists, across the political spectrum, from Adam Smith, Locke, Hume, Voltaire, Jaucourt, Turgot, Saint-Simon, Taine to Karl Marx, theorized on money's role in social development. Ironically, the most influential work of economic theory, Marx's *Communist Manifesto* (1848), was almost totally ignored and *Das Kapital: A Critique of Political Economy*, finally edited and published in 1867 with the help of Friedrich Engels, originally garnered critical attention only among small groups of intellectuals. In the 1870s, it was assumed that Auguste Comte, Saint-Simon, Hippolyte Taine, and certainly Hume and Locke would be household names in the next centuries, rather than an impoverished, rambling, prophetic German Jew living in exile in London.

Where Marx transformed the concepts of value, commodity, and money in relation to labor, production, and society by establishing dialectical divergence rather than convergence, the German philosopher Georg Simmel in *The Philosophy of Money* (1900), set forth for the first time a sociological and philosophical interpretation of money as key determinant in societal and cultural development. Simmel, influenced by Berlin's Americanization (nicknamed Chicago on the Spree), urbanization, economic development, and speculative fever in the 1880s and 1890s, delved into the existential role of money as abstract possession and its psychological implications within society. Considered highly controversial, his work influenced Lukács, Weber, Durkheim, and Max Adler, and in the 1930s was discussed in parallel to Marx.

Lukács' study of the role of culture in capitalist societies placed Simmel's stratification of money, alienation, and objectification (reification) within a larger historical dialectic. Critics argued over whether Simmel was an extension of Marx or a parallel study within the boundaries of traditional exchange and transactional relationship, but Simmel, like Marx, emphasized from different perspectives "the alienation of man from his products and from the culture that he has himself produced" (Simmel, 1978: 27). Simmel understood that "Where a historical dimension is absent, the effects of money and the money economy become the fate of all culture" (Simmel 1978). As society became more bureaucratized and anonymous, he was the first to observe that a civil servant's "salary no longer has any quantitative relationship to his various achievements, but is supposed to grant him an appropriate standard of living" (Simmel 1978). Closer to liberal socialism than hard core capitalism, Simmel viewed money as a means of re-establishing the rank and security of the individual, through the intermediary of the state, quoting the conditions in the French Constitution of 1791, which, for the first time, adopted the daily wage as standard of value. Every qualified citizen had to pay a direct tax of at least three days work and, in order to vote, required an income of 150 to 2000 labor days (see the "Constitution of 1791" in Simmel 1978: 357).

Simmel's objective was to apply socio-philosophical methodology to "the phenomena of valuation and purchase, of exchange and the means of exchange of the forms of production and the values of possession" (Simmel 1978: 93). Like Hume in 1752, Simmel postulated that

> Money is measured by the goods against which it is exchanged and also by money itself. For not only is money paid for by money, as the money market and interest bearing loans show, but money of one country becomes the measure of value for the money of another country as is illustrated by foreign exchange transactions.
>
> (Simmel 1978: 123)

Unlike other areas of production, creation or development, the field of finance and money carries misconceptions so deeply embedded in popular imagination that science, logic, and factual proof cannot dislodge them. As money is inherently intangible and dependent on authority and power to give it value, it remains strange, mysterious, and dangerous. From usurers to goldsmiths to hedge fund managers, those who deal in money are seen as possessing knowledge and skills which are not available to the population at large, therefore associated with foreigners, strangers to the community, the "Other."

In the nineteenth century novel, money is part of the fabric of social interaction, but it is also given biblical attributes in a universe where the Stock Exchange becomes the temple of a new religion. Biblical metaphors abound in the last page of Zola's *L'Argent*, as he justifies and sublimates the worst excesses of capitalism, precursor to Joseph Schumpeter's "creative destruction."

> L'argent etait le fumier dans lequel poussait l'humanite de demain; l'argent empoisonneur et destructeur, devenait le ferment de toute vegetation sociale, le terreau necessaire aux grands travaux qui facilitaient l'existence [Money was the dung heap from which emerged future humanity; money, poison and destroyer became the fertilizer of all social vegetation, the earth necessary to all great works which facilitate human life].

(Zola 1972: 497)

2.2 Anti Semitism to anti capitalism

> You did not cause the anti-Semitic insults about Jews and money, but you caused them to be revived.... I am not comfortable with the fact that so many of the articles about you specifically identify your prominent place in the Jewish community. Ken Lay of Enron shame was never identified as a "prominent Protestant energy broker."

(Gellman 2009)

From the start of the financial crisis in the summer of 2008, the Internet was awash with anti-Semitic comments blaming alleged Jewish investment firms, bankers, and financiers. Since June 2008, scurrilous remarks on Yahoo message boards against Lehman Brothers and Goldman Sachs, accused Jews of shorting the market, provoking the oil crisis and being disloyal and greedy. The year ended with the Bernard Madoff scandal, in which a prominent American fund manager, formerly director of NASDAQ, was revealed to have run a vast, global Ponzi scheme, involving losses of almost US$65 billion. Investors and victims of the fraud, involving major global banks in Europe and the United States, small private banks, hedge funds, and private equity firms, included major Jewish philanthropies, foundations, universities, and charities. In an environment rife with the need for scapegoats, the alleged rather than actual fraudulent actions, deception and major losses to individuals and institutions attributed to one Jewish financier, revived and validated the worst atavistic responses.

Long before the term or concept of anti-Semitism entered European mainstream culture, Jews were accused of engaging in usury, manipulating money and only serving their own communities' interests. In the corrupt and venal world of the late Roman Empire, Jews were already ostracized as political and moral outsiders. Juvenal's *Satire 14*, in its virulence and contempt, establishes the anti-Semitic stereotypes of otherness, arrogance, and avarice which will reverberate throughout the next two millennia. Jewish work ethic and intellectual endeavor are also mentioned but distorted through the prism of contempt to reflect vice rather than virtue.

Those whose lot it was that their fathers worshipped the Sabbath....

Circumcised, not as the Gentiles, they despise Roman law, but learn and observe and revere Israel's code, and all from the sacred volume of Moses.... Young men need not be taught to imitate most of the vices

Only avarice seems to oppose their natural instinct. Here is a vice, for once in the shape and shade of a virtue,

Gloomy of mien and dour indeed in dress and expression

The miserly man is praised, of course, as if he were frugal.... Add the fact that the people thinks of the man whom I mention

As an artist at gain: estates increase with such foremen

And they increase every way, becoming bigger and bigger.

The anvil is never still and the furnace forever is blazing.

(Juvenal 1958: *Satire 14*)

By the Middle Ages, the association of Jews and usurious practices was firmly ensconced in the popular imagination. Expelled from England in 1290, Jews remained part of the psychic folklore which did not need the actual community to propagate the stereotypes. Accused in Germany of poisoning wells and bringing about the plague in the 1340s, they were expelled from Nuremburg and Munich. Ostracized from the centers of commercial and urban activity, they depended on the whim or need of the ruler. Jewish law forbade moneylenders from receiving interest from another Jew, "Thou shalt not lend upon usury to thy brother ... Unto a stranger thou mayest lend upon usury" (Deut. 23:19–20), reinforced the element of distrust and disloyalty inherent in the portrayal of this minority. After expulsion in 1349, many cities on the Rhine missed "die Finanzquelle des Judenregals" (the financial skills of the Jews), allowing them to return by 1372, but by the sixteenth century they had been reduced to pawnbrokers, moneychangers, rag dealers, and peddlers, except in the city states of Hamburg and Bremen, members of the Hanseatic League.

Interestingly, Dante, in his attack on the corruption and venality of the Church, sends all financial practitioners to purgatory or inferno but makes no specific mention of Jews. Braudel stressed that the Cahorsieans and Lombards as well as Eastern minorities, Greeks and Armenians, were also involved in money changing and money lending, but the myth was pervasive regardless of the facts. Shakespeare, in *The Merchant of Venice*, adapted the stereotype firmly codified in the English mindset. Each subsequent generation's interpretation of Shylock, from primal anti-Semitism to subtle analysis of his humanity and conflicted nature, asked the question whether he is guided by greed, paternal concern, economic necessity, or revenge. Ironically, the title refers to Antonio as merchant of Venice, not to Shylock. Antonio, who contrary to the custom in fifteenth-century Venice and sixteenth-century England, has not taken out maritime insurance, is in a sense a parody of the young aristocrat's total contempt and ignorance for all pecuniary transaction. Shylock's first words: "Three thousand ducats" (1974: Act 1, Scene 3), repeated "as the price of the loan on three months and Antonio bound," were familiar to the English audience. There is an extraordinarily sophisticated casuistic on the definition of "good man" between Bassanio and Shylock, as the distinction between moral and economic worth is put into play, assuming that for the Jew, the economic equates morality, while for the Christian morality cannot be economic, but as Shylock proves he has value and values: "my ducats and my daughter" (Shakespeare 1974).

> My meaning in saying he is a good man is to have you understand me that he is sufficient, yet his means are in supposition: he hath an argosy bound to Tripoli. Another to the Indies ... he hath a third at Mexico, a fourth for England and other ventures he hath squandered abroad ... The man is notwithstanding sufficient.
>
> (Shakespeare 1974: Act I, Scene 3)

At issue is not the excessive interest or the pound of flesh, but the dialectical semantic shift between good and sufficient, between reputation based on externality versus the moral compass. Shylock, despite his prejudices and insularity in his community, represents modernity, homo economicus versus Antonio, and Bassanio, still within the confines of the medieval world, where the worth of the individual is in relation to God rather than secular world.

England and Holland, far more pragmatic and tolerant on grounds of economic necessity, included affluent Jewish, often Sephardic, shareholders, stockholders, and directors in East Indies companies, the Bank of England, and major commercial enterprises. In Germany, Frederick William I, despite comparing Jews to locusts, created conditions in which the richest and best were allowed to remain in Berlin. As the King was in constant need of cash, he sold Jews the privileges of residency, abolished the yellow patch, and, in 1715, granted the right to build a synagogue. With the same mindset, Frederick II, the "so-called philosopher king" (Elon 2002: 17), needing money for wars, employed minting and banking firms such as Veitel Ephraim and Sons, who became one of the first

German court Jews granted privileges for their financial services. The Oppenheim bank, created in 1789, prominent in helping fund the German state from 1870, was the first bank to be targeted in 1938 when the Nazis come to power. About to celebrate its 150 jubilee, the bank was officially ordered to change its name to Pferdmenges and Co., the name of a non-Jewish German partner: "We inform you that hereafter that our enterprise established since 1789 from here on will be known under the name of Bankhaus Pferdmenges and Co., signed by Sal Oppenheim on May 1938" (Sal Oppenheim Jr. and Cie-Geschichte einer Bank und einer Familie, March 2004).

In German folklore and early literature, money is not part of popular imagination or culture. Relegated to merchants, often Jews and foreigners in urban areas, it is redolent of foreignness and disrepute. Ferguson, in the introduction to *The Cash Nexus*, interprets Wagner's Ring of the Nibelung "as another romantic critique of capitalism" (Ferguson 2001: xiv). The mythological epic, filled with giants, dwarfs, holy objects, maidens, and sacred quests, is based on the quest for the golden ring symbolizing perpetual need and obsession, which can never bring emotional happiness. Marx's, like Wagner's apocalyptic imagery and dialectical symbolism, sets labor against capital, and evil against good, establishing a moral dichotomy in the material world. Poverty is good because capital and capitalism are inherently evil, wealth is bad because the workers alone deserve to be rewarded and the wealthy punished.

Federated Germany seemed to promise greater assimilation, as Jews would be integrated among other regional groups of Saxons, Prussians, Hessians, and Silesians. Partly in response to the instrumental role Jewish bankers played in unifying Germany in 1871, the new Reich State's emancipation law abolished all restrictions on civil and political rights based on religion. Between 1871 and 1878, 36 Jews (12 converts) were elected to the Reichstag, including the banker Oppenheim from Köln. But by 1873, in the wake of the transatlantic market crash and recession, anti-Semitism reappeared openly;

> Jews were held responsible not only for the crisis but for capitalism itself: Judaism was "capitalism in the extreme." No less than 90 percent of all "capitalist promoters" in Germany were said to be Jews. Under their auspices, capitalism was generating a materialist society that consumed the hard earned savings of good Christians.
>
> (Elon 2002: 213)

New phrases were coined in German: "Judenparasitenokonomie, Juden weltherrschaft [Jewish parasite economy, Jewish world domination]" (Elon 2002: 215). Bleichröder and other Jewish bankers, known as the small group of Kaiser Juden, were the subject of the first vicious wave of anti-Semitic culture and prototyping. In 1879, led by Prussian historian Heinrich von Tretschke, anti-Semitic slurs specifically targeted Jews in finance, and linked together the peddler and the banker: "the inexhaustible Polish cradle spawns hoards of ambitious young men who come pushing across our border to peddle their trousers and whose children and grandchildren are supposed to one day dominate the German stock market and German newspapers" (Elon 2002: 217). Within a few years this propaganda receded and blatant anti-Semitism ebbed, retreating into what Stefan Zweig called the "Golden Age of Security" for wealthy, assimilated, educated, native German or Austrian Jews. By the 1890s, Jews prominent in all aspects of the booming German economy held seats on the boards of Deutsche Bank, Dresdner, and Darmstatter. However, underlying suspicion and fear of Jewish financial conspiracy remained in the arts and press as in 1900 Berlin, of the 200 richest families, 40 were Jewish or of Jewish extraction, and half the private banks were in Jewish hands.

Throughout Germany and Eastern Europe, Jews were portrayed in articles and art as privy to the secrets of stock markets, as portrayed in small statues of two Jews whispering, sharing stock market information, which reinforced the image of secrecy and conspiracy in creating or manipulating finance (Jewish Museum of New York, permanent exhibits). Germany's post-war economic debacle, provoked by reparation demands, coupled with the appointment of Jewish financier Walther Rathenau as Minister for Reconstruction and Foreign Minister, gave the anti-Semitic right a scapegoat and a victim. Rathenau was assassinated in June 1922 and although "the immediate response was an affirma- tion of the [Weimar] republic and the government passed emergency decrees against defamation" (Stern 2006: 65), the damage was irreparable. The atrocious inflation which spiraled upward through 1923, worsened by ineffective policies and panic, quickly sought out Jews as causing and exploiting the situation; "For those on the political right, all the profiteers were Jews, all Jews profiteers" (Stern 2006: 65).

In France, fear and hatred of Germans after the Franco-Prussian War con- flated Germans and Jews as agents of foreign finance in the writings and speeches of Deroulede, Barres, and Maurras. This culminated in the virulence of Drumont's *La France Juive* (1892) and rabid anti-Semitic articles in *La Libre Parole*. Prior to the Dreyfus Affair, the Panama scandal in 1892 involved a rich Jew of German origin, Baron de Rheinbach, accused of defrauding the French government, thus reinforcing the concept of wealthy Jews manipulating the government.

The myth of Jewish power and international networks was perpetuated by family dynasties and intermarriage, which by 1900 connected many German Jewish families. Harold James illustrated how familial relationships and family dynasties, at the heart of European banking, served as guarantors against disloyalty, shifting of loyalties, betrayal through fraud, absconding with funds, misappropriation of assets or unwise speculation. The Roth- schilds, Oppenheimers, Bischoffheims, Bleichroders, Bambergers, Warburgs, and Foulds family alliances intersected Europe like the railroad lines that they helped create between 1840 and 1890. Primarily patriarchal, with few excep- tions, from father to son and son-in-law, politics, law, philanthropy, and arts intersected with finance. Fortunes remained within the family, creating a unique combination of caution, sound business practices, and thrift with calculated ostentation. Wealth represented the individual and the company name. Religious identity in the major Jewish banking families acted as a shield, but tragically was often misperceived as a conspiratorial cult where outsiders were not allowed.

Through the ascent of old private banks and newer investment houses in Germany, France and England, Jewish bankers evolved from marginal money-lenders to the banking elite, "la haute banque." Under the Napoleonic decree of July 20, 1808, "The brief legal emancipation of Jews during the Napoleonic wars released unparallel economic, professional and cultural energies," similar to the relationship of Jews to the kings of Castile before the Inquisition (Elon 2002: 6). But Revolutionary and Napoleonic tolerance and integration brought about a backlash of violent diatribes in political discourse and literature against the nefarious affect of republicanism, foreign influence and money. Balzac, staunch monarchist, anti-republican and anti-capitalist, in his opus *Comédie Humaine*, referred to his own irresponsible financial odyssey, earning large amounts from books and articles, borrowing and spending extravagantly on advance income. Heavily indebted, outraged by the demands of his creditors, the novel reflects his hatred of banks and bankers. *Illusions Perdues* (1844), based in part on Balzac's legal difficulties, almost losing his home and being thrown into debtors prison in 1836 when his publishing house failed, devotes entire chapters to the vilification of banks and bankers:

> Si une grande maison de banque a tous les jours en moyenne un Compte de Retour sur une valeur de mille francs, elle touch tous les jours vingthuit francs par la Grace de Dieu et les constitutions de la Banque, royauté formidable inventée par les juifs au douzième siecle. Et qui domine aujourd'hui les trônes et les peoples [If a major banking house, every day on average has one Compte de Retour for the amount of 1,000 francs, it earns every day twenty eight francs by the Grace of God and the constitutions of the Bank, formidable royalty invented by the Jews in the twelfth century, and which today rules over thrones and nations].
>
> (Balzac 1961a: 592)

In *La Maison Nucingen* and other works, the Baron de Nucingen, immensely wealthy, ennobled, jowly, prominent Jewish banker, with a German accent and lack of refinement, caricatures the Rothschilds, perceived as symbol and agent of anti-French interests and international conspiracies. Zola's *L'Argent* (1891), gives his banker, Gunderman, the same characteristics. *L'Argent* was inspired by the saga of l'Union Generale Bank created in 1887 by Catholic aristocrats, with Vatican and French government backing, as a counterweight to Jewish and Protestant banks. It failed due to bad investments in the Ottoman Empire and poor management, but blamed its demise on the power and international contacts of the Rothschilds.

The Rothschilds bear a unique role in financial history as name and image of modern investment banking and international finance, but unlike their contemporaries, they also became the symbol of the Jewish banker in popular imagination, art and literature throughout the nineteenth and mid-twentieth century. Established by 1815 in Paris, Frankfurt, and London, the family dynasty dominated European industrial and commercial development, becoming a ubiquitous presence through their associations with other banking families. Ferguson, in his biography explains the cultural impact of the fortunes in London where their homes "were advertisements for Rothschild power, five star hotels for influential guests, private art galleries: in short centers for corporate hospitality" (Ferguson 1999: 554). The geographic scope of the Rothschild banking empire, and their immense fortune and power allowed them a voice in major financial decisions across Europe, and added to the mystique and contempt. In Vienna they played a role in concessions for coal and iron ore in Silesia and founded Credit Anstallt. Instrumental through the 1850s in the underwriting of railroad bonds throughout Europe, their interests later turned to copper, rubber, and oil. They built large portfolios of undervalued stocks in Royal Dutch and British Shell, granting them vast holdings of Royal Dutch Shell after the 1907 merger, as mentioned in Proust. In February 1889 in Vienna, they intervened to calm the market panic that followed the announcement of the death by suicide of Crown Prince Rudolph at Mayerling. As the economic situation worsened through the spring, there was a resurgence of anti-Semitic literature and diatribes, accusing Jews of overpricing and usury – a manifestation rarely seen in the diverse and tolerant Vienna of Kaiser Frantz-Joseph (Morton 1979: 245). In 1891, when Russia tried to recall massive gold loans on the open markets, creating a mini panic, the Rothschilds withdrew guarantees in response to pogroms in Russia. Extending their influence to the arts, they lent their name to French vineyards and racing stables from the 1880s, commissioning world renowned artists, often friends and protégés, to create labels with the Rothschild logo for each year's cru. (see Sotheby's Wine Auction catalogue and exhibit, 2007).

In 1899, Zola's defense of Dreyfus was a political call for justice for a military man and a French citizen. Anti-Semitism against a French citizen for Clemenceau, Monod, Reveille, and Leon Bloy was an affront to French rationalism and republicanism. However, it did not preclude judging Jews as a profiteering and corruptive influence in France's economy. Zola's *L'Argent*, like Jean-Richard Bloch's *Et Cie* (1917), and Anatole France's *L'île des pingouins* (1908), includes anti-Semitic tirades that emphasize Jewish bankers' supposed international contacts, excessive venality, and subversive beliefs. Jules Claretie's *Le million* (1882) and Alphonse Daudet's *Le Nabab* (1877), dealt with the realm of finance as a mythic battlefield of conflicting moral and theological values. Barres, Bourget, and later Maurras in *l'Action Française*, conjoined Jews, Germans, and American as agents of capitalist abuses. Serving as inspiration for their modern counterparts, Le Pen and the rhetoric of le Front National in 2002, virulent anti-Semitic and Islamophobic tirades in Houllebecq's novels, the association of Jews with international investment, oil money, global corporations, and borderless banks are once again described as antithetical to the values and traditions of the French nation.

Despite greater overall tolerance and opportunities for Jews in finance in America, there is a long history of adherence to the same stereotypes. Steve Fraser explains in *Every Man a Speculator: A History of Wall Street* (2005: 58), that by 1857 "Elements of xenophobia and anti-Semitism found their way into the Southern aversion to Wall Street, but were by no means confined to that region." Auguste Belmont, related to the Rothschilds by marriage, arrived in New York in 1837 and was immediately targeted as part of this international conspiracy. In Edith Wharton's *House of Mirth*, the more subtle references to foreign influences in *Age of Innocence* give way to the Balzacian character of Simon Rosedale "the novel's shylock is no mere plunger, but a man of infinite deliberation in whose hands speculation becomes 'patient industry,' very Morgan-like" (Fraser 2005: 236), as he tries to conquer the elusive and damaged heroine. Blatant anti-Semitism attached to populism, found its true champion in Henry Ford in his tirades in the *Dearborn Independent*, against the power, reach, and specifically the international nature of Jewish financiers. Echoed in the sermons of Father Coughlin, populism in the 1930s hated Wall Street, not only for abuse of power, but for its international bankers who, in the tradition of French right-wing demagogues, saw finance as antithetical to the true values of the heartland.

On Wall Street itself, despite maintaining quotas and latent bias against hiring Jews in WASP (White Anglo-Saxon Protestant), white shoe banks through the 1970s, there was overall tolerance of German Jewish bankers. The house of Kohn, Loeb, Warburg, and Oppenheim were part of the Wall Street establishment. Smaller Jewish banks in the mid-West, and a few institutions catering to poor emigrants from Eastern Europe in New York, remained marginalized, but tolerated. Yet a subtle religious snobbism pervades American institutions and their portrayal in literature. Tom Wolfe's satire of elite Protestant bankers, traders, and lawyers reappears in his article on hedge fund managers for the first issue of *Portfolio* magazine:

> Many prominent hedge fund managers are Jewish and on Round Hill Road and Pecksland Road in Greenwich as well as on Park and Fifth in Manhattan there has arisen ... the sibilant sound of people with social cachet whispering to one another ... variations on the theme "Some of my best friends are Jewish but..." Mercifully, such statistical breakdowns don't exist but it would appear that no extraordinary fraction of hedge fund managers is Jewish.... The common denominator is something else entirely: that status fixation.
>
> (Wolfe 2007: 271)

The tone is witty and derisive, yet it is clear that the stereotypes are still in place.

The crisis of 2008 resurrected myths of Jews having infiltrated Wall Street. Invoking the Protocols of the Elders of Zion (ur-text of global anti-Semitism concocted in Russia in 1910), accusations of a Jewish cabal running global finance has been invoked on radical Islamic sites and press. The names of Lehman, Bear Stearns, and Goldman Sachs were assumed at face value to be Jewish run firms, counter to actual fact or information, just as after September 11, 2001, rumors circulated and are still given credence in the Muslim world that Jews had prior knowledge of the attack on the World Trade Center, seen as symbol of global American financial power.

2.3 Women and finance

> My pride, not my principle, my money, not my virtue kept me honest.
>
> (Defoe 1965: 115)

If the Jew is feared and scorned as outsider and foreigner, women are feared and scorned as insidious, corruptive, and seductive forces. Historically women's association with finance as usurer, banker, money dealer or market speculator is uniformly condemnatory and pernicious. Few women usurers are found in literature, art or theater, for the combination of the female and usury is almost too unholy. When Raskolnikov, hero of *Crime and Punishment* commits his act of murder, Dostoevsky grants his hero the possibility of redemption by creating as victims Alyona Ivanova, a repulsive old woman usurer, and her poor sister, parasites on society and therefore so despicable that their murder can be absolved. The presentation and perception of women in finance is fraught with moral and emotional obstacles.

Through the twentieth century and until the 1970s, very few women entered the profession of finance or banking. Once women breached the ramparts, they advanced rapidly on brains and merit, yet by the late 1990s their progress began to stall. Sexism, gender discrimination, and inherent bias persist on Wall Street, but the causes and immediate reasons appear far more complex and nebulous. Is there a deeper fear of women in finance as they are already seen as more susceptible to temptation or sin, or is inherent sexual power dangerously increased if they also gain control of finance? Being considered part of property, a possession, when women transgressed into ownership did they threaten the established order of things? Why has the negative image of women and money dominated through the ages and why has it still not found full resolution in the financial workplaces of the twenty-first century?

In most societies it is presumed that women are responsible for household finances, but any relationship to money, outside of the home is either reprehensible to society, forced upon them due to destitution, the death of or abandonment by the male figure, or unnatural. Women in finance are depicted as old, ugly, deformed, somehow cursed by nature, or luring, the siren who must be curbed and ostracized: crone or prostitute. The French banking historian Petit Dutaillis, in his work *Portraits de Banquiers* (1982), calls his first chapter "les Banquieres," only to denigrate the term which should not exist in French. Speaking of Madame de Tencin, often called the first woman banker of the eighteenth century, he describes "pillow talk [elle parlait d'affaires entre deux draps]" and says that women who play the market "are thieves who do not deserve the name of banker [sont des voleuses et ne meritent pas le nom des Banquieres]" (Petit Dutaillis 1982: 10). In France, women were not entitled to have a bank account, to vote or to have control over their inheritance or dowry until 1946. Images of women and money always play on a complex dichotomy between values of thrift, self sufficiency with inherent propensity toward abundance, and spending. Women figure in mercantile literature by the 1550s, in bourgeois novellas and plays, but their functions are as keepers of household finances, "marchande," or given title of their husbands (presidente or tresoriere). Although women are not creators of profit or investors, they are endowed with very shrewd knowledge of the value of money, the value of goods, and the ability to wrangle money out of men. The role of dowry is essential to the social contract: women bring money, but can neither control, invest nor remove it from the marriage as, since Merovingian times, the dowry given by the father belongs to the husband. Therefore, the only control exerted on their creative power and spirit of initiative occurs within the erotic realm. Novels which focus on the transformational power of the merchant classes from the seventeenth century, describe the role of the couple as a set of commercial arrangements, which further the male's societal position and insure his business dealings. Businessmen, bankers, and merchants are very rarely lovers. Therefore, the adulterous schema within each novel becomes a means of transposing knowledge (woman's body) and wealth (the act of possession) from the all powerful business financier to the economically repressed hero. Adultery is another type of transaction: a form of credit operation, a bill of exchange with its bearer, drawer, and intermediary financial agent (the banker husband), yet an operation whose inherent nature implies fraud. Where the banker cannot be used or reduced, he can be manipulated or transformed into another archetypal comedic figure of the wronged husband. Sexual interaction, like semantic interaction, becomes an exchange of commodities.

Throughout literature, women's inherent relationship to money is internal as she is herself a commodity. Women and money are directly associated to women and prostitution. The female protagonist starts as an innocent young girl sold for "fifty guineas peremptory for the liberty of attempting me and a hundred more at the compleat gratification of his desires" (Cleland 1985 [1748]: 17). In *Moll Flanders* (1722), Daniel Defoe depicts the protagonist's pursuit of her career through the use of economic terms such as "dues," "shares," "commodities," and "prices." Moll Flanders' activities, including her numerous marriages, are defined as transactions in which she is treated as a commodity and is evaluated strictly in terms of the profit that she can generate for her marriage partner.

The novel's subtitle tells it all:

> The fortunes and misfortunes of the famous Moll Flanders who was born in Newgate and during a life of continu'd Variety for Threescore Years ... was Twelve Year a Whore, five times a wife..., Twelve Year a Thief, Eight Year a Transported Felon in Virginia, at last grew Rich, liv'd Honest, and dies a Penitent.
>
> (Defoe 1722)

In each of the multiple relationships, they are straightforward transactions, how much she has, how much is lost through profligacy, bad investments, theft, and how much remains. After two husbands, at age 20, she writes

> I had saved about L100 more, but I met with a disaster … that a goldsmith in whose hands I had trusted it, broke, so I lost L70 of my money, the man's composition not making above L30 out of his L100.
>
> (Defoe 1722: 116)

Every relationship is carefully described in terms of potential gains and losses. Moll is not only focused but knowledgeable of finance.

In France, depictions of prostitution abound in the novels such as Prévost's *Histoire du Chevalier des Grieux et de Manon Lescaut* (1965 [1731]), Sade's *La Nouvelle Justine ou les Malheurs de la Vertu Suivi de l'Histoire e Juliette , sa Soeur* (1797), and Restif de la Bretonne's *Les Nuits de Paris* (1960 [1788]), which places the female protagonist within the economic structure. In Sade's six-book opus the corrupt Juliette's body is described as a commodity: "the same merchandise was sold to 80 persons who paid." Describing Juliette's education in vice, she begins by learning the advantages of theft and larceny from Dorval, one of a myriad of corrupt wealthy lovers, as a form of social retribution:

> But who are greater thieves than our financiers?…There were then in the realm nine hundred million in specie; toward the close of the reign of Louis XIV, the people were paying 750,000,000 in taxes per annum and of this sum, only 250,000,000 found the way into the royal exchequer; which means that half a billion went yearly into the pockets of thieves. They were very great thieves; do you suppose these thefts weighed heavily upon their conscience?
>
> (Sade 1968: 124)

Histoire du Chevalier des Grieux et de Manon Lescaut (Prévost 1965 [1731]) underscores the dialectical tension between Des Grieux's ignorance of and scorn for the acquisition of money, and Manon's knowledgeable manipulation of the corrupt bankers and financiers who "keep" her. In these works, personal relationships are expressed in the semantics of exchange in which persons and objects interrelate according to their current market value, and even a character's downfall can be cushioned by previous financial dealings. Manon's wealth, like that of Moll Flanders, acquired through fraud, larceny or prostitution, is used to secure better living conditions even when she falls into prison. In eighteenth-century France's vast output of pornographic literature, money is a sub genre where women functions as commodity, trader and seller of her person. Even for virtuous, proper heroines in the Victorian era, the female body is an object of negotiations. Jo in *Little Woman* like the heroine of O. Henry's *Gift of the Magi* sell their hair, the only commodity in which they can transact within the norms of society, in order to help family finances or buy a gift for their husband.

There are women speculators in the Mississippi Bubble, including Alexandre de Tencin, mother of d'Alembert, who had her own "bureau d'agiotage:" Lady Mary Wortley Montagu, the Duchess of Rutland and Marlborough, and as "revealed by the presence of thirty five ladies (out of the eighty-eight names) on Lord Sunderland's list for the Second Money Subscription" (Chancellor 1999: 79). A ditty by Edward Ward, "South Sea Ballad," describes how in Change Alley "Our greatest Ladies hither come ... /Oft pawn their Jewels for a Sum ... / Young Harlots, too, from Drury Lane ... /To fool away the Gold they gain/By their obscene Debauches" (Chancellor 1999: 79).

In seventeenth- and eighteenth-century literature, female protagonists are also archetypes of a fluid, mobile servant class which indirectly emancipates women by allowing them to engage in business transactions in which the single, independent, strong willed and shrewd young woman steals, defrauds, cajoles or sells in order to change her status in society, gain financial independence, and succeed without the benefit of a father or husband. Legally, in England and across Europe until the 1920s, women had to have a male signature in order to access their finances, open accounts or dispose of property, unless designated as sole heir or widow with full legal rights. Although women were not active participants in finance, it was the lady of the house, the matron, mother, and wife who took active part in financial decisions on household matters, and on increasing family fortunes through marriage and dowries. Colonial America imposed strict moral coda on the behavior of women, as seen in Hawthorne's works. However, the rigorous geographic, physical and economic demands of colonial life necessitated women to take a more active role in finances.

Modesty was often cited as it was deemed unladylike for a woman to have to haggle and discuss her finances, but there were no specific theological interdictions, allowing greater flexibility in the application of these moral norms. Robert E. Wright, in the essay "Women and Finance in the Early National US" (2000), provides a unique insight into how, in eighteenth- and nineteenth-century America's vibrant financial sector, women were directly involved in financial and commercial transactions. "Women held loan and deposit accounts in many northeastern banks in the early national period. They also owned significant amounts of corporate stock and other financial securities" (Wright 2000). The demands of colonial America, with husbands often away for long periods, with few male relatives, and the need for economic self sufficiency, allowed women by necessity to take on commercial and transactional functions. According to historian Laurel Ulrich, "almost any task was suitable for a woman as long as it furthered the good of her family and was acceptable to her husband" (Ulrich 2000). In the 13 colonies, and later in the Western territories, women often lived in isolated rural areas overseeing large properties, which required a variety of skills including knowledge of revenues and costs.

Despite a few legal barriers, most women, even married ones, could engage in business on their personal account. Originally a London custom, *feme sole* status was codified by some American colonies or states. A *feme sole* trader, in other words, was a married woman conducting business on her own, with her husband's permission, but without his aid. ... Women owned a large percentage of the small volume of government bonds issued during the colonial era.

(Wright 2000)

Bank stock was seen as a sound and conservative investment: Wright quotes correspondance from a young woman, Marie Nichols during the War of 1812:

"Now, mamma has not been well for some two or three weeks," Nichols explained to Mrs. James Bayard, "and it was a little difficult to determine the cause of her malady; but the nature of her disease declared itself upon her rapid recovery when the United States Bank declared a dividend." "This is an excellent Bank," Nichols continued, "last quarter they paid 3 percent – this 3½ percent – next they hope to pay 4 percent." Wright also noted that "considerable numbers of women owned equity stakes in banks, insurance companies, and other joint-stock companies."

(Quoted in Wright 2000)

As America grew richer and as society established stricter rules of conduct for middle and upper class women, based on the examples of Victorian England, ladies did not engage in commerce unless absolutely necessary. In *House of Mirth*, Lily Bart's flirty interest in business matters is a sign of her somewhat dubious social standing. Jane Austin, Louisa May Alcott, and George Sand granted their heroines an interest in dowries and their husband's business interests, but never did they venture into the world of making money. Since the Middle Ages, merchants' wives are pervasive in literature and theater, offering good sense and greater business acumen than their husbands, but never given a role in decision makings. Margaret Mitchell's portrayal of Scarlett O'Hara in the American classic, *Gone With the Wind* (1936), describes her transformation from Southern belle in the plantation, emblematic of a pre-economic Eden, into a crass and wily business woman as wife of lumber merchant Frank Kennedy in post-Civil War Atlanta. Tough and able to buy and sell as well as any man, she betrayed the ethos of Southern womanhood epitomized by the philanthropic, sickly, and economically dependent Melanie.

By 1864, in the United States ladies publications warned of women ruined by engaging in speculative activities. In Zola's *L' Argent*, women lurking in the corridors of the Exchange, trying to engage in stock speculation, were judged as grotesque and amoral. In Theodore Dreiser's *The Financier* and *The Titan*, Flaubert's *Education Sentimentale*, and Henry James' *The American*, women are the desired prize for the financier, speculator hero or anti-hero.

Despite vast advances, in the glamorized world of investment banking in the early 1980s, New York and London merchant bankers "recur in gossip columns with beautiful women in tow (they are not supposed to be women themselves, and although I know that women investment bankers hold senior positions, I didn't come across any)" (Ferris 1984: 37).

Women were barred from engaging in speculative activity under the guise of societal, biological and moral standards. "Wall Street was a man's world; women were considered by nature to be ill suited to its rigors, lacking in the brains, emotional equanimity, and masculine reserve that the life of the speculator demanded" (Fraser 2005: 100). The exception was the Quaker heiress Hettie Howland Robinson Green, who managed through conservative investments in railroads, real estate, and US greenback dollar holdings, to increase a US$7 million fortune in 1864 to close to US$200 million at her death in 1916. Notoriously stingy and increasingly paranoid, she worked out of Seaboard National Bank, refusing to deal with other bankers. Although she was respected at the time (she participated in the New York City loan in 1907), she entered financial lore as the "Witch of Wall Street."

Despite the massive losses of manpower and the entry of women into the work force after World War I, banking and financial professions remained a male bastion. In America, between 1880 and 1920 the proportion of women in the work force rose 50 percent, yet finance was not an appropriate or desirable profession unlike medicine, law, academia or even journalism. Women are better represented in small Nordic countries as demonstrated in Iceland in the 2008 financial collapse when women bankers, Chief Executive Officer of Glitnir, Birna Einarsdottir, and Elin Sigfusdottir at Landesbanki, were appointed to resurrect the two largest nationalized banks.

Outside of the Nordic countries, which achieved political and economic gender equality, in most of Europe, especially in Germany and the Mediterranean countries, the assumption is that women only work as an interim measure before marriage and children, and that they engage in traditional female professions: teaching, medicine, the arts, and retail. France took a giant step forward in emancipating women within the realm of finance with the appointment in 2007 of its first female Minister of Finance, Christine Lagarde, attorney, economist, and former managing director at McKinsey in Chicago, positions she might not have attained in France. In Germany, Italy, and Japan, very few women ever attain management positions in finance. In Japanese investment banks, Nomura, Daiwa, and Yamaichi, in the 1980s women could only be employed as clerks, secretaries, and assistants. Yet there was a unique female work force outside of the institution's organizational chart. Nomura employed nearly 2,000 housewives as sales staff to sell government issued bonds and other safe, fixed interest securities to housewives in the suburbs. This personalized marketing approach was seen as an acceptable avenue for women to sell securities, earn small commissions, and increase the client base without actually integrating them within the structure of these institutions (see Ferris 1984: 169–172).

In Germany, as in emerging economies, there still is a latent prejudice – such that once Germany regained economic stability during the economic recovery years 1957–1970, there was a sense of national pride that women no longer needed to work. In the European Union, women reach high level political positions, and under European Union rules there has to be equal opportunity, and in many countries equal representation of women in Parliament, but in the field of finance women are still very much in the minority.

The case of Muriel Siebert epitomizes the trajectory of women in American finance. In 1967, a middle class Jewish woman trained at Bache and Co., decided to break the barriers and asked for a loan to buy a seat on the New York Stock Exchange. As described in her autobiography and in countless interviews and speeches, against all odds, bucking discrimination, indifference, and hostility from Bernard Lasker, then chairman of the NYSE, Muriel Siebert became the first woman among 1,365 men to have a seat and the only female owned broker-age house on the New York Stock Exchange (Siebert 2002). In 1972, Juanita Kreps became the first woman director of the NYSE. In 1977, Siebert was appointed New York State Superintendant of Banking.

Between 1972 and 1975, a socio-cultural shift occurred on Wall Street as a generation of women lawyers, MBAs, and PhDs in economics, arrived in the work place. For the first time women demanded, and were offered, positions on trading floors, account departments, correspondent banking, and client relations. Graduates of top schools, they were not willing to settle for executive secretary, marketing or human resources positions. Entering a boisterous male culture, they adapted, slowly transforming the financial workplace. Through the 1980s, the transition was remarkable and fraught with difficulties as women broke through gender stereotypes. The profile of the banker radically changed as minorities entered the arena. American popular novels, such as Arthur Hailey's *The Money Changers* (1975), Emma Latham's (pseudonym of Mary Latsis and Martha Hennissart) mystery series involving John Putnam Thatcher, the conservative "WASP" banker-detective (1961–1979), and *Cashing In* by Antonia Gowar (1982), incorporated the mechanics and concepts of high-technology banking and depersonalized administrative structures, as well as the specialized terminology and jargon of computerized trading centers and boardrooms. They also presented a new phenomenon: the woman banker and banking executive. But Hailey's Edwina d'Orsay or Gowar's Lisa Gould did not change the image of the banker; instead, they grafted the traits of monomaniacal ambition, amorality, and disillusion onto a female character. Unlike in eighteenth- and nineteenth-century literary works, which treated women as merely another form of commodity, assets, profit, or as a tangible prize for the male financier, women in these novels move from objective to subjective status. Yet they do not transform the genre – they merely reverse sexual roles and update the stereotype. At Lazard Frères, as described by William D. Cohan in his in-depth study of the firm, an entire chapter is devoted to the cultural, generational, and institutional barriers against women bankers. In the 1980s, the firm decided to hire a second woman banker, a senior partner, assuming that the first one is therefore being fired, has to be told that "this would be a second woman." Glanville's response was "I thought the EEO meant we only had to have one" (Cohan 2007: 392).

In 1997, Martin Mayer could write that "banking has a higher percentage of female officers than any other industry" (Mayer 1997: 19), but within the next decade the overall numbers would fall. Women would populate administrative, clerical, and low level account positions, but in trading rooms in London, Paris, and New York gender and ethnic disparities remain striking: traders are mainly white men; the back office is heavily populated by minority women.

Why have women not progressed further in boardrooms since the 1990s? October 23, 2006, the Hotel Pierre in New York was the venue for "A Celebration of Excellence, the Most Powerful Women in Banking," dinner and award ceremony. This ranking started in 2003 by *US Banker* magazine was, as described in the program "to pay tribute to women executives whose outstanding corporate performances were underscored by how they used their social and professional capital to bring about change." The event honored Jessica Palmer who, since the 1970s, broke barriers at Wells Fargo as head of the fixed income capital markets group, and at Citicorp for 22 years as head of the international investment banking group. Other honorees included women from Bank of America, Wells Fargo, US Bancorp, and Wachovia, as well as smaller banks, Umpqua Bank, Amegy Bank of Texas, with Citi leading in the number of women including Chief Financial Officer, Sallie Krawcheck; Chief Executive Officer of Treasury and Security at J.P. Morgan Chase, Heidi Miller; and Executive Vice President of Consumer Credit Group, Doreen Woo Ho at Wells Fargo. According to *US Banker*, October 2008, HSBC USA, Wells Fargo, Citi, and ING continue to have the largest number of women in senior management positions (Sraeel and Scott 2008).

If retail banks showed definite progress, in 2007, US private equity firms had less than ten women in positions of management. The Blackstone Group, Kohlberg, Kravis, and Ceberus Capital Management do not have any women senior dealmakers. These causes are myriad:

> They lack the networks of their male counterparts; some of them leave work to raise a family; there are simply fewer women getting M.B.A.s and going into finance in the first place ... The real problem is that the proverbial glass ceiling is self reinforcing. The traits that a woman must develop to duke it out on the trading floor will come back to haunt her as she ascends the ranks of management.

> (Hagan 2008)

Law suits filed against the financial sector refer to deeper prejudices and stereotypes. The law suit brought by six senior bankers at Dresdner Kleinwort Wasserstein in 2006, based on discrimination in promotion and bonuses "also cites instances of lewd behavior toward the women, entertainment of clients at a strip club and repeated examples of scaled-back opportunities for women after they returned from maternity leave." Lawsuits filed against Merrill Lynch, Morgan Stanley, and Salomon Smith Barney often resulted in large settlements (Andersen 2006).

There is a similar trajectory in the United Kingdom, where women were first allowed to trade on the London Stock Exchange in 1973, and the first women director at a bank was appointed in 1982. In 2008, Marjorie Scardino at Pearsons, Helen Weir at Lloyds, and Joanne Dawson at HBOS are among the highest paid women directors. How they will fare, as these banks are partially or fully nationalized has yet to be decided. Clara Fuse, Head of the London Stock Exchange since 2001, is the only woman to head the world's oldest and most prestigious exchange in its 235-year history. However, despite these prominent success stories, an April 2007 study in Britain showed 92 women on Britain's list of 1,000 wealthiest people, up from 64 in 1997. Although larger percentages of women derive wealth from their own earnings, "most British millionairesses will still be wives, daughters and divorcées" ("Sex and Money" 2007). Women are directors of ten of the FTSE-100 firms, and around 10 percent of the Forbes 500 list. In US and UK firms, the number of top female senior managers has dropped since 2002.

As the caustic *Financial Times* businesswomen commentator stated, when praising the choice of women to resolve Iceland's crisis,

> Of course there are plenty of women in banking, especially retail banking. I suspect half the workforce of Britain's retail banks is female. A career as a bank teller is one that sits supportively with family life. But women in charge of a bank? There are very few.
>
> (Mrs Moneypenny 2008)

In emerging and underdeveloped markets in Africa, women often serve as intermediaries between rural barter economies and post-colonial urban finance through the use of micro-credit geared specifically toward women. However, in the Islamic world, legal and theological restrictions against women fully participating in the workplace hinder economic progress. According to a 2007 World Bank Study and the *Financial Times Special Report* "Leading Businesswomen in the Arab World" in 2007 and 2008, the same names appear of exceptional highly educated, Western trained, prominent women in banking, holding companies, Stock Exchange, and financial institutions. In 135 of 4,000 companies, in seven Middle East countries, women are principal owners with over 15 percent share. Although affluent women are often highly educated, the opportunities to put these skills to use outside of the home or family owned businesses remains very limited. The *Financial Times* survey of 26 women leaders, highlights retail, cosmetics, educational software, and banking and investment ventures. However, these women in top positions, especially in finance, are all part of a very small group of foreign educated wealthy women. Members of leading or ruling families, they have the protection and contacts which allow them to function outside of societal and political restrictions. In Morocco and Jordan, where women are far more emancipated and interactive in the economic life of the country, Hynd Bouhia became director of the Casablanca Stock Exchange in March 2008, a Harvard PhD, she worked at the World Bank. Nezha Hayat is head of private banking, Société Générale Marocaine des Banques; Reem Badran, daughter of a former Jordanian prime minister, is chief executive officer of Kuwaiti Jordanian Holding Company. But banks themselves are not yet attuned to seeing women as a client base. International Finance Corporation report that very few women use formal bank credit to finance small business, depending rather on family or personal savings. They fall into the trap of all disenfranchised groups in relation to formal financial networks: as they cannot offer collateral and do not have a credit history, banks refuse to grant them credit. In Saudi Arabia, women must have a husband or father as guarantor of a loan, a practice common across Europe until the late nineteenth century. Egypt is starting to create products geared toward this sector: credit cards, life insurance, and consumer lending, started by Commercial International Bank in 2002. Dubai Bank is planning a similar endeavor. One exception is India where there are opportunities for women in banking. India's largest private bank, ICICI appointed Chanda Kochhar as chief executive officer in December 2008, part of an elite cadre of female bankers in charge of domestic and major foreign banks, including HSBC, J.P. Morgan, and UBS. Two other women executives head state banks and two of the four deputy governors at the central bank of India are women. Highly educated, often from American or British schools, they are fully accepted in the business community. ICICI "has a growing tradition of awarding senior roles to women who occupy about 40 percent of the top positions at the bank" (Leahy 2008).

The crisis of 2008 reinforced the vulnerability of women on Wall Street, as Zoe Cruz at Morgan Stanley, Chief Financial Officer at Lehman, Erin Callan, and Chief Financial Officer at Citigroup, Sallie Krawcheck, were among the first to be demoted to less visible positions and then summarily dismissed. As described by Krawcheck "most at Citicorp are treated as a 'condiment' rather than a 'main course' she also said that she had no regrets about her experiences there" (Fabricant 2008). Since 2008, despite unprecedented losses in global banks, very few chief executive officers have resigned or been asked to step down. They have chosen to forego bonuses, as at UBS and Goldman Sachs, to promise reforms, and to profess a sense of culpability, but they have retained their positions. The issue is not if women in top positions bear the same share of responsibility for lack of oversight and prudence, but, unlike their male counterparts, they were unable to muster the necessary support and approval within the board, the institution at large and their chief executive officers.

2.4 Paper money and counterfeiting

Even Adam Smith, a defender of banknotes, stipulated that if paper had to replace coinage, "a Law indeed might lay restraints and threaten Penalties, but it can't change Men's minds, to make them think a piece of paper is a piece of Money" (Smith 1776). Modern financial crisis began in the 1700s, with the issuance and distribution of paper notes, shares, and the start of a gold for paper speculative market. Preceded by a surge in speculative activity between 1704 and 1715, conducted "by small time sharks, back street usurers" (Rude 1971: 547), in paper to gold transactions, a vast unregulated market fed on rumors of convertibility of paper into gold, silver, and even copper coin as strength and confidence in paper notes fluctuated on a daily basis. Literature, art, theater, pamphlets, and tirades against agiotage exposed and reinforced the fear and lack of confidence in this illusory and corruptible form of exchange. In contrast, in each financial crisis the price of gold surges as there is an atavistic, physical need for tangible value. Between 2005 and 2008, gold increased over 50 percent in value, reaching nearly US$1,000 per ounce as stocks, esoteric instruments, and even bonds began to appear vulnerable and prone to wild fluctuations. Lack of confidence in paper in modern markets is revealed in the flight to safety, that is, a rise in the price of gold and commodities. Since the French Revolution, when émigrés smuggled or sent gold to London, in subsequent wars, revolutions, and major economic crisis (including Jewish refugees escaping the Nazis in Germany and France, Hungarians in 1956, and Iranians in 1979), women often smuggled out gold as personal jewelry, once notes, stocks and bills were no longer accessible or convertible.

In 2008, derivatives have been excoriated for their complexity, esoteric nature, and inaccessibility that even bankers, traders, and chief executive officers have had to admit ignorance. These instruments are all the more nefarious as they were based on the most basic and oldest asset: a home mortgage. Marc Shell distinguishes between scriptural ("created by process of bookkeeping,") and fiduciary money or bank notes, both separate from specie. In all countries the issuance and distribution of paper money has been met with extreme wariness and fear, as the process itself resembles alchemy more than science: Rumplestilskin spinning straw into gold. In 1809, Goethe, obsessed with the John Law fiasco and having personally observed the failure of the French Revolution's assignats, never trusted paper issuance in Germany. In *Faust II*, he attributed to the devil, Mephistopheles, the skill to cure economic crisis by transforming the natural order of goods and services for cash into a new form of alchemy in which paper replaces gold in turn used to pay expenses and cancel debts. The Intendant of the Treasury explains to the bewildered Emperor how his signature alone has transformed mere paper into gold:

Remember, thou the note didst undersign

And just last night! …
So that a like advantage all might claim
We stamped at once the series with thy name,
In Tens, in Fifties, Hundreds all prepared.
Thou canst not think how well men since have fared!

The Emperor amazed and relieved exclaims: "And with my people does it pass for gold?/For pay in court and camp the notes will hold?/Then I must yield, although it seems amazing" (Goethe 1962: 55). A century later, in the aftermath of World War I, the societal and political repercussions of Germany's devastating hyperinflation of June 1922 to November 1923 were accelerated by the printing of worthless bank notes. In a desperate attempt to create new notes to replace the discredited Reichsmark, the Rentemark, issued following the occupation of the Ruhr in January 1923, immediately devalued in an inflationary spiral which changed prices twice a day in the summer of 1923, confirming the worst fears of the German right on the fragility and corruptibility of paper money. Georges Grosz and Otto Dix with brutal, grotesque painting and drawings of industrialists, bankers, and money – New Objectivism (Neue Sachlichkeit) – revealed the horror of a world where all personal and economic value and identity, money, land, assets, stocks, titles had been rendered worthless. As the currency lost value there was a desperate quest for foreign currency, a pattern which recurred after World War II and in the post-Soviet era as a black market in foreign exchange became a shadow economy. The total loss of faith in the government's ability to control prices and protect assets and land, focused on distrust of paper and foreigners as agents of economic chaos. The right-wing press and Hitler's populist rhetoric found its scapegoats in the black market where Eastern Europeans and Jews dealt in dollars. Faith in bank-issued notes and paper only returned to Germany once the Deutschmark was created on June 20, 1948, formally establishing a sound currency. Within the next two decades, the Deutschmark would become the anchor of the fledging European monetary system.

John Law, architect of the Mississippi Bubble, was an early advocate of paper money as credit, in the form of shares backed by the value of land to be redeemed on demand in silver coin. Although treated in the innumerable satires of the time as smoke, mirrors, wind, and deceit, Law firmly advocated that a paper and specie economy, allowing circulation of capital regulated by a central bank, could replenish the Treasury. First coming to France in 1705, he was "banished in 1706 for having asserted that paper money was superior to gold and silver" (Kindleberger 1993: 98). The psychological impact of the Mississippi Bubble was profound distrust of paper, of bank notes, of all transactions outside of specie. Montesquieu, in *Lettres Persanes* (1961 [1720]), saw in currency transactions an operation which functioned as illusion without the sound, tangible security of specie. "If he has only one million ecus in his treasury and he needs two, all he has to do is persuade them that one ecu is worth two and they believe him" (ibid.: letter 24). After the fiasco of the Law scheme, examined in the next section, the experience of paper notes during the Revolution was even more devastating.

Mirabeau's tirades against paper money called it theft and exploitation, but by 1790 without a central bank and no fiscal system in place, paper money was the only solution. The concept was to create notes backed by confiscated Church lands. Issued in large denominations of 100, 500 and 200 livres, they did not respond to the needs of the population and as smaller notes were issued and their actual value fluctuated throughout 1792, "they also embedded paranoia about paper money and banks more deeply in the French subconscious" (Kindleberger 1993: 101).

Talleyrand, clergyman under Louis XIV, republican minister under Napoleon, and monarchist diplomat under the Restoration, best described the failure of the assignats:

> You will ensure that an assignat of 1000 livres must be accepted as payment for the sum of 1000 livres. But you will never be able to force anyone to give 1000 livres in ecus for an assignat of 1000 livres.
>
> (Talleyrand quoted in Furet 1989)

As émigrés smuggled gold and silver abroad and as church bells were melted for hard currency, the Jacobins persisted in printing notes even after the most fervent revolutionary Saint Just, disciple of Robespierre decried: "I no longer see anything in the State, but misery, pride and paper" (Furet 1989). Napoleon understood, upon coming to power that faith in the currency and in a stable note issuance had to be established. The Bank of France, created in 1800 with sole privilege of issuance of 500 and 1,000 franc notes, officially defined the French franc as 322.56 milligrams of gold or five grams of silver and all notes convertible into gold. But it was not until 1856 that checks were introduced and began to be used between 1893 and 1913.

In America, plagued by counterfeiting from the 1860s until 1913, politicians railed against paper: "You send these notes out into the world stamped with irredeemability. You put on them the mark of Cain and like Cain, they will go forth to be vagabonds and fugitives on the earth" (Pendleton 1829 quoted in Shell 1982: 7). Poe's *Gold Bug*; Mark Twain's *100,000 Bank Note*; Hawthorne's, *Seven Vagabonds*; Ralph Waldo Emerson and Washington Irving each saw in paper deviousness and corruptibility. The fundamentals against speculation and paper currency are rooted in their ability to convert money and profits from the void, riches from air. It also reinforced the initiated, esoteric, and, by extension, alchemic nature of the operations involved, from bills of exchange to agiotage to speculation to hedge funds. Since the Great Depression, fear of speculation is associated with loss of paper value in stocks and bonds, which translate into loss of real value. In the Crash of October 1987, the market lost 22 percent of value in one week, in September 2008 erratic losses and gains of nearly 1,000 points, caused losses of nearly 9 percent in market value mid-month, with continuous gyrations through 2009, wiping out over US$1 trillion on paper. In 2008, the complexity, diversification of risk, number of buyers, number of trades executed, and turnover of these instruments created a unique situation in which banks holding these assets could no longer estimate true valuation nor differentiate between the healthy and the toxic. Mortgages, the oldest and most reliable of financial instruments, based on written deeds for land and estates, had metamorphosed into fragmented, indefinable, and dangerous chimeras.

2.5 Counterfeiting

> I am Capocchio's shade – the counterfeiter
> Of metals by alchemy; if I trust my eyes
> You recall how good I was at aping nature.
> (Dante 1994: Canto XXIX)

Counterfeit derived from "contra facto" (against the fact), is a more generic term than the French term "faux monnayeurs," specifically referencing those who create false or fake money, who violate the basic trust between buyer and seller. In French literature, Andre Gide's *Les Faux Monnayeurs* represented moral and emotional identity theft, where appearance and reality merge and submerge for purposes of fraud. In his widely read and acclaimed novels, Gide, in perpetual religious and sexual conflict between what he perceived as vice and virtue, was fascinated and horrified by the power of money. In *Les Caves du Vatican*, another counterfeit hero, Lafcadio learns of money from a German banker Heldenbrock, who teaches him about interest, exchange, and speculation as a multilayered identity and financial fraud is set up to deceive and rob the Church (Gide 1948).

Distrust of paper money is not only from fear of its inherent ephemeral nature and dependence on outside contingencies, but also the ability to replicate these instruments, to create identical yet worthless copies. The fear of counterfeiting first applied to coinage, which was reputed to be verifiable by the sound, the ring of the coin, and the hardness of the metal if bitten down on. In Dante's age, counterfeiting the Florentine ducat was punishable by death and in *Inferno* Dante relegates all "falsifiers" to the eighth circle of hell, where those accused of sins of fraud including hypocrites, flatterers, thieves, and "false counselors," suffer the agonies and mutilations through eternity.

As the United States was the first nation to issue paper currency in 1785, counterfeit notes were a persistent problem for the new nation's economic well being. During the Civil War there was an urgent need to fund the Union, including a first income tax proposed by Salmon Chase, Treasury Secretary, and approved by Congress, but paper currency had to be printed in order to supplement the dwindling supply of gold reserves. Like France and Germany, the United States went through a psychological, political, and cultural debate as the pros and cons of paper and specie dominated the financial discourse. As issuance remained under the state system, banks issued notes of different appearance and apparent value, counterfeiting was rampant and there was minimal control. Stephan Mihm in *A Nation of Counterfeiters* (2007) described how the proliferation of banks issuing paper money rose from 200 in 1815 to over 300 by 1830. By the 1850s, more than 10,000 different kinds of paper currency circulated across the states and territories, making it extremely hard to differentiate real from fake. Without a central bank and one source of issuance, once Jackson did not renew the Charter of the Second Bank of the United States, new note issuing banks sprang up.

> As Hezekiah Niles [editor of one of the first financial publications in 1818] recognized, both bankers and counterfeiters issued bills or notes with little or nothing in the way of assets backing their promises to pay and both drew their energy from the same boundless faith that slips of paper could pass as good as gold.
>
> (Mihm 2008)

But as the country and the demands for goods and capital expanded, these notes were accepted and circulated.

> Many people in the business of banking viewed counterfeiting as a small price to pay for a system of money creation governed not by the edicts of a

central bank or the fiscal arm of the state, but by insatiable private demand for credit in the form of bank notes.

(Mihm 2008)

Only the demands of financing the Civil War brought about currency reforms and banned the issuance of notes by state chartered banks. However, by the 1880s, rampant counterfeiting recurred and the first financial sheets, including the Dow-Jones newsletter, offered daily warnings where and which bills and notes were genuine or counterfeit.

Since the 1990s, the proliferation of money laundering and large scale drug trafficking across borders, coupled with access to sophisticated technology has engendered an international industry in counterfeit currency, specializing in the US dollar, requiring different denominations to be issued and re-issued, with more built in security and anti-replicating measures.

2.6 Financial manias, panics and crisis

To execute a perpetual egg dance among more or less dangerous debit balances.

(Rothschild's comment on Emile Pereire's skill at the failed
Credit Mobilier bank, 1857)

In 2008, the financial world rediscovered Charles Kindleberger's *Manias, Panics and Crashes* (2005), the latest edition published posthumously in 2005. Kindleberger in this definitive study of the causes and repercussions of financial catastrophes lists the "big ten financial bubbles" as follows:

1 The Dutch Tulip Bulb Bubble 1636,
2 The South Sea Bubble 1720,
3 The Mississippi Bubble 1720,
4 The late 1920s stock price bubble 1927–1929,
5 The surge in bank loans to Mexico and other developing countries in the 1970s,
6 The bubble in real estate and stocks in Japan 1985–1989,
7 The 1985–1989 bubble in real estate and stocks in Finland, Norway and Sweden,
8 The bubble in real estate and stocks in Thailand, Malaysia, Indonesia and several other Asian countries 1992–1997,
9 The surge in foreign investment in Mexico 1990–1993,
10 The bubble in over-the-counter stocks in the United States 1995–2000.

(2005: 9)

Over a period of time each of these events provoked financial instability, excessive speculation, lack of oversight, and caused both liquidity and currency crisis. The housing bubble, which overvalued real estate prices from 2000 to 2007, imploded into a liquidity and solvency crisis in major insurers, banks and credit markets within six months in 2008. The year began and ended with vast losses through trading fraud and the largest Ponzi scheme committed by Bernard Madoff, with losses of US$65 billion. Kindleberger in "Frauds, swindles and the credit cycle" (ibid.) examines each of these issues, but one applies to all and especially to Madoff: "The supply of corruption increases in a procyclical way much like the supply of credit … In the absence of more credit, the fraud sprouts from the woodwork like mushrooms in a soggy forest" (Kindleberger 1993: 165). Defining the degree of criminality in financial fraud is complicated by the complicity of the investor seeking higher earnings and the banker, financier or analyst looking for better yields and therefore higher compensation and rewards.

> Much of the fraudulent behavior initially had occurred in the mania phase as stock prices were increasing but was obscured in the froth of the bubble; high risk borrowers were able to refinance their maturing loans because the lenders were eager to increase their total loans and assets … customers old enough to vote presumably were capable of looking out for their own financial interests.
>
> (Kindleberger 1993: 166)

Ponzi schemes from the original to Ivan Kreuger to BCCI to Madoff, depended on the same principles as the Mississippi and South Sea Bubbles, an endless number of investors willing to believe in endlessly positive returns. Kindleberger's examination of historical rationale for past follies and excesses questioned whether crises were created by monetary and credit markets "or are they real – war, the end of war, good and bad harvests, waves of investment based on innovations such as the canal, railroad, automobile? Could they be either? Both?" (Kindleberger 1994: 264). He refers back to Adam Smith who defined the stages of financial manias: "overtrading" followed by "negligence and profusion," then "revulsion and discredit." Hyman Minsky theorized that since the Renaissance, financial crises were the effect of "displacements": wars which created instability provoking monetary displacement, gold to silver, excess or sudden reduction of currency, devaluation or revaluation of the currency (Minsky 1993: intro). From 1551 to 1866, financial crashes occurred approximately every ten years. However, in the last 20 years, as technology and availability of information increased, financial crises have occurred in 1987, 1995, 1998, 2000, 2002, and 2008. Walter Bagehot, following the precepts of Smith and Lord Overstone, cited the cycle as "quiescence, improvement, confidence, prosperity, excitement, overtrading, CONVULSION [Bagehot's capitals], pressure, stagnation, ending again in quiescence" (quoted in Kindleberger 1993: 268).

An exact cause or one precise moment when the scale tips and overvaluation and overtrading become a crisis is hard to pinpoint, but often there is a confluence of events. In 1866, a drop in cotton prices at the end of the Civil War affecting textile markets from India to Egypt, impacted shares on the London Stock

Exchange, with contagion spreading to finance companies in Austria, Prussia, and Russia. The near failure of Barings in 1890, contained through the Bank of England's rapid intervention, still had repercussions on lending to other parts of the empire and in the United States. Often the failure of one institution could be the catalyst: Overend, Gurney and Co.'s failure in 1866, Ohio Life and Trust Company of New York's US$2 million embezzlement, the Mires bank failure in Paris in 1857, Drexel Lambert in 1989, Bear Stearns in March 2008, and Lehman in September 2008.

Crises occur once larger and larger segments of the population, despite being knowledgeable of the vagaries of the market, become persuaded that a certain product, instrument, transaction or future investment will bring them immense wealth: "Before the mysteries of structured credit there were the mysteries of witchcraft; before investment banks used initial public offerings to turn dotcom concepts into billions of dollars alchemists claimed to turn base metals into gold" (Kay 2008). Treating this symptom as anthropological rather than economic, Kay interpreted this behavior as irrational and destructive as any other manifestation "of collective psychosis or group think in which profit or power no longer allows individuals or leaders to step away from the precipice."

Speculation in objects as disparate as tulips, securities, railroads, real estate both real and fictitious follow a trajectory "when euphoria and speculation spread from object to object and place to place," heightened by the fact that "greed or less pejoratively, appetite for income is highly infectious" (Kindleberger 1993: 265). The tulip mania, the South Sea Bubble, and the Mississippi Bubble became imprinted in European cultural memory. The exotic nature of the ventures, the ability to attract investors of all social classes and to provoke disastrous losses of wealth, reputation and faith in the market, attracted condemnation and commentary by politicians, intellectuals, and artists in the immediate aftermath. The tulip mania in Holland from 1620–1637, mentioned in contemporary Dutch, French and English pamphlets by the 1720s, was incorporated into etchings and drawings of the Mississippi and South Sea bubbles, illustrating temptations and dangers of speculation. Charles Mackay popularized the tulip mania in *Memoirs of Extraordinary Popular Delusions and the Madness of Crowds* (1852 [1841]), describing how from the 1620s, "the demand for tulips of a rare specie increased so much in the year 1636 that regular marts for their sale were established on the Stock Exchange of Amsterdam, in Rotterdam, Harlaem, Leyden, Allmar and other towns" (ibid.: chapter 3). By 1637, the folly was over and just as quickly the government had to intervene to control the market. The original schemes in London and Paris, which engendered the speculative frenzy and subsequent losses known as the South Sea and Mississippi Bubbles, began as well-founded efforts to increase and improve public finances. In 1711, John Blount established the South Sea Trading Company to help settle the national debt by issuing shares in potential trading profits and selling the shares at reasonable valuation. By 1718, encouraged by John Law's takeover of the Banque Royale, the South Sea Company vastly expanded, with share prices increasing from a safe 100 pounds to 1,000 pounds in six months, based on rumors of immense dividends and future riches. As Alexander Pope, one of the few skeptics wrote, "Statesmen and patriots plied alike the stocks/Peeress and butler shared alike the box" as "Britain was sunk in lucre's sordid charms" (Pope 1752). The South Sea Bubble became subject of factual and allegorical literature, tracts, press, and art. It inspired French and Dutch satirical prints, like Chatelain's *The Great Mirror of Folly* and *Island of Mad Head* with a giant jester's cap filled with the names of the exchanges, participants, and vices. In England the most famous representation was William Hogarth's *South Sea Bubble*, a sharp rebuke to religion, false beliefs, and the corruptive influence of money. Working on a companion piece entitled *The Lottery*, Hogarth honed in on gambling and speculation with the same compendium of vices and virtues: misfortune, sloth, fraud, despair, folly, pleasure, and industry.

John Law, returning to Paris in 1715, at the death of Louis XIV persuaded the Regent that a bank could help alleviate the public debt of 3,500 million livres tournois. The Conseil Extraordinaire agreed to let Law set up the first French state bank, Banque Generale in 1716, with limited note issuance in order to restart commercial lending to industry and trade. By 1718, the bank under the Regent, Philip d'Orleans, became Banque Royale whose primary function, in conjunction with the Louisiana Trading Company, was to issue stock in the Mississippi lands. Law issued 200,000 shares at 500 livres tournois apiece, taking over monopolies of minting, tobacco sales, and taxes. By 1718, the Banque Royal could issue notes to circulate as money but once the shares became dangerously overvalued and were being sold and resold for 18,000 by end of 1719, they could no longer be redeemed. Within two months, in the summer of 1720, "with 550,000 claimants for 2.2 billion in notes and 125,000 shares with a nominal value of 250 million, worth five times that amount at the market's peak. The claims were written down to one-twentieth of their stated value" (Kindleberger 1993: 99). The ensuing losses and recriminations assured that the public and the Crown would steer away from banks and issuance of notes. At its peak the Mississippi Bubble as described in the Memoires of the Duke of Saint-Simon:

> The Bank was first established in the rue Quincampoix where Law resided. It was necessary to lock down the street. A bell announced the opening and closing of the bank. The crowd was so thick that there was not room for a pin ... and clerks passed the notes through the windows. Everyone co-mingled, valets and noblemen.
>
> (Saint-Simon 1879)

At first the profits were amazing and Paris "had never before been so full of objects of elegance and luxury" (Saint-Simon 1879). But in early summer 1720, the powerful Prince of Conti, annoyed at his inability to purchase more stock, decided to be reimbursed in cash. The amount was so great that the Bank requested that he return part of the gold, but soon rumors spread that the bank could not redeem the shares and panic set in. Speculation at its height had reached a point where shares worth 500 livres were being sold for 20,000. The bank had issued notes for 3 billion livres, but had only 500 million in cash. In October 1720, the government closed down the Bank, refused to honor the notes and Law, fearing for his life, escaped to Belgium. All at once the illusion of wealth was replaced by endless recriminations and accusations of fraud. A popular ditty of the day revealed the speed and range of the losses:

> Monday, I bought shares
> Tuesday I earned millions
> Wednesday, I fixed up my house
> Thursday, I bought a horse and carriage
> Friday, off I went to the ball
> Saturday, to debtors' prison
> [Lundi, j'achetai des actions
> Mardi, je gagnai des millions
> Mercredi, j'arrangeai mon ménage
> Jeudi, je pris un equipage
> Vendredi, je m'en fus au bal
> Samedi, a l'hopital].
>
> (Lagarde 1963)

On some level, France never recovered. "French experience with John Law was such that there was hesitation in even pronouncing the word bank for 150 years thereafter – a classic case of collective financial memory" (Kindleberger 1993: 100).

In each financial crisis from 1857, 1873, 1882, 1893, to 1987, references to Law resurface as French journalists, novelists, and later media warn of the dangers of speculation and putting trust in foreigners. Nineteenth-century crashes caused by over speculation in railroad stocks in 1846, bubbles in grain prices causing the Crash of 1848, the impact of the Gold Rush on global markets by 1857, crashes in the United States and Europe in 1866, 1873, and 1893 had a major economic impact but did not necessarily enter the collective imagination.

Until fall 2008, the most significant event in American financial culture was the Crash of 1929, metaphor for financial collapse and disaster on a global scale. The fascination with the market and Wall Street permeated all aspects of American culture through the 1920s best described in Galbraith:

> By the summer of 1929 the Market ... also dominated the culture. That recherché minority which at other times has acknowledged its interest in Saint Thomas Aquinas, Proust, psychoanalysis and psychosomatic medicine then spoke of United Corporation, United Founders, and Steel. Only the most aggressive of the eccentrics maintained their detachment from the market and their interest in autosuggestion and communism.
>
> (Galbraith 1954: 77)

Once panic spread to Europe in 1932, enthusiasm and optimism in American finance was replaced

By a new kind of financial mirror giving back a more sinister image of business – for example the Australian born Christine Stead's House of All Nations (1938) about derring-do and chicanery in a Paris based international bucket shop. Few reformist novelists of the 1930s – not even John Dos Passos in his trilogy U.S.A. – directly addressed the well-publicized malfeasances of American business of the previous decade.

(Brooks 1984)

The crash itself was not reprised or depicted in literature as America sought entertainment and only wanted peripheral references, especially in the new popular genre of cinema.

Frothy fantasies, *Topper* (1937); musical extravagances, *Gold Diggers of 1933* (1933) where a millionaire composer rescues unemployed actors; and glamorous social comedies like *My Man Godfrey* (1936); responded to the country's need for catharsis and entertainment. *My Man Godfrey*, despite its zany portrayal of the idle rich Bullock family, shows the conditions of the destitute and homeless, where the heroine finds her future butler and love interest. The lovely improbable ending – where the butler, Godfrey (William Powel), is discovered to be a wealthy gentleman with a good business sense who wisely regains the family's fortune after major losses in the market, marries the daughter (Carole Lombard), and uses his fortune to help his former vagrant buddies – exonerated the follies of capitalism in the name of good American virtues and sense of justice.

Although there were hearings and indictments, it was hard to pinpoint one culprit as so many had invested so much in the market. Debunking a myth that one individual or a select group of individuals provoked the Crash of 1929 (a popular conspiracy theory in left-wing media in the 1940s and 1950s) Galbraith wrote:

No one was responsible for the great Wall Street crash. No one engineered the speculation that preceded it. Both were the product of the free choice and decision of hundreds of thousands of individuals. The latter were not led to the slaughter. They were impelled to it by the seminal lunacy which has always seized people who are seized in turn with the notion that they can become very rich.

(Galbraith 1954:4)

But Galbraith's statement resounds as it did in 1954: "For a decade, whenever Americans have been afflicted with doubt as to the durability of their current state of prosperity, they have asked: 'Will it be 1929 all over again?'" (Galbraith 1954: 4).

In 2008, analogies with 1929 are hyperbolic at best, fear mongering at worst. From October 1929 to Roosevelt's first fireside chat on March 4, 1933, over 10,000 banks failed, people lost US$2 billion in savings as there was no federal deposit insurance, unemployment rose to 23 percent in 1932 (without unemployment benefits or protection), stocks lost nearly 80 percent of their valuation. In

2008, Chairman of the Federal Reserve, Bernard Bernanke (a scholar of the Depression), the United States Treasury, and European governments acted quickly to staunch the bleeding by lowering interest rates, maintaining open markets, injecting massive amounts to salvage the banking system, and calm the markets. Yet all facts withstanding, analogies comparing President Obama to Roosevelt, and the crisis to the Depression continued in the press and media.

In France President Sarkozy led the rhetorical battle to impose moral values and to equate rampant, unfettered market activity with a devaluation of moral standards expressed by the Minister of Policy Planning, Eric Besson: "Those who want to defend the virtues of free market capitalism must at the same time demand a balance of rights and responsibilities from top executives. Setting an example matters" (Hall 2009). The title of the article, "France Steps up the Drive to Sell Morality to Markets," encapsulates the difficulties of defining the relationship between markets and morality. Is selling morality an oxymoron, an exercise in virtual trading? But if morality cannot be valued by markets, then how can markets and capitalism ever be justified?

3 Metamorphosis

Materialism to capitalism

> Europe's development gradient ran from west to east and north to south, from educated to illiterate populations, from representative to despotic institutions, from equality to hierarchy. It was not resources or money that made the difference, nor mistreatment by outsiders. It was what lay inside – culture, values, initiative.
>
> (Landes 1999: 252)

Simultaneously, Europe shifted geographically, economically and culturally from the fourteenth to the sixteenth century, as Italy began to fade, despite retaining some of its prestige as a manufacturing, banking, and commercial center. After the wars of religion and the Protestant Revolution, German city states, the United Provinces led by Amsterdam, Antwerp, and finally London, took over as financial and commercial centers. Paris occupied a unique place in European economic history: innovator and guide in principles of nationhood and political philosophy, it was a reluctant and wary latecomer in institutionalizing economic and monetary policies. Paris, recognized as theoretician and mentor never took on the role of Genoa, Florence, Amsterdam, London, or Frankfurt. Despite establishing a successful mercantilist model in the monarchist-corporatist symbiosis under Colbert, it always maintained an undercurrent of condemnation and wariness of business and finance.

Following Max Weber's premise that capitalism was an outgrowth of Protestantism; historians have debated whether Protestant doctrines, especially Calvinism, lend themselves better to money creation and capital accumulation, or was it that individuals inculcated in these beliefs felt justified and socially rewarded in the quest of gain and profit? The premise has also been reversed in so far as capitalism, its fundamental principles established in late fifteenth century Europe gave rise to Protestantism or that Protestantism mainly appealed to those who respected and sought out mercantile values. Tawney, in *Religion and the Rise of Capitalism*, rejected symbiosis between religion and economic development: "that religion and economic interest form two separate and co-ordinate kingdoms, of which neither without presumption can encroach on the other" but conceded that new religious beliefs "shielded tradesman and manufacturers against ... genteel contempt. It gave them a sense of dignity and righteousness, armor in a world of anti commercial prejudices" (Tawney 1953: 176). Secularization, urbanization and gradual democratization of the benefits of trade, exchange, and wealth creation propelled economic progress. Landes, Braudel, Morrison, Schema, Boorstin, and Birdzell stress innovation: "the West's system of economic growth offered its largest financial rewards to innovators who improved the life style not of the wealthy few but of the less wealthy many" (Rosenberg and Birdzell 1986: 27). The unique phenomenon in Europe outside of Russia was to synchronize technological and structural advances with greater autonomy and individual responsibility. The Osmulu Empire in Turkey, the Sultanate of Delhi, and the Manchus in China remained locked in medieval societal structures, despite immense wealth in commodities, specie, and potential human capital. Government by divine right, rigidified class and rank distinctions, and vast ineffective bureaucracy hampered increase in wealth distribution and the integration of merchants and bankers into positions of power.

China's bureaucratic and autocratic structure, which demanded absolute loyalty to the seat of power, placed intrinsic limitations on technological and scientific innovation and knowledge. Enforced centralization in China, caste and class bureaucratization in India, restriction of individual freedoms and initiatives, despite a vibrant merchant class in the Ottoman Empire, combined with lack of stock exchanges, public agencies, and economic stewardship created barriers to economic development. In the monarchies of Central and Eastern Europe, trade and commerce came from outside or outsiders: Jews, Greeks, Armenians, and German minorities which were simultaneously needed and resented.

The first case of economic shock therapy, applied by Peter the Great (1689–1725), unified, modernized, and Westernized Russia within two decades of massive military, maritime, urban, and industrial construction. Inspired by Louis XIV, he brought French style, Dutch engineering, German printers, and English laws, establishing a global power in rivalry with the kingdoms of Sweden and the rising forces in Prussia. Catherine the Great (1762–1796), friend and mentor to the philosophers and artists of the French Enlightenment, continued the tradition of importing European culture, without allowing corollary values of individual initiative, political dissent, social mobility or independent middle class to take root.

By the end of the eighteenth century, Russia remained hampered by serfdom, spendthrift nobility, weak consumer demand, and little export or development of indigenous industry. Most commerce, even in the highly lucrative fur, timber, and commodity trade often depended on barter. Under the long reigns of Alexander I (1801–1825) and Nicolas I (1825–1855), Russia became a world power militarily after defeating the armies of Napoleon and gaining a seat among the victors at the Council of Vienna in 1815. Economically, Russia remained in the late Middle Ages, although it dealt in sophisticated financial operations, including issuance and circulation of paper money as early as 1768. Finances, including extension of credit to the peasants, industry or small merchants, and structuring of loans and conditions of repayment, were entirely dependent on the state:

As late as 1839 savings banks were most often restricted to large estates as "aid banks," equivalent of the medieval "monts de piete" where the poor could accumulate funds and recover interest of 3–4 percent. But deposits were limited to no less than 50 silver kopecks and no more than 50 silver rubles.

(Cepiene and Jasiene 2001)

Wealth was land based and inherited; knowledge of modern finance was restricted to the tiny educated aristocratic and merchant elite in Moscow and St Petersburg. In this environment, references to money and financial operations were limited to the evils of gambling in Pushkin's *Queen of Spades* (1833); satire of the impoverished nobility or merchant's abusive get rich quick schemes in the sale of dead serfs in Gogol's immensely popular *Dead Souls* (1997 [1842]), or ironic tragedy in Gogol's "The Overcoat" (1999 [1842]), describing the exploitation of pathetic low level bureaucrats in newly prosperous St Petersburg:

There is in St Petersburg a mighty foe for all who receive a salary of four hundred roubles or about that sum. That foe is none other than our northern frost, although it is said to be very good for the health.

(Gogol 1999 [1842]: 240)

Although after the emancipation of the serfs and the creation of the Bank of Russia in 1860, Russia became a financial partner in European global finance, autocratic state ordained and state controlled banks, and credit facilities with limited reforms remained in place until 1917.

3.1 Secularization, science and literacy: reading the market

Galileo and Bacon, like Newton, called upon to stabilize the silver content of the English pound sterling in 1699, understood quantitative and scientific innovation to be a secular process. Merchants, tradesmen, moneylenders, and bankers, complemented by notaries, judges, clerks, and scribes in order to succeed in an increasingly competitive environment, had to be knowledgeable, literate and well versed in the complexities of financial instruments – from letters of credit, bills of exchange, and promissory notes, to insurance contracts and different types of mortgages. They had to understand and implement financial processes such as double entry bookkeeping, formulated in Benedetto Cotrugli's *Della Mercatura et Del Mercante Perfetto* (1458), and elaborated on by Luca Bartolomes Pacioli in *Summa de Arithmetica, Geometria, Proportioni* (1494).

Respect for literacy and scientific progress, measures of time, and clocks as a component of the work ethic, helped mitigate inherent prejudices toward tradesmen and bankers. Acquisition of knowledge, through the progression of written language, from Latin to the vernacular, was no longer a rarified activity granted to the Church and the nobility for its own prestige and pleasure. William Caxton, wealthy textile merchant and financial advisor to the court of Edward IV, became instrumental in the transformation and reform of written English, publishing the first French–English dictionary and translations of French texts in the 1470s. Du Bellay's *Defense and Illustration of the French Language* (1549), validated French as a language worthy of all categories of literature; Martin Luther's translation of the Bible into "Hoch Deutsche," German of Saxony helped harmonize the numerous dialects in the Germanic principalities and city states. The secularization of written texts helped propagate knowledge of commercial terms and operations.

From the 1580s to the 1650s, manuals, pamphlets, and references in novels devoted to commercial activity, procedures, and theories proliferated in French, English, German, Dutch, and Spanish, adding to the earlier literature in Italian.

> In one picaresque novel, *El Diablo Conjuelo [The Lame Devil]* by Velez de Guevara (1641), there is an "expert" who is so excited by his fight against rising inflation that he sticks a pen into his eye and goes on writing without noticing what he has done.
>
> (Quoted in Vilar 1976: 9)

The works of Tomas de Mercado on value, Bernardo Davanzati on gold, Jean Bodin on monetary supply, Thomas Gresham on rates of exchange, and Nicolas Barbon's very popular *A Discourse of Trade* (1690), on economic ethics and social development, influenced merchants and princes alike. Bookkeeping and ledgers became part of business practices, as merchant houses meticulously recorded all commercial activity, establishing rules and procedures of accounting and accountability. Ledgers were so heavy and large that transcription by the keepers of the books had to be done in a kneeling or standing position. By the end of the sixteenth century, the public at large in urban centers readily recognized terms of commerce, exchange rates, and different currencies. The London audience at Shakespeare's *The Merchant of Venice* in 1609, was familiar with ducats, florins, guilders, and sterling, and understood the conditions of the loan discussed between the Jewish moneylender, Shylock, and Bassanio, representing the young merchant nobleman. Antonio:

> Shylock: "Three thousand ducats, well"
> Bassanio: "Ay sir, for three months"
>
> (Riverside Shakespeare 1974: Act I, Scene III)

Presented at the Globe in 1606, Ben Jonson's *Volpone* would have great success throughout the seventeenth century. A social satire on greed, the shrewd miser dupes the greedy by pretending to be dying and watching his community grovel and scheme to be his heirs. Volpone comments on his wealth, acquired by hoarding rather than labor or commerce:

> Yet I glory
> More in the cunning purchase of my wealth

Than in the glad possession, since I gain
No common way. I use no trade, no venture
I wound no earth with plowshares, fat no beasts
To feed the shambles; have no mills for iron,
Oil, corn or men to grind'em into powder;
I blow no subtle glass, expose no ships
To threat'nings of the furrow-faced sea;
I turn no money in the public bank,
Nor usure private.
      (Jonson 1963: Act I, Scene I lines 34–40)

Literacy greatly contributed to the shift in perception and attitudes toward wealth and social mobility. Gutenberg's printing process allowed an exponential increase in the production and distribution of books and in the spread of literacy. Before Gutenberg, books were a rare luxury limited to a few thousand in Europe, by "1500 there were probably about ten million printed books circulating" (Boorstin 1983: 534). In the late 1400s, the number of copies averaged less than 500, by the seventeenth century, books were published in editions of 2,000 and in the 1750s, "the Europeans of that day were already interested in records. Mark here the difference between hieratically literate and generally literate societies. The Europeans for all the analphabetism of the populace were of the latter category" (Landes 1999: 164). Protestants were expected to be able to read the Bible rather than have it read to them within the pomp and ceremony of the Church.

When Spain closed its doors to foreigners, imposing rigid restrictions against scientific discoveries, literacy, and the flow of information, it was reduced to an impoverished rural back drop of Europe through the nineteenth century. As late as 1900, Spain had a 56 percent illiteracy rate, Italy 48 percent, and Portugal 78 percent, compared with 3 percent in Great Britain. In the Russian, Mongol, and Ottoman empires, even at the height of industrial and financial strength, the population remained largely illiterate.

As books, pamphlets, essays, written plays, novellas, and novels were made available, and could be read by a broadening public, these flows of information began to influence attitudes toward commerce and money. Literature, like art, was still subject to censorship, litigation, and prison in France and even in England in the years after the South Sea Bubble. Voltaire could only publish *Lettres Anglaises*, in praise of English religious tolerance and commercial acumen, in Holland, and was forced into exile after distributing *Le Mondain*, in praise of luxury and materialism. After revelations of the corrupt and inept practices of the wealthy in the South Sea Bubble, Swift, Pope, and Defoe used literary contrivances and moral parables to convey political and economic criticism. Hogarth in *Harlot's Progress*; *Rakes Progress*; and *The South Sea Scheme* incorporated moral parables while John Gay's immensely popular *Beggars Opera* (1728) portrayal of the criminal underclass as mirror of the rich and famous, was accused of glamorizing criminality and inciting unrest.

The development of the novel runs parallel to societal dynamics of mobility, circulation, and transaction. The novel (unlike classical theater and other noble genres, poetry, oration, and classical history), is a work in motion, as the protagonists must achieve a trajectory, interact, and transact in order to move the plot. But more importantly, it dealt with different social classes, and slowly would be read by or read to rich and poor alike. During the long reign of Louis XIV (1661–1715), French literature, art, and architecture had to adhere to specific rules on themes and style, which emulated classical genres. Only low genres, less restricted or unrestricted by the rules of literary propriety: comedy, farce, and vaudeville, could portray the merchant class and its foibles. However, despite periods of repression and censorship, the tenets of European culture and religion allowed for individual initiative and innovation, even within regimented state or nation structures.

3.2 Wealth distribution and mobility

England was at the forefront of shifts in financial culture and theory. In 1545, confronting the teachings of the Catholic Church, Henry VIII abolished the law against usury, allowing interest on loans not to exceed 10 percent. This measure transformed the profession of money changing, no longer limited to Lombards and Jews, the goldsmiths could practice their trade within the confines of society.

In 1560s England (followed by France a decade later), merchants, goldsmiths and bankers, fearing rampant inflation, began to implement forms of regulation on foreign exchange and to formulate policies on the interrelation between trade, money supply, and control of exchange rates. Mistrusting Italian and Spanish exchange dealers as Catholic plotters and spies, Sir Thomas Gresham advocated control of exchange rates, setting up the royal exchequer, in 1576, and Royal Commissions against foreign manipulation of the rate. France, under Henri III, established monetary tribunals and account money in the "ecus de marc" and "ecus de soleil" to combat inflation caused by excessive silver currency smuggled in from Spain.

In the seventeenth century, as faith, rituals, and fundamental institutions of the Church and the Crown were tested and questioned across Europe, money, profit, transactions, and markets moved from the actual to the potential, from the present to the future. In the Amsterdam market of the 1640s, for the first time "the speculator was in fact selling something he did not possess and buying something he never would" (Braudel 1982a: 536), what the Dutch called "windhandel," trade in the wind. Such transactions were similar to today's financial futures where "people were not content simply to buy and sell shares, speculating on their possible rise or fall, but where one could by means of various ingenious combinations speculate without having any money or shares at all" (Braudel 1982b: 101).

Long distance trade, "Fern-handel," required merchants to acquire an entire new set of skills, from calculating exchange rates, converting weights and measures to working out simple and compound interest, and being able to communicate in long detailed letters with their home offices and representatives in foreign countries. Merchants conducting foreign trade also established monopolies and vast warehouses in foreign and rare commodities, non perishables and textiles:

> The rule was always the same: buy goods directly from the producer for a low price, in return for cash or, better still, advance payments; then put them in store and wait for prices to rise (or give them a push).
>
> (Braudel 1982b: 419)

By the start of the eighteenth century, wealth was no longer primarily an inherited privilege and entitlement. It could be earned, increased, and invested as well as squandered and gambled away. The literature of the 1720s to the 1750s is replete with beneficiaries and victims of social mobility from Lesage's *Turcaret*, Marivaux's *Paysan Parvenu*, and Fielding's *Tom Jones.*

> A capitalist might be an investor, a manufacturer, a financier, a banker, or a tax farmer or manager of public funds. Therefore, it was possible to advance by stages within capitalism: a merchant could become a banker, a banker could become a financier, and both could become capitalist "rentiers," – thus surviving as capitalists for several generations.
>
> (Braudel 1982b: 480)

However, it is important to note that despite the flow of money, goods, and global commerce, the penetration of wealth and benefits of capitalism remained very limited within societies at large.

> Conspicuous at the top of the pyramid is a handful of privileged people ... This is the group that governs, administers, directs, takes decisions, sees to the continuity of investment and thus of production. To this group flows all goods, services, currencies. Below it ranges the multitude of economic agents, workers of every rank, the mass of the governed. And below everyone else, stretches that huge social scrapheap, the world of the unemployed.
>
> (Braudel 1982b: 466)

Braudel provides the following figures:

> What is striking is that despite the increase in wealth, the distribution remains very limited. In Venice before 1575 the nobili were about 10,000 (5% of the population of 200,000); in Nuremberg in the 1500s about 43 patrician families; in 1688 England 36,000 families with income exceeding 200 pounds when total population is about 1.4 million families.
>
> (Braudel 1982b: 467)

By the 1650s, very wealthy non nobles could aspire, outside of birthright, to acquire titles and accede to political power, creating an urban class of "aristocracy of the robe" versus aristocracy of the sword. Gradually the preordained differences between merchants and nobles demanded to be reevaluated. Across Northern Protestant Europe these traits allowed Denmark, Sweden, and Finland to flourish economically and to progress toward prosperity versus late industrial development in Italy, Spain, and Portugal, hampered by religious and intellectual intolerance: "religious zealotry and Counter-Reformation cultivation of ignorance" (Landes 1999: 248). The Church's promotion of censorship, trials of heresy against Galileo and Bruno, the expulsion of the Jews and merchant banking class from Spain and parts of Italy created isolationist and regressive societies where inherent prejudices remained in place for the next 300 years.

3.3 Amsterdam

During the seventeenth century, Genoa and Venice among the Italian city states, retained their position in capital markets as the Genoa lire di banco, an account money was still considered a hedge against rate inflation and domestic currency fluctuations, holding a constant weight of 0.328 grams of gold from 1675 to 1793, encouraging investments in France, Austria, Bavaria, Lyon, and Amsterdam (Braudel 1982c: 173). But the lire and the Florentine florin were rivaled by the British pound sterling and the Dutch guilder across European money markets, as the center of European international trade and money markets shifted to Antwerp and Amsterdam.

In Amsterdam in 1631, the great building of the Amsterdam Exchange opened opposite the East Indies Company. "What was new in Amsterdam was the volume, the fluidity of the market and the publicity it received, and the speculative freedom of transactions" (Braudel 1982b: 101). More importantly, the vibrant Amsterdam exchange institutionalized futures trading in commodities: "forward buying of herring before it has been caught and wheat and other goods before they had been grown or received" as described in Joseph de la Vega's satirical account of trade and speculation, *Confusion de confusiones* (1688).

The Dutch money market also dealt in securities and stock offerings. The flourishing market encouraged new forms and venues of social interaction among Dutch and foreign speculators, brokers and merchants, who frequented coffee houses where Dutch and Levantine coffee was sold along with gaming tables, books, and tobacco. Without any official quotation of prices, brokers dealt in the Exchange with small as well as big capital holders and savers. A 1643 traveler's guide described Antwerp as "into which there flowed every year 500 million in silver, 130 million in gold not counting exchange currency which comes and goes like the tide" (Braudel 1982c: 31). For Dutch burghers, the concept of life annuities and the use of annuities as a steady form of income originated in this period.

By the 1620s, real estate speculation, inflated property prices, and bubbles in rare commodities and esoteric instruments appeared in the United Provinces. Although historians debate the extent of the damage caused and the number of speculators involved, in the 1620s, Tulip mania introduced short selling, a futures market in tulips on the Amsterdam Exchange and the need for government intervention to quell market panic once the bubble burst in 1637. The boom economy of the 1620s triggered construction, speculation, and investment in real estate in Amsterdam and specifically in the Herengracht canal front property market where wealthy burghers built the canal areas and small angular mansions between 1628 and 1633. Within three years, following the crash of the Tulip mania and an outbreak of plague in the mid-1630s, in which nearly 14 percent of the population perished in 1636, housing prices dropped precipitously. Yet by the 1640s, the market recovered, reaching new heights with a spurt of lavish construction. Jan Gossaert Mabuse's painting *Girl Weighing Gold*, showing a goldsmith's daughter, wealthy, well fed, well dressed, pre-adolescent, holding the scales is a snapshot of prosperous, comfortable early sixteenth century Holland (Braudel 1982b: 425).

The Dutch East India Company, chartered in Amsterdam in 1601, became "the most remarkable contemporary edifice of commercial capitalism," dominating trade between Europe and Asia through the seventeenth and eighteenth century (Bowen 2002: 21). Its structure allowed it to flourish as "de facto, a department of state," as well as the largest import export company, declaring annual dividends for its stockholders with annual elections, quarterly meetings of stockholders, and weekly meetings of directors. Personnel were hired for life and "further core strength was established by the commercial bookkeeping and accountancy practices changed little over a century or more" (Bowen 2002: 31). Dutch and English merchants were fierce competitors until after the Glorious Revolution of 1688, when both countries allied against France. Trade occurred in non metallic precious materials, including a vast international gem market in London for pearls, emeralds, diamonds, sapphires, and rubies. The East India Company dominated not just trade but the entire development of commercial processes, instruments, and industries that depended on it:

> Longer terms of credit, low prices, forswearing of freight and related charges, offers of full insurance, substantial advances, new arrangements for pay involving half bill and half bond: such became the stock in trade for merchants eager to acquire a piece of the growing India traffic, and was in line with what was being done in London.
>
> (Hancock quoted in Bowen 2002: 164)

The Dutch East Indies company "in the record years of 1657 and 1658 sent to the Far East two million florins in gold, silver, ingots," and had on its books by 1691 over 100 ships (Bowen 2002: 64). The company also returned massive dividends of 20–22 percent between 1620 and 1720. Although according to Braudel, it was difficult to assess the actual amount of profits earned by the company and by individual investors; Dutch international trade was a key component in the overall wealth accumulation and consumption patterns in seventeenth-century Holland. The United Provinces had numerous mints, setting up categories of currency for international trade: gold thalers for trade with Poland and the Baltic's, gold ducats for Russia and silver for China and Indies.

The Bank of Amsterdam, founded in 1609, accepted deposits listed in the grand ledger, any bill of exchange in Amsterdam had to be paid in at the bank which guaranteed payment, in turn guaranteed by the municipality. The bank did not discount notes nor extend credit. By 1683, it began to give advances to individuals, credit operations and by 1722 deposits exceeded 28 million florins, due in part to capital flight from France after the Law debacle and ensuing panic.

The United Provinces, like England and later Japan, were small, constricted, besieged geographical entities, lacking in natural resources, but benefiting from harbors, maritime strength, and political pragmatism. Despite periods of repression and fanaticism during the Wars of Religion (see Poorvliet 1991), Holland was favored by a unique cultural determinant, Braudel called toleration:

> Toleration meant accepting people as they were, since whether workers, merchants or fugitives, they all contributed to the wealth of the Republic. It is in any case hard to imagine the centre of a world economy as anything but tolerant, obliged to take all the men it needed, from wherever they came.
> (Braudel 1982c: 185)

This "toleration" extended to a large Jewish community of Sephardic Jews, many who would later in the century emigrate to England with William of Orange. Demographically, Amsterdam grew from 50,000 in 1600 to 200,000 in 1700, with a melting pot of Flemings, Walloons, Germans, Portuguese and French Protestants, who emigrated after the Revocation of the Edict of Nantes in 1685. In the fifteenth and sixteenth centuries, the Jewish merchant class in Spain, forced into conversion, had fled to Holland to escape the Inquisition where these Marranos often reverted to Judaism, integrating into the Dutch middle class, with direct links to Spain and Portugal. Similarly, French emigrants continued dealings with their contacts in Bordeaux, La Rochelle, and Paris. The Flemish School painting by Quentin Metsys, *The Banker and his Wife*, Rembrandt's paintings of *A Jew*, and *An Old Jew*, Breughel the Younger's detail in *Paying Taxes*, depicting apprentices, servants, a table strewn with bundles of bank notes, letters, documents, and the tax collector as calmly studying the documentation, portray those engaged in or associated with money professions respectfully and with deep humanity.

Although in 1776 Adam Smith considered Holland a wealthy nation, based on its abundance of capital and ability to borrow capital cheaply, it was no longer an economic power, beleaguered by industrial stagnation, especially in cotton, tobacco processing, and loss of the manufacturing sector to German provinces and England. There were still large fortunes in Holland but investment was more passive and localized: "The Dutch merchant seemed to be dozing off on the soft cushions of formerly gathered riches" (Landes, quoting Peter Klein, 1966: 477).

3.4 London

Within one generation, England went through the throes of anarchy, the end of divine right of monarchy, and violent retribution, as illustrated in Hobbes's

Leviathan and Milton's *Paradise Lost.* The cataclysmic events of the 1640s, the Cromwell Revolution, the beheading of Charles I in 1649, dissolution of Parliament, death of Cromwell and the Restoration under Charles II in 1660, followed by an outbreak of bubonic plague in 1664, which killed nearly 75,000 in London alone. England, hardened, pragmatic, and cynical needed to regain a sense of stability, prosperity and self sufficiency.

The creation of Puritanism, "schoolmaster of the English middle classes" (Tawney 1953: 176), encouraged and unfettered the use and creation of money, but it also instilled a sense of discipline and community in financial and commercial undertakings. Richard Baxter, in his *Christian Dictionary or a Summa of Practical Theology and Cases of Conscience*, expounded on the triumph of economic virtues, long distance trade conducted on credit, iron manufacture's need for capital, and the reconstruction of London after the Great Fire (Tawney 1953: 189). Under Charles I, the state promoted capitalism closer to the French Colbertian model espousing exports, protecting domestic markets, economic interests and professions, specifically the goldsmiths or bullion brokers.

In *Cash Nexus* (2001), Ferguson states that:

> This book's central conclusion is that money does not make the world go round.... Rather it has been political events – above all wars – that have shaped the institutions of modern economic life: tax collecting bureaucracies, central banks, bond markets, stock exchanges.
>
> (Ferguson 2001: 13)

Nearly two generations of volatility, followed by the Nine Year Wars (1689–1691), forced England into undertaking major financial reforms and establishing institutional and regulatory structures. The wars required increased dependency on financial markets and goldsmiths which led to augmented taxed revenue, greater participation in domestic bond issues, lottery schemes, life insurance and other instruments justifying the need for a centralized financial institution which would serve as intermediary, monitor and guarantor of these different sectors of the economy.

Between 1691 and 1699, the London Stock Market boomed, the Bank of England was chartered (1694), and Sir Isaac Newton spearheaded the reforms of the pound (1699).

By the eighteenth century, cultural intersections of wealth, power, political connections, and, when necessary, unscrupulous business dealings, were as firmly entrenched as confidence in the Exchequer, the Bank of England, and the pound sterling. Within this culture, England and then America, unlike the rest of Europe and Russia, would evolve and flourish with amazingly few transformative psychological shifts through the twentieth and the first decade of the twenty-first century.

Despite political, economic and historical upheaval, a fundamental faith in money, wealth and finance as agents of betterment and progress has not diminished. Britain led the way in the industrial revolution, based on what Landes described as "the nonmaterial values (culture) and institutions" (Landes 1999: 215). These institutions were rights of private property, personal liberty, and enforcement of rights of contract, responsive, stable, and relatively honest government. These principles included the ability to promote industry, freedom of expression, the ability to enjoy fruits of labor, and relative social mobility. Adam Smith commented that in Great Britain "industry is perfectly secure" and freer than elsewhere in Europe (Smith 1776). Defoe, Montesquieu, and Voltaire described England as far more prosperous as a nation than France. "A comparison of British and French history in money and banking indicates that Britain was a century ahead of France in evolving most of its financial institutions" (Kindleberger 1993: 76). In wages, living conditions, and urban development, England also surpassed most of Europe. In 1640 to 1660, France and England both depended on poorly executed tax collection, but where France would remain static, England, after the Revolution of 1688, jumpstarted its economy including state control over custom duties, excise tax, and by 1714, a Treasury Board, which supervised the flow of revenue to the Exchequer. Interest in English, Scottish and Irish joint stock companies, and the purchase and sale of shares rapidly increased between 1687 and 1691 (Scott 1910–1912).

Prosperous, confident and stable, by 1715, London's Exchange Alley became the center of international commercial and money markets as aristocrats, members of the Crown, as well as the landed gentry enthusiastically participated in the new joint stock companies, becoming shareholders, investors, and businessmen. Initially the South Sea Bubble was the result of faith in the government and merchant bankers to generate wealth and profits, and to offer sound, long-term investment strategies. In 1711, John Blount and the Chancellor of the Exchequer, Robert Hurley, decided to set up a new trading company, which in a debt for equity exchange would take over the government's floating debt. Between 1711 and 1719, shares rose steadily, influenced by 1718 by the rumors of potential riches touted in John's Law Mississippi land scheme in Paris.

Research in the journals and ledgers of a financial broker, Charles Blunt, between 1692 and 1720, recording his business activities, investment decisions and subsequent involvement in the South Sea Bubble, offers a unique window into the financial Zeitgeist (Murphy 1997).

Charles Blunt was symptomatic of the financial entrepreneur of the period, as described by Daniel Defoe. Originally an upholsterer, like many bourgeois who made fortunes in the textile trade (satirized in Molière's *Bourgeois Gentilhomme* 1670), by 1692, he decided to become a financial broker lured by easy profits. Cousin of John Blount, one of the architects of the South Sea Bubble, his contacts were in place. In a unregulated market, which thrived on rumors and lack of information, charging ten shillings per share, Blunt dealt with the East India, Hudson Bay, Royal African trading companies, and the Bank of England, earning over 2,000 pounds in brokerage fees in 1693. The creation of the Bank of England encouraged investors to turn from stock trading to government bond trading, which began to reduce the need of stock jobbers. British merchants practiced diversification of assets, an investment strategy similar to Jacob Fugger in

Augsburg a century earlier. Charles Blount became one of the directors of the South Sea Company. Blunt by 1718, "held between one-half and two-thirds of his capital either in tangible assets like property and land or fixed income instruments such as annuities or government debt." He had an active share portfolio but remained extremely cautious: "confined his investments to the larger and safer joint – stock companies – the East India Trading Company and the Bank of England" (Murphy 1997: 15). As described and derided in Richardson and Fielding's works, acquisition of wealth led not to more investment, but to a decision to retire and become a country gentleman where status mattered as much as, if not more than, money.

By October 1720, when the overvalued shares precipitously collapsed from 1,000 to about 200, Charles Blount committed suicide. Swift compared the South Sea Bubble to a shipwreck in which 462 members of the House of Commons and 112 peers had been deluded and defrauded. Robert Walpole, never a proponent of the scheme, was brought in as Chancellor of the Exchequer to restructure the national debt by creating an early bailout package involving the South Sea Corporation, the Bank of England, Treasury and a new reserve fund to salvage remaining assets.

William Hogarth (1697–1764), like Swift, Defoe, Pope, and Gay, depicted the transition from medieval to modern financial culture and society in England, combining classical satire with the new genre of political and social satire. Hogarth's father (like Dickens' father a century later), jailed in a debtors prison, participated in the call for Fleet prison reforms. In *Rake's Progress*, Hogarth shows a frantic character in the Fleet, who drops a scroll: "Being a New Scheme for paying ye Debts of ye Nation, together with another marked Debts" (Lindsay 1979: 11). *Harlot Progress*, like the South Sea series, was based on "faits divers," local news stories and scandals in which the wealthy and powerful were implicated in their dealings with prostitutes, brothels and crooks. George Lillo's *London Merchant* in 1731, Richardson's *Clarissa*, and Defoe's *Moll Flanders* presented temptations and dangers of a dynamic, but relatively lawless society.

The ability of all social classes to congregate together and engage in the Law and South Sea investment schemes had profound implications in England and France. Investing in shares, equally partaking in the gains and losses broke through social barriers and created a new language and imagery of money. Under the guise of imparting moral lessons, the novel reflected new societal fluidity and mobility. Servants and domestics of all provenances, including bastard children and foundlings, were portrayed having social acumen, ambition, and a better sense of value and monetary gain than their aristocratic masters. The popularity of the novel became a social watershed as the lives, mores and foibles of the middle class and the poor became a subject of study. *Tom Jones, Pamela, Clairissa, Moll Flanders, Joseph Andrews, Rodrick Random*, as well as Sterne's *Tristam Shandy* were not only experiments in new forms of narration, realism and character development, but reflected these movements in urban society. The basic plot line for both male and female protagonists, precursor of the Bildungsroman, presents a trajectory from a rural, static, predetermined existence to the shifting, morally perilous but potentially rewarding urban environment. By the 1760s in France, Beaumarchais, Lesage, Sedaine, Marivaux, Diderot, Restif de la Bretonne, and Sade broke through social conventions to portray the energy, dangers and freedom of individual action. Money was the subtext, the ability by hook or by crook to move beyond specific class and rank, but these works also offered first glimpses into the lives of the previously invisible poor. The poor included semi or unskilled day laborers, servants, and porters which differentiated from the destitute and migrant. There was a vast increase in the urban domestic class, as military and domestic service became conduits for social mobility. The intelligent valet, a comic archetype found in Cervantes, Shakespeare, and Molière, is emblematic of shifts in the relationship between the social classes, as the equivalent of street smarts begins to gain credence.

London's population grew from 575,000 to 900,000 during the course of the eighteenth century. Georges Rude's *Hanoverian London* (1971) mentions that there were close to 400 trades and professions, including tailors, carpenters, shoemakers, peruke-makers, chandlers, bakers and distillers, high end luxury trade milliners, seamstresses, coach makers, lace makers, book sellers, card, and clock makers to service and benefit from an increasingly wealthy and expanding urban merchant class and landed gentry. Rude (1971) quotes the class rankings Defoe delineates in the *Complete English Tradesman*:

> The great who live profusely. The rich who live very plentifully. The middle sort, who live well. The working trades who labor hard but feel no want. The country people, farmers, &c., who fare indifferently. The poor who fare hard. The miserable, that really pinch and suffer want.
>
> (Rude 1971: 37)

The aristocracy in Britain derived wealth from traditional sources of inheritance, land and vast real estate holdings, but also "intermarriage with the mercantile plutocracy such as the alliance cemented in 1695 between the future Duke of Bedford and the granddaughter of the fabulously wealthy London banker and East India merchant, Sir Josiah Child" (Rude 1971: 39). Wealth also came from trade, financial speculation, and holdings in banks and trading companies. Among owners of Bank of England stock were members of the oldest noble families: Pembroke, Marlborough, Stanhope, and Lady Elizabeth Germain, who left her heir Lord George Sackville a "legacy of 120,000 pounds in funds in 1769, a fortune heavily accumulated from holdings of combined stock in moneyed companies. In 1751 Bank of England proprietors included 29 noblemen, their widows or their wives" (Rude 1971: 40).

The next rank of the gentry and lesser nobility: baronets, knights, esquires, and gentlemen, on average increased their incomes two and three times during the course of the seventeenth century, derived from rents, estates, inheritance, and financial interests. When Defoe spoke of the rich he meant the "great mercantile and financial bourgeoisie of the City of London" (Defoe 1726), founders of the Bank of England, loyal to the Hanoverian monarchy, and intermarrying with the aristocracy: "our merchants are princes, greater and richer and more powerful than some sovereigns" (Defoe 1726).

In England as early as 1575 to 1630, according to Braudel, nearly half of the peerage was investing in long distance trade. Among the large East India Trading Company directors in 1720, were listed Sir Isaac Newton and members of Parliament. Elihu Yale, who endowed Yale University in 1703, was a wily Welsh American gem merchant, governor of Madras who, through the East India Trading Company, amassed a fortune in diamonds of about £200,000. Removed from his post in 1692 after allegations of corruption, he returned to England and continued to deal in diamonds. Among the vast fortunes linked to banking and overseas trade was a subgroup of extremely wealthy Sephardic Jewish merchants with offices in the City: da Costa, de Medina, Henriquez, Rodriquez, Ximenes, and de Matteos, originally of Spanish, and Portuguese Ladino origins. In 1750, the financier Samson Gideon was worth in corporate stock £76,450, and died leaving an estate of half a million pounds (Braudel 1982c: 53–54). Bankers of all denominations flourished in 1764, when Quakers Taylor and Sampson Lloyd opened Lloyds.

But what specifically set England apart from the rest of Europe was the vast increase in the professional class, comprised of merchants, lawyers, clergymen, surgeons, civil servants, brokers, and apothecaries. In the course of the eighteenth century "working trades," scientists, artists as well as ship owners, manufacturers, innkeepers, grew from 82,000 to 254,000 (Rude 1971: 57). Hogarth achieved middle class status, as did Sir Joshua Reynolds, who earned for his portraits £6,000 a year in 1762. Writers, essayists, and artists, such as John Gay, Alexander Pope, James Boswell, Joseph Addison, and Henry Fielding through patronage, marriage, and payment were able to attain upper middle class status and life style. *The Beggars Opera* by John Gay, produced and directed by John Rich in 1727, took a lively look at London's low life, crooks, and poor, running for 62 nights, which "made Gay rich and Rich gay" as went a ditty of the day (Rude 1971: 65). Painting was still a pursuit limited to the aristocracy, but there was an active art market in French art, as documented by the sale of Watteau's paintings in the 1720s.

Fascination with finance also extended to gaming and gambling. The gaming clubs in St James Street: Old Club at Whites, Boodles, Almack, which became Brooks, "it was here that the largest stakes were placed and the largest fortunes were lost and won. Charles James Fox, when only 24, lost 140,000 and had his debts paid for him by his wealthy father, Lord Holland" (Rude 1971: 71). Here originated the "martingale," gambling technique of doubling bets after every loss, a technique quoted by the "rogue trader" Jerome Kerviel of Société Générale, in 2008, as explanation for the serial increase in hedging derivative futures.

The Stock Exchange (model for the New York Stock Exchange in 1792) emerged from the Exchange coffee house in 1773, where merchants involved in domestic and foreign trade congregated. London was at the forefront with newspapers: the *Daily Courant* in 1702 (le *Journal de Paris* only appeared in 1777); Steele and Addison founded *Tatler* in 1709; the *Spectator* in 1711; and *The Times*, started in 1785. By 1800, there were 278 newspapers, journals, and periodicals in London.

Poverty was still rampant and, according to Rude, as London expanded one-eighth of the population in 1797, about 115,000 persons, was composed of vagrants, beggars, part time domestics, including Jewish and Irish peddlers, and the "underclass," which became the core of the Industrial Revolution's exploited factory and manufacturing sector. In 1779, a journeyman, with a wife and three children, on a weekly budget of 20 shillings, spent about four on bread. However, in times of bad harvests, the price of grain rose inciting a rise in robbery, prostitution, and urban violence in the late 1720s and 1740s. Political riots and the rise of a rebellious working class in 1737, and later in 1763, caused massive destruction of property in wealthy areas and an attack on Fleet prison, the Marshalsea, freeing the inmates of the notorious debtors' prison. As Rude notes, in 1780

> Another constant element is that of an underlying class hostility of the poor against the rich which led the attack on the Royal Exchange and Bank of England, not only by the poor but by well organized armed working class.
>
> (Rude 1971: 226)

By the end of the 1780s, unrest and political volatility worsened once the French Revolution began to impact England. In 1793, at the height of the revolutionary period of terror, London suffered a financial and economic downturn, with sharp declines in trade and shipbuilding, and increases in bankruptcies. In 1797, the reserves of the Bank of England were severely depleted due to large scale loans and foreign losses. However, England had huge advantages in industrial production, and foreign trade rose from £41.5 million in 1792 to £69 million in 1800.

At the start of the nineteenth century, London's population exceeded one million. The poor were still in miserable conditions, but overall London and England had progressed from the Great Revolution through the eighteenth century, in fairly linear fashion, toward economic and social progress. Financial innovation, money, trade, profit, and enrichment were acknowledged, encouraged by the mores of the time, and largely unrestricted by government, church or citizens.

3.5 Paris

For French intellectuals, England was a model of economic innovation, progress, and tolerance. Voltaire wrote *Lettres Philosophiques* during his exile in London, in 1727–1728, having to publish the work in Amsterdam, in 1734, to escape censorship. Devoting the first seven letters to the Protestant sects, in letter six ("Sur les Presbyteriens") he observes the following:

> Entrez dans la Bourse de Londres, cette place plus respectable que bien des cours, vous y voyez rassembles les deputes de toutes les nations pour

l'utilite des hommes; la, le juif, le mahometan et le chretien traitent l'un avec l'autre comme s'ils etaient de la meme religion, et ne donnent le nom d'infideles qu'a ceux qui font banqueroute [enter the London Exchange, this arena more respectable than many courts, here you will find assembled representatives of all nations in the service of man; here, the Jew, the Mahomatan and the Christian treating one another as if they all practiced the same faith, giving the name of infidel only to those who go bankrupt].

(Voltaire 1961: 16)

In letter ten "Sur le Commerce," Voltaire extols British merchants:

Le commerce qui a enrichi les citoyens en Angleterre a contributé a les rendre libres, et cette liberté a etendu le commerce a leur tour; de la s'est formé la grandeur de l'état [commerce which enriched England's citizens has helped make them free and this freedom has in turn expanded commerce, here from derives the power of the state].

(Voltaire 1961: 27)

It is in letter ten that Voltaire throws down the gauntlet to the rigid French class structure which denigrates and ostracizes the merchant class:

Je ne sais pourtant lequel est le plus utile a un état, ou un seigneur bien poudré qui sait precisement a quelle heure le roi se leve, a quelle heure il se couche … ou un négociant qui enrichit son pays, donne de son cabinet des orders à Surate et au Caire, et contribute au bonheur du monde [I do not know which is more useful to the state; a well powdered bewigged aristocrat who knows at precisely what time the king arises, at precisely what time the king lies down … or a merchant who enriches his country, from his office sending out orders to Suarta and Cairo and contributing to worldwide happiness].

(Voltaire 1961: 28)

France, under Louis XIV, was a study in sharp contrasts between the extravagance and expenses of the monarchy in Versailles, whose cost had exceeded all the other royal palaces of Europe, and depression in textile production, weak harvests, fluctuating prices of grain, and reduced specie in circulation. The king's relationship with financiers can be bracketed between the trial of Nicolas Fouquet, in 1661, and the disgrace of Samuel Bernard, in 1709. Louis XIV, upon assuming the throne realized that he was dependent upon about 200 extremely wealthy "traitants," largely of provincial noble stock, who dominated the collection of all taxes and could set conditions of loans to the often depleted royal treasury. Surintendant Fouquet invited the young king to his sumptuous chateau, Vaux-le-Vicomte, seemingly flaunting his wealth and causing his downfall, trial, and imprisonment. Louis XIV was not merely vindictive, but understood that, if left unchecked, the monetary power of the tax collectors would allow them political power. "In fact France had no public finances at all, no centralized system; so neither control nor forecasting were possible" (Braudel 1982b: 537). In the late 1660s, under royal stewardship, Colbert established policy and control over state expenditures to industry and commerce, but the king continued to depend on the financiers to fund the never ending wars. Samuel Bernard, a Protestant banker who had been favorable to establishing a public bank with note issuance (similar to Law's proposal in 1705), was called upon to lend the king nearly 50 million livres between 1703 and 1708 "when he refused further advances ... was cut off from payments on the outstanding debt and unable to repay his draft" (Kindleberger 1993: 97). He went bankrupt, but recovered very quickly and, by 1715 was again immensely wealthy.

The monarchy's unwillingness to create a banking system, modernize or democratize tax collection, share or relegate financial control, or encourage investment paralyzed French economic progress for two centuries. Yet despite hierarchal restrictions, censorship and embedded prejudices, theater and novels produced subversive and critical responses to changes in financial culture. During the seventeenth century, monetary operations, actors, and instruments became popular themes, encouraged by a rapidly prospering urban bourgeoisie who began to see their economic power surpass the declining aristocratic classes. For medieval and Renaissance historiographers and philosophers like Montaigne, economic issues had no legitimate function in political or historical philosophy. By contrast, as early as the 1630s, the comédie de moeurs, such as Corneille's *Place Royale* (1961 [1633]), began to include realistic financial and commercial terms and situations in a theatrical context.

In Molière's *L'Avare* (1668), the miser protagonist, Harpagon, sets out the dichotomy between avarice and prodigality, when money as obsession replaces all other values or emotions, but also sets father-lender, son-borrower dichotomy. Molière emphasizes that Harpagon is truly rich: "10,000 livres en bonnes especes: bons louis d'or et pistols bien trebuchants, [10,000 livres in good currency, good gold louis and high quality pistols]" (*L'Avare*: Act V:1). Savings and hoarding took on political dimensions, as the aristocracy was impoverished, and overtaxed on land. Harpagon sees himself as representing the sound values of the past against the excesses of nouveau riche bourgeois. France was in the throes of extreme consumerism and without a sound economic structure, where money constituted security but only in its most tangible form, yet the inability to invest, place, and entrust money to authority placed this security at risk. Harpagon's miserliness and obsession with gold is juxtaposed against his social pretensions and his desire to impress an aristocrat.

In Molière's *Don Juan* (1665), a creditor is an economically impotent object of mockery in the scene between Monsieur Dimanche, the merchant, and the dissipated aristocrat. The disdain shown by Don Juan for Dimanche, in refusing to honor his debt, plays upon Dimanche's bourgeois subservience and his inability to enforce his economic rights. The formal clichés of Don Juan's aristocratic discourse distract Dimanche from the economic reality of his situation and precipitate his retreat for the palpably foolish reason that: "it is true that he shows me so many considerations and gives me so many compliments that I could not ask him for money" (*Don Juan*: Act IV, Scene III). In *Le Bourgeois Gentilhomme* (1670), the wealthy tradesman, Jourdain, becomes a figure of farce as he seeks to purchase prepackaged social graces and aristocratic skills to sublimate his economic identity and to integrate himself into an unwelcoming aristocratic class.

Between 1680 and 1715, financiers, tax collectors, and usurers appear in plays dealing with themes of bankruptcy, money lending, public utilities schemes, and gambling debt. Two of the most successful plays were Champmeslé's *La rue St Denis* (1682), set on a street of retail trade in Paris, where a prosperous Jewish usurer, Sabatin, receives stolen goods, and N. de Fatouville's *Le Banqueroutier* (1687), where the financier Persillet is involved in fraudulent operations, removal of assets, and tricking creditors, abetted by his notary, M. de la Ressource. These works helped to incorporate financial and commercial terminology into literary discourse, while, from a psychological perspective, Furetière's *Le Roman bourgeois* (1666) and La Fontaines' *Fables* (1668–1694) considered the tension between personal happiness and the approbation of society versus the acquisition of wealth.

One of the most revelatory works was Furetiere's short novel, *Le Roman Bourgeois* (1666), which created a social tableau of the era with financial underpinnings of the nouveau riches:

> Sachez donc que la corruption du siecle, ayant introduit de marier un sac d'argent avec un autre sac d'argent, en mariant une fille avec un garçon, comme s'il s'était fait un tariff lors du decri de mérite et de la vertu, il lui fait un tariff pour l'évaluation des homes et pour l'assortiment des parties [Know that the corruption of this age, has introduced the idea of marrying a bag of money with another bag of money, marrying a girl and boy, as if a tariff had been set up based on merit and virtue, so there should be such a tariff to evaluate men and the joining of interested parties].
>
> (Furetiere 1666)

Furetiere provides a table, "Tarif ou Evaluation des Partis Sortables," starting with a dowry of 2,000 to 6,000 livres, representing a merchant or clerk, up the scale of 30,000–45,000 livres, for an auditor of the Treasury or tax collector (Auditeur des Comptes trésorier de France ou payeur des Rentes), to 25,000–50,000 ecus for an attorney (un Conseillier de la Cour des aides), to the highest amount of 100–200 ecus, for "un président au Mortier, vrai marquis, surintendant, duc et pair [a regional president, a real marquis, high commissioner, duke and peer]". Beneath the satire and sharp humor is the implication that aristocrats are for sale, that titles and position can be bought and sold (Furetiere 1666).

By the end of the reign, satire and farce become sharper, as the money supply is depleted, prices rise and there is unregulated speculation on paper and gold values in 1704. Hedging on differences in price between paper notes and gold, this process, called "agiotage," embodies the suspicion and fear of speculative activity. The most popular play on this topic was Dancourt's *Les Agioteurs* (1710), which ran for an exceptional 20 performances. The complicated plot involved a usurer Zacharie, his son Trapolin, a wealthy widow, a peasant, and a maid who overhears that paper can be changed to gold. The speculation is explained as follows,

> Paper is a better bet and specie is rare, better lower the price of paper to eight hundred, when we sell off our share, we can buy it back or raise the price if possible [puisque le papier nous gagne et que l'espèce est rare, il est bon de baisser aujourd'hui le papier de huit pour cent: quand nous serons défait du notre, on le remettra sur le même pied, ou on le rehaussera, s'il est possible].

> (Dancourt 1710: Act I, 8)

The transactions are shady, the players underhanded, and the prime motive is profit – the highest short-term returns on investment, at the mercy and goodwill of the moneylenders.

In 1713, in a play by Legrand, *L'usurier Gentilhomme*, satirizing *Le Bourgeois Gentilhomme*, the hero, Mannaville, is a usurer as well as agioteur, who wants his son to marry the daughter of a nobleman. Mme. Mannaville, the wife, is a farcical, crude nouveau riche. The play was a major success until 1789: "to audiences that reverenced as an ideal a stratified society, free from usurers and from persons who sought to change their class" (Lancaster 1945: 249).

The best known work is Lesage's *Turcaret* (1973 [1709]), about a tax collector, his wife, a shrewd unscrupulous Baroness, counterfeit money, and the introduction of money on stage, a breakthrough in the rules of propriety.

However all representations are not solely derogatory. The financier-merchants Aurelly and Melac in Beaumarchais' *Les deux amis ou le négociant de Lyon* (1770), are endowed with altruism, a sense of honor, and generosity, qualities previously only associated with members of the aristocracy. Beaumarchais' play incorporates a broad spectrum of financial terminology, which the playwright evidently expected to be understood by a general audience. Slightly earlier, Sedaine's *Le philosophe sans le savoir* (1765), presented the banker as a sympathetic figure in the character of Vanderk, a nobleman by birth who chooses to be "a financier and takes pride in his chosen profession" (Sedaine 1765). In the face of his son's protests, he defends his calling and praises his fellow practitioners as "the silken threads" who link nations together (Sedaine 1765).

Economically, France never went beyond the Colbertian premise that "the strength of a country depends on the amount of gold in its central coffers" (Kreinin 2006: 21). By the mid-eighteenth century, Smith and Ricardo demonstrated that trade and circulation of capital were principles essential for the development of merchant capitalism. "The primacy of money in the service of power found expression in economic thought. Mercantilism was not a doctrine, nor a set of rules. It was a general recipe for political-economic management: whatever enhanced the state was right" (Landes 1999: 443). The rigidity of the court and rules of conduct limited or prohibited the participation of the land rich aristocracy in the economic professions and transactions leaving France in a financial backwater long after even Hungarian, Danish, Polish, and Italian nobles became involved in merchant activities and investments in trade.

France's first experience with paper money was short and disastrous, the repercussions long and traumatic. Nearly a century after Italy and England had confidence in treasury or bank notes, France, without a banking system, suffered such severe shortage of specie that, in 1685 and in 1709, playing cards had to be accepted as legal tender. The excessive minting of gold coins, incited inflation in grain prices and heavy speculation on the value of gold and paper notes.

In 1715, after being forced out in 1705, the Scottish financier and gambler John Law returned to Paris, persuading the Regent that a bank could help alleviate the public debt of 3,500 million livres tournois. The Conseil Extraordinaire agreed to let Law set up the first French state bank, Banque Generale, in 1716, with limited note issuance in order to restart commercial lending to industry and trade. By 1718, the bank under Philip d'Orleans, the Regent, became Banque Royale, whose primary function, in conjunction with the Louisiana Trading Company, was to issue stock in the Mississippi lands. Law issued 200,000 shares at 500 livres tournois apiece, taking over monopolies of minting, tobacco sales and taxes. By 1718, the Banque Royale could issue notes to circulate as money but once the shares became dangerously overvalued, being sold and resold for 18,000 by end of 1719, they could no longer be redeemed. Within two months, in the summer of 1720: "with 550,000 claimants for 2.2 billion in notes and 125,000 shares with a nominal value of 250 million, worth five times that amount at the market's peak. The claims were written down to one-twentieth of their stated value" (Kindleberger 1993: 99).

Many of the investors in Law's scheme were tax collectors, financiers, and "fermiers generaux," chartered under Colbert in 1669 as syndicates of tax collectors. As a group profoundly hated and feared (34 fermiers generaux were executed in the Terreur of May to July 1794), their syndicate had about 40 members in 1787, with "near monopolistic hold ... A fantastic share of the nation's wealth remained in the hands of the tax farmers" (Braudel 1982b: 540). They received vast amounts of monies which some redistributed in manufacturing and commercial endeavors, but unlike in England and the Netherlands, and even in eighteenth century Cadiz, distribution was uneven and did not benefit the economic health of the nation at large. Therefore, the tax collector came to be perceived as an exploiter rather than part of an economic system of exchange and reinvestment. Unlike England, French financiers and wealthy merchants belonged to a few families.

> Take for instance the powerful family of money –lenders in Languedoc, the Castiniers in the time of Louis XV... Some of them farmed the taille in Carcassonne, others were directors of the French Indies Company, their sons

and nephews were members of the Toulouse parliament, before becoming state ministers. There were Castanier manufactories in Carcass. In Paris there was a Castanier bank.

(Braudel 1982b: 534)

France was a country wealthy in land, gold, luxury goods and inherited fortunes, underused and under invested. In 1754, Paris with a population of one million (of whom about 200,000 were domestic servants) had less shops, companies, merchants, and bankers than London. Montesquieu, like Voltaire, observed how the poor in London ate better, were better shod and dressed, and lived healthier lives, even at the lowest level of society.

This fundamental dichotomy between Adam Smith's principles of wealth generation and Colbert's mercantilism, differentiated British and French economic and financial culture: "The correspondence of merchants moreover abundantly proves that Louis XIV's France was full of unused capital 'kicking its heels' as J. Gentil da Silva puts it for want of employment" (Braudel 1982c: 327).

From the 1750s to the 1780s, Parliament rejected modest proposals for fiscal reform including Necker's call for a banking system as the deficit grew to ten million livres by 1781. In 1789, the expenses of Marie Antoinette exceeded 100,000 livres a year. The National Assembly rejected Necker's plan and began printing paper money, the notorious assignats, which would be totally devalued within three years. In the last desperate years before the Revolution, there were only a few French bankers, such as Etienne Delessert, among the founders of the Caisse d'Escompte in 1776, to help facilitate commercial ventures. Fermiers generaux such as Augeard, attributed to bankers lack of loyalty: "to have two homelands, one where they find money cheap and one where they sell it dear [d'avoir deux patries, l'une ou ils trouvent l'argent a bon marche et l'autre ou ils le vendent fort cher]" (Petit-Dutaillis 1982: 180).

The revolutionary constitution of 1791 did not mention finances, the revised constitution of 1793 mentioned accounting and oversight functions for errors and abuses of the Treasury, administered by "agents comptables." In 1795, the new constitution of the Montagne, the radical left, incorporated Title XI – Finances, with state control over finances, expenses and payments for each department. By 1794, there was so little metal left that the silver of convents and bronze church bells were melted down. In 1799, Article 45 of the revised constitution for the first time granted the state the function of minting and issuance of coin of the realm, and recognizes the merchant class.

There is a pervasive myth that France disdains money and bankers as detrimental to the best interests of the nation state. Banking is seen as a function, it is not granted the dignity of being a profession. In American history and literature, the bank as institution may be regarded as inherently evil or antithetical to the good of the community, but the individual and his right to enrichment is not condemned. In France the institution, the bank, can be absolved in the name of its function and purpose for the state but the individual, the banker, is judged to be untrustworthy and evil. From John Law to President Sarkozy's comment that the crisis of 2008 originated in America, when France engages in corrupt or failing financial practices, the assumption is that foreign influences were at work and that the key players were foreign or had succumbed to Anglo-American influences and tactics.

3.6 Consumerism to luxury

Luxe, calme et volupte.

(Baudelaire, *Fleurs du Mal*, 1857)

It smells, in a word rich, which these days has its appeal.
(Nelson 2008, on a new perfume from perfumer Antoine Lie for the French Japanese fashion label, Comme des Garcons, called 8 88, packaged in a gold bottle selling for $135)

The transition from mid-eighteenth century middle and upper class accumulation and generation of wealth, to mid-nineteenth century spending and display of wealth, changes the culture of finance from the purchase and ownership of durable consumer goods, to shopping, disposing, and renewing newer, more exotic, rare and sought after products. Availability of discretionary income, creation of stores and department stores, and a female demographic encouraged to buy and display wealth fostered a shift in culture, which slowly led to greater democratization of production, distribution and use of non essential products, in turn provoking an endless quest for new, more expensive, and more specialized luxury products. From Rome in the days of Petronius and Juvenal, to Florence under the Medicis, luxury dominates the popular imagination as it represents the obtainable for a chosen few and the desire to obtain for all others. Luxury as cultural determinant in financial history represents creation, consumption, and distribution of rare, desired and expensive goods, as in each era and country the definition of luxury changes and allows new and unknown products to enter the mainstream. Jules Michelet in *Le Peuple* (1965 [1842]) described the shift of supply and demand created by new consumers and new products. Cotton bought at lower prices by the poor instigated "a revolution in cleanliness ... people had bed linen, body linen, linen for the table and the windows: it was now possessed by whole classes who had never had any since the world began" (Michelet 1965 [1842]). As Braudel wrote, "luxury goods might be lightweight, but they were spectacular and much talked of, money flowed towards them and obeyed their dictates" (Braudel 1982b: 178). As trade and society expanded and evolved, sugar, alcohol, tobacco, coffee, tea, and cotton joined the silks, spices, and furs which had entered Europe in the Middle Ages. In 1606, Lope de Vega describes Madrid as a town full of shops, as Defoe a century later describes London with about 400 luxury shops. Once money became more respectable, mobile, and visible the very rich and the newly ennobled desired a different standard of living in their homes, furnishings, attire, and superfluous objects which declared their rank and wealth.

Money in the eighteenth century also brought about the concept and sense of worth to private spaces and larger living spaces. Wealthy merchants and bankers no longer conjoined work and living space as stores, offices, and business establishments became separate from residential areas. Stalls in fairs and markets evolved into self standing shops in the center of towns and cities. Small boutiques, specializing in luxury or exotic goods, opened under protected arcades in Paris, Bologna, Florence, and London.

Retail commerce entailed a new system of payment and repayment based on credit and installment payments. Respect for commerce and honest gain facilitated this shift in transactional relationships, but in France and Spain, class distinctions, privileges of the nobility, and an inbred disdain for monetary activity propagated a precarious structure of indebtedness as the merchant class extended credit, often long term , to the aristocracy who rarely paid on time or in full. The urban merchant class needed to serve the aristocracy, which alone could afford new and expensive goods, as they were trendsetters, interested in exotic and rare items and possessions. However, in order to stimulate economic activity and allow the purchase of goods, the merchants had to be paid. In France, the court paid late, sporadically, and under duress. The vast debts incurred by Marie Antoinette in the 1780s, were symptomatic of a life style which appreciated the products, but totally ignored the correlation between creation, distribution, and circulation of luxury goods and capital.

In 1752, David Hume wrote an apologia of luxury, and in the *Encyclopedie* (1986 [1751]) Saint Lambert's article "Luxe" justifies luxury as necessary to the welfare of the state, economy, and happiness of the individual:

> "C'est l'usage qu'on fait des richesses et de l'industrie pour se procurer une existence agréable" and adds "sans luxe, il y a moins d'echange et de commerce" ["this is the use that one makes of wealth and industry in order to attain a pleasant existence" adding "without luxury, there is less trade and less commerce"].
>
> (*L'Encyclopedie ou dictionnaire raisonne des sciences, des arts et des metiers* 1986 [1751]: 215)

Voltaire wrote his apologia to luxury, progress, and unabashed materialism in two verse pamphlets,the first of which, *Le Mondain*, caused such a stir in late 1736 that, fearful for his safety; he fled to Holland for two months. Returning in 1737 with a *Defense du Mondain*, he had to justify his work against the defenders of the so called edenic state of pure nature:

> J'aime le luxe, et meme la moellese,
> Tous les plaisirs, les arts de toute espece
> La Proprete, le gout et les ornaments: ...
> Tout sert au luxe, aux plaisirs de ce monde.
> Ah! Le bon temps que ce siecle de fer!
> Le superflu, chose tres necessaire,

A reuni l'un et l'autre hemisphere
[I love luxury and even lassitude
All pleasures, all arts
Cleanliness, taste and ornaments ...
All for the benefit of luxury, the joys of this world
Ah, how good is this age of iron
The superfluous, most necessary thing
That has brought together both hemispheres].

(Voltaire 1961: 203)

He extends his praise to paintings, tapestries, carriages, dinner ware, silver, per-fumes, cuisine with fine wines, and champagnes, which improve and embellish daily life, and in turn benefit industry and commerce. In the *Defense du Mondain*, he sets out an elitist but pro-business industrial policy:

Sachez surtout que le luxe enrichit
Un grand Etat, s'il en perd un petit.
Cette splendeur, cette pompe mondaine
D'un regne heureux est la marque cetaine.
Le riche est ne pour beaucoup depenser
Le pauvre est fait pour beaucoup amasser...
Le gout du luxe entre dans tous les rangs;
Le pauvre y vit des vanites des grands
[Be aware that luxury enriches
An important state, if it can imperil a weak one
This splendor, this worldly pomp
Is the sure sign of a happy reign.
The rich is born to spend
The poor is destined to accumulate
Taste for luxury penetrates all ranks
The poor lives off the vanities of the powerful].

(Voltaire 1961: 209)

Voltaire enounced the principles of spending and consuming as engines of economic growth, a sentiment echoed by many from Adam Smith to Alan Greenspan. Consumption, creation, and development of luxury brands mirror the quest for visible symbols of status and wealth leading to acceptance and approval of capitalist culture. Post-World War II Japan, Korea, and, in the last five years, China, followed stages of industrial resurgence from initial production of infe-rior quality products for export, opening of markets and availability of foreign luxury items, growth in market share for foreign luxury firms through develop-ment of the indigenous luxury market. From total suspicion and rejection of Western materialism, Beijing artist Lang Lang stated in an interview in "How to Spend It' as part of describing his weekend:

And then I'll go shopping in Wangfujing, which is the Fifth Avenue of Beijing. I very much like Armani and the Zegna store, and Versace. And my mother loves Louis Vuitton, though my father is more interested in porcelain. He's a serious collector of pots from the Ming, Tang and Qing dynasties.

(Lang Lang 2008)

Does materialism and taste for luxury denote prestige, as in the sumptuous costumes created for the classical dance sequences at the Beijing Olympics in summer 2008? Does it, as in Voltaire, denote pride in appreciation of foreign and domestic culture and art? Is it a fundamental transformation of ideology, or a rejection of ideology in the guise of materialism? According to an Ernst and Young report (2005), global luxury goods industry went from $103 billion in 2000 to $174 billion in 2005. In 2005, 41 percent of global luxury sales were in Japan, 17 percent in the United States, 16 percent in Europe, and 12 percent in China.

In Russia, where extreme poverty and wealth coexisted, only the Court and aristocratic families with vast land holdings could afford a level of sumptuous consumption rivaled only by Oriental potentates. By the 1780s choosing primarily French as the fashion, language, and standard of behavior, court costumes for the royal family, including even nightwear and children's garments, emulating and exaggerating the French court, were trimmed with sable, ermine, and rare jewels. (Victoria and Albert Museum exhibit, "Magnificence of the Tsars," fall 2008). Since 2000, Russian oligarchs, seeking to once again flaunt immense wealth, sought out the most expensive fashion brands, buying rare global treasures, acquiring and commissioning extraordinary jewelry, houses, and cars. As in the late nineteenth century, this display of immense luxury was not reflective of greater democratization of wealth or, as seen in 2008, of sound economic fundamentals, but rather a declaration of entitlement to luxury. In the case of Russia was it a rejection to 70 years of deprivation of consumer goods, or is extreme ostentation and ownership of luxury products an aggressive and regressive act as only few can benefit but all are made aware of the status and privileged life of the exhibitor?

In times of economic distress and unequal distribution of wealth, the question arises of when conspicuous consumption becomes a negative social or political force? When does the consumer become the debtor? When does the extension of credit work as counter to the good of society as a whole? "Their wealth would alone excite the public indignation and the vanity which almost always accompanies such upstart fortunes, the foolish ostentation with which they commonly display that wealth, excites that indignation still more" (Smith 1776: Book 5, 976). Condemned by the Church, the state or the public, the very rich in Venice, Naples, Amsterdam, and Poland under the Radziwill exercised restraint and modesty. Through the 1830s, the ostentation of the Ancien Regime would be counteracted by a scrupulous show of modesty and a veil of silence over one's finances in France after the Revolution. Outside of Paris and across France post-World War I, this attitude prevailed, as displays of wealth were deemed vulgar and potentially dangerous to social stability. The excessive consumption of the late 1990s and 2003–2008 suddenly reverted to modesty and frugality in the crisis of 2008.

China had reveled in its few newly minted millionaires and even one billionaire, Huang Guangyu. However in the middle of the crisis of 2008, *Financial Times* correspondent Geoff Dyer wrote:

> "To get rich is glorious," Deng Xiaoping once told China. "But maybe not too rich." With a fortune of $6.3, from electronic retail chains, the billionaire was forced to suspend trading and was arrested for stock manipulation, provoking rumors that he had been silenced or worse as a symbol of a new awareness of economic slow down and disapproval of excessive materialism.
>
> (Dyer and Anderlini 2008)

3.7 The individual and the state's economic impulses

Max Weber looked at the "economic impulse" as the base of most human activity in the most basic trading function but, "if the economic impulse in itself is universal, it is an interesting question as to the relations under which it becomes rationalized and rationally tempered in such fashion as to produce rational institutions of the character of capitalistic enterprise" (Weber 1961: 261). The argument is that natural resources alone are not conducive to wealth generation or enterprise, therefore as Landes argued Africa, Russia, Brazil, and the Middle East, despite vast resources, have not achieved long periods of sustained economic independence or continued cycles of prosperity, in fact, often becoming victims as well as benefactors of these resources. Europe, Japan, India, and America sustained periods of economic development when governments allowed economic activity to thrive under a combination of autonomy, regulation, and fostering of individual initiative across larger segments of society. Once the Treasury was no longer the sole domain of the Crown, institutions could evolve which would serve both the state and its citizens.

In *The Wealth and Poverty of Nations* (1999), Landes addresses the issue in his subtitle "Why Some Are So Rich and Some So Poor." Industrial innovation, from clean water to washable cotton to mass produced soap, better farm implements, the water wheel, the mechanical clock, printing, eyeglasses, to gunpowder, scientific advances allowed the pursuit of personal wealth but also vastly increased the amount of time, previously allocated to basic living functions, which could be dedicated to wealth generation and the concept of leisure.

Rosenberg and Birdzell in *How the West Grew Rich* (1986), traced a gradual growth out of poverty to wealth, completed in the nineteenth and twentieth century, due to what they define as "an institutional mechanism, built deep into the structure of Western economies and continuously seeking out and adapting growth inducing changes" (Rosenberg and Birdzell 1986: 6). Marx called this determinant a "capitalist engine" derived from a "driven pursuit of personal riches" (Marx 1977), proving Spengler, Malthus, Dystopias, and contemporary doomsayers wrong.

As Europe and America evolved from merchant to industrial to corporate societies, from the 1780s through the nineteenth century, they did not sanction, sanctify, or even approve of all aspects of capitalism, but there grew a fundamental acceptance and comfort level with its risks and rewards. Financial activity was propelled forward not only by secularization, but by the ability to accept it as a necessary evil which must be integrated into the fabric of society. The genius of Dutch merchants, English traders and goldsmiths, economic advisors, and economists, from Sir Thomas Gresham and Newton, to Smith, Say, Ricardo, Guizot, from Hamilton to Greenspan, Brown, Trichet and Bernanke, has been to seek a point of equilibrium between the state and market forces, both in times of growth and in times of crisis, from the South Sea Bubble to the subprime mortgage crisis.

Financial culture implied collective pride in economic accomplishments. From the burghers in Bruges and Antwerp to the bankers in London and New York, in large or small nations like Japan, Finland or France, where wealth and financial success were seen as reflecting on and adding to the prestige of the nation, there was a sense of pride. After the Nazi era, Germany could only reassume identity through economic achievement. The economic miracle, the Deutschmark, and the Bundesbank were the only acceptable sources of national pride in the economic miracle years through the 1980s. Since the eighteenth century, America and Britain benefited from the least tormented and least complex relationship to money, profit, speculation, and business. Capitalism or the integration of finance within the cultural framework of a nation or region, requires a spirit of competitiveness and acceptance of inequality in the name of dynamic evolution.

Russian and Chinese tycoons, like the robber barons in nineteenth century America, have accumulated vast fortunes in a very short time. They want to spend and show their wealth, but at present they appear more willing to buy foreign luxury goods than to invest in their national cultural heritage or to build museums, schools, and hospitals. They have accepted with glee the principles of materialism and consumption, but still turn to the state for investment and infrastructure. The greatest challenge of the post-2008 crisis will be whether these semi-autocratic or totalitarian regimes can continue to foster economic growth in a weaker and more volatile financial environment, whether the principles of economic initiative and endeavor have taken root, or whether they revert to far greater government control, restrictions, and anti-capitalist ideology.

3.8 Community to state capitalism: central banks

The Bank of England, its creation, evolution and role as model and paragon for all other central banks, epitomizes the transition from merchant banks to state banks, from lending to the government at will to lender of last resort, from responsibility for commercial and credit transactions to responsibility for monetary policy, stability, and prestige. As central banks must act as representative of, but not beholden to their governments, they reflect the cultural perception of the state–financial sector relationship to the public at large.

The origins of the Bank of Amsterdam (1609), Bank of England (1694), Bank of France (1801), the Reichbank (1875), and the Federal Reserve (1913) reveal how public perception and confidence in these institutions defined their respective country's interpretation of banking independence and the bank–state relationship. Unlike commercial or investment banks, central banks functioned as financial diplomats, reflecting their governments' historical and political reactions to finance, money, banking, and markets. Over the course of their history, central banks have at times been required to subsume their decision making process to a government. The unique creation of the European Central Bank in 1998, reversed the premise as to whether institutions would be able to subsume their national identity, a far more complex and psycho-historically disruptive process. In centralized and ideologically paternalistic France, issues of separation from the state, whether in the form of privatizations, denationalization or independence, were interpreted within a context of historical, rhetorical, and socio-political rather than economic considerations. The decision of the United Kingdom to remain outside of the European Monetary Union and the tutelage of the European Central Bank was a political and cultural statement on the historical as well as economic predominance of the Bank of England. As a member of the European Union, the United Kingdom respected the requirements of the Maastricht Treaty, officially declaring independence of the Bank of England in 1994, yet upon its 300-year anniversary it retained its unique status and never surrendered autonomy to the European Central Bank. The crisis of 2008, which required the Federal Reserve and the European Central Bank to act as lenders of last resort, and assume additional supervisory and monitoring roles over government injections of capital and bailouts, called into question the relationship of the state, the banking sector, and central banks. Examining central banks from 1694 to 1913, from the inception of the Bank of England to the creation of the Federal Reserve, provides a window into the changing nature, the functions, power, and public perception of state capitalism and its institutions.

The first European state guaranteed bank, the Bank of Amsterdam, founded in 1609, in competition with private and municipal banks, functioned as a deposit bank, accepting deposits in any currency above a value of 300 florins and registering it in the Great Ledger. The origins of the Bank of Amsterdam, as the Bank of England, stemmed in part from the government's increased inability to control and regulate powerful merchants:

> The city authorities became convinced that "cash keepers," many of whom were merchants as well as money changers and who had taken on a variety of banking functions, including the acceptance of deposits, the transfer of funds and the extension of credit caused the value of circulating silver coins to rise above the official rates, and create a scarcity of "good" coins.
>
> (Schull 1999)

Monetary diversity in Holland had mints producing coins for different trade routes, talers for the Levant, rijksdaalders for the Baltic and Poland, gold ducats for Russia, and silver ducats for India and China trade. Holland, unlike France, readily exported and imported currencies. Able to control minting, distribution, and the price of currency, the merchants in Amsterdam, like the goldsmiths in London, risked rivalling the power of the state. In Amsterdam, the government decided that establishing the bank standard would only be possible by establishing a government bank where any bill of exchange had to be paid in at the bank, creating a monopoly on instruments of trade. By 1683, the bank began to levy a small charge for payments and transfers. By 1699, the bank was tied to the prestige of Amsterdam as "the foremost in greatness, wealth and the extent of her trade" (Vilar 1976, quoting van Dillen 1934: 207). Between 1686 and 1691, deposits grew from seven million to 13.5 million in standard florin. Although Amsterdam ceded lead position to London in the 1720s, following the bubbles in France and England, and in the 1790s during the Revolution, there was capital flight to Amsterdam as it continued to be recognized as a political and economic safe haven.

In 1668, Sweden chartered Sveriges Riksbank, the only public bank governed exclusively by the Swedish Parliament. Johan Palmstruch, a merchant, was given the right to establish a lending bank. Among the four estates represented in Parliament, nobility, burghers, and clergy approved, while the peasants remained wary. The Riksbank "evolved like most early forerunners of central banks as a commercial bank with the government as its biggest customer" (Deane and Pringle 1995: 37).

Originally, the Bank of England, like state banks in Amsterdam, Stockholm, and Barcelona, was conceived to regulate and harmonize banking operations from private banks. The state was overly dependent on goldsmiths and, in the 1690s, needed money and loans: "The Crown and the great London merchants therefore united in accusing the gold merchants of speculation, usury, clipping coins and even insolvency" (Vilar 1976: 215). William Patterson, a Scotsman, familiar with the bank in Holland and supported by the powerful merchants of London, suggested that a bank be set up to provide domestic financing to the Crown for the wars with France, bypassing dependency on the goldsmiths. Arranging a loan of £1.2 million at 8 percent interest, subscribers to the loan were incorporated as governors of the first joint stock bank. The bank, led by Sir John Houblon, descendant of French Huguenots, opened in July 1694. Within the next five years, monetary reforms had to be implemented following the Great Recoinage of 1696 which undervalued silver. The danger was scarcity of coinage and use of unregulated paper notes, which led to the worst excesses of agio speculation in France. Until 1717, silver was the monetary standard, although due to the extent of trade and inflow of currency, London was flooded with gold, which created currency value disequilibrium. In 1696, John Locke, in *Further Considerations Concerning the Raising of the Value of Money*, premised that there be one standard and issuance of all coins in full weight. Isaac Newton, Master of the Mint, was ultimately responsible for the value of the gold guinea in 1717, but until 1774 England retained aspects of bimetallism until finally settling fully into the Gold Standard with "recognition that silver was a subsidiary coinage" (Kindleberger 1993: 61).

At its creation in 1695, the bank was seen as a response to "almost crush'd several sorts of Blood suckers, mere Vermin, Usurers and Gripers, Goldsmiths, Tally Jobbers, Exchequer Brokers and Knavish Money Sciveners and Pawn Brokers with their Twenty and Thirty percent" (Plender 1994). Within a decade, the Bank was granted vast privileges: in 1706 direct agent in circulating exchequer bills, by Act of Parliament in 1708 monopoly of note issuance, and management of government securities in 1717. "It was given a monopoly of joint stock banking, the handling of the government's account, the right to deal in bullion, to discount approved bills of exchange ... and to issue notes" (Deane and Pringle 1995: 39). Its directors were implicated in the losses of the South Sea Bubble in 1720, and "the Bank of England came to the rescue of the South Sea Company belatedly and at a punishing price, in order to dispose finally of a dangerous rival" (Kindleberger 1993: 92). The intervention averted further panic but could not contain nor reimburse massive losses.

The repercussions of this action continue to reverberate in the crisis of 2008: when is it appropriate and deemed necessary for a central bank to rescue failing private sector companies which risk to destabilize the entire financial system? The concepts of contagion, domino effect, and "too big to fail," attributed to the public–private financial relationship, were tested by the Bank of England's approach in 1720, in the 1890 Barings bailout, in the 1995 decision to let Barings fail, in the Johnson Matthey Bankers, a firm dealing in gold bullion that was rescued in 1984, the Northern Rock, mortgage lender, bailout in 2006, and in the capital injection package and partial nationalization of Barclays, HBOS, Royal Bank of Scotland, and Lloyds in October 2008. The Bank of England's extreme caution, combined with the need for timely action, its ability to avert major crisis and to reassert confidence in the banking sector has been the cornerstone of its philosophy and public image. The bank's role, as custodian and guarantor of the nations gold reserve, was tested in the crisis of 1797 when the British economy, severely impacted by capital flight of gold and silver from France, suffered through currency appreciation and sudden depreciation as the French paper assignats collapsed in 1795. The Bank of England "somewhat lost its head and was given permission to suspend convertibility of bank notes into coin well before its reserves had run out" (Kindleberger 1993: 63). The Bank Restriction Act, finally repealed in 1821, which was cause of numerous debates led by monetarists such as David Ricardo and bankers such as Alexander Baring, led to acceptance of the Gold Standard as sole basis and support of the currency.

Moving to Threadneedle Street in 1734, the bank took on the nickname "Old Lady of Threadneedle Street." Manager of the national debt, the power of the institution rested on its dual role as commercial and government bank: "Right from the start, the Bank had to balance the demands of shareholders looking for profits in a private company with a requirement to pay attention to public benefit" (Deane and Pringle 1995: 40). The Bank Charter Act of 1844, the Peel's

Act, established its predominance in setting monetary policy and sole right of issuance over all other banks, establishing the standards for all other central banks as both the government's bank and the banker's bank.

The Bank of the United States in 1790 and 1816, the Bank of Spain first chartered in 1782, the Bank of France in 1800, the Reichbank in 1875, the Bank of Japan and the Federal Reserve in 1913, all looked to the Bank of England as paragon of credibility, stability and order. By the mid-nineteenth century, London was world leader in trade financing, money markets, and banking: "The Bank was not only the government's bank but had become the banker's bank too; other commercial banks used accounts with it to settle claims between themselves and kept their reserves with it" (Deane and Pringle 1995: 42). Since the nineteenth century the governor, deputy governor and directors of the Bank of England serve for limited terms (four and five years), appointed by the Crown in coordination with the prime minister and chancellor of the exchequer. Directors traditionally came from elite investment banks.

> It [the Bank of England] is, in all respects to money as St Peters is to the Faith. And the reputation is deserved, for most of the art as well as much of the mystery associated with the management of money originated there.
>
> (Galbraith quoted in Deane and Pringle 1995: 38)

4 World bankers
Ambivalences of modernity

The analysis by Alfred Chandler, Harvard business historian, of administrative and managerial structures in industrial capitalism characterized the British model as "personal," the Germany model as "cooperative," and the American model as "competitive." Within this pantheon, the French model's unique cyclical private–public relationship should be added and defined as ambivalent.

From 1815 to 1914, the influence of British, French, and post-1870 German finance and banking institutions extended far beyond the worlds of commerce, monetary policy, stock exchanges, and banks. Engine of expansion and reform in productivity, income, urban demographics and longevity, money permeated all aspects of civil society and culture. In England, begrudgingly accepted within the Protestant ethos yet judged morally reprehensible, depictions of finance tread a fine line between the gentleman banker and the avaricious, murky financier or speculator, all the while aware that both were essential to the growth and prosperity of the nation. English finance and financiers were an inescapable evil, yet part of the social fiber. In post-revolutionary France, displacement of French values, overtaken by economic forces, called for a new topos to describe and formalize operations and instruments. The archetypal manor, palace, and church gave way to bank, exchange, trade, mines, and railroads. Never able to fully reconcile the moral and the economic, even in the name of state prestige, French literature and art reflected the ambivalence and deep-seated distrust of these new economic forces. Being a French banker, even when French banks had achieved global status and prestige, was somehow tainted or amoral, often depicted as foreign or influenced by foreigners. Under Bismarck's unification and centralization, Germany moved from merchant autocracy to modern capitalism within a decade. However German society and intellectual life remained aloof, xenophobic, and wary of economic cosmopolitanism. In Germany, economic progress was validated in the name of military power and the industrial–financial nexus.

The internationalization of European finances, led by a close network of family dynasties from France, Germany, the Low Countries, and Switzerland, interspersed with English and Jewish family alliances, lent credence to the myths of foreign interests at play, not necessarily detrimental but also not genuinely loyal to national interests. Eighteenth-century English literature dismantled the classical barriers between the economic and cultural spheres, between literary text and economic context. Fielding, Defoe, Sterne, Gay, and Pope propagated the semantics of commerce, the depiction of all aspects of transactional activity, as their texts were meant to serve as mirror rather than antidote or deflection of the evils of social mobility and secularization. They set the stage for English realism and for the French schools of Realism and Naturalism in literature and Impressionism in art. An increase in literacy among the urban working class, the serialization of novels in newspapers, book publishing, distribution, and leisure time among the middle and upper middle classes allowed the representation of economic ideas and images to permeate the public discourse. Education, even when limited to small elites in Spain, Italy, Prussia, Poland, and Russia, was rigorous in the learning of classical and modern languages, specifically French as the language of diplomacy, intellectual, and political discourse and English as the language of international commerce. Therefore, Heine, Chekov, Turgenev, and Tolstoy read Balzac, Stendhal, Flaubert, and Goncourt in the original.

France and England set the paradigm for incremental modernization of political ideology and secularization of social thought, but most European nations and empires remained entrenched in profound economic passivity. Inherent dynamism coupled with pro-growth and pro-business government policies was largely limited to France, Britain, and after the 1880s, Germany, the United States and Japan. French and British finance in the boom years of the 1850s to 1860s, injected capital and investment across Europe; united Germany and the United States became economic powerhouses in the second industrial revolution in the 1880s and 1890s, generating a new wave of growth and industrial financial expansion. Russia opened the door into the modern economic world with the emancipation of the serfs in 1861, to be completed on imperial lands in 1866, the creation of the Imperial Bank of Russia in 1860, modeled on the Bank of England, and plans for monetary reform under the enlightened reign of Alexander II. However as in previous (and future) periods of economic and social reform, the momentum was short lived and impacted only a small segment of the urban population.

Britain, France, the United States, and Germany showed that for the first time in history, economics trumped theology, republics and democracies trumped absolute monarchies, bankers and politicians synchronized policies and politics, yet underneath this surge of economic activity and stability, societies never addressed the resentments, fears, myths, and hatreds engendered by money and its omnipotence. After the Revolutions of 1848, the rise of capitalism paralleled the rise of socialism, as the newly enfranchised middle classes and the permanently disenfranchised but newly organized and literate working classes, intersected and diverged. At the height of the economic boom in France and England in 1864, Société Générale, the second largest French deposit bank with international clients opened in Paris; the International Workingman's Association, the First International, assembled in London attended by Prudhon, Blanqui, and Karl Marx.

4.1 British universalism

> Everyone is aware that England is the greatest moneyed country in the
> world; everyone admits that it has much more immediately disposable ready
> cash than any other country.
>
> (Bagehot 1897: 4)

Eminent British economist, Walter Bagehot's statement in the 1870s expressed
common knowledge among all educated citizens of the world: the British Empire
was the unquestionable economic, financial and political leader. British finance
set the global standard for financial institutions, central banks, international and
domestic transactions, and monetary policy. England was the world's largest
lender: "because she possesses an unequaled fund of floating money, which will
help in a moment any merchant who sees a great prospect of new profit"
(Bagehot 1897: 15). Banker to Europe, London functioned as "clearing house to
foreign countries" (Bagehot 1897: 33), with Lombard Street as intermediary
between international commerce and British finance.

Starting in 1848, when all bond markets except the English were severely hit
by domestic revolutions or fear of uprisings: "Clearly the market as a whole had
no expectation of a revolution in London which was used as a safe haven by
many continental investors" (Ferguson 2001: 274). A generation later, during
and after the Franco-Prussian war in 1872, England again became safe haven for
continental European fortunes. Bank deposits in London in 1873 reached £120
million versus £13 million in Paris (due to wartime hoarding of gold, the actual
amount of French wealth was underestimated). Kindleberger judged England in
1815 to be a century in advance of France and continental Europe in financial
development and implementation. Its political and military clout indisputably
validated at the Council of Vienna, from the end of the Napoleonic era to World
War I, England waged wars abroad, morphing into the British Empire, but unlike
continental Europe, the United States, and South America, wars were not waged
on British soil, allowing uninterrupted economic progress, expansion, and wealth
generation based on long-term geopolitical and financial policies. Domestic
turmoil and civil disturbances in the Chartist movement, inciting strikes and riots
in the late 1830s, large demonstrations over the protectionist Corn Laws,
repealed in 1846 in support of free trade, the Kennington Common demonstrations in 1848 for workers rights, indicative of growing militancy in the disenfranchised urban poor, never grew into full fledged rebellion or organized
revolution. Parliament always granted just enough reforms to modulate the level
of anger and the dominant business classes returned to order.

France never attained an analogous sense of long-term security, constantly
besieged by political upheaval from the revolts of 1830 and 1832 (subject of
Victor Hugo's *Les Miserables*) to the attack on the Tuileries by the enraged populace in February 1848, followed by the brutal repression of June 1848, to the
popular uprising of the Paris Commune of March 1871, and massacres in late
May 1871. Although economic philosophy, from Guizot, finance minister to

Louis Philippe to Thiers, first president of the Third Republic, was relatively consistent, political instability left profound scars in the national psyche, unlike England where the assumption was that during the extraordinarily long Victorian era (1837–1901), money invested or deposited would be guaranteed for generations.

The Industrial Revolution resulted in the largest urban working class populations in northern and western England but, as historian Robert Carson Allen demonstrated, they were also beneficiaries of higher wages, lower energy costs, due to the efficiencies of the coal industry, and the unique British synthesis between technology and capitalism: "that technology was invented by people in order to make money. ... First inventions were investments where future profits had to offset current costs" (Allen 2005). Wages in England throughout the nineteenth century were higher than in any other country in Europe or Asia, therefore even in bad circumstances, the average wage earner was able to buy better food, clothes, and benefit from a higher level of health and sanitation.

The success of capitalism in England was not a question of wealth but of will. France, Prussia, Sweden, and Russia were very wealthy countries but they never resolved the deep ambivalence between money and worth, between the ruling classes' bestowed right and the merchant classes' earned rights. England achieved fiscal harmonization, use of banknotes, and bank deposits which: "spread through Britain beginning about 1826 and quickly after 1850, slowly in France after 1875" (Kindleberger 1993: 116). By 1855, England and Wales had 409 banks and 1,185 banking offices, while in "1863 three-quarters of France lacked access to banking" (Kindleberger 1993: 116). London led in insurance houses, joint stock banks after 1854, and the number of banks outside of London increased, led by Lloyds and Midlands.

After the banking reforms of 1844, all banks in England depended on the Bank of England, which assumed greater power as the sole joint stock company permitted to issue bank notes and as "the last lending house" (Bagehot 1897: 53), formulating the lender of last resort principle. Bagehot advised that the Bank of England's reserves never go below £10 million, and in case of a crisis (referencing 1866) he offered a prescient remedy for averting panic and loss of confidence:

> A panic is a species of neuralgia, and accordingly to the rules of science, you must not starve it. The holders of the cash reserve must be ready, not only to keep it for their own liabilities, but to advance it most freely for the liabilities of others. They must lend to merchants, to minor bankers.
>
> (Bagehot 1897: 51)

Laying out the conditions for a sound economy (still applicable in 2009): "much loanable capital, good credit, and the increased profits derived from better used labour and better used capital" (Bagehot 1897: 149), Bagehot defined the bank's directors as "trustees for the Public" (Bagehot 1897: 35), "a board of plain, sensible, prosperous English merchants" (Bagehot 1897: 174).

4.2 The British Gold Standard

The symbol of sound practice and the badge of honor and decency.
(Kindleberger 1993: 131, quoting Joseph Schumpeter (1954) on Austria's
decision to join the Gold Standard in 1892)

The Gold Standard, synonymous with control over global monetary policy, reinforced the power of the British Empire. Decisions to unilaterally peg the pound
sterling to gold occurred in stages over the course of two centuries, culminating
in the universal Gold Standard from 1880 to 1914. During the 1815–1860 period,
England's flexible Gold Standard and France bimetallism worked well to assure
cooperation on currency fluctuations, especially in the volatile period following
the American Gold Rush in 1849, and the Australian Gold Rush in 1851. As
gold production rose nearly ten times, creating destabilization of currency
markets, provoking in part the Crash of 1857, the Bank of England and the Bank
of France coordinated efforts to maintain stability in the inflows and price.
France was sole economic rival to England in the 1860s, when the Second
Empire oversaw a surge of production, construction, and investment as underin-
vested, hoarded and repatriated French assets were reintegrated into the
economy. In June 1865, the French franc's proven stability and prestige gave
Napoleon III the political clout to convene in Paris an international conference
calling for a "etalon universel," a universal monetary standard pegged to the
franc. Britain maintained the supremacy of sterling and the Gold Standard with
the support of the newly internationally involved United States. The Latin Monetary Union, as alternative to the pound, pegged the Swiss and Belgium francs,
the Italian lira along with Spanish, Finnish, Bulgarian, Romanian, Serbian, Ven-
ezuelan, Columbian, and Haitian currencies to the Franc. Functional until 1875,
the International Monetary Conference of 1878 led to a realignment of European
currencies, and the acceptance of a universal Gold Standard in 1880. Under the
Gold Standard, the French franc, Reichsmark and dollar were aligned in parity
with pound sterling: £1= 25 francs; 1 mark=1.2 francs; $1=5.18 francs. Coupled
with low inflation, stable purchasing power, currency parity remained in place
until 1914.

4.3 British and French bankers to the universe

Under the guise of fundamental belief in European superiority and established
hegemony, international banking was neatly divided among the realms of the
French and the British Empires. From the 1860s, British and French banks established branches, representative offices, and subsidiaries in their respective colonial empires to finance railroads, mining, diamonds, and trade in rice, cotton,
sugar, tobacco, tea, and silk. Standard Bank of British South Africa, established
in 1862 by James Patterson, helped finance diamond fields and gold mining in
Johannesburg. The Charter Bank, established in 1853, six years later had offices
in Bombay, Calcutta, Shanghai, Hong Kong, and Singapore – Standard Charter

was created by the 1969 merger. Hong Kong Shanghai Bank (HSBC), founded in 1865 by Thomas Sutherland, Hong Kong Superintendent of the largest navigation company, saw the need to create a separate bank to help finance the growing trade between China and Europe, and to explore the new potential for China–United States trade, opening the first branch of a British bank in San Francisco the same year. Instrumental in railroad financing in India and China, within a decade the bank also opened offices in Yokohama and Kobe in Japan, and expanded across China, with opulent buildings in Shanghai on the Bund, and Hong Kong on the harbor in 1885. In 1889, HSBC took a stake in the newly opened Imperial Bank of Persia. Commonwealth Bank Corporation, founded in Australia in 1912, extended Commonwealth presence through the Pacific Islands.

> Jew Rothschild and his fellow Christian Baring.
> Those, and the truly liberal Laffitte,
> Are the true lords of Europe. Every loan
> Is not a merely speculative hit,
> But seats a nation or upsets a throne.
>   (Byron 2004 [1823]: Canto XII)

Within Europe, the power of Barings was only rivaled by Rothschilds, outside Europe, Barings led in the Americas and Rothschilds extended their reach into Russia and the Ottoman Empire. As early as 1823, Lord Byron's vicious ditty epitomized the perception of international banking: an omnipotent, stateless force led by markets and speculation, capable of upending or transforming nations at will. Barings, according to an apocryphal anecdote circulated as early as 1817, was the sixth great power in Europe following England, France, Prussia, Austria, and Russia (Fay 1996). Francis Baring, descendent of German wool merchants in Bremen, founded the bank in 1762, lent to the Crown during the American Revolutionary War, and solidified his fortune during the Napoleonic wars. Alexander Baring, shrewd, cautious, and willing to make bold decisions in financing international trade, transformed the bank into a major international house by 1815. During the railroad boom, the house speculated on its own account in French and Russian bonds, Austrian stocks, and American railroad shares. Partnering in syndicated loans and bond issues across Europe, with Rothschild, Bischoffsheim, Cassel, and Oppenheimer, and in New York and Boston with Kidder Peabody and Morgan, the bank became America's lead correspondent banker. Its reputation was undisputed until the near fatal decision to invest in the volatile Argentinean market in 1890. Ned Baring, granted the title of Lord Revelstoke in 1885, decided to underwrite a £2 million share issue for Buenos Aires Water Supply and Drainage Company, the funds were sent to Argentina where the market collapsed amid political chaos in South America, rendering the shares worthless and leaving Barings heavily overcommitted. In November 1890, Barings was bailed out by a consortium established by the Bank of England, the Bank of France, the Imperial Bank of Russia, and the Rothschilds.

The damage was contained and the bank saved, but Lord Revelstoke's career was over and his personal estate had to be liquidated. By 1896, the bank was repossessed by the family and would become far more conservative and cautious. Banker to the monarchy, by 1928 succession passed between members of the family and outsiders, but by 1971 succession passed back to the Barings heirs. Like most City banks, it expanded in the 1970s and following Big Bang in 1986, engaged in corporate finance and trading activities. Run by Nicholas and Peter Baring, the bank entered the cutthroat world of currency trading, without fully comprehending the risks and dangers involved (see Chapter 5).

French international banking developed under three separate and intersecting venues: international deposit and corporate banking; cross regional investment banking; and specific colonial banks. In the first category, Crédit Lyonnais chartered in Lyons in 1863 and Société Générale in Paris in 1864, within a decade began establishing branches and offices abroad. In 1867 Crédit Lyonnais had over 2,500 client accounts, including 38 in Africa, 18 in Asia, and 12 in America. Sensitive to the political tensions between Prussia and France, Henri Germain, head of Crédit Lyonnais, by 1868 began to transfer the bank's assets abroad, opening the first foreign branch of a French credit facility in London in 1870. By carefully monitoring the bank's assets and lines of credit during the Franco-Prussian War and Paris Commune, Crédit Lyonnais, unlike Credit Foncier, and Société Générale, did not require any aid from the Bank of France and by the end of 1871 had returned to pre-1870 levels of profitability. Its financial position was so sound that it was asked by the new government of Adolphe Thiers to participate in the first war reparation bond issue with the Banque de France and Rothschild. The second issue, in 1872, included Société Générale and the brand new Banque de Paris et des Pays Bas. By 1875, Crédit Lyonnais had branches in Cairo and Alexandria to finance cotton, Constantinople for the wheat trade from Ukraine, and in Smyrna, Jerusalem, and Jaffa. The first branch in Russia opened in 1878 in St Petersburg, followed by Moscow in 1881, and Odessa in 1892. As broker bank for Russia's industrial transactions it extended credit facilities between Russia and the Ottoman Empire, in areas with vast resources, but very little available capital or even cash-based trade (Morin 1983). Crédit Lyonnais was closed out of only two major markets: India due to the hegemony of British interests, and the United States due to protectionist tariffs against foreign banks and the position of Barings.

Paribas, founded in 1872 in the immediate aftermath of the Franco-Prussian war, would become the premier international investment bank in Europe under French home office and directorship. Integrating in one institution Landes' categories: "banque de depots" (retail, corporate bank) and "haute banque d'affaires" (investment bank), the bank offers a microcosm of intra European alliances and dynastic partnerships. Its founding charter in 1872 was a unique example of cross-border cooperation: "to German signatures were added French, Swiss, Belgium, Dutch, and Danish signatures; Jewish signatures next to Catholic and Protestant signatures; Paris is associated to London, Brussels, Amsterdam and Geneva" (Buissiere 1992: 28).

The founders and original investors, the German banking family of Bischoff-sheim, established since the early 1800s in Amsterdam, Antwerp, and, through marriage, with the Goldschmidt bank in London, opened a small private bank in Brussels after Belgium declared independence in 1830, and a bank in Paris during the July Monarchy. In 1850, Bischoffsheim was one of the founders of the Banque Nationale de Belgique. Related to the Bamberger family (directors of Deutsche Bank and the Reichbank in 1870), they were also allied with Maurice de Hirsch, co-investor with Rothschild in Austro-Hungarian railroads. The Swiss bankers Hentsch, in Paris since 1812, added a connection to Geneva. Bischoffsheim and Goldschmidt were among the initial shareholders in Crédit Lyonnais in 1863, Société Générale in 1864, and Banque de l'IndoChine in 1875. Leaving the board of Société Générale, in 1869 they set up the third major deposit bank in France, Banque de Paris, which included Henri Cernushi, Italian banker associated with Credit Mobilier. War reparation payments imposed by Bismarck in 1871, required bond issues – mainly underwritten by the Rothschild bank and the Haute Banque. Crédit Lyonnais took on the first bond subscription, but there was a need for more banks to participate in order to offset the lead of the Rothschild. Willing to step into the fray and participate in 1871, Banque de Paris and Banque des Depots des Pays Bas decided to merge, and raised capital of 125 million francs (compared to the 25 million for Crédit Lyonnais in 1863). One of its first acts was to underwrite the second bond issue in 1873, which helped France to pay back the 5 billion gold franc war indemnity nearly two years ahead of schedule. France was judged to be so wealthy and financially stable, despite having lost the war, that the bond issue was oversubscribed from all of Europe, Russia, the Ottoman Empire, the United States, and even Germany itself. In 1878, Paribas moved into a magnificent town house on rue d'Antin, a few steps from the Palais Garnier, site of the Opera of Paris. Henri Germain decided to move Crédit Lyonnais' headquarters to Paris in the same year. In Paris's most fashionable location, Crédit Lyonnais, Société Générale, and Paribas, surrounded by the opera, theaters, cafés, and newly created department stores, symbolized the ornate, ostentatious style of French wealth, economic power, and international prestige.

Withstanding initial losses in the crisis of 1873, affecting world markets, through its voluminous foreign connections Paribas within five years became lead bank in Russian, Swedish (through connections with the Wallenberg banking and industrial dynasty), and American bond issues. Ernest Cassel, descendant of a Cologne banking family related to Bischoffsheim, established in London and correspondent for Schiff and Kuhn Loeb in New York, helped Paribas with connections to Barings and the Americas. With branches in Amsterdam, Brussels, and Geneva, Paribas participated in the creation of the Russo-Chinese Bank in 1896, in order to help finance railroad and mining projects in Siberia and Manchuria (see Buissiere 1992: 51). Rival and partner in international syndications with Crédit Lyonnais and Société Générale, the bank was the leading French investment bank through the twentieth century. Briefly national-ized in 1983 to 1986, the bank merged with BNP in 1999 to become France's largest universal bank, best positioned in Europe, with HSBC and Deutsche Bank, to withstand the financial crisis of 2009.

In the last category, banks specifically created to finance colonial interests, Banque Suez and IndoChine functioned as political vehicles for the interests of the state, guaranteeing French financial sovereignty. Major banks brought prestige, presence, and served as conduits for trade and investment in the empires, but in reality neither the branches of the two major banks nor the colonial banks added that much to the prosperity of the nation, nor its investors. Already by the 1880s there began debate in France over whether the colonies were in fact a burden or an asset to French prosperity. After the emergence of Germany and the United States, France receded to fourth place in industrial power, railroad, canal, infrastructure, roads, tunnels, and urban construction, retaining its position as "banker to the universe" (see Beltran and Griset 1988).

4.4 Political–financial matrix

The psycho-cultural and economic myths and stereotypes surrounding the Rothschild family are examined in Chapter 2. It is also important to note their specific contribution to cross-border banking transactions: "As key player in the world's biggest market, Rothschild was the prototype financial master of the universe" (Ferguson 1999: 271). Between 1848 and 1870, railroad expansion in France grew from 3,000 to 20,000 km, from 6,000 to 19,500 in Germany, and from 10,000 to 25,000 km in Britain, fueling a vast market in government bonds. In 1868, 14 countries "turned to the Paris market for the sale of 2.127 million francs worth of their government bonds" (Ferguson 2001: 205), the largest percentage issued through Rothschild banks, subsidiaries, and affiliates. Austrian railroads were funded through Rothschild and Credit Anstallt, Lombardy, Piedmont, and the Papal States in Italy, pre- and post-unification, depended on French finance. The railroads requiring government and private sector cooperation and joint financing (for the first time outside of military operations), equivalent to the information technology revolution in the twentieth century brought about a major shift and expansion of industrial production. "In the nineteenth century, the future of finance lay in long term ventures; firstly in the promotion and negotiation of government stocks and secondly, in the promotion and support of private enterprise" (Landes 1961: 117). The Rothschilds, and to a lesser degree Barings, bridged the gap between being banker to the Crown, banker to the state, and partner or guarantor to other banks. In 1852, at the start of the Second Empire, understanding the need for a French version of the British joint stock bank, they helped the Péreire Brothers fund the first French investment bank ("banque d'affaires"), Société Générale du Credit Mobilier, in direct competition with the Bank of France. Credit Mobilier set the stage for joint stock, limited partnership banks, which did not need the authorization of the state.

If medieval monies were priced according to harvests, displacements of monarchs, and local fairs, "nineteenth century investors priced bonds in response as much to political news as to less accessible fiscal or monetary indicators" (Ferguson 2001: 275). More than price indexes or ministerial decisions, the responses of the Rothschilds was judged a crucial indicator of political and economic conditions. In the advent of the July Revolution in 1830, a journalist, Ludwig Borne, wrote of Louis Philippe's relation with the haute banque and the Rothschilds: "[he has] taken the title of Emperor of the five per cents, King of the three per cents, Protector of bankers and exchange agents" (quoted by Ferguson 2001: 276). In 1872 at the founding of Paribas it was understood that in order to succeed: "the bank had cooperated harmoniously with the Rothschilds, whom under the aegis of James, the great Baron, exercised since the 1840s a sort of unofficial rule over the financial market in the capital" (Bussiere 1992: 23). In the fragmented Austro-Hungarian Empire, Spain, and Italy under quasi-French rule, the Rothschilds controlled investments into and out of these dependent impoverished markets.

The Mediterranean countries lagged far behind Northern Europe: "Rural-urban backward economies could not be salvaged by banks without an adequate sociopolitical matrix of laws, regulation and custom in which they operated and appropriate government policies" (Kindleberger 1993: 151). Banking in Spain began in the 1770s, but under French dominance through the end of the Napoleonic era, the country remained in thrall to the all powerful Church, aristocracy, estates, and feudal structure. There was residual suspicion of currency, lack of faith in paper money, and very little participation in the banking sector outside of a few major cities. As in the rest of Europe, the land and railroad boom in the 1850s to 1860s brought about a short period of foreign investment and modernization. In this environment, the Botin family founded Banco Santander in 1857, which still remains Spain's oldest, wealthiest, family owned bank. After joining the Latin Monetary Union in 1865, Spain hoped for further support, but interest waned and Spain retreated into a backward, rural, semi feudal economy, and nearly illiterate population.

Italy, foremost commercial power of the Middle Ages, by the post-Napoleonic era had become a besieged, backward, group of desolate regions united into one kingdom in 1861. Italian economist, Francesco Ferrara, in January 1866 described the state of Italy:

> The nation is tied to its past; the spark of progress has not touched it; it tills the soil as it used to, it plies its ancient crafts; … a thoughtless and inept generation succeeds one which was servile and indolent. The world around us moves in feverish strides; new inventions, new methods, the needs of everyday social life help to regenerate all branches of industry, but Italy just looks on and admires and buys if it can.
>
> (Luzzatto 1969)

A weak, decentralized state apparatus remained dependent on foreign, largely French, banks and investment. Italy did not participate in the huge surge of railroad construction and expansion which opened up rural France, Germany, and

England to new industry and distribution of goods, and accessibility to larger domestic markets. Stuck in almost medieval conditions in tax collection, land ownership, and ecclesiastical privileges, Italy remained anachronistic in its distrust of industrial and agricultural investment, and in the use of banks. Although there were numerous savings banks, deposits were modest, as the population, even in the North, kept money out of formal institutions. The only modern lending banks in 1862 were Cassa Generale and Cassa di Sconto in Genoa, and Cassa del Commercio e delle Industrie in Turin. Between 1863 and 1866, in the hope of attracting more intra-European trade, new banks were created, including the Anglo-Italian Bank and Societa Generale di Credit Mobiliare, modeled on the French Credit Mobilier, chartered in June 1863 with members of Credit Mobilier on its board. The Banca Nazionale, created in 1861, suffered through the currency crisis and economic downturn in 1866 when, as in Spain, this crisis forced France to withdraw investment, worsening the lack of confidence and trust in banks and paper money, and increasing hoarding across Italy. The country remained profoundly fragmented with separate economies, poor, rural, land bound, and almost feudal in the isolated South, slow but steady progress toward industrialization and monetary economy in the North. In the aftermath of unification, Rothschild helped develop Piedmont and Liguria as well as Genoa, but dependency on the textile industry and lack of industrial diversification hampered economic progress. Poverty remained endemic, with workers earning daily wage of two lire on working days, about 300 a year, while woman and children barely had starvation wages. Illiteracy in Spain and Italy remained exceptionally high throughout the century, with weak penetration of schooling, entirely under the aegis of the Church. Despite the creation of a large network of local and regional banks, financial institutions in Italy remained formally and informally, locked into arcane familial, Church and state affiliations and obligations through the 1980s.

4.5 Cosmopolitan finance: the stranger among us

The role of international finance, esoteric in nature, conducted among a small interrelated group of bankers, able to conjure vast amounts of capital, and to influence governments in the process, persisted, and reinforced conspiracy theories and accusations of disloyalty to the nation. Less prevalent in Britain, the image of the banker as foreign or foreigner permeated French literature. Traumatized by the Mississippi Bubble scheme, the banker as a stranger whose interests are not aligned with French values remained deeply embedded in the collective psyche. Balzac set up the model in the Baron of Nucingen, a parody of Rothschild in title, appearance, and assumed accent (see Chapter 2), evoking the anti-Semitic stereotype of usurer and foreigner: "Alsacien banker, the son of some Jew or other, converted by ambition" (Balzac 1961: 291).

After the defeat in the Franco-Prussian War in 1871, German and Jewish bankers were further tainted as part of anti-French international cabals. The bankruptcy in 1892 of Union Generale, a Catholic bank, founded in part with

Vatican support in order to counteract the monopoly of the Rothschild bank, became the object of conspiracy theories and the basis of Zola's *L'Argent* (1891). Involved in speculation in Ottoman Empire investment schemes, the bank failed due to over-leverage, poor management, and lack of sufficient capital, but its demise reinforced the insidious myth of foreign finance interfering with true Catholic interests. Right-wing essayist and novelist, Maurice Barres wrote: "Capital speculates, destroys, becomes more and more international and aspires no longer to be in solidarity with the destiny of France" (Barres 1954).

In England, reflecting the sentiment on the continent, Anthony Trollope in 1875 completed *The Way We Live Now*, offering in 100 chapters a bitter, scathing attack on financial fraud, business, and unscrupulous bankers, with anti-Semitic asides and moral condemnation of the bankers' stateless status. The hero, Augustus Melmotte, a foreign born financier (his origins are never specified but assumed to be German, perhaps inspired by German-French banker, Auguste Belmont), sets up a scam on fictitious American and Mexican railroad shares, luring in an affluent English family. Unmasked, he recovers his money, is elected to Parliament, engages in other fraudulent deals until, finally bankrupt and having alienated even his own daughter, he commits suicide. The subtext of the melodrama has the victimized British family vindicated and the evil, foreign banker destroyed: order re-established.

4.6 Forging institutional culture home and abroad

The concept of a corporate identity, of a set of behavioral and social criteria applied to an institution rather than a family or a state, took shape as a byproduct of capitalism. The size, scope, and international prestige of large banks and industrial conglomerates forged their identity and position within the state and society. By 1900, these banks had mastered the concept of logo recognition, marketing, and sponsorship. At the World's Fair in Brussels in 1910, Crédit Lyonnais, chief sponsor of the fair, was honored with the title of world's largest international bank. A few years earlier, one of France's most famous glassmakers, Jacques Graber, was commissioned by Crédit Lyonnais to create for the main office in Nancy, an exquisite blue and gold stained glass window. A traditional, circular floral configuration, it bears the bank's logo, "C and L," intertwined at the center, in place of a religious symbol (Montella 1987), the window's sacred opulence, a true "Gilded Age" metaphor for France's conversion from church to temple of money.

Anti-capitalist journalist and novelist, Anatole France, parodied the French state in *Penguin Island:* "The penguin state was democratic, three or four financial companies exercised broader and especially more effective and better known power than the masters of the republic" (France 1908).

At home and abroad, these banks built or moved into splendid buildings on main strands or avenues, replicating in foreign branches the décor, dress codes, and working conditions of their home offices, insuring that they were also exporting British and French culture. Banks were the first service industry, unlike other sectors which at the lower levels required manual labor and off-site operations. Based on office functions, they required literacy and basic mathematical skills, creating in their wake a bureaucratic gradation of positions, from lower-level clerk to bank manager. Even if lower-level positions paid badly and required long hours at the mercy of the next echelon and capricious management, working in a bank was considered a first rung in social advancement, and carried a level of pride and accomplishment. The large banks in turn, capitalized on their position to set up an environment which encouraged worker loyalty and sound practices. In the French and British colonial empires, if these banks financed colonial expansion, and at its worse colonial exploitation, in the rubber, tea, and rice plantations, and textile factories, they also employed segments of the population and provided a sprawling administrative and educational framework. Unlike German and Belgium colonial empires in Africa, which were built solely to exploit natural resources, without establishing a civil and societal framework, and horrifically abusing local populations and decimating local cultures, the French and British century-long presence often juxtaposed rather than superimposed its cultural imprint.

By hiring local employees at various levels, England was far more open to incorporating indigenous workers at all but management levels; working for foreign banks was a sign of social prestige and middle class status in India and even China. Lower-level clerical positions offered salary and conditions worthy of the middle or merchant class. In order to impose Western codes of behavior, Western dress, manners, and sports were inculcated. HSBC in India and China sponsored rugby and cricket soccer teams and matches, captured in carefully posed photographs in the 1880s and 1890s (see *HSBC Wall of History Archives*).

Introduced in France, and later implemented in all branches abroad, Henri Germain, head of Crédit Lyonnais from its inception in 1863 until his death in 1905, established strong, progressive labor policies and benefits. Germain, a moderate, post-1848 Catholic republican, and lifelong disciple of Saint-Simon, advocated that the entire community had to benefit, and that expansionary capitalism had to keep faith with democratic and community obligations. Crédit Lyonnais became the first financial institution to provide annual free medical examinations and paid leave for personnel from 3 p.m. on Saturdays. In the home office, amenities included separate lunch cafeterias for male and female employees, in respect of Victorian mores, with a garden for the ladies at the head office, and "spittoons for hygienic purposes," as well as a convalescent home and a vacation site. As early as 1875, Director General Jacques Letoumeur expounded: "Credit Lyonnais is an institution, but thank heaven, Credit Lyonnais is more than that, it is a family" (Montella 1987). Banks and large industrial corporations in France, Britain, and later Germany cultivated employee loyalty through "cradle to grave" policies and, from lower-level employees to senior management, encouraged employment from generation to generation.

The same principles were applied to the client base. Germain and his successor Mazaret developed the first marketing campaign for a bank, advertising its services in local newspapers and brochures, always ready to follow up with personal visits to local businesses. These new deposit banks differentiated themselves from the Bank of France, Banque Laffitte, and Rothschild Bank in name, concept, and client base. They would be called "credit," "comptoirs," "caisse," or "societe." They extended credit facilities to "newer capitalists," offered crossover services between the traditional activities of "haute banque" and "banque d'affaires," investment, and commercial banking. By 1865, Crédit Lyonnais and Société Générale were in direct competition with the Bank of France, being able to attract private capital by offering advantageous conditions, better levels of interest, and willingness to work "at any price and at all prices" (Bouvier 1961: 167). Its goals were

> To create a large client base in all classes of the population, as well among the craftsmen and small capitalists as among business merchants and rich industrialists. We want loyalty in our relationships, quick and efficient execution of transactions and fair conditions.
>
> (Bouvier 1961: 153)

Although the railroads democratized international and domestic finance by requiring greater numbers of subscribers, the new French industrialist class had to be coaxed and courted to entrust their private fortunes to banks. Henri Germain understood that in order to succeed, he would have to overcome profound distrust of banks, and provide a sense of institutional security more than a promise of profits. Henri Germain described this environment in a speech to shareholders in 1865: "The money today deposited in our bank, was in large part stashed away in drawers, providing no interest for those who safeguarded it, nor usefulness for society" (Bouvier 1961). Although there were large withdrawals after each financial crisis or drop in market value (1866, 1871, 1873, 1882), Germain always demanded that depositors be given absolute guarantee that there were significant reserves to cover any losses, and avert any panic run (Montella 1987).

T.S. Elliot was, from 1917 to 1920, an employee of Lloyds Bank, dealing with foreign exchange, acceptances, and documentary bills. A very senior banker meeting an acquaintance of Elliot expressed the following upon hearing of his reputation as poet and critic:

> You know, I myself am really very glad to hear you say that. Many of my colleagues wouldn't agree at all. They think that a Banker has no business whatever to be a poet. They don't think the two can combine.

He proceeds to approve of "his hobby," however emphasizing "we think he's doing quite well at the Bank. In fact, if he goes on as he has been doing, I don't see why – in time, of course, in time – he mightn't even become a Branch Manager" (Sutherland 1975: 244). This charming anecdote can serve as parable for the British and French financial sector through World War I. Functions, positions, and duties remained clearly defined and had to be clearly executed. Major financial institutions represented stability, longevity and social order against the dangers of an increasingly volatile world.

4.7 Monetary bipolarity

British, French, and German banks and credit institutions were the engine of extraordinary economic progress across Europe, and served as models for national banking systems and fledging capital markets from Brazil to Japan, from the United States to India and Indochina. Able to generate and control massive flows of capital, to stabilize and coordinate policies when necessary, and to insure monetary stability, banks and bankers should have enjoyed unadulterated levels of respect and admiration. Yet the very qualities which served them best, knowledge of esoteric instruments and market intricacies, cross-border contacts and the ability to provide funds for foreign governments and projects, close familial and long-term business alliances and connections, immense personal wealth and social connections fostering direct communication with governments, were the very qualities which were caricatured, criticized, and even demonized in the collective culture. British and French finance and stock markets ran the world, but banks, bankers, markets, and traders only affected a very small percentage of the overall demographic. For large swathes of the population, monetary transactions were limited to payments in cash, pawn brokers, bill collectors, moneychangers, usurers, and local markets and shops.

The nineteenth century formalized the irreconcilable differences between money as subject and money as object. Despite the anti-clericalism of the Revolution and the legacy of the Enlightenment, despite the republicanism and burgeoning democratization across Europe, the social mores of the aristocracy and inculcated principles of Christianity kept intact contempt and discrimination against monetary operations, agents and their instruments. The new middle classes seeking to emulate the aristocracy followed its rules of behavior in clothing, décor, manners, and proper subjects of conversation as studiously as Moliere's M. Jourdain in *Le Bourgeois Gentilhomme*. President of France, Francois Mitterrand, recalled how as a child: "In the family of little Francois, it was indecent to speak of money at the dinner table" (Daniel 1987). In France, as in Victorian England, inherent prejudices against money as unworthy made it an unacceptable topic in polite society or at the dinner table in respectable households, paradoxically judged to be too serious and too vulgar. Money was discussed in peasant and less refined households, but as a subject of complaint, dearth or need. Intellectuals, novelists, poets, artists, and playwrights propagated these attitudes and behavioral norms. Heroism and capitalism were dialectically opposed set of values, as reflected in the cult of Napoleon. La Martine, Stendhal, Hugo, and Byron could never reconcile the Napoleonic myth with the Napoleonic legacy of financial reform, the franc, the Bank of France, administrative, educational, and civil bureaucracy. Money as object, whether the basis of economic progress, exploitation, production, distribution or speculation, framed the political and social discourse of the nineteenth century. For the upper and middle class, beneficiaries of capitalism defined by accumulation and generation of wealth, property, and possessions, bipolarity of money-subject, open to condemnation and money-object, open to pragmatic justification, could never be fully resolved. They could function on parallel and separate tracts within the social coda, but in reality money-subject and money-object were inextricably inter-linked. Where Voltaire and the Encyclopedists had to justify "luxury" as good for the state (see Chapter 3), by the 1820s increased production, distribution, and accumulation of discretionary goods and income was proven beneficial to manufacturing, industrial and financial growth, and to society at large. In a passage strikingly relevant to the attacks against the compensation and life styles of top executives in the crisis of 2008, Karl Marx derided but brilliantly understood the effective power of materialism derived first from avarice and greed:

> But the progress of capitalist production not only creates a world of delights; it lays open in speculation and the credit system, a thousand sources of enrichment. When a certain stage of development has been reached, a conventional degree of prodigality, which is also an exhibition of wealth and consequently a source of credit, becomes a business necessity ... Luxury enters into capitals' expenses of representation.
>
> (Marx 1971a: 308)

For the next century, at the antipodes of economic and social theory the Church and Marxism would condemn capitalist accumulation as morally reprehensible. The banker was condemned by the right for democratization of capital and commerce, devoid of any national loyalty, and by the left as personification of greed and exploitation of the masses in the name of profit. In Hardy, Thackeray, Trollope, Dickens, Balzac, and Flaubert, acknowledgment or knowledge of monetary value, the working of business and finance was seen as a sign of crassness and middle class origins, yet lack of knowledge signified naïvety, and the potential victimization in an increasingly money based society.

Thackeray's Becky Sharp and Barry Lyndon, both unsavory charming parvenus, but Becky Sharp, her generation's better educated and better mannered Moll Flanders, understood relationships in terms of worth, Lyndon, weak and gullible, ended up in Fleet prison. Hardy's victim protagonists, the ironically named proletariat heroine, Tess d'Urbervilles, and the wistful and tragic, Jude the Obscure, pretend through false identities and names to move beyond their class. These works, like Flaubert's *Madame Bovary*, were condemned as immoral and licentious, for they violated moral and economic codes of behavior. Sex with those outside of one's rank was forbidden, as it translated into stealing into the middle class or lower aristocracy. Emma Bovary, victim of materialism, romanticism, and greed more than lust, attempts to transcend economic as well as social barriers, unable to do either Flaubert must give her a dramatic death in order to maintain her integrity and heroic identity. However, Flaubert's vicious sense of humor intervenes and the end of Madame Bovary is a more systematic condemnation of a money ruled society, as her husband dies destitute and the neglected ugly daughter is sent to the poorhouse. Nineteenth-century literature, immersed in sex and money, mirrored a society where social mobility, dependent on money, transformed all familial, sexual, and matrimonial relations into economic transactions.

4.8 Devalorization of value

In England, universal faith in the currency and the Bank of England should have evoked a sense of reverence and respect for finance but, in fact, only the institutions themselves were exempt from moral condemnation or ridicule. Under the restrictive moral and social codes imposed by the Victorian regime, sex and money were morally reprehensible subjects, therefore they had to be sanitized, purged, and transmuted into worthy endeavors: economic and physical procreation by increasing the wealth/demographics, aiding the poor, and improving social conditions. This paradigm, which permeated European literature in an early form of anti-capitalism under the guise of religious or moral values, extolled genteel poverty, characteristics most often attributed to female characters in Hugo, Dickens, Trollope, Balzac, Zola, and Dostoevsky. Exuberant pragmatism, tolerance, and bemusement expressed by eighteenth-century intellectuals toward merchant bankers, money men and brokers, regressed into snide morality and contempt fraught with hypocrisy.

> Our age is no better than we are; we live in an era of greed; no one troubles himself about the intrinsic value of a thing if he can only make a profit on it by selling it to somebody else; so he passes it on to his neighbor. The shareholder that thinks he sees a chance of making money is just as covetous as the founder that offers him the opportunity of making it.
>
> (Balzac 1961: 331)

Voltaire and Montesquieu, shunned in France, had to travel to London to find appreciation of the merchant class (see Chapter 3). By the 1850s, a subtle reversal occurred, as France eagerly embraced the principles of British capitalism, while British culture quietly acceded to French distrust and disdain of capitalism, its agents, operations, and even its institutions. Protestant pragmatism and Catholic ambivalence found common ground in the burgeoning left and entrenched right-wing political responses to finance, its practitioners and operations.

In order to reconcile these divergent societal responses, distinctions began to appear between the representation of banks and markets, separating bankers from traders and banking from speculation. Addressing the dilemma between the need for and the disgust with money, caught in an endless loop of moral recriminations and justifications, French authors needed to interpret financial success as a reflection of French prestige, while British authors had to look for rationale in the role of money in society. Balzac, Dickens, Heine, Trollope, Flaubert, Chekov, Turgenev, Dostoevsky, and Zola personally detested finance and money makers. Although intermittently successful and even well off, they had recurrent money problems, indebtedness, near foreclosure, bad investments, and dependency on inheritances, inciting a sense of insecurity and fear of business ventures and money, reflecting the woes of the middle classes across Europe. The world was stable, but individual fortunes were vulnerable to the whims of the market, unscrupulous business men, speculators, and personal losses in gambling and loss of family fortunes. Journalists, essayists, academics, and philosophers were even more at the mercy of ill paid jobs, loss of patronage, and lack of stable income.

Attitudes were also tinged with envy and anger, as the social mobility visible in English society in the Hanoverian period and promised to French society through the Revolution and Napoleonic meritocracy, receded into greater social calcification and rigidity. Discrepancies in wealth distribution increased in England and, after 1840, in France between the very wealthy and the middle class: "Merchants, industrialists, proprietors and rentiers held 53% of all wealth in Paris in 1820" (Ferguson 2001: 191). The figure rose to 81 percent in 1911. The British economy between 1850 and 1880 grew 130 percent, average earnings by 25 percent. The wealthy left estates so huge, they were equivalent to part of the national gross domestic product. In England Hardy and Trolloppe, in France, right-wing monarchist writers from Balzac to Taine, Bourget, Barres, and Drumont, judged bankers and financiers detrimental to the true ethos of hard work, labor, and land based dividends rather than profits gained by manipulating capital.

When, an impoverished and indebted Karl Marx, in London in 1848, compiled his lectures on economic theory in *Das Kapital*, codifying the semantic and philosophical relationship between money, commodities, labor, and society, he reflected a deep set antipathy and lack of trust in financial transactions, banks, stock markets, and all those employed in these professions. For Marx, the banker is a "hoarder" of reserves of capital, who acquires wealth produced by the labor of the exploited working class. His function as intermediary destroys the direct transactional relationship between the producer and the user of commodities. By introducing the question of private property, the *sine qua non* of the industrial/financial class emancipation from feudalism, and the greatest fear of the bourgeoisie, having witnessed or known of the disastrous re-appropriation of property during the French Revolution, Marx destabilized the frame of reference. As Niall Ferguson wrote, referring to Marx's Communist Manifesto:

> The notion of a fundamental conflict between morality and Mammon also informed the most successful "secular religion" of modern times. To Karl Marx and Frederich Engels, what was odious about their own class, the bourgeoisie was its ethos of "naked self interest" and callous cash payment.
>
> (Ferguson 2001: 1)

4.9 Dickensian capitalism

Dickens, on his first visit to America in 1841, was both shocked and impressed at the callousness of American business, comparing Wall Street to Lombard Street: "This narrow thoroughfare, baking and blistering in the sun is Wall Street: the Stock Exchange and Lombard Street of New York. Many a rapid fortune has been made in this street and many a no less rapid ruin" (Dickens

1842: 80). Dickens, on his return to New York in April 1868 as an honored author, expressed his admiration for America's progress in a public dinner speech , emphasizing the "amazing changes [...] vast new cities, changes in the growth of older cities almost out of recognition" and praised "the national generosity and magnanimity of Americans" (Dickens 2001: Addendum)

However in offering his panoramic view of contemporary British mores, Dickens responded to the ambivalence and distrust inherent in the public:

> "Papa, what's money?" ... Mr. Dombey was in a difficulty. He would have liked to give him some explanation involving the terms circulating medium, currency, depreciation of currency, paper, bullion, rates of exchange, value of precious metals in the market, and so forth; but looking down at the little chair and seeing what a long way down it was, he answered: "Gold, and silver, and copper. Guineas, shillings, half pence. You know what they are?"
>
> "Oh yes, I know what they are" said Paul. "I don't mean that, Papa. I mean what's money after all. I mean, what can it do?"
>
> (Dickens 1848: 92)

To Dickens, financial transactions such as speculation in stocks and currency fluctuations were symptoms of moral depravity. *Nicholas Nickleby* (1838–1839), *A Christmas Carol* (1843), and *Hard Times* (1854), present the acquisition of wealth as inimical to emotional fulfillment or moral worth. The financier is an impotent and solitary figure who finds solace only in his worldly possessions. Josiah Bounderby is cruel and tyrannical, Ebenezer Scrooge only shows affection for his bill-discounting business, and Dombey can only experience the sentiments of fatherhood once he becomes bankrupt and leaves the financial community. Nicholas Nickleby's Uncle Ralph is a notorious usurer who corrupts and defrauds in order to increase his hoard of riches. In *Martin Chuzzlewit* all characters are tainted by money in the enterprise of Anglo-Bengale Disinterested Loan and Life Assurance Company, where the morally bankrupt become worshippers of wealth and commerce for its own sake. Once money is deemed to be inherently evil, the speculator, banker, and businessman who cannot justify or redeem his profession has to be suitably punished. In *Little Dorrit* (1855–1857), Mr. Merdle's "wonderful bank" derives from usurious loans and shady dealings, Merdle's narcissism and megalomania reflected in his dishonest business practices. After his death, his banking empire is proven to be based on fraudulent accounts and fictitious assets. Dickens panorama of British finance placed the banker within a more insidious social structure: the banker as part of a bureaucracy of finance in which firms, banks, and all functions, from clerical to management, are interrelated.

The constant appeal of *A Christmas Carol* resides in translating the economic into a moral parable: Marley, unrequited miser is condemned to eternal damnation, Scrooge is redeemed after being terrorized by the demons of past genteel poverty, present infernal greed and selfishness, and future destruction through

lack of Christian charity. The story's enduring popularity was reflected in the
success of film versions created in England and Hollywood in 1938, 1951, 1970,
and 1984 and on television in 1999.

4.10 Balzacian to Saint-Simon capitalism

It is part of the folklore here that land and Catholicism have left the French
unfit for capitalism.

(Jane Kramer, *New Yorker*, August 6, 1984)

Decimated, exiled, and enraged, French aristocrats and clergy fostered an anti-
Revolutionary movement which fed on anti-capitalist and anti-republican sentiment. For Bonald and De Maistre, and their English sympathizers, Carlyle and
Edmund Burke, the Revolution had been a satanic abomination instigated by
dangerous mobs and money obsessed foreigners. Holding latent but pervasive
influence over major French intellectuals and novelists, they expounded against
commerce, banking, the newly emancipated middle class as usurpers and
idolaters. Balzac, fanatically monarchist, created a fictional universe in
which the impoverished nobility is the victim of careerists, rapacious financiers, and dangerous opportunists. where all financial transactions were vari-
ants of usury. In the rural setting of *Les paysans* (1844), Rigou and Soudry
purchase land in order to subdivide it for resale at usurious rates to their
debtors; In *Illusions perdues* (1843), the hero-victim Lucien de Rubempré's
perennial status as a debtor is cause for a lengthy diatribe against banking (see
Chapter 2). In *Le père Goriot* (1834), *Eugénie Grandet* (1833), *La Maison Nucingen* (1838), *Gobseck* (1830), and *Un homme d'affaires* (1845), banking functions solely for the purpose of enriching the individual banker. Social and
physical intercourse functions in a context of financial accumulation: dowries,
bonds, debts, and real estate. Balzac's *Comédie Humaine*, revolving around an
economic axis, introduced Rastignac, member of the impoverished nobility, who
willingly violates the ethos of his class and rank. Embracing the modern version
of medieval knighthood, financial rather than courtly conquest, Rastignac
embodies ambitious financial opportunism. In *La Maison Nucingen*, allowing his
hero to choose as model Nucingen, the most despicable embodiment of foreign
influence and raw financial manipulation, Balzac decries moral bankruptcy:

No creature whatsoever can be made to understand that the Baron yonder
three times did his best to plunder the public without breaking the letter of
the law, and enriched people in spite of himself. No one has a word to say
against him. If anybody should suggest that a big capitalist often is another
word for a cut-throat, it would be a most egregious calumny. If stocks rise
and fall, if property improves and depreciates, the fluctuations of the market
are caused by a common movement, a something in the air, a tide in the
affairs of men subject like other tides to lunar influences.

(Balzac 1961: 358)

Victor Hugo, great liberal novelist, essayist, and politician, in *Les Miserables* constantly refers to money in endless expositions of poverty and destitute characters. Jean Valjean, melodrama hero in his mythopoeic journey from misery of the ex-convict to the bourgeoisie to the moneyed middle class, distributes sous, francs, and livres, the different currencies still in circulation in post-Napoleonic France. When he rescues the little orphan Cosette, he gives her a large doll and a 20 franc gold piece, a vast fortune. Money for the poor is materiality as well as value, the tangible sound (argent sonnant) and feel of the coin. The new intangibles of monetary activity, balances, income, inheritance, and dowries, are abstract and meaningless. Money on paper and paper money cannot be trusted after the assignats and the Revolutions. Hugo, bitter enemy of Napoleon III, finished the work in 1860–1862, at the height of the Second Empire economic boom, but the story ends in 1833, the year of Guizot's propulsion of the French economy into the age of the railroad and industrial expansion. Jean Valjean leaves Marius and Cosette an inheritance of 630,000 francs, and one financial instrument, a "traite de 20,000 francs sur New York." He has converted the money of the poor into the money of the middle class.

Under the July monarchy of 1830–1848, the reigning middle class had not resolved its inherent sense of inferiority and identity. Guizot lent wealth creation respectability, on condition that it was used for the betterment of the state. The philosopher Auguste Comte set out the tenets formulated by his disciple Saint-Simon that a post-revolutionary social system had to have bankers, industrialists, and entrepreneurs in order to create capital mobility. But capitalist practices had to enrich the nation and its citizens, not serve as an end for personal gain.

Saint-Simon defined the ideal state as ruled by a small oligarchy, which would include scholars, artists, industrialists, scientists, and members of Parliament elected in free elections. Aligned with the old aristocracy by birth and modern socialism by belief, Saint-Simon wrote *l' Organisateur* and *Le Catechisme des industriels* in 1823, inspiring a generation of politicians and industrialists from Guizot to Napoleon III. Minister Guizot identified these leaders as enablers ("capacities") who would produce and govern in a society where industry, technocracy, and philosophy would coexist. Although clearly Utopian in its literal form, the application of these principles, as practiced by Saint-Simon's disciples, called for the acceptance of wealth and the reinvestment of private funds into banks, in order to promote and develop industrial, scientific, and technical enterprises which would benefit all social classes. By legitimizing wealth creation and prosperity, it granted the merchant class personal and social validation formerly reserved only for the aristocracy. This philosophy also called for centralized, oligarchic control over new national initiatives, such as railroads, mining, banks, financial press, and stock markets.

In May 1863, the government passed legislation which allowed companies with a minimum of 20 million francs to become "SARL" (limited liability in corporate statute) shareholder corporations. Napoleon III also recognized the importance of economic activity outside of Paris. The charter of Crédit Lyonnais was approved on July 27, 1863, with the initial capital subdivided into 40,000 shares. Lyon, for centuries an economic and trade hub, regained stature with the opening of the first deposit bank granted under the new legislature. The original shareholders from the ranks of government, industry, and finance included Henri German, Charles Sautter, who became the first director of Paribas in 1872; future president of Banque Indosuez, Arles-Dufour; Charles Hentsche, founder of Paribas and brother of Edward Hentsche, first president of Indosuez; Teissier director of the Lyons branch of the Banque de France; and Jacques Brettmayer, director of Docks et Entrepots de Marseille (Bouvier 1961).

In 1864, Société Générale's initial offering included 3,000 shares held by Crédit Lyonnais shareholders. After suffering important losses, following the precipitous drop in share value and ensuing bankruptcy of the Union General bank in 1882, Henri Germain limited portfolio exposure, tightened credit lines, reduced staff, and announced that the bank would mainly focus on short-term credit operations (Montella 1987). Crédit Lyonnais retained its independence until 1946, was nationalized under De Gaulle with Société Générale, was privatized in 1999 (see Chapter 5). The bank lost autonomy and identity in 2003, in the merger with Crédit Agricole (originally a mutual bank created for rural loans in 1894). Between 1830 and 1890, despite political turmoil, the Franco-Prussian War and market crashes of 1857, 1866, 1873, 1882, France maintained steady growth, a stable franc, and increased its gross domestic product from 9 billion French francs to 17.5 billion French francs (Beltran and Griset 1988).

In opposition to, and in parallel to, the Saint-Simon model of enlightened oligarchy and paternalistic industrial policy, concentrating on the expansion and prosperity of small and medium enterprises and banks, benign paternalism, France saw the rise of more radical forms of social systems, distribution, and production, led by Prudhon who opposed all interest bearing instruments, and Charles Fourier's utopist movement. The implementation of industrial and financial policy dictated by the state in the name of democratization and betterment of the nation, preserved Colbertian principles of economic nationalism. For Marx, Prudhon, Fourier, Valles, and Taine, broaching the subject from diametrically opposed points of view, the danger of capitalism resided in its displacement of the natural order. Despite the extraordinary speed and effectiveness of entry into the ranks of modern economic powers, the surge of activity is limited to a fraction of the population; in 1861 about 150,000 Frenchmen had listed shares in their portfolio. France still remained a nation of landowners, with a firm belief in gold and land and a deep distrust of paper and market instruments. The rapid industrial and financial transformation of France from the 1850s to the 1880s, established in the cultural sphere an economic typology, a mythic universe with a new theology within the capitalist pantheon. By the 1830s, popular culture, literature, and the arts had become obsessed with monetary, transactional, and commercial issues.

Napoleon III, under the tenets of Saint-Simon, like Marx, railed against Pauperism, a byproduct of capitalism, as detrimental to social order, but Marx's originality and potential danger was to understand that those marginalized by the forces of capitalism could also be energized as a countervailing force:

The greater the social wealth, the functioning capital, the extent and energy of its growth and, therefore also the absolute mass of the proletariat and the productiveness of its labor, the greater is the industrial reserve-army, [describing] the absolute general law of capitalist accumulation.

(Marx 1971: 346–347)

4.11 The middle class: ascension, ambivalence, nostalgia

Reflective of society's ambivalence toward the permeation of finance in personal and professional activities, British and French intellectual condemnation was in fact behind the curve throughout the century. Where monarchies, nobility, and merchant classes remained locked in adversarial and ambivalent class struggles in Eastern and Southern Europe, South America and Asia, England reached a comfortable consensus on the integration of industrial, financial, and commercial wealth at the highest echelons of society. England would be the standard bearer for the merchant, tradesman, banker, financier, tax collector, and insurance and stockbrokers' ascension from the alleys and back rooms, the ghettos and moneychangers stalls, to the exchanges, commercial houses, banks, and investment firms. Unique in its tolerance of landed gentry, new and old aristocracy, and wealthy merchants sharing power, it brought about a total realignment of urban social stratification and political power. European monarchies, after the French Revolution and the beheading of Louis XVI, no longer able to claim divine right, had to grudgingly concede to a public interdependency between money and power. As economies developed, the wealthy merchants, bastions of the new middle class with its own gradations between lower and upper middles class, "petite et haute bourgeoisie," became the engine of economic growth, standard bearers of financial development as well as financial culture. The wealthy merchant, able to buy land, property, title, and political power was no longer dependent on the favor or need of the monarchy. Yet centuries of rigid class distinctions and societal barriers could not be eliminated by economic contingencies or even violent political upheaval. The English or French tradesman, granted a title through recognition for his wealth creation, and through awareness of his newly gained political clout, never overcame a sense of atavistic insecurity and "nostalgie de la monarchie." Through the 1840s, despite proclamations of meritocracy and republicanism, despite the cult of Napoleon, which resonated throughout Europe, literature portrayed an affluent middle class in quest of elusive nobility:

Sir William Lucas had been formerly in trade in Meryton where he had made a tolerable fortune, and had risen to the honour of knighthood by an address to the king during his mayoralty. The distinction had perhaps been felt too strongly. It had given him a disgust to his business and to his residence in a small market town; and quitting them both, he had removed with his family to a house about a mile from Meryton, denominated from that period Lucas Lodge, where he could think with pleasure of his own importance, and unshackled by business, occupy himself solely in being civil to all the world.

(Austen 1922: 240)

With elegant sarcasm, Austen gently ridiculed the pretensions and the sudden aversion to the very activities that now allowed a life of leisure. The goal of this new class of knighted merchant is to bask in their mythologized version of the life style of the landed gentry.

Stendhal in *Le Rouge et le Noir: Chronique de 1830*, created a more sophistic-ated version of this conflict in the juxtaposition of an anachronistic set of values. M. de Renal underwent a similar metamorphosis: "Since 1815 he was ashamed to be an industrialist: 1815 made him mayor of Verrieres" (Stendhal 1960: 35). For Stendhal's hero, Julien Sorel, money is only acceptable as an unspoken, invisible security shield which allows higher moral values of honor and heroism to flourish. Stendhal's narrative intervention in chapter II superimposes a monetary subtheme on the thematic and semantic structure of the novel: "To Earn Income" (ibid.: 38), the repetitive and capitalized emphasis on this term asks the reader to displace the initial presentation of the young romantic hero into a specific socio-economic framework. Julien is offered numerous forms of accommodation with his society (his salary, described in precise sums), a position with his accountant wood mer-chant friend Fouquet: "You will keep the books. I earn big in my business" (ibid.: 98), and finally a chance to achieve his goal of social ascension through the Marquis de la Mole: "10,000 francs ... and land" (ibid.: 438). Julien himself is treated as a commodity, bought by M. de Renal from his father, and bought for Mathilde de la Mole by the Marquis, in exchange for giving Julien a new identity as titled M. de la Vernaye. From illiterate, vulgar peasant stock, Julien Sorel could now bask in his grand title, but Stendhal in order not to compromise his hero's integrity, can only kill him off in an extravagant death reminiscent of a baroque drama. In the societal structure of 1830, economic survival and idealism are anti-thetical and the hero must choose moral or financial bankruptcy.

Three decades of political vacillations of empire to monarchy to republic to empire, provoked reverse discrimination and opportunism, described in Flau-bert's brutal social satire, *L'Education Sentimentale*, describing the banker M. Dambreuse in the 1840s:

M. Dambreuse's real name was the Count of Ambreuse, but from 1825 on, dropping little by little his title and party, he turned toward business, and attuned to all businesses, a hand in all enterprises.... He had amassed a seemingly considerably fortune; furthermore he was officer of the Legion of Honor, member of the general assembly of the Aube region, deputy, soon to be "Pair to France."

(Flaubert 1951 [1869]: 55)

The reigning middle class, not born to privilege, rank or inherited fortune, was constantly in the process of simultaneously acquiring and justifying its attempts to gain wealth and power. Jean-Paul Sartre in *L'Idiot de la Famille: Gustave Flaubert de 1821 a 1857* (1971), interpreting Flaubert through the prism of Marxist psychoanalysis, viewed his contempt for the bourgeoisies as the leisured middle class ambivalence toward earned versus inherited wealth. The themes of inheritance and dowry, which permeate the works of Austen, Dickens, Trollope, Thackeray, Balzac, Flaubert, Maupassant, and Zola as well as Westernized Russian authors, reflected a conflicted capitalist society in transition between being born to the manor and buying the manor. The importance of arranged marriages, dominant social determinants since Shakespeare's comedies and *Le Roman Bourgeois'* transactional marriage scale (see Chapter 3), equally affected noble families and the ranks of the bourgeoisie. In transition third to first world economies, India, South East Asia, South America, and the Middle East, arranged marriages, complex inheritance litigation, and limited rights for widows continue to permeate the culture as they affect economic mobility and ensure that fortunes are preserved within family dynasties.

4.12 The gentleman banker

Literature and intellectuals condemned the banker, portraying him as a formulaic caricature, yet popular representation simultaneously revered him as a model of decorum emblematic of British business ethos and mores. The "British banker" impressed itself upon the collective imagination throughout the nineteenth century and continued well beyond the actual hegemony of British finance into the 1980s, associated with the investment houses in the City. "In 1983 English bankers are still English gentlemen, yet aware that the winds of change are coming, even at Warburg" (Ferris 1984: 209). The last Barings to run the bank before its dramatic demise in 1995, was Peter Baring, named chairman in 1989: "he was well liked by his peers in the City and was one of the last gentlemen bankers. But his grasp of details was sometimes tenuous. Even when he was finance director, he occasionally got lost among the figures" (Fay 1996). Bastions of sound policy, based on stable, long-term relationships with Treasury, the Crown, in the person of Queen Victoria, and the public, the institutions and gentlemen of Lombard Street were not only guardians of the British economy, they were models of comportment and behavior which reflected these principles.

The Degas paintings *A la Bourse* (1878–1879), and *The Cotton Exchange at New Orleans* (1873), depict brokers and bankers in the "coulisses" of the Paris Exchange or the floor of the commodity exchange sharing rumors and tips, checking price sheets in the crowded hallway, all garbed in identical fashion as the portraits and photographs of Baring, Rothschild, Peabody, Morgan, Casel, Bischoffheim, Bamberger, Germain, Lazard, and Warburg. Men of finance observing certain rules of fashion, whether slightly disreputable brokers, traders and speculators, or highly respected bankers, all show striking homogeneity in appearance and dress: large, portly, impeccably tailored, middle aged men in black suits, silk cravats, and top hats, sporting elegant mustaches or beards, they impart solidity, calm, imperviousness, and trust. Around the world, for over a century, all bankers became British bankers in appearance, with few modifications in the cut of the suits and homburgs replacing top hats. Even when history long surpassed the image, reducing it to stereotype and even caricature (the fathers in J.M. Barrie's *Peter Pan* (1904–1911) and P.L. Travers' *Mary Poppins* (1934) are Victorian bankers), they are regarded with nostalgic solicitude, representative of a past age of economic and financial stability.

Banking and finance in the nineteenth century changed from a series of functions and operations to a profession. Evolving from separate trading, brokerage, stock jobbing, commercial lending and credit facilities, banks became depository institutions, and custodians of private fortunes, establishing formal distinctions between private, commercial, and credit and thrift institutions. In 1879, HSBC established an "Institute of Bankers" which standardized training for apprentice bankers. In order to graduate, the students had to pass a written examination in political economy, practical banking, commercial law, arithmetic and algebra, and bookkeeping, a comprehensive curriculum for the functions involved in middle management and account officers ranks. Paradoxically, as the profession became more technical and esoteric, market and banking terminology was researched and incorporated into literature, theater, and the press, precise technical and numerical references to foreign exchange, bonds, ledgers, contractual agreements, dowry, land income, stocks, trading options, arbitrage, and rate of exchange proliferated.

The characters Merdle, Melmotte, Nucingen, Dambreuse, Saccard, and even M. de Renal, and the Marquis de la Mole, modeled on real bankers and international financiers, are depicted as overbearing adversaries who hold total control over institutional power, money and politics. They are father figures, mentors and protectors, yet by these very characteristics they can also deny the means of advancement or control success. Often appearing older, sedentary, posed in their offices and homes, surrounded by their wealth, like the medieval merchant with his gold coins and strongbox:

> A valet appeared, and introduced Frederic into a small room where one could clearly see two deposit boxes.... From afar because of his thin size, he could appear still young ... A merciless energy resided in his steely eyes, colder than glass.
>
> (Flaubert 1951 [1869]: 55)

Zola's Saccard seems younger, imbued with a nervous energy: "his black creased puppet face with pointed nose and small shiny eyes" (Zola 1891: 13).

In the archives of HSBC, a book of cartoons was discovered drawn by a clerk at London Joint Stock Bank *circa* 1895, entitled *Bankers at Play*, showing a charming scene of four spry bankers playing tennis, one in boating attire with stripped jacket and straw hat, the other three in proper vest, ascot, striped pants and spats; two of them still wearing their top hats although divested of their coats. Like W.H. Hamilton's cartoon nearly a century later in the *New Yorker*, it offers a rare glimpse of the dual nature of this creature and creation (HSBC History Wall c. 1895).

4.13 La Banque de France: hate the banker, revere the bank

But while the banker could be reviled, the bank was revered as a stable institution which guaranteed the nation the security and strength it sought to project. The tragic misalignment of the ideals of the Paris Commune and the interests of the Banque de France epitomized the paradox and the ambivalence which would characterize French attitudes toward bank and banker for the next century.

When the Franco-Prussian War broke out July 14, 1870, France's financial, political and industrial nexus functioned under the banner of "chateau, banque, usine" (palace, bank, factory). Treasury and government officials had joint appointments in the largest companies and on the Board of directors of the Bank of France. Eugene Schneider, head and founder of Creusot, was Regent of the Banque de France, president of the Legislature, and advisor to Empress Eugenie. In February 1871, after the bitter, famine ridden siege of Paris, in a fit of patriotic fervor, the populace and Paris National Guard refused to surrender its last canon, officially declaring its autonomy in the Commune on March 18, 1871. The bourgeoisie at first outraged by the capitulation remained in Paris, but once the Commune asserted its power, retreated to Versailles. The Communards, composed of disgruntled soldiers, naïve intellectuals, enthusiastic journalists, and thousands of workers, tried to construct a peoples' republic, to implement separation of church and state, and educational reforms, but within two chaotic months they turned violent, killing an archbishop, and were unable to fend off the return of the Army to Paris in May 1871. Troops marched into Paris on May 21, and in one week killed almost 20,000 mainly unarmed Communards. The event suppressed in French history books, became a symbol of socialist resistance for Lenin, Marx, and Brecht, but a theme of horror and fear of mob rule for right and center right intellectuals including Flaubert and Hugo, Taine and Zola.

The Commune government finance committee elected Jourde, former employee of the Bank of France, to act as intermediary with bank officials in Paris and Versailles. Jourde, unable to confront Rouland, the governor of the Bank, and despite the urgent need of the Commune, consistently opposed any rash measures, absolutely refusing to confiscate the reserves in the vaults of two billion gold francs and 214 million francs in securities. The Commune asked Rothschild for a loan of 500,000 francs, while the City of Paris had on the books a credit of nine million francs. While the Bank promised neutrality, it actually provided loans to Versailles of 257 million francs in order to replenish the army and combat the Commune. Beslay, commissioner in charge of finances of the Central Committee insisted: "Is it not established that the Bank as the depository of wealth and the center of credit represents the national patrimony, whose vitality is a matter of interest not only to France but to the whole civilized world?" (Lissagaray 1886). Lissagaray, historian of the Commune, observed that while the Commune held Versailles hostage, in reality the Communards were duped by Versailles into believing that any attack on the Bank of France would endanger French industry, commerce, and that promissory notes would be worthless. The Commune also refused to nationalize factories and private businesses, and kept the tax structure intact. Respect for the institution was greater than revolutionary fervor as the Commune was literally and figuratively starved for lack of funds. Beslay protected the assets of the bank, insisting until the end that consumer and general confidence resided in the bank: "la finance sacro-sainte." Marx, in his writings to Engel on the Paris Commune, *The Paris Commune of 1871* (1971) praised the concepts but regretted that the Commune had not heeded his advice: "The only social measure which the Prudhonists put through was not to confiscate the Bank of France and this was partly responsible for the downfall of the Commune" (letter to Engels, January 1873). Whether the Communards could have survived longer with the funds of the Bank was never resolved, but what remains more troubling is that, out of respect and faith in the institution, they never even tried. The lessons were learnt as Lenin appropriated the reserves of the Imperial Bank of Russia in 1917, and Fidel Castro, Chase Manhattan's assets in Havana in 1959.

4.14 Traders, speculators, brokers: the evil of the market

In England and France, as in the United States after the Civil War, the market is a source of deep ambivalence, as speculators are both sharks and innovators, benefiting the economy by investing in new inventions, railroads, industry, factories, and urban and maritime investment. However, a distinction has to be made between pure speculation and investment.

> Look at these public works, these manufacturers, factories, credit institutions who help spread affluence. Wealth, which improves and consolidates the living standards of all working classes and tell me whether this transformation is not due to the principle of which agiotage is the extreme point, that speculation is not ... the linkage which unites all these resources and multiplies the power.
>
> (Courtois quoted in Plessis 1983: 45)

There was an irreconcilable dilemma, as intellectuals condemned and admired the importance of finance and financial activity. There was a sense that, by allowing all to participate, the agent de change was truly an agent of change in the societal and psycho-cultural sense. An active financial press of 4,000–5,000 copies with six daily sheets, offered quotes and information. Most of the population was far too poor to save, much less invest or begin to acquire shares. The average salary of small shopkeepers, civil servants and clerks was 1,500 francs a year, the average share cost approximately 250 francs. Yet this small income for an individual or a family represented the middle class, as the poor or the educated working class "proletariat de bacheliers," receiving an unexpected inheritance or stipend were thrilled to have 40 francs a month in 1879, as described by former Communard, Jules Valles, who offered a rare glimpse into an itemized monthly budget:

> Tobacco 4.50; newspaper 1.50; library fee 3; candle 1.50; laundry 1.00; soap .20; sewing kit .10; rent 6 ... Food lunch time, half meat 0.20, 2 rolls

0.10; evening meal half meat 020; vegetables 0.10; 2 rolls = 0.70 daily, 21.00 per month, extraneous expenses 1.20.

(Valles 1970: 68–69)

The middle and upper middle class tended to be very conservative, investing in real estate and in land and large farm holdings. The country was 70 percent rural, a figure which remained in place through the 1950s. Although all social classes could take part in bonds, stocks and shares holdings, in reality most wealthy outside of Paris limited their investments to land, and had to be coaxed into opening accounts in the new deposit banks like Crédit Lyonnais, Société Generale, and Crédit Agricole. Treasury bonds, seen as the safest, were more prevalent. By 1870, the number of shareholders of companies listed on the bourse was about 150,000. In 1861 a bond issue by the Bank of France for rail-roads attracted over 53,000 subscribers, about one-third in Paris; only a very small group of very rich invested in foreign bond issues. There were 16,000 Bank of France stock holders and 1,000 for Crédit Lyonnais. Shares in valued old companies and in railroad bonds were passed on as part of inheritance.

Overall, France remains averse to market speculation, a combination of post traumatic disorder since the Law scandal, reinforced by the lack of faith in paper after the assignats, and further hardened by the moral climate expressed in literature and popular culture, which analogizes speculation to gambling:

A menace to the established order as the regent Lafond, denounced to his colleagues of the Bank of France in 1852 "the fury of gambling" which he says "inflames deplorable urges and insatiable venality which not the least feeds into socialism."

(Bellet 1983: 56)

In 1834, a play entitled *L'Auberge des Adrets* created the character of Robert Macaire, played by the famous actor Frederick Lemaitre, and his witless victim, M. Gogo. These characters become the prototype for the persuasive, dishonest speculator and the gullible investor, appearing in Charles Philippon's drawings, Paul de Kock's 1844 novel, *M. Gogo a la Bourse*, and the best known illustrations in the satirical paper *Charivari*, where the brilliant cartoonist Daumier publishes his satirical lithographs, capturing the dealings of brokers, traders, swindlers, and investors. Prudhon, Dumas, and Feydeau repeat the leitmotiv, which dominates popular representation of money, finance, and market stereotypes. The stock market, the bourse, becomes a place of diabolical maneuvers and lost innocence. Roger Bellet wrote: "the attraction of the Bourse was that of a foreign land, an exotic population, an isolated world within Paris, an ethnic entity with its own customs, pathology" (Bellet 1983: 54). There are vaudeville farces like Clairville's *La Bourse au Village*, Ponsard's satire on capital flight from the country to Paris, and important serious treatises. Prudhon's *Manuel du Speculateur a la Bourse*, published in 1854, sold more than 22,000 copies, attracting a wide audience despite its 420 pages, technical information on operations, instruments, including attributing to the bourse prophetic and conspiratorial elements. Decades before Zola's analogy of the Stock Exchange to a temple, Prudhon wrote:

> La politique a ses palais, la religion ses églises, l'industrie ses manufactures et ses chantiers, le commerce a ses ports, le capital a ses banques: pourquoi la Speculation seriat – elle demeurée a l'etat de pure abstraction? La BOURSE est le temple de la Speculation. La Bourse est le monument par excellence de la societe modern [politics has its palaces, its religion, its churches, industry its factories and construction sites, commerce its ports, capital has its banks: why should Speculation remain pure abstraction? The STOCK EXCHANGE is the temple of Speculation. The Stock Exchange is the one real monument of modern society].
>
> (Prudhon quoted in Bellet 1983: 56)

In 1857, the radical journalist Jules Valles published a satirical diatribe against the stockmarket, *L'Argent par un homme de lettres devenu homme de Bourse*, subtitled *L'argent: rentiers, agioteurs, and millionnaires*. The cover had an enlarged picture of an ecu d'or worth five francs surrounded by the phrase: "J'en vaux cinq au controle et cent dans la coulisse," mockingly dedicated to the Jewish financier Jules Mires. Valles, who had worked for a broker, knew the inner workings and language of the Parisian stock market he described as the "City Hall of the New Republic," where knowledge of financial operations, brokerage, deals, and money markets replaced humanistic values.

Alain Plessis and Roger Bellet analyzed how the French stock market reopened after the Revolution in 1796, established in the Palais de la Bourse in 1826; it began with little fanfare and only 30 listed companies. Losing most of its value in the market collapse and crisis of 1848 it only regained momentum in the coup of December 2, 1851, which brought Napoleon III to power. The Second Empire started a long bull market through the mid-1860s. Between 1852 and 1857, the market boomed, based on easing of credit and lowering of discount rates at the Bank of France window. Despite some setbacks in the ensuing years of 1858–1869, the number of stocks quoted rose from 118 in 1850, to 407 in 1869, mainly in railroads, banks, and insurance. France, like England, was home to immense personal fortunes, no longer limited to land or inherited wealth but in stocks, bonds, and diversified portfolios. In 1866, at his death, the Regent of the Bank of France left his only son a diversified portfolio of over one million francs in bank shares, including National Life and Fire Insurance shares, Russian, Austrian and Egyptian securities, and a stock portfolio of railroad shares.

Finance was dramatized and satirized in the theater, explained in lengthy treatises, and discussed in salons and cafés. Among the most popular and well received were: Oscar de Vallee, *Les Manieurs d'Argent, etude historique et morale 1720–1857*; Edmond About's play, *Ces coquins d'agents de change* (1861); a legal treatise by Bozerian on *La Bourse, ses operations et ses operateurs* in 1859; Ernest Feydeau, of society farce fame, *Un coup de bourse* (1868), and in 1873, *Memoires d'un Coulissier;* Dumas fils' play *La question d'argent* (1857), which

Jules Mires took as a personal attack, had a resounding success, as did *l'Honneur et l'Argent* by Ponsard, lauded personally by Napoleon III for its morality.

Both left and right were deeply ambivalent about speculative activities. On moral grounds, the basic paradox was that speculation, even short-term stock speculation on gold against paper shares, "agiotage," so bitterly attacked in the eighteenth century, was an essential part of market activity which moved forward industrial and commercial infrastructure urban expansion across France.

After the Franco-Prussian War, anti-capitalist literature took on xenophobic and nationalistic stridency. Jules Claretie's *Le million* (1882), Alphonse Daudet's *Le nabab* (1877), and Emile Zola's *L'Argent* (1891), dealt with the realm of finance as a mythic battlefield of conflicting moral and theological values. Jean-Richard Bloch's *Et cie* (1917), and Anatole France's *L'île des pingouins* (1908), highly regarded authors taught in French schools included anti-Semitic tirades and digressions that emphasized Jewish bankers' supposed international contacts, excessive venality, and subversive beliefs.

Flaubert's retroactive analysis of the events of 1840–1848 in *L'Education Sentimentale* (1951 [1869]), has the protagonist, Frederic Moreau, undertook the prototypical journey/quest of intellectual, emotional, professional, and commercial endeavors only to systematically fail at each one, yet managing to survive, by a compromise toward mediocrity which involved acceptance of financial contingencies. Like speculators in the market, Frederic ignores the present in anticipation of possible future gain. When temporarily disinherited, he sees his identity as potential lover demolished, whereas a new inheritance reestablishes not only his financial status, but his very ability to identify himself as a lover, a financial, and therefore a sexual achiever.

> Twenty-seven thousand pounds of income! and a frenzied joy overtook him, at the idea of seeing once more Mme. Arnoux with the sharpness of a hallucination. He saw himself seated next to her, in her home, bringing her some gift wrapped in silk paper.
>
> (Flaubert 1951 [1869]: 129)

When Frederic invests in stocks, the rise and fall of his stocks take on a psychological dimension:

> Three days later, at the end of June, the shares of "Nord" went up 15,000 francs, as he had bought 2,000 last month, he found himself enriched by 30,000 francs. This kiss of fate gave him new confidence. He told himself that he didn't need anyone.
>
> (Ibid.: 260)

But,

> At the end of July, an inexplicable fall brought down the shares of "Nord." Frederic had not sold his: he lost 60,000 francs all at once. His income was

substantially reduced. He would have to either cut back his expenses, take up a position, or make a good marriage.

(Ibid.: 266)

Frederic himself has no personality; he is reduced to a puppet that reacts according to monetary pressures, amounts, and trends which he cannot even control.

If French financial discourse of the Second Empire opens with Valles' *L'Argent* in 1857, it closes with Emile Zola's *L'Argent*, part of his great panorama, *Les Rougon-Macquart, Natural and Social History of a Family under the Second Empire* in 1891.

Zola's completely negative portrayal of the Stock Exchange, offers no naïve young protagonist to counteract or be corrupted by the venality and amorality of the banker hero: Saccard. The myth of chivalry, erotic quest or military heroism does not need to be displaced into the secular realm, as the entire text represents a mythological rendition of a modern version of hell. The Stock Market is analogized to the temple of a pagan, sacrificial cult where all moral and ethical considerations have already been eliminated. Saccard functions within a descending spiral of financial success, stock manipulations, rapid reversals, collapse, fraudulent dealings, disgrace, and eventual resurgence. Zola's linear narrative transcends the individuals involved, focusing on condemnation and eventual salvation of the instrument itself: money.

In Zola, after catastrophe strikes the participants in Saccard's fraudulent stock manipulation, the building alone remains intact, an abandoned mausoleum, the sole survivor in the apocalyptic metaphor:

And the Exchange, grey and dull, stood out, in the melancholia of the catastrophe, which, for a month had left it deserted, open to the four winds, like a market emptied by famine. It was the fatal epidemic, intermittent, its pillage sweeping through the market every 10 or 15 years, the black Fridays, as they are named.... It takes years to rebuild confidence, to reconstruct banking houses till the day where, the passion for the game slowly revitalized, ignites anew and the adventure starts again, bearing a new crisis, destroying all in a new disaster.

(Zola 1891: 413)

In France and Germany, since 2000 there has been the slow dismantling of nineteenth-century corporate governance, closed doors, incestuous boards, arcane accounting, opaque supervisory mechanisms, and a gradual acceptance of the role and voice of shareholders. Large multinational corporations have accepted cultural shifts, however, the assumption remains that structural changes should be brought about by the government not the private sector, hence the schism and the paradox. In the financial crisis of 2008, the reassertion of government influence and outright control has been more a source of comfort in France, but a source of deep ambivalence in Germany, as expressed by Chancellor

Merkel's hesitancy to impose government run bailouts, and the extreme reluctance of German banks to accept bailouts. In France, although profit is now more openly recognized as a motive for the French corporate class, social responsibility remains a subtext in the political and corporate discourse. The population at large has never crossed over from the sense that the government is still creator and guarantor of jobs and security: an emotional lender of last resort. In the past decade, despite an almost totally privatized corporate, financial, and media sector, France remains highly ambivalent about the Anglo-American model of non-state intervention. A survey in April 2006, at the University of Maryland showed that only 36 percent of French are in favor of "free enterprise and market economy as the best system for the future." Of 20 countries surveyed: United States = 71 percent, Germany = 65 percent, China = 74 percent, Spain = 63 percent, United Kingdom = 67 percent and Russia = 43 percent, France has the lowest score in overall faith in the system.

This is not a new paradox, nor a new battle, the lines in many ways have been drawn since the early nineteenth century, a constant push and pull between the Revolution and "nostalgie de la monarchie," which still dominates French political, social, and economic life. The *New York Times* article on February 17, 2008 (Schwartz and Bernhold), on the Jerome Kerviel trading scandal and losses at Société Générale: "Where the Heads no longer roll," describes the closed elite circle of the Club of 100, created in France as a gastronomy society of wealthy Parisian businessmen in 1912. This club is "a close knit brotherhood – it's nearly all male – that shares school ties, board memberships and rituals like hunting and wine tasting." The members include Daniel Bouton; Claude Bebear, retired founder and CEO of AXA; Fourtou, head of Vivendi; and Michel Pebereau of BNP. Bebear remarked in the article: "the CEO of a French company is more of a monarch than in the US [monarque eclairé]." Often called "godfather of French capitalism," Bebear was replaced in 2000 at AXA by Henri de Castries, also a graduate of ENA. De Castries' ancestor was naval minister under Louis XVI, and his grandfather was ambassador to the United States under De Gaulle. Over half of France's "CAC 40" is run by graduates of ENA and or Polytechnique. Like Bouton, the new head of Société Générale, Francois Oudea, is a graduate of ENA and Polytechnique whose prior positions include the Ministry of Finance, Economy and Budget from 1987 to 1995. In France as in Germany, many bankers at major institutions have lifelong careers; many have second or third generation or alliances through marriage to their institutions. It is part of a French tradition since the Restoration and July Monarchy of 1830 that top officials move between positions in industry, high finance, and government, often maintaining government positions simultaneously with board memberships in each of these sectors.

Chirac, in his first term 1995–2002, was ineffective in combating this inbred system, alienating rather than integrating the business community which put him in power. He tried half heartedly and failed to undo what an article in the *Banker* (January 1996), described as: "A system of cross shareholdings, interlocking boards and shareholder pacts that permits them to exert control, even though in the minority at the expense of profitability." The insiders waltz or "pantouflage" continues. The term refers to the word for slipper, a metonym for cozy, familial arrangements.

In the 2008 crisis, France has proven that it can respond efficiently and aggressively to the demands of the market. But the conundrum remains: in order to be effective, it has to define its own version of capitalism, which respects elitism, oligarchy, and dirigisme, in the name of French competitiveness and prestige. It is a form of capitalism which rewards innovation, creativity and risk taking, but within a tightly structured societal and intellectual framework:

> We are very suspicious of money and any sign that you possess too much of it, while at the same time there is this inventiveness, creativity, willingness to become an entrepreneur which is not often seen as a strength of our country, but which I think is.
>
> (Dickey 2009)

In Britain, the extraordinary success of the past decade and the weight of history in favor of individual initiative and profit have created a severe crisis of confidence, as the government has had to intervene and rescue the stars of British finance. The crisis of 2008 invoked the ghosts of pre-Thatcher, economically depressed, and government dependent markets and industrial sectors. It has proven that the economy has become too finance-centric and too willing to follow the United States in methodology and culture. However, fundamentally Britain has long, solid financial traditions, and the prestige, weight, and power of its banks has proven their historic resilience and ability to withstand global shocks and to recuperate.

4.15 Prussian to German financial power

In 1815, each of Germany's 35 principalities and four free city states had full sovereignty over their coinage and monetary systems. Economic historian Carl-Ludwig Holtfrerich makes the following point:

> The feudal – albeit often enlightened – elites governing the principalities were interested in the preservation of local traditions not only because they hoped to advance the economic cause of their own state..., but also because they had a vested interest in defending independent fiscal revenue sources for the prince and his court in a period when bourgeois strata of society had already ... curtailed the prince's free hand in taxation matters.
>
> (Holtfrerich 1989)

A large array of coins circulated, including French, Russian, Danish, and British monies with little or no parity. The thaler in Prussia and the gulden in the South and Austria dominated, linked to silver, while Bremen as a port city had to adopt the Gold Standard. The states issued paper money of dubious convertibility, moneychangers, and banks benefited from the high cost of these transactions but it hampered industry and cross regional commerce. The Zollverein Treaty of 1835, followed by the Munich Coinage Treaty in 1837, established that the gulden was to have legal tender status in all states. A Dresden Coinage Convention in 1838 extended the zone and the government of Saxony proposed a fraction of the Prussian thaler as legal standard for all member states. Although rejected at the time, in order to facilitate gulden and thaler exchanges, a so-called "Champagne Thaler" (the price of a bottle of champagne) was suggested. The reference implied that this was the realm of the rich, but as more and more German commerce was denominated in paper notes, the thaler gained support as daily currency. Austria, on a paper standard with a fairly well functioning central bank, passed the Vienna Coinage Treaty of 1857, linking its coinage to the Zollverein.

Paper money was not readily accepted nor trusted, as illustrated in Goethe's interchange in *Faust II* (see Chapter 3). Different principalities issued notes, but they were not convertible across Germany and the army and the population had to be paid in coin. By the mid-1860s, powerful bankers and industrialists called for a new currency, the mark, and introduction of the Gold Standard, in order to link the German currency to the British pound. The unification of Germany under Bismarck, rapidly followed by the defeat of France in 1870, and the issue of French war reparations of five billion gold francs, settled the currency issue and consolidated monetary policy. Pushed by bankers, Bamberger and Soetbeer, Germany accepted the Gold Standard in the Coinage Act of December 4, 1871. Currency standards based on the value of the mark were established in 1873, and the Banking Act of March 14, 1875 established the Reichbank, modeled on the Bank of England. Unlike the Bank of France and the Bank of England, the Reichbank was subordinate to, rather than in cooperation with, the government. The Banking Act named the Reich's chancellor as head of the Reichbank, giving Bismarck unsurpassed power over financial and political institutions. This formulation remained in effect through the Third Reich. The disastrous consequences of this consolidation post-World War I and during the Nazi era led the charter of the Bundesbank to declare itself totally independent, the principle upon which the European Central Bank would be established.

German financial culture is intricately linked with the rise of independent banking houses, mostly Jewish, in the eighteenth century. These banking dynasties, the Rothschilds; the Goldschmidt who originated in Frankfurt; the Oppenheimer in Cologne; and Bischoffsheim in Mainz, through marriage and family alliances established correspondent banking houses in Brussels, Paris, London, and Vienna in the Napoleonic era. "There was something asymmetrical in almost every aspect of German Jewish coexistence: disproportionately prominent in the free professions, in law, medicine and journalism, a major presence in trade and banking; disproportionately wealthy" (Stern 2006: 20). In finance, fully assimilated but never fully accepted by the Kaisers and German bankers, German Jewish bankers benefited from their international contacts which offered greater security when necessary and the ability to finance major cross-border projects. Salomon Oppenheim, born in 1772, like Barings, expanded his father's trading house in oil, cotton wine, and tobacco, setting up a bank and currency exchange business in Cologne. Therese Oppenheim, his wife, became renowned for her own banking acumen from 1828 to 1842. Their son, Simon von Oppenheim, granted a title by the Kaiser, financed German industrial undertakings including the Rheine railroad consortium and insurance, with the powerful Fould family in Paris. Marrying into the Rothschild family in 1834, their joint interests led to diversification in French German assets after the crisis of 1848. German and German Jewish banks worked in unison, such as the Schiffs and the Speyers. In New York, the transplanted houses of Kuhn Loeb, Lehman maintained close interrelations with Morgan and Deutsche Bank through a network of representatives. Banker and philanthropist Otto Kahn, trained with Deutsche Bank's London office, took a position at Speyer and Co., and married into the Kuhn Loeb family. Like their French and British counterparts, these bankers sat on each other's boards, on the boards of their clients, built palatial residences and offices in Cologne and in Paris, and were instrumental in the welfare of their workers and the improvement of their cities.

4.16 German financial ethos and practice

German literature, melding Teutonic mythology and effusive Romanticism in the Sturm und Drang and Biedermeier movements, created insurmountable firewalls between intellectuals and businessmen. Goethe's epic poetry, Shiller's historical drama, Holderlin, and Novalis' mysticism inspired the Romantic Movement in France and England, but in contrast French and British Realism and Naturalism has little resonance in Germany. Goethe condemned money, finance, and social aspirations as satanic. Heinrich Heine, Jewish poet, essayist and playwright, gently mocked his society inspired by Stendhal. Ironically, at the end of the century the most controversial and seminal texts on money in all its complexities and permutations were written in German: Marx, Simmel, Freud, and Thomas Mann's first novel, *The Buddenbrooks*, published in 1901. Describing the rise and decline of a wealthy merchant family in Lubeck in the 1835–1877 period, Mann, inspired by Stendhal and Tolstoy, presented the portrait of an age in which art and business, creativity, and money were contiguous and irreconcilable. Like his other panoramic novels, Mann delves into the minutiae of an oppressive, rigidly structured, order obsessed society ensconced in its drawing rooms, parlors and gardens, insulated from and frightened of the outside world.

Germany won the Franco-Prussian War, established its military and economic prowess, but the German psyche never adjusted. Jumping in one generation from conservative regional merchant societies to fully fledged international capitalism; Germany became a world power with small town, rural values, never resolving the profound feelings of ambivalence and insecurity. In the three decades before World War I, Germany asserted itself as leader in science, education, culture, philosophy, yet already harbored a "strident militaristic ethos" (Stern 2006: introduction).

Banking and corporate historian, Jeffrey Fear, in his study on German corporate governance and institutional banking culture, attributes Germany's wariness and extreme caution to the Crash of 1873 (Grunderkrise), which, coming soon after unification, influenced German attitudes toward stocks and speculation. But where France regressed and shut down financial progress for nearly a century after the Law fiasco, Germany instead sought to regulate and put in place measures to curb and protect investor excesses, starting with the charter of the centralized Reichbank and the 1884 Corporation Act. Through the 1920s Germany was upheld as an intellectual model in corporate governance, central bank management, insurance, and industrial policies. J.P. Morgan studied in Germany and the Warburgs, once in the United States, would set out the initial rules for the creation of the Federal Reserve inspired by the Bank of England and the Reichbank. German investors were astonished at the laxity of banking regulation in the United States, and at the lack of concerted cooperation between industrial and financial sectors (see Chapter 6). Fear offers the premise that despite both Germany and the United States having strong populist movements, antagonistic to big business, bankers and speculators, "the political and social reaction to these crises differed greatly in the two countries because of different underlying collective attitudes toward big business, banks and capital markets" (Fear 2008: 7). Germany was comfortable with cartels, while America tolerated trusts. Industrial banking interests working in concert, similar to the Japanese bank-corporate conglomerates, maintained a sense of regional and institutional loyalty and long-term relationships, but it also fomented fragmentation and insularity: "Americans made banks a symbol of the 'money trust' while Germans made banks dedicated to long term owners or advisors to firms and regulators of stock markets" (Fear 2008: 9). Regional traditions and loyalties remained firmly engrained in the banking sector, promoting support for small local banks, thrifts and savings, unlike in the United States where local banks mainly fended for themselves. The post-1948 structure of Landesbanken, Sparkassen retained the regional relationship, limiting the reach of the few major banks to under 35 percent of the domestic market through the twentieth century. German banking through 2007 remained provincial, fragmented and unable to achieve successful domestic mergers, only becoming more competitive when the Landesbanken were coerced under European Union regulation to agree to domestic consolidation.

By 1900, the Berlin Stock Exchange was booming, Berlin was called "Chicago on the Spree," and German investors became active in railroad securities, electrification and transportation, coke and coke technology in coordination with Bethlehem Steel. However, business practices in Germany were geared against joint stock companies and speculation: "leading to calls for a system in which stability, solidity, reputation and respectability became paramount virtue – classic burgerlich (bourgeois) values" (Fear 2008: 10).

4.17 German banks abroad

Deutsche Bank was established in 1870 by George Siemens, of Siemens and Halske, as a joint stock company "by a group of small banks and investors for the purpose of representing German financial interests on international markets" (Kobrak 2008: 5), to clear transactions, absorb foreign debt, and take positions in foreign firms. From 1876 to 1899, like Crédit Lyonnais, Deutsche Bank expanded activities inside and outside the country with offices in Bremen, Hamburg, and London, followed by holdings in French and New York banks, and branch offices in Shanghai and Yokohama (which closed in 1875). However, as the market in Asia and Asian transactions were represented by British banks, Germany decided to focus on South America. Seeing opportunities in the flourishing American market, Deutsche Bank's American representatives, Henry Villard and Edward Adams, worked closely with Morgan, Warburg, and Speyer as well as the Rockefellers. By 1913, Germany was almost on par with America and England: Deutsche Bank's assets grew: "from 1870 to 1913 business volume grew from 239.3 million Mark to 129.2 billion Mark" (Kobrak 2008: 19).

The great German banks: Deutsche, Dresdner, Commerz, Discontobank, and Darmstadter, created in the 1860 to 1870s boom years, were at the "hub of creating new companies and financing old ones" (Kobrak 2008: 2). The "Bleichroder–Rothschild–Bismarck triangle" (Stern 2006: 230), was the tip of the iceberg, as all major European banks shared initial financing, founding directors, boards, and major shareholders. Bleichroder, Disconto Gesellschaft, and Paribas participated in the first bond issuance in Romania in 1881, in Argentinean bonds, and South American railroads in conjunction with Barings. German finance was instrumental in Austria, Switzerland, and Sweden. Creditanstalt, established in 1855 by Anselm de Rothschild, financed the railroad boom. Austria saw a boom in banking in the 1860s, although, according to Bleichroder, the market remained underbanked and immature. Sweden, also dependent on German, French, and British money, saw a surge of banking activity in the 1850s and 1860s.

Switzerland, symbol of international finance after 1930, had mainly small private institutions catering to the domestic market: wealthy German clients out of Zurich and long-established French connections out of Geneva. Swiss Bank Corporation was established in Basel in 1895 by the merger of two cantonal banks. Switzerland, contrary to popular belief, did not attain any reputation as a banking center until 1930 (see Chapter 5).

4.18 Europe on the eve

On the eve of World War I, Russia, India, China, Persia, and the Ottoman Empire – great civilizations and cultures – had barely entered the age of modern capitalism. South America and Brazil were just beginning to adopt European financial practices, but fortunes remained land and family based. Forced or imposed upon by foreign empires, these vast nations had accepted the conditions and practices of the West in very small dosage within restricted geopolitical perimeters. Most of the world's population had never encountered paper money, banks, stocks, bonds or commercial contracts. Gold, silver, and copper currencies circulated in exchange for tangible agricultural and artisanal products in markets and urban centers, as they had for centuries. Barter still existed at the core of commercial transactions. Enormous progress in transportation, living conditions, literacy, education, science, and communication, benefiting from advances in markets and finance, impacted a small segment of the urban demographic in Europe and the United States. Yet in Britain, France, and Germany there was deep seated belief, in the best tradition of the Enlightenment, that progress was linear and that civilization, as they had defined it, could and would improve all nations. In hindsight, tainted by the horrors of the twentieth century, this perspective has been called hubristic, arrogant, and exploitative, but at the start of the century,

> Decade after decade had seen increasing political freedom, the progressive spread of democratic institutions, the steady lifting of the standard of life for the masses of men.... In financial matters the good faith of governments and central banks was taken for granted. Governments and central banks were not always able to keep their promises, but when this happened they were ashamed, and they took measures to make the promises good as far as they could.
>
> (Andersen (1949) quoted in Alan Greenspan 2007: 364)

5   Capitalism is dead, long live capitalism?

> Your ancestors were the princes of Cleves and Juliers since 647; God wanted in
> his infinite goodness that you possess almost all the shares of the Suez Canal and
> three times as much Royal Dutch as Edmund of Rothschild; your ancestors ...
> date back to the year 63; two of your sisters-in-law are empresses.
>
> (Proust 1989: 427)

Marcel Proust mockingly attributed the Princess of Parma's sense of duty and
generosity to a diversified portfolio of blue chip stocks, a necessary precondition
to maintaining, rather than simply having, the finest social credentials. Proust,
whose personal fortune derived in part from American railroad bonds in Union
Pacific, Pennsylvania and Southern Pacific, understood that transatlantic flows of
capital, investment in commodities (Royal Dutch Shell invested in oil exploration in Oklahoma), railroad bonds, and major bank stocks were essential components of the first Gilded Age's international economy. Juxtaposing references
to Suez, Royal Dutch, and Rothschild, and description of the purest of noble
French lineage, Proust revealed the contradictions at the very heart of European
capitalism. Wealth and its corollaries, power and prestige, could no longer be
self contained; by nature it had become international, tainted by foreign operations, agents and instruments. Where England and America accepted and incorporated these conditions in their collective psyche, continental Europe would
struggle through a century-long tormented relationship with theory and practice
of financial activity.

Financial culture in the twentieth century, a unique paradox of total adulation
and propagation of market economies, financial innovation, and wealth creation
coexisting and then superseding total negation of the very principles of capitalist
activity and motivation, is so complex that any overview needs to be narrowed
to specific years and major events which instigated or best characterized these
behavioral and geo-economic shifts. Unlike the recessions, financial panics and
downturns of 1837, 1847–1848, 1857, 1873, and 1891: "the twentieth century,
which experienced the most rapid and widespread economic development in
history, was also a century in which capitalism engaged in a series of struggles
with itself, with its inherent weaknesses" (Emmett 2003: 23). Coordination
among central bankers in the 1890s and 1907, which held panics and bank runs

in check, was neither sufficient nor flexible enough to maintain financial stability in the impoverished, fragmented nation states of the 1930s. The Great Depression, as damaging as it was to the United States, proved far more dangerous, once it reached global proportions in the 1930s, creating in its wake totalitarianism and fascism. In the post-World War II period, increased demand, and unregulated supply, putting nations at the mercy of oil rich autocracies and dictatorships, led to economic instability in the 1970s. The crises of the 1990s, instigated in the United States, were market rather than economy based, as overall stability and prosperity increased even in the developing world. Capitalism, judged cause and solution of all social and political ills, presented as the grand antithesis to Marxism, socialism, Communism, and fundamentalism, has been demolished, left for dead and resuscitated nearly every 20 years from 1905 to 2008.

The crisis of 2008 revealed major fault lines in the core Anglo-American principles of corporate and financial capitalism, which had come to represent the most successful global model in the last decade. Governments, media, academics and the public at large, frightened at the unprecedented loss of real estate, securities and commodities valuation within less than a year, turned upon this model as cause and scapegoat. But the challenge will now be, as phrased in an American aphorism: to not throw out the baby with the bathwater. The opacity of instruments used to create the subprime mortgage crisis, repackaged and sold to large banks unwilling and seemingly unable to attest as to their actual value, the esoteric nature of transactions enacted by hedge funds and private equity, the ineffectiveness of government regulation, and the over dependency on self-regulation has proven to be part and parcel of general financial misinformation and misperception, what Chief Executive Officer of the NYSE Euronext, Duncan Niederauer, dubbed "financial illiteracy" (Museum of American Finance 2009a). Led on by an overly enthusiastic press, media, and Washington policies, similar to the 1920s, 1980s, and late 1990s, the American public propelled the global race into the stock market without a clear understanding of the actual valuation of assets, their potential risks, and the immensity of potential losses. Hayek, Friedman, Chandler, Sylla, and Phelps, in their seminal work, have attributed the success and resilience of capitalism and specifically of American capitalism to dynamic forces of innovation, mobility, flexibility, and privatization. Braudel, Landes, Ferguson, Galbraith, Kindleberger, Wallenstein, and Eichengreen, have examined the delicate balance of trust and interdependency between governments and financial institutions, between civil societies and central banks as issuer and guarantor of the money supply, between individuals and credit institutions. The crisis of 2008 created a spiraling loss of confidence in the market, but does it risk, as former Chairman of the Federal Reserve, Paul Volcker, mentioned in many interviews, bringing about a loss of faith in these institutions and the end of "financial capitalism as we know it?"

Between September 2008 and spring 2009, financial markets, international banking, and credit on a global scale have suffered such traumatic disruptions that the very definition of capitalism is being reexamined. In this time of existential mutation, when the nature of banks and the functions of bankers, as well as the culture of consumption and materialism are being called into question, are there certain immutable collective and individual responses to financial crisis based on nation, community, and society? The question should not be whether capitalism is dead, but whether once resuscitated, it undergoes a structural and philosophical transformation or merely reforms some of the excesses and within a decade or less reverts to levels of dynamism, private initiative, and creativity leading back again to "irrational exuberance."

A conference hosted by the Capitalism and Society Center at Columbia University on February 20, 2009 brought together academic, finance, and political leaders to examine reforming and regulating the financial sector, adjustment of international balances, and solutions toward regaining "dynamism and inclusion." George Soros, Joseph Stiglitz, Robert Mundell, Martin Wolf, William McDonough, and Christine Lagarde, among other members of the international financial community, sought to underscore the importance of cooperation and dialogue, and the need to integrate the needs of the wealthy and the developing countries in the debate. Edmunds Phelps, Nobel Laureate in Economics (2006), theoretician of "dynamic capitalism," based on the creativity of entrepreneurs, the skill of financiers, and the ability of managers to evaluate the applicability and positive impact of privatization to move capitalist endeavor forward, to revive and continuously regenerate it, opened the discussion. Paul Volcker, economic advisor to President Obama, at the Sixth Annual Conference at the Capitalism and Society Center, Columbia University, February 20, 2009, stressed that this crisis was "a challenge to capitalism," calling for the creation of banks that specialize in, and are dedicated to, long-term lending to business: "stable strong banking institutions, relation centered, service oriented … operations … done without enormous risk … prohibiting institutions from sponsoring proprietary trading, hedge funds, equity firms," prohibiting high risk activities with "enormous conflict of interest," and calling for the end to "financial engineering."

The words written in 1865 by Adrian Mazaret, French businessman and banker, director of Crédit Lyonnais resonate:

> For a bank the first quality is wariness: it is necessary to be systematically wary of every person, every deal. It is necessary to always question what is the motive, what is the reason and if one is not totally satisfied, to not hesitate to abstain.… The resistance of the banker must be proportionally equal to the insistence of the client.

> (Montella 1989: 36)

As American and European governments have rolled out series of complex rescue plans for the banking, insurance, and industrial sectors, the public and the media have responded with increased frustration at the lack of clarity and lack of results.

In European cultures, imbued in principles of collective responsibility, loss of honor and loss of face in the community, financial calamity has proven far more insidious and threatening than simple loss of money or even fear of bankruptcy, penalties and risk of imprisonment.

In January 2009, in the wake of the Madoff scandal, a German businessman Adolf Merckle, "a parsimonious billionaire" who built a German industrial empire in a small town, Blaubeuren, committed suicide by walking onto train tracks. A solid citizen, in lifestyle and appearance the epitome of the German burgher, he lived by a "Protestant ethic and way of life." He had built a pharmaceutical and cement family business into a global distribution network, accumulating through his wife's family holdings a vast fortune. But unbeknown to his family and associates, he enjoyed playing the market for high stakes. Investing in Porsche, when the credit crunch hit the DAX, he bet the wrong way on the Volkswagen Porsche merger and lost a fortune. His assets diluted, he needed a bridge loan, which required divesting of his core pharmaceutical business. Unable to justify this loss of power and negligence of his sense of duty to his family business: "stepping out of the cozy world of German capitalism into high octane derivatives on VW and Frankfurt's Dax 30 index, he saw his life's work unraveling," he signed the bridge loan and walked to the train tracks (Milne and Wilson 2009). On December 23, 2008, Thierry Magnon de la Villehuchet, a prominent hedge manager, well respected in the New York French corporate community, learned he had lost US$1.4 billion in funds he had invested for his clients with Bernard Madoff. He committed suicide in his office by slashing his wrists and biceps with a box cutter. Villehuchet felt that he had betrayed friends and clients who had invested in his firm, Access International Advisors, which managed US$3bn in assets for French and American clients. Descendent of old Brittany aristocracy, former head of Crédit Lyonnais' investment banking arm, and member of the Yacht Club, his brother explained that he had felt that his personal honor and name had been compromised beyond redemption (Kouwe 2008).

Tragically in both cases there were possible resolutions, a number of feeder funds are in litigation and have or will partially recover losses. In the case of Merkle, the German government was on the verge of offering him a less stringent financing deal. Neither of these businessmen were about to suffer overwhelming personal losses, therefore objectively the facts did not merit the outcome, but a more complex set of atavistic responses provoked these extreme reactions. Honor and trust within the community or the family as the basis of financial relationships, the shame of having breached this trust and having lost respect, the inability to face clients and creditors, the loss of control, characteristics embedded in the collective French and German psyche, transformed monetary loss into loss of self worth. Interestingly, American bankers of diverse geographic, ethnic, and educational backgrounds, pilloried in the press and media, accused of pilfering their institutions and abusing public trust, have chosen to tough it out: unless forced out, none have resigned and none have cracked under pressure.

5.1 The first and second Gilded Ages: 1905 and 2005

Looking back from the perspective of the global financial crisis of 2008, the first and second Gilded Age in London, Paris, Berlin, New York, and Moscow, in 1905 and 2005, were eerily similar, signaling the beginning of the end of the last great eras of capitalism, characterized by excesses of materialism, disposable wealth, the hubris of Western powers, and the belief in a new economic system which would guarantee ever increasing market and corporate growth.

1905 was a year of exceptional technological progress and innovation, with the inauguration of the Parisian metro, America's boost in automobile production with the first car shows at Madison Square Garden, and, in January 1905, the Tran-Siberian Railroad, linking Paris to Vladivostok in 21 days. Teddy Roosevelt elected for a second term, declaring the convertibility of the dollar and reinforced American economic clout abroad as he began anti-monopolistic inquiries at home against Rockefeller and Standard Oil. Japan, after winning the Russo-Japanese War, proving its naval and industrial power, exposed the underlying fragility of the Russian military. Between 1890 and 1900, annual growth of 3.8 percent in gross domestic product in the United States surpassed Western Europe with 2.2 percent. In less than a decade before World War I, Germany surged ahead of France, Italy, Japan, Russia, and even Britain, in industrial, commercial, naval, military strength, and coal production. French economic strength resided in banking, finance, iron, steel, and chemicals, led by Schneider, Renault, Michelin, and Rhone Poulenc. Britain, as global financial and currency leader, retained competitive military, naval and industrial power, yet its 22 percent share of total world manufacturing output in 1880 would decline to 13 percent by 1911–1913.

1905 ended on a stable but nervous note, the American economy in full boom, although suffering from trade balance problems, the overall population growth, income, and employment figures in positive territory, despite unhealthy wage differential between top managers and workers across too many sectors, and a surge of investment mergers and real estate construction. The largest firms in France and Germany were extremely profitable, especially the banks: Société Générale, Crédit Agricole, Paribas, Deutsche Bank; the pharmaceuticals and chemicals sector, Bayer, Hoechst, and Rhone Poulenc; the industrial and new automotive sector, Siemens and Daimler. Europe was calm, but there was fear of weakening economic activity. Within a range of minor fluctuations, the major global currencies, sterling and the dollar, were stable with strong central banks. London continued to be the uncontested financial center. Russia had a very unstable year, and despite solid economic growth the underpinnings of social stability appeared fragile.

Amazingly, a century later, despite physical devastation, economic ruin, political dissolution, and reconstruction, the largest European companies by market capitalization listed in the *Financial Times* "Survey of Most Respected Companies" (2007) include seven German companies, all in play in 1905: Daimler Benz, Siemens, Allianz, Deutsche Bank, Bayer, BASF, and Hoechst; the Dutch company, Royal Dutch, and the French companies Total (from Elf Aquitaine), and Sanofi-Aventis (formerly Rhone-Poulenc). The top French banks, BNP/ Paribas (merged in 1999) and Société Générale and CALYON (combining Crédit Lyonnais and Crédit Agricole in 2003), were established between 1863 and 1900. In 2007, nearly one-third of the French CAC 40 were founded before 1914, including Lafarge, Vivendi-Veolia (former Compagnie Generale des Eaux), Schneider, Suez, Michelin, Sanofi-Aventis (former Rhone Poulence-Hoechst), Dexia, AXA, and Saint Gobain, created under Colbert in 1665. On the German DAX, most corporations had been dismantled, divested and totally reconstituted after 1957, yet nearly half of the 30 were incorporated before 1914: Allianz, Bayer, BASF Commerzbank, Continental AG, Daimler, Deutsche, Post bank, Henkel, Siemens, Munich Re, and Thyssen-Kruppp. On the London FTSE (FOOTSIE) 100, among the top 25 firms in market capitalization, over half were established in the eighteenth and nineteenth centuries during the height of the British Empire. These included Royal Dutch Shell, Standard Chartered, AngloAmerican, Royal Bank of Scotland, Rio Tinto Group, HSBC, BP, British American Tobacco, Barclays, and Lloyds. Only in America, did the list of blue chip companies, growth sectors, and most respected firms totally change during the course of the century, with the exception of GE, Citibank, and J.P. Morgan. But what remained the same in the first and second Gilded Ages, were the levels of excessive consumption, self indulgence, vulgar luxury, and fraudulent profiteering.

5.2 The last waltz of the empires

In the depth of the winter of 1913, at the height of pre-Lenten carnival, the Vienna Bankers Club gave a Bankruptcy Ball at the opulent Blumensaal hall. Some ladies appeared as balance sheets, displaying voluptuous debits curving from slender credits. Others came as inflated collateral.

(Morton 2009)

Frederic Morton evokes this outrageous display of financial hubris and humor as the glittering, fragile, decentralized Austro-Hungarian Empire under beloved Kaiser Franz-Joseph coasted on the edge of disaster. Galbraith, in *A Journey through Economic Time* (1994), described the Austro-Hungarian Empire as "an incoherent assemblage of ethnic, religious and language groupings created by territorial acquisition [that] had long been verging on dissolution" (1994: 15).

Geo-strategically, in the decade before World War I, the world was divided between the Great Powers, their weakened colonial empires, the faltering Austro-Hungarian, Ottoman, Chinese, and Russian empires, and fledgling nations across Asia, Africa, and Latin America. Post 1918 beneficiaries and victims of short lived democratic independent nationhood between the wars, Central and Eastern Europe became a pawn in the grand geo-strategic game between fascism and communism. Newly formed and reconstituted nations struggled to assert economic and political independence, with very little aid or international support.

Fledgling parliamentary democracies in Poland and in Czechoslovakia, in the remnants of the Ottoman Empire in Rumania, Bulgaria, and Serbia were doomed from the start, plagued by weak central banks, non-convertible currencies, bouts of hyperinflation, encroaching protectionism, a multitude of ethnic demands, flows of refugees, and the pull of socialist and incipient communist parties.

Emerging from behind the Iron Curtain in 1989, these nations were frozen in economic time. Barely able to reform in the 1930s, two generations lost to war and Communist rule, within 15 years of the dissolution of the Soviet Union, and reassembled into independent nations, they joined the European Union in the expansion of 2004. Once again a powerful regional power was to offer them the subsidies, strategic support, and economic renaissance, a short lived apotheosis which nearly disintegrated under the impact of the 2008 crisis as nearly all former East Central European non-Eurozone countries required European Central Bank and International Monetary Fund emergency assistance.

Till 1939 the role of global superpower belonged to the British Empire, but there were signs of weakening alliances, vast inequalities in the scope and penetration of economic prosperity:

> The weary Titan [staggering] under the too vast orb of its fate ... the United Kingdom by itself will not be strong enough to hold its proper place alongside of the United States or Russia and probably not Germany. We shall be thrust aside by sheer weight.
>
> (First Lord of the Admiralty, Joseph Chamberlain, quoted in Kennedy 1987: 229)

A bankrupt Ottoman Empire encompassed what would become the Middle East, Turkey, and the Black Sea region. Inherently tolerant of merchants, minorities, and open to flows of emigration, the Ottoman Empire carried a 400-year history of immense wealth, military power, and merchant dynasties, impeded by fragmented, inefficient, economic stewardship. The inability to cohesively assimilate or govern the complex national and ethnic groups within its boundaries never allowed it to meet the competitive demands of modern capitalism. Dismantled and reconstituted in the Treaty of Sevres in 1919, only the Turkish Republic under Kemal Ataturk created a secular Western-styled society imposing Western political, social, and business practices. Orhan Pamuk, in *Istanbul: Memories and the City* (2005), describes the ambivalent relationship between the wealthy and the state: the fear of being ostracized, exiled or penalized. Unlike other empires, the Ottoman "state had no hereditary aristocracy, but with the coming of the Republic, the rich worked hard to be seen as its rightful heirs" (Pamuk 2005: 191). The power and monopolistic control of the banking, industrial, media, sports, and cultural sectors under Turkey's wealthy dynasties, led by the Sabanci and Koc families, has been a double edged sword: beneficial in its largesse in all aspects of urban and rural infrastructure, educational, and cultural projects and guaranteeing continuity and stability, but regressive in its noncompetitive policies, exclusion of foreign interests and insularity.

In 2005, recovered from the financial and banking crisis of 2001, Turkey was in the process of bank reform and belated opening of financial markets. Constantly thwarted in its attempts for full membership in the European Union, under moderate Islamic rule, Turkey reasserted itself as leader in the Black Sea Region and as major geo-strategic and economic partner for the Middle East. Istanbul literally and figuratively bridges Europe and Asia, criss-crossing the Bosporus, from the medieval bazaars of the old city, to the European side's modern towers housing banks and corporations, the bridge to Asia, isolated rural communities, and the World Trade building near the ultramodern airport, emblematic of a delicate balance of traditions, histories, and ethnic economic cultures.

The revolutionary movement gained prominence in Russia in 1905. Czarist Russia could have moved toward a parliamentary oligarchy, monarchy, and market economy. In 1905, Russia began serious legislative and social reforms under a weakened and frightened Czar Nicolas II, and economic reforms under the aegis of a strong, respected central bank with the world's largest gold reserves. On January 22, 1905, Bloody Sunday, the first workers' uprising in St Petersburg was brutally repressed by the police instigating the first Revolution; in February Governor General of Moscow, Grand Duke Sergei, was assassinated; in July, during the revolt on the Potemkin, the sailors hoisted the red flag. Trounced by the Japanese Navy in the Russo-Japanese War, Russia began a downward spiral of economic and political implosions leading to 1917.

In 2003 to 2007, Russia repeated the same pattern of rapid emancipation: Western funded and modeled projects, large scale Western investment, and a commodity fueled economic expansion, manifested in excesses of luxury consumption in a money bloated Moscow:

> Everywhere Socialist era edifices, former state stores and even onetime academic institutes are being purged of their pasts and transformed into hot spots glimmering with Italian furniture, French chefs, European fashions and DJ spun music.... Russian taste for old world opulence clearly did not perish with the Romanovs.
>
> (Sherwood 2007)

Had Moscow in its new found wealth adopted the financial culture of the West, or was it returning to a love of extreme wealth, luxe, and opulence functioning in synch with an authoritarian regime, which allowed capitalism to flourish separate from democratization of business practices and concepts? In the crisis of 2008, once oil and gas prices plunged, the trappings of excessive consumption disappeared, or were severely curtailed. Moscow became suddenly dour and closed as the era of extravagance ended, leaving quasi-repressive rule under Prime Minister Putin firmly in place. The culture of ostentation has retreated and anti-capitalist rhetoric has gained new validation, as Russia again needs to define its economic objectives.

South America, after decades of war, rebellion, and independence movements, finally enjoyed a decade of relative calm, benefiting from global financial and currency stability following the emerging market crisis of 1890, centered on Argentina. Although infrastructure and urban development improved, wealth remained concentrated in old Spanish, Portuguese, and British colonial families, the Church, and corrupt governments vacillating between populism and aristocratic led oligarchy. Argentina would be in constant fluctuation between various dictatorships, lurching from currency crisis to full blown banking crisis in the 1990s and 2002, incurring runs, insolvencies requiring International Monetary Fund intervention (De Negro and Kay 2002). In 1905, Brazil, 15 years after the end of the empire and declaration of the Republic of the United States of Brazil, was in a period of modernization, full economic expansion, and liberalism under a constitutional democracy which would remain in place until 1930. After a period allowing unregulated note issuing banks to expand from eight to 67 in the previous decade, bank reform, coupled with currency stabilization fixing exchange rates to gold, ushered in a period of financial prosperity. A vast, sparsely populated nation, financial power remained ensconced in dynastic coffee, land, and commodity fortunes. From the 1940s, suffering from erratic economic progress under military regimes, hit by hyperinflation in the 1986 to 1994 period, Brazil, despite immense natural resources and potential, seemed to be relegated to permanently emerging economy status. Since 1994, under stringent currency reforms eliminating the devalued cruziero and reinstating the real (equal to 100 centavos), sharply curtailing inflation in coordination with the International Monetary Fund and Washington led policies during the Clinton Administration, Brazil proved its critics wrong. The economic turnaround was helped by a consolidated public–private banking sector with top banks led by Banco do Brasil, Banco Itau, and Unibanco, owned or in close coordination with the government, under the regulatory and supervisory regime of the independent Banco Central do Brasil, established in 1964. Modeled in part on the French banking sector, it successfully combined government ownership or shareholdings with cautious, profit generating, competitive free market strategies. Since the major currency reforms in 1994, reinforced by the center left election of President Lula du Silva in 2002, Brazil has proven that socialism and capitalism can achieve successful partnership and economic stability. In 2008, Brazil has withstood the financial crisis with less damage due to relatively low exposure to real estate derivatives and losses, large reserves, and, despite the global recession, a normal increase in retail spending (Banco do Brasil 2009). Traditional family, class, and religious value systems, and inherited fortunes, a leisure and service oriented lifestyle encourages an avid shopping and spending culture among the wealthy and affluent middle classes. Yet this culture of materialism and dynastic, land-based wealth has never fully accepted nor desired the dynamics and risks of capitalism. Across Latin America, the extraordinary literary output of Borges, Cortazar, Marquez, Vargas Llosa, and Fuentes depicted the bourgeoisie and the wealthy immersed in phantasmagorical pagan and Christian mythology, frozen in economic and historical time.

In the Americas, still part of the British Commonwealth, Canada followed British and American financial models. The Bank of Montreal, founded in 1817, became the first foreign bank in the United States in 1859. Canada enjoyed decades of booming economic growth, following the discovery of gold and railroad expansion. The Stock Exchange opened in 1874 and the Canadian Pacific Railway was completed in 1885. Although rich in natural resources, with oil and gold deposits, the largely rural, under populated regions were severely impacted by the Great Depression and United States tariffs. When the Bank of Canada, modeled on the Federal Reserve and the Bank of England, opened in 1934, Canada was in the throes of nearly 30 percent unemployment. But Canadian banks since their inception have worked in close coordination with the government. A basic philosophy of social responsibility, community lending, large reserves, and guarantees, has encouraged cautious investment and relatively little exposure to United States or European excesses. In the crisis of 2008, Canada had been nearly unscathed, having avoided exposure in mortgage or Ponzi schemes.

By 1905, Asia remained divided between the British Empire on the Indian subcontinent, French Indochina, China, and a strong, modernized militaristic Japan. Having defeated China, in the Sino-Japanese War of 1894, having gained control of Korea and Taiwan, Japan's victory over Russia in the Russo-Japanese War established its position as a formidable military power. Japan opened to the West in 1859 after two centuries of isolation, ending the Edo reign of the Shogunate era, where financial activity was limited to merchant banks. During the Meiji Restoration, from 1871 to 1882 Japan established the yen under the New Currency Act of 1871, the oldest national bank Dai-Ichi in 1873 (joining with two smaller banks in 1971 to create Dai-Ichi-Kangyo DKB), and the Bank of Japan (Tamaki 1995). According to Tamaki, Japan was not a bank-centric society, but rather encouraged growth through a combination of banks and capital markets which worked with the industrial conglomerates, the zaibatsu. Like France under Napoleon III and Germany under Bismarck, Japan from the 1870s to 1905 quickly adapted and assimilated modern market procedures and ideology. The large industrial dynasties, often in coordination with their own banks, Mitsui, Mitsubishi, Somitomo, and Yasuda, retained prominence through the twentieth century. Historically, its ancient and insulated civilization encouraged merchant dynasties and granted strong political power to a conservative, highly structured mercantile class. However, imperial interdictions on foreign trade between 1638 and 1868 created impenetrable firewalls between the arts and commerce, encouraging literature and philosophy to scorn the mercantile profession. Similar in philosophy and corporate structure to the German model of industrial–financial symbiosis with emphasis on heavy industry, military expenditures, almost xenophobic rejection of foreign banks, and majority shareholdings, both nations post-World War II, despite years of occupation and American imposed standards of recovery, maintained the same large companies and family ownerships in place. As late as 1999, Japanese bankers, already enduring five years of economic stasis, were unwilling to accept any foreign buyouts or to allow major banks to close or fail. Japan became a major economic power from the 1980s to the early 1990s, with lead position in global banks. In 1990 to 1991, Japan led with seven out of ten largest banks in asset capitalization. But following the recession of 1991, Japan gradually retreated into a "lost decade" of relatively low growth and inefficient "zombie" banks and industries, despite maintaining its position as one of the top five economic global powers. In 2008, the Japanese economy has been severely impacted by the global curtailing of exports, although its banks have suffered a lesser degree of exposure to high risk loan portfolios. But an odd phenomenon was observed in political financial circles, as Japanese officials declared a sense of nostalgia for the pre-Meiji period before the intrusion of Western capitalism. "Eisuke Sakakibara, the former Vice-Finance Minister indelibly branded Mr. Yen, describes a country that was peaceful, orderly, unspoilt, and friendly: 'That was what pre Meiji Japan was like. We should go back to that,'" (Pilling 2009). The sentiment echoes French responses to views of an idyllic, rural French past, resurrected in every period of crisis or perceived foreign economic incursion. Japan like France, honoring and revering its cultural heritage, always tends to view capitalism as somewhat discordant with its intrinsic set of values and professed destiny.

India, first under the Mogul Empire, then under the British Empire, creating and codifying the vast Indian civil service administration, remained and after 60 years of independence still remains locked into an endless loop of immense progress and total paralysis, a perpetual First World power and Third World emerging market. Even when India entered the modern age in the 1960s, in terms of education, technological innovation, industry, and social progress, two-thirds of a nearly one billion population remain imbedded in feudal caste and class structures. During the eighteenth century, "the brilliant courts were centers of conspicuous consumption on a scale which the Sun King at Versailles might have thought excessive" (Kennedy 1987: 13), yet through the twentieth century urban and exurban poverty continued at levels inferior or equal to the most impoverished nations in the world without basic sanitation, waste management or infrastructure in place. Banking and finance, following a long tradition of merchant castes, in coordination with British rule established a complex regional network of banks since the early nineteenth century, including the State Bank of India, and the Central Bank of India, the first bank totally under Indian control and management, founded in 1911. Most banks nationalized in 1969 continue, despite privatization and international presence in the last decade, to function under regional, local, and state interconnecting boards and shareholdings. A sprawling democracy under center left governments for decades after independence, maintained British financial culture with banks often run by a British educated managerial class. Since the 1990s, banking services have been slowly democratized, with an increase in community and regional banks offering more local grants, loans, and services. The self-contained economy and insulated banking system has, in 2008–2009, spared India severe collateral damage from the financial crisis.

China in the last decade of the corrupt Qing dynasty, overthrown in 1911, was divided into French, British, and German concessions. A mercantile system of guilds and banks used as remittance institutions, were the most prevalent in

Shanghai, which also housed the largest number of foreign banks. John King Fairbanks compares the financing of Chinese trade to the Hanseatic League guilds (see Fairbanks 1992). Pingyao had the first bank since 1823, Ri Sheng Chang, which today houses a museum in the ruins of the old town. As the city was situated on the trade routes between Beijing and Xian, traders and merchants needed a local bank, which granted the city the reputation of a banking center. In 1900, Pingyao had 22 banks with hundreds of branches, and the town had become home to wealthy financiers with vast mansions. By the 1890s, Europeans introduced British and French style banking, commerce, and industry, as foreign banks opened branches throughout China (see Chapter 4), with French banks retaining dominance through the 1930s. Although the economy remained 65 percent rural, under the first republic instituted in 1921, the new middle class founded local banks. By 1920, Shanghai: "had 71 old style native banks. Specializing in short-term loans, they handled the funds of opium merchants and the dye trade in chemicals. A stock exchange and a national bank were still lacking" (Fairbanks 1992: 271). By 1927, in Shanghai, Peking, and Tianjin, bankers were making fortunes by lending to the government and underwriting loans. The court of Qing defaulted on huge loans, the economy was in shambles and after the Japanese invasion, by 1937 the last of the old banks closed. Victim of atrocious deprivation and hyperinflation in the aftermath of World War II, the nationalists in 1948 instituted the gold yuan: 4 yuan = 1 dollar (1992: 333). For the next 30 years, under Chairman Mao the country disavowed all commercial banking enterprise as capitalist exploitation. The first measures of opening markets and acceptance of mercantile activity occurred under Deng in 1978, providing some scope for private enterprise and market forces, a slow decentralization of banking system and greater flexibility in loans. Banking in China became part of a state run bureaucracy in the name of economic improvement and social progress. The largest government owned bank, Industrial and Commercial Bank, had 3,000 branches, employing 300,000 people, with small loans available for working capital and industry.

In 2005 to 2007, China appeared to have adapted economic principles of markets, exchanges, banks, and even credit cards, encouraging vast construction and infrastructure projects, and mass emigration from rural to urban centers. China seemed in barely a decade to have made a quantum leap from closed communist demand economy to viable market economy. But the paradoxes are many and the incongruities of an authoritarian, Marxist one-party system promoting Western style economic ideology will remain irresolvable and possibly irreconcilable for decades.

5.3 Dancing on the edge

In 1905, the wealthiest families and individuals in Britain and France were worth multiple millions in dollars, pounds or francs, leaving vast estates and inheritances. Fortunes were carefully diversified in stocks, bonds, gold, art, and above all property. Across Europe, despite the French Revolution, the revolutions of

1848, and the democratization and urbanization of finance, large estates, manors, palaces, castles, town houses, and hôtels particuliers were still at the core of familial holdings. In Russia, Poland, Italy, and Spain, as in South America, vast land holdings were often the sole source of support for the lesser nobility, as they remained outside of the scope of commercial and financial activity. In the United States, although new fortunes, especially in the West, possessed vast tracts of land, and great American fortunes owned lavish estates in Boston, New York, and Newport Rhode Island, these homes were only a small part of diversi-fied portfolios. Money at the turn of the twentieth century was tangible and accountable. Within a century, money and currencies became ephemeral, illu-sionary, and virtual. In the aftermath of two world wars, forced dispossession, and appropriation of Russian, Polish, German, Jewish, Chinese, and former colo-nial families and fortunes, accompanied by total devastation of property and the entire reconfiguration of Europe and Asia, the established rules of inheritance, and stable, multigenerational wealth had largely disappeared. And yet at the height of the boom in 2005–2006:

> Boston Consulting Group estimates total assets managed by the private banking business reached around $96, 400bn by the end of last year (2006), an increase of 8% over the previous 12 months ... The estimate markets permitting, based on a 5% yearly growth, was projected to reach almost $116,000bn by 2010 ... The other change is that while a generation ago private banking catered largely to inherited money, they now deal with global entrepreneurs ... In the plutocracy that is America, success in private banking hinges on having a winning strategy for getting, keeping and man-aging the assets of the very rich as US households with net worth of 5 million or more rose to 1.14M.
>
> ("Private Banking" 2007)

According to estimates in 2009, nearly half of global wealth had been lost in the financial crisis of 2008. This data leaves unanswered a number of questions: How much money has been withdrawn from the markets and is being hoarded as in other periods of crisis? If, as proven, private wealth increased manifold in the 2002–2006 period, how and to where has this money evaporated? If large parts of this wealth were virtual or on paper, did entire swaths of the population in developed countries enter into debt or take on obligations based on illusionary future dividends? Clearly the financial bubble was larger and deeper than ever before, but do the basic rules of boom and bust still apply as they have on a much more modest scale since the 1850s?

5.4 Post-World War I financial chaos, inflation, depression

Some 500 years of economic progress, where wealth generation and accumula-tion led to enhanced social status and political power, assuring a place in the social hierarchy, and national identity, was brutally and irrevocably destroyed between 1914 and 1945. The ravages of the post-war Germany traumatized in the hyperinflation in 1922–1923, the loss of monetary hegemony and stability in Britain and France, the Crash of 1929 and the Great Depression left in its wake a loss of trust in the inevitability of economic progress.

Since 1880, under the Gold Standard and stable currency parity, nations and business communities had unmitigated confidence in the major currencies, central banks, and large banks. Money, a literary and intellectual construct, could be depicted as amoral, seductive, dangerous, but the currency, legal tender of major nations, was sound, stable and constant.

In 1919, the Treaty of Versailles imposed upon Germany conditions and schedule of war reparations, under the false pretense that Germany could emulate France in 1870 and be able to meet its obligations. The devastation of the German industrial base and the repercussions of the implosion of the Austro-Hungarian Empire were seen as corollary damage instead of focal reasons why Germany neither would nor could ever meet these conditions. While the Allies could raise capital in the United States, German assets were expropriated under the October 1917, Trading with the Enemy Act: "On July 1, 1914 Germans held $1.1 billion of long-term US investments. By December 1918, thanks to sales and expropriations, German holdings amounted to nothing" (Kobrak 2007: 197). Liaquat Ahamed's *Lords of Finance* (2008) describes the inherent flaws in the positions of European and American central bankers, Emile Moreau, Montagu Norman, Benjamin Strong, and Hjalmar Schact, who tried and dismally failed to structure a viable coordinated system. Limited by history and the constraints of their countries' policies and monetary traditions, they never fully grasped the potential danger of allowing Germany to default, and the risks of uncoordinated piecemeal responses to each crisis.

Between 1919 and spring 1921, the exchange rate of the mark to the dollar remained steady until the Allies delivered the ultimatum to Germany requiring 121 billion gold marks in reparation by October 1921. The next year proved disastrous, when, in June 1921, German Minister of Foreign Affairs, Walther Rathenau, negotiating with the Allies to alleviate the reparation schedule, was assassinated. The government, unable to quell rising strikes and social unrest, began printing money to pay the Ruhr miners on strike:

> Inflation which had turned sharply upward in June 1922, reached hyperinflationary levels and in real terms, the money supply shrank as printing presses failed to keep up with prices ... By August the mark exploded and was replaced in November by an entirely new currency, the Rentemark.
>
> (Kindleberger 1993: 293)

The rate of the mark to the dollar spiked from 275 in May 1922 to 370 in June 1922, to 400 on July 1, 1922, and 2,000 by August, reaching 7,000 by November. People sought foreign currency abroad at any price as described in Stead's *House of All Nations* (1966 [1938]), when German Jews, in search of dollars, desperately sought out American relatives. The Reichbank continued to print money in higher and higher denominations until the 100 trillion marks in November 1923. Real estate, banking assets, pensions, and salaries had all become worthless paper, sold for fractions to German and foreign speculators. Hjalmar Schact, hapless governor of the Reichbank, at first hailed as a hero, temporarily reestablished some coherence in the German economy at the worst of the hyperinflation of November 1923 with the creation of the Rentemark. But the damage had been done; the markets remained extremely jittery in conjuncture with an explosive rise in unemployment. There was an inherent disconnect between the top banks, the impotent Weimar Republic, and the public. Throughout the trauma of devaluation and hyperinflation, Deutsche Bank remained largely unscathed and was involved in the sale of American securities in Europe. The Rentemark was a temporary measure, followed in 1924 by the American led Dawes plan, which reinstated a new Reichsmark. By 1928, Germany had regained levels of industrial output equal to 1928 and a period of relative calm. In June 1931, the Federal Reserve, Bank of England, Bank of France, and the newly formed Bank for International Settlements organized to lend the failing Reichbank US$100 million: too little, too late.

Brutal bouts of inflation and hyperinflation in Germany, Austria, Hungary, China, Argentina, Brazil, Turkey and Chile provoked economic and social destabilization, but more importantly, and long after the resolution of the financial impact, it caused psychological dislocation and inherent loss of confidence in the value and durability of the currency. At its most basic level, hyperinflation is a betrayal of the bond between the government and the market, between each individual's purchasing needs and purchasing ability. As Milton Friedman explained, inflation is an economic phenomenon, hyperinflation a political one. Between 1946 and 1948, hyperinflation impeded the start of recovery in Germany and Hungary and created disastrous famine in China. In 1946, the Hungarian National Bank issued a 100 quintillion pengo, at which point paper becomes virtual, a sign of complete collapse of any tangible relationship between currency, issuer and recipient. Like playing cards in 1704, the actual currency in Germany's occupied zones, Displaced Persons (DP) camps, and bases became American cigarettes.

> In the extreme disequilibrium system of Germany from 1945 to the spring of 1948, cigarettes were one form of money and soluble coffee and silk stockings other, but less satisfactory substitutes.... Cigarettes came in cartons of ten packages, packages of twenty cigarettes and individual cigarettes, which were occasionally divided.
>
> (Kindleberger 1993: 443)

The occupation forces sold cigarettes on the black market against the Reichsmark. In these circumstances, transactions were also conducted in ration cards, and the barter of coal for potatoes and bread grains. Ludwig Erhard formulated the German monetary reform, which set up one Deutschmark to ten Reichsmark, in coordination with the American occupation forces. A year before statehood was granted to West Germany, the Deutschmark, imposed on June 20, 1948, became the symbol of Germany's painstaking and cautious recovery and reacceptance into the world community: "I regard the German monetary reform of 1948 as one of the great feats of social engineering of all time" (Kindleberger 1993: 407). The impact was almost immediate, as all debt had to be paid in Deutschmarks. Within a decade it became the anchor for all European currencies until 1999, under the jurisdiction of the Bundesbank, established in 1957, which instituted a policy of total independence and intransigent anti-inflationary policies.

World War I left France in a state of socioeconomic shock. The bourgeoisie, wealthy, scared and hoarding gold, retreated into conservative seclusion and nostalgia for an idealized past, where stigmas of bankruptcy still prevailed, as described in the memoires of Raymond Barre and the novels of Marguerite Duras. Weak post-1919 governments refused to acknowledge the extent of industrial losses, the costs of reconstruction, and the ascendancy of the dollar in global competition. Between 1919 and 1926, the dollar fell from US\$1 = 5.18 francs to US\$1 = 2 51 francs. Despite a resurgence of French industry, the Bank of France's inability to quickly bolster the franc in the crisis of 1924 (when Lazard Bank had to intervene on foreign currency markets) shattered faith in the franc's ability to withstand speculative shocks. Emile Moreau, head of the Bank of France, forced through a cheap franc in order to encourage exports, entrenched in the classic Colbertian model of importing specie and exporting French goods. This policy calmed the "Mur d'Argent," but was unable to control volatility and speculation against the franc. In June 1928, when Poincaré restored the Gold Standard, it seemed that France alone would be able to withstand the aftermath of the October 1929 crash, because of its anachronistic conservative policies of protectionism and less dependence on international markets. But by 1932, heavy speculation against the franc, lack of political cohesion, a drop in industrial production, coupled with a policy of political appeasement toward Germany, led to popular and political turmoil. In this environment the Socialists came to power in 1936, in a wave of newfound optimism and idealism under the brilliant but naïve Prime Minister, Leon Blum. Blum, Jewish, an outsider to the power elite which had supported and granted special powers to Poincaré in 1928, became a tragic scapegoat for the deteriorating political situation. Unable to gain the support or cooperation of the banking sector and afraid to attack the commercial banks, Blum chose to push through a massive devaluation on September 28, 1936, by reducing the gold content of the franc by 30 percent, nationalizing industry, creating the 40-hour work week, and implementing "democratization" of the Bank of France. This impacted on the direct influence of the 200 main shareholders, striking at the core oligarchy upholding the values of the nation. Each stockholder, regardless of his holdings, would have one vote, and there would be an open selection of the board of directors, a violation of the secrets of the "economic priesthood." The government–bank relationship of closed cooperation and respect was replaced by sudden intervention, which created an unconditional adversarial relationship for the first time in the Bank's history. In the Popular Front, Blum hoped to govern "to the left in social matters, to the right in financial ones" (Lacouture 1982) a paradoxical reconciliation of social idealism and economic pragmatism, but the combination in 1936 was doomed to failure. The devaluation of the franc, meant to coordinate with the pound and the dollar, was not seen as a means of strengthening the domestic economy but rather as a lack of resistance to foreign influences. Unlike De Gaulle's successful devaluation in 1958, and Mitterrand's "realignments" in 1981–1984 under the European Monetary System, Leon Blum did not receive the necessary support from the establishment and was forced out of office in 1937. Under Vichy France, he was kept under house arrest, sent to Buchenwald in 1943 and transferred to Dachau in 1945 where, in the special political prisoner section, in one of the bitter ironies of history, he met the disgraced former Hjalimar Schacht, head of the Reichbank.

Absorbing the lessons of the popular front, De Gaulle understood that monetary policy had to reflect France's prestige. Like Napoleon, aware that the money is foremost a symbol of sovereignty, De Gaulle refused to allow the circulation of American army-issued "billets de liberation," which were dollars denominated in francs, demanding that Eisenhower replace them with Bank of France bills. In 1946, the bulk of gold bars smuggled out of the vaults of the Bank of France to Lisbon and London returned, and the Bank of France was among the first central banks able to re-establish a viable currency.

The omnipotent British Empire refused to admit that despite winning World War I, it had lost its undisputed economic hegemony. Suddenly rivaled and surpassed in industrial output and monetary influence by a victorious hyperexuberant American market economy, Britain depended on Montagu Norman, the eccentric and obsessive governor of the Bank of England, who, in 1925, persuaded Churchill to revert to the Gold Standard until 1931. Norman remained adamantly convinced of the invulnerability of gold and sterling, which could not withstand the shocks of disjointed monetary policy and weak economic fundamentals. Yet, as the fledgling democracies of the post-World War I era gave way to the ravages of totalitarianism and fascism, Britain alone offered a sense of security in the continuity of Lloyds, Barings, Barclays, the Bank of England, and the pound sterling, which retained its prestige as global trade currency until 1939.

5.5 Marxism: the agony and the ecstasy

> The inherent vice of capitalism is the unequal sharing of the blessings. The inherent blessing of socialism is the equal sharing of misery.
> (Churchill, as quoted by Risk Capital Partners chairman, Luke Johnson, *Financial Times*, May 21, 2008)

The creation of the Soviet state and the destruction of the capitalist model proposed a system which would be the antithesis of financial history and culture. The ideal state of man would be one in which money, profit, gain, enterprise, banks, money markets, stock exchanges, and financial instruments, as means of exchange and commerce would no longer exist, thereby obliterating and rewriting economic history.

Where for centuries economics had been attacked on moral grounds, the realization of the Soviet Union gave the disillusioned, agnostic, and dispossessed World War I generation the means to condemn economics on political grounds. Capitalism was not just a moral abomination; it was now a political and moral abomination for the right and the left. By outlawing and systematically destroying the means of production and possessions of the aristocracy, the privileged, the bourgeoisie, by re-appropriating lands, real estate, and holdings of these classes, Marxism sought to eradicate the culture of consumerism, materialism, and profitability. The notorious re-education campaigns of the Russian Gulag or the Maoist purges against intellectuals, merchants, professionals and aristocracy sought to remove by force all interest, desire or aspiration to possess any object not allotted by the state to the collective body politic. In the aftermath of World War I, Marxism in the formulations of Lenin and Stalin, even in the heresies of Trotsky, offered in principle the realization of the dreams and hopes of the disenfranchised, not the apotheosis of the exploited masses, but the power of the "proletariat des bacheliers," the educated workers, and embittered intellectuals to create a pure anti-capitalist state.

Even when these goals had been discredited and proven untenable, European intellectuals saw Marxism as the antidote to the sordid trio of state, industry, and finance, which had dominated politics and policies since the 1840s. Like Napoleon, Communist leaders Lenin, Mao, and Fidel Castro created their own mythology, revered and honored as heroes. The disdain of intellectuals toward money, its agents, and institutions in the nineteenth century became a source of revulsion at the heart of a new ideology. For the Marxist state, wealth was not only morally reprehensible, but now it was politically subversive and destructive to the nation. For Marxist and socialist writers of the 1920s and 1930s, the banker reverts to stereotype, ferociously depicted by George Grosz, Max Beckmann, and Otto Dix in the Neue Sachlichkeit School (New Objectivity School) of realistic art. Capitalism is totally cannibalistic and exploitative, with no redeeming features in the devastated economy of post-war Germany where the rich have to consume the poor, figuratively and literary, in order to survive and thrive. In French poet Louis Aragon's *Cloches de Bâle*, John Steinbeck's *In Dubious Battle*, Bertolt Brecht's *Die Dreigroschenoper* [*The Threepenny Opera*] where bankers in morning coats post the bail for their new director, McHeath, king of the underworld, the banker is symbol of exploitation of rural and urban working classes. The fragmented collage narrative in John Dos Passos' *The Big Money* presents a "camera eye" of historical and fictional events. The United States is defined as consisting of "holding companies, trade unions, radio networks ... stock quotations rubbed out and written in ... USA is a set of big mouthed officials with too many bank accounts" (Dos Passos, 1937). To Dos Passos, financial transactions and the desire to make a killing in the market were a sublimation of primitive urges toward aggression and violence.

Conscious of the brutal disruption and fragility of political and economic continuity, fascinated and frightened by the lure of Marxism, yet repulsed by the vulgarity and perceived amorality of capitalism; influential European and American authors choose detached elegant commentary on the social and sexual mores of the affluent. Huxley, Gide, Mann, Fitzgerald, Christie's Miss Marple series, P.G. Wodehouse's Jeeves series, and Colette offer exquisite commentary on the doings of the idle rich with sharp inklings of discomfort. Money and art, like money and literature split ways. In the deconstruction and reformulation of literary and artistic genres, from Cubism, Dadism, and Surrealism to James Joyce, there is a fascination with machines, inventions, new laws of physics, medicine, science, and psychoanalysis but very few references to money. The sufferings of the starving poet living in a garret, unable to afford coal in winter or decent food, gave way to the myth of glamorous poverty, where intellectuals and artists living in cheap hotels in Greenwich Village in New York, Montparnasse, Montmartre, and the Left Bank in Paris frequented cafés, jazz clubs, and restaurants in a seemingly endless round of drinks and affairs. Writers, artists, and musicians flocked to Paris from the increasingly repressive regimes across Europe and Asia, and the oppressive conservatism of Middle America. The cheap franc provided good food, mobility, and easy credit, supplemented by the patronage of rich American expatriates like Zelda Fitzgerald, Gertrude Stein, and Anais Nin.

Descriptions of finance are usually associated with a real or imaginary America, embodiment of free market activity devoid of any redeeming features. Celine's brutal, scatological *Voyage au bout de la nuit* [*Journey to the End of the Night*] (1932), follows Bardamu's journey to New York and Detroit, the antipodes of capitalism and socialism. Wall Street is portrayed as a secular church dedicated to the sacred ritual of "the Dollar, a true Holy Ghost, more precious than blood," but the sanctuary of the bank is also the scene of ritualistic use of public toilets and defecation. Kafka, in his novel *Amerika* (1946 [1927]), describes a phantasmagoric journey where the hero Karl, meets Mr. Pollunder, a New York banker and symbol of American efficiency. Karl's experiences with finance and exchange of commodities are dehumanized, anonymous transactions within a bureaucratic robot like structure.

The rare case where the bank, although dehumanized, is placed in a specific political context occurs in *La Condition Humaine*. Andre Malraux, novelist, art critic, and future minister of culture under De Gaulle (whose socialist credentials remained ambiguous as he benefited from sundry business ventures in Indochina) won the prestigious Prix Goncourt in 1933 for his elegy to existentialism and Marxism. The novel reveals the bitter fractures within the Chinese Communist party in 1927, and the tragic antithesis between the forces of colonial capitalism and Marxism. But the seventh part, separated from the rest of the text, mirroring the geopolitical detachment of the Bank of Indochina, transfers the action to Paris, to prove that (as in the case of the Paris Commune) the *sine qua non* of the success or failure of the revolution is money. The ideals of Marxist rebellion and the basest instincts of capitalism are juxtaposed. The businessman banker Ferral is called to Paris, accountable for the actions of a consortium of banks in China, to seek a restructured consortium with sufficient funding. He meets with representatives of the Bank of France, Treasury, finance inspectors, and bankers from Crédit Lyonnais, described as caramel chewing, elderly, nameless, caricatures of aristocrats with their monocles and white moustaches. But in turn Ferral is viewed as an outsider to the banking establishment, not a true banker, an unmarried womanizer, suspected of opium addiction, having refused the Legion of Honor, a lone wolf speculator: "Ferral always wants a bank to be a gambling den [Ferral veut toujours qu'une banque soit une maison de jeu]" (Malraux 1933: 328). Ferral's methods are speculative but his intentions are societal and political therefore worthy, theirs are only numerical as the discussion references assets, balance sheet: "language chiffre." The consortium will be bailed out even if "deficitaire" (ibid.: 329) in order to protect French interests with the least liabilities. The consortium is compared to Mitsubishi in Japan (the most prominent keiretsu in the 1920s), looking solely to protect its own interests under Chiang Kai Shek without any intention of helping develop China or aid in its reconstruction. Naïvely, Ferral announces the end of the communist rebellion, but there is no interest to provide further funding as one minister understands it in quashing a movement has not quashed Communism. The novel reflected the concerns in France, which had lost nearly 40 billion francs in shares and loans invested in the colonies since 1919, and the desires of the French banking establishment, "Mur d'Argent," to recoup any losses and close ranks.

5.6 Limousine liberals to Louis Vuitton

Great heroism, coupled with the devastating losses Russia suffered in World War II, granted the Soviet Union immense goodwill and exculpation among European and American intellectuals, lasting through the Hungarian uprising of 1956, the first information on the Gulag in the 1960s, and even in the immediate aftermath of the Prague Spring, 1968. Even when Gide, Malraux, Orwell, Koestler, Gunter Grass, Milan Kundera or the archetypal Russian dissidents Pasternak and Solzhenitsyn, would reject the abuses of communism, they never accepted capitalism, materialism or free market ideology as a societal solution. Sartre, Camus, and Beauvoir, the most influential voices of the post-World War II era, demanded that intellectuals take pride in inherent contempt for material wealth, emphasizing its corruptive influence. In *Les Mandarins* (1953, translated 1954), Simone de Beauvoir sends her heroine to Chicago, recreating her relationship with the impoverished drug addicted Nelson Algren, a Chicago of dark, dank apartments, sordid bars, and back alleys, a world where the intellectual is underappreciated and exploited. The phrase "limousine liberals," coined in the 1970s in the United States, was picked up in France a decade later as "gauche cavier," satirizing the wealthy left which sought to reconcile Marxist ideology and capitalist lifestyle. Black revolutionaries in Park Avenue penthouses and French Socialists in the salons of Neuilly were subject to ridicule, but underneath the satire they proved that the quest for luxury was just as potent as the belief in equal wage distribution and state imposed distribution of goods. The only effective melding of Socialist principles, wage allocation, and social equality with a restrained Western consumer culture occurred in the Nordic countries. These homogeneous, insulated societies with few markets, needing to balance their commercial interests between the Soviet Union and Europe, flourished through the 1980s. Although admired, Sweden, Finland, Denmark, and Norway remained outside of the larger intellectual debate. Their significant contribution to film was heralded; the social welfare "Swedish model" was touted by economists but largely ignored by the European Community intelligentsia.

The first expressions of freedom in the Soviet Union, East Germany, East Central European countries, and newly enriched China since 2004 were manifested in an extravagance of conspicuous consumption in luxury goods, property, and tangible assets. Across the former Soviet Union and satellite states, the suppressed instincts of materialism burst in a true wave of "irrational exuberance," as if to make up for 75 years of deprivation. In order to succeed, Marxism had to persuade or coerce its citizens to believe that equitable distribution of wealth and its corollary, equal scarcity of goods, services, and consumer choices, was preferable. Satirizing the 1989 period, the German tragicomic film *Goodbye Lenin* (2003), captured the overwhelming lure of consumerism and the remnants of ideology in the tale of a staunch communist woman who falls into a coma the night the Berlin Wall comes down in November 1989. Coming out of the coma a few months later, her family, persuaded that she could not handle the shock of the new consumer driven Germany, tries to replicate the food, products, and events of the Communist era.

The Marxist state, by assuming all responsibilities for the welfare of its citizens, took paternalism from benign oligarchy to authoritarianism, as the state would both provide and control the entire chain of financial transactions, from production to distribution, eliminating the market and competition. By dictating quantity and quality, it removed choice in the name of equality, and collective instead of spiritual virtue. The fascination with the objects of consumer culture, made available to the small elite as rewards, smuggled or, in the short periods of détente, sent from abroad, consistently undermined the power of ideology to overcome desire of material possessions. Gorbachev, in the twin concepts of perestroika and glasnost, provided the West, led by Chancellor Kohl, an opportunity to basically buy out the Soviet Union by assuming the costs and burden of its vast empire, as described in Timothy Garten Ash's *In Europe's Name, Germany and the Divided Continent* (1993). Gorbachev understood that the Soviet Union was about to collapse under its own weight, and that a restricted market economy, with full support and massive capital injections in Deutschmarks and dollars, was the only solution. In a sense, the end of the Soviet Union was the greatest initial public offering in history. In 2008, Gorbachev, elder statesman of Russia's return to market economy, revered more abroad than in Russia, took his role to its ultimate ironic conclusion, becoming one of the faces of Louis Vuitton, hyper-expensive luxury leather goods advertisement campaign. Sharing the role with Madonna, the "material girl," he symbolized the end of ideology in the name of consumption.

5.7 Paradox of post-Marxism

> Less than seventy-five years after it officially began the contest between
> capitalism and socialism is over: capitalism has won. The Soviet Union,
> China and Eastern Europe have given us the clearest possible proof that
> capitalism organizes the material affairs of humankind more satisfactorily
> than socialism; that however inequitably or irresponsibly the marketplace
> may distribute goods, it does so better than the queues of a planned
> economy.
>
> (Heilbroner 1989)

Since 1991, the former Soviet Union, both satellite countries and parts of greater
Russia, shared one goal: to enter the West literally and figuratively. The West, a
mythological variant of the American dream, was in fact a vision of Europe
based on rapid accumulation of wealth, consumer goods, and democratic institutions. The economic boom of the 1990s further accelerated these objectives, as
technology seemed to herald a new era of continuous growth and profit. Joining
the European Union in 2004, Former Soviet Union (FSU) and Central and
Eastern European (CEE) countries, which within the last decade barely recon-
structed their own historic identity, had to persuade their citizens of the advantages of this new supra structure. Despite politicians enthusiastically celebrating
the European Union enlargement, in May 2004, regionalization implied loss of
national sovereignty and complex standardization of commercial products and
financial practices. Just as developing nations chafed against the conditions of
the International Monetary Fund and World Bank loans, and technical assistance, factions in new member countries chafed against the reforms and monitoring imposed by European Union authorities in Brussels.

In 2009, the unraveling of Eastern Europe in both European Union and non
European Union countries, from Latvia, Estonia, Hungary, Czech Republic, to
Ukraine, revealed that the transition may have occurred too quickly and much
more superficially than assumed.

> Capitalism as it had emerged in the Atlantic world and Western Europe over
> the course of four centuries was accompanied by laws, institutions, regula-
> tions and practices upon which it was critically dependent for its operation
> and its legitimacy. In many post Communist countries such laws and institu-
> tions were quite unknown – and dangerously underestimated by neophyte
> free marketers there.
>
> (Judt 2005: 689)

The fallacy of instantaneous transformation from command to market economy
was encouraged by the Clinton administration's well meaning but naïve economic and development experts. Investment, trade, aid missions, and advisors
from European nations, led by France and Germany through the European Union
PHARE (Pologne, Hongrie Assistance à la Reconstruction Economique)

program and the European Bank for Reconstruction and Development (EBRD), from America through the departments of State and Commerce, and USAID, all sought to bring Western know how, financial methodology, and management programs into these newly reconstituted countries, and into the even less ready Newly Independent States (NIS). The assumption was that education, retraining, and funding would allow privatization to occur on a national scale. The reality was that privatization became "kleptocracy," as the old group of state bureaucrats adopted new democratic titles and proceeded to loot their state treasuries.

The creation or reinstatement of domestic currencies and the explosion of banks were among the first indicators of major discrepancies between enactment and implementation of sound policy. Between 1990 and 1992, every newly liberated country declared its autonomy by establishing its own currency, reinstating national symbols, and opening a Central Bank. But these currencies were only symbols. When Erhard established the Deutschmark on June 20, 1948; Napoleon, the franc in 1803; and De Gaulle the nouveau franc in 1958, they understood that a currency had to be defined by strong government support, stability, and convertibility. Transactions in the East Central European countries continued in Deutschmarks or in dollars as in the Communist era black market. Slavenka Drakulic (*Café Europa*) journalist, wrote a reportage of these transitional years in which the simplest tasks such as buying a vacuum cleaner became a symbol of the clash of cultures. Wanting to buy the appliance to take back to their summer house in Croatia, she details the bribes necessary at the border, the problem of buying one in Croatia due to huge overpricing, rampant corruption, and smuggling of foreign goods. "In that respect nothing has changed since the communist times. But obviously such traffic poses a problem for our already devastated nation and economy ... as millions of German marks are spent abroad each month" (Drakulic 1997: 111). Capital flight out of Russia, the Newly Independent States, and East Central European countries impeded accountability on how and where aid money was spent. Central banks, well intentioned and often manned by Western educated economists, were unable to manage long-term policies, fearing inflation, and at the mercy of foreign investment. Even in 2008, real estate speculation and exposure in Hungary and Latvia was largely denominated in euros and Swiss francs, revealing a basic lack of faith in local currency denominated instruments.

The opening of Eastern and Central Europe and former Soviet Asian republics provided huge new markets, but like Asia or Mexico under NAFTA, the great fallacy of the 1991–1998 period was that open markets meant receptive, responsible, and stable markets. The move from totally regulated to deregulated economies, was translated as free for all capitalism, the principles of a market culture, with its risks, rewards, and obligations left unexplained. In financial and business practices, the lack of basic information was overwhelming. All operations, from the role of the individual in every process of the chain of command, the role of service and service industries, finding and keeping clients, functions of banks versus credit agencies, loans and contractual obligations in countries without any commercial code, sales tax, and capital gains tax, had to be reconsti-

tuted. In East Germany and Hungary, the first reforms had to resolve appropriation and reappropriation of private property confiscated in 1947–1954. The
concept of bankruptcy, last detailed in pre-1917 Russia, had to be explained, the
basic functions of checking accounts and other bank functions had to be re-
introduced.

From 1917 to 1989, Russian banking had four state owned banks: Gosbank,
state bank of the USSR which presided over allocation of credit; Vneshtorgbank
for foreign trading operations; Stroibank for long-term capital investment under
the Five Year Plans; and Sberbank, the only deposit savings bank for Soviet citizens (Fitch Ratings 2007). Once individuals were given the right to create
banks, "this led to a huge increase in the number of small banks from less than
one hundred in 1988 to nearly 2,500 at the end of 1995" (Fitch Ratings 2007). In
reality in the mid-1990s, less than 200 actually qualified as banks, according to
United States and European Union. By 2007 the system had been reformed and
restructured with about 1,100 banks, of which the four largest, which accounted
for 40 percent of the market, are state owned. There are few private banks and
only a few foreign institutions led by Raiffeisenbank, Citibank, and HSBC.
French banks were the first to return to Russia. Crédit Lyonnais, the largest bank
in St Petersburg in 1917, had lost vast assets in railroad bonds, yet immediately
after World War II, it began to re-establish contacts. In 1972, it was the only
Western bank granted permission to open a representative office in Moscow. In
October 1989, actively involved in leasing and joint ventures, it helped establish the International Moscow Bank with Crédit Lyonnais, as shareholder,
with three Soviet and four other foreign banks. Over-invested and under-
regulated, on August 17, 1997, Russia devalued the ruble after defaulting on
Treasury bills. When the International Monetary Fund refused a bailout liquidity
dried up and foreign investors panicked and retreated. In the United States, this
led to the near collapse of Long Term Capital Management hedge fund (LTCM),
which by the end of August lost US$1.9 billion in assets and 45 percent of its
capital. Its entire hedging strategy had been based on the belief that exogenous
events could not undermine a perfect model, even when dealing with barely
functioning post-Soviet economies.

Following the Asian and Russian currency crisis of 1997–1998, it was clear
that the banking sector was immature, inefficient, poorly capitalized, and prone
to corruption and lack of regulatory oversight. Within five years, the banking
sector in East Central European countries had been taken over, nearly 80 percent
by European Union banks. Austrian, Italian, Swedish, and French banks injected
capital; provided credibility and trust in retail networks; and improved efficiency
and technology, which allowed a smooth flow of foreign investment and trade.
Once absorbed into the European Union in 2004, these new member countries
could neither claim history nor any advantage for small indigenous institutions,
therefore fledgling and formerly state-owned institutions were bought up by
large core European Union banks. These takeovers have brought modernization
and name recognition, but they have also engendered resentment, as in the case
of Poland in 2006. In 1998, Rolf Breuer, former chairman of Deutsche Bank,

discussing the impact of European Economic and Monetary Union on the banking sector, stressed that French, German, and Italian banks would undergo "massive consolidation" under pressure from the euro, electronic banking, and globalization. Although he predicted that there would be greater acceptance of foreign bank takeovers, he foresaw the cultural obstacles:

> But countries' emotional and psychological objections to deals involving big foreign banks could be mitigated if these were in specialized areas such as retail or investment banking. That would be more likely to be successful than if a big elephant comes along and the small one says: "My God, that's the end of my 100 year history."
>
> (Breuer 1998)

When the crisis of 2008 accelerated, and over-leveraged and over-exposed major banks in Austria, Italy, Sweden, or even France came under domestic pressure, one of the concerns was whether they would withdraw, siphon off these assets, or reduce stakes. As these countries falter, their currencies in free fall and their bonds downgraded, outside of Slovenia, which having joined the Euro in 2007, they are not formally under the jurisdiction of the European Central Bank. Therefore, without formal obligation they depend on political good will to rescue them. The core countries, France and Germany, having carried the burden of subsidies and aid to concentric groups of "new" member countries since the inception of the European Community in 1958, and having brought in the countries of East Central European and the Former Soviet Union with generous subsidies in 2004, are now feeling the brunt of the financial crisis, and are far less willing or able to extend concerted bailout packages. One of the most troubling ramifications of the 2008 financial crisis is whether these countries, integrated into the European Union in 2004 and 2007, but unable to meet European Economic and Monetary Union criteria, feeling as economically betrayed by the West as they had been politically betrayed or ignored in the 1930s, may revert to extremism in nationalism or other forms of authoritarianism.

In Russia, still a global nuclear power, the greatest damage has been inflicted by the brutal drop in the price of oil from $140 a barrel in summer 2008, to less than $40 a barrel by March 2009. The large oligarch fortunes, based on commodity monopolies in nickel, copper, oil, and gas, have been severely depleted. The Russian Stock Market, re-established by 1995 with two exchanges, the Moscow Interbank Currency Exchange (MICEX) and the Russian Trading System (RTS), was heavily weighted in oil and gas companies, led by Gazprom, Lukoil, and Rosneft, which carried nearly 65 percent of the market before fall 2008.

Do the former countries of East Central Europe and the Former Soviet Union, depressed and disillusioned, look again to Russia, already able to exert control through Eastern Europe's dependency on Russian gas and oil? If Russia, despite its own volatile economy, is able to offer aid and rescue packages, under what conditions will help be offered? Niall Ferguson, in a lecture in February 2009, compared the state of Austrian banks' near insolvency to the failure of Credit Anstalt, the largest Austrian bank in 1931, a shock to the markets that accelerated the Depression in Eastern Europe and subsequent disasters. This comparison may be too dire and yet....

5.8 Wartime finances

The war found Germany with an economy at full employment and with a high civilian use of industrial capacity.

(Galbraith 1994: 127)

The ruthless, draconian conditions of Nazi occupation derived from the deep hatred for the humiliation imposed on Germany in the period following World War I. The goal of German war-time finances was to despoil and bankrupt all occupied countries, by bleeding dry their financial reserves. Kindleberger cites the report "France During the German Occupation 1940–1944" that France had to reimburse Germany for the occupation on a daily basis to a: "sum of 20 million Reichsmarks, calculated as 400 million francs, payable in advance every ten days," to pay expenses of lodging and quartering the troops on French territory. The Reichsmark was set at 20 francs "it bore no relation to the true value of the two currencies at that time, the mark being worth barely over 10 or 12 francs," also included were additional military charges of advances calculated in 1944 to reach "165,000 million francs" (1993: 393). Almost half of World War II expenses were raised by taxes from the occupied countries outside of Eastern Europe. The occupation troops also had their own banks, Reichkreditkassen, issuing notes for German authorities and troops. Occupied countries returned to Germany between 85 billion and 104 billion Reichsmarks. France claimed 862.5 billion francs, and Belgium between 70 billion and 100 billion francs. Occupied countries functioned with dual economies, German imposing exchange rates and prices forcing a grey economy in which even the Germans participated, with rationing for the occupied civilian populations, and barter.

The Aryan myth of "ubermenschen," based on Nietschean and Wagnerian philosophical and literary conceits, was intrinsically anti-capitalist, reverting to an idealized past of virtuous and glorious heroic exploits. But as in Grimm's fairy tales, the real quest is for lost, stolen or retrieved gold, and power. Priding itself on anti-materialist values, the Third Reich, by portraying the Jews as purveyors of capital, stolen or hoarded, could justify purging and purifying Europe by genocidal policies. Once the Jews were stereotyped and dehumanized as propagators of destructive capitalism, they could be murdered; their possessions removed and even their body parts transformed into spoils of war or objects of use to the war effort. In this context, the victims of Nazism helped fund their own extermination. Economic justification was one of the greatest horrors of the wars, the use of slave labor, the vast industrial complex of death machines in which nearly 30 million lives were lost, including six million Jews and 20 million Russians.

Extending the original role of finance to provide money for war, banks in Germany and Japan became the conduit for the funding of occupation, extermination, and prison and death camps. As banks did not employ slave labor, or partake in any specific campaigns of brutalization, it was not an issue of direct physical culpability, but rather knowledge, abetting, and funding the companies which sat on their boards in interlocked directorships. Hermann Abs, in top positions at Deutsche Bank since 1938, was aware of the Aryanization campaign, which forced Siegfried Warburg to escape to London, nearly penniless, of the Oppenheim bank being forced to change its name and relegate its management to Nazi party members. Accused of collaboration in 1946 but reinstated in 1948, he became America's favorite German banker, overseeing the administration of the Marshall Fund, invited to the White House after 1957: "he represented Germany in much of its financial dealings with the United States" (Kobrak 2007: 262). However, aware of the political implications, Deutsche Bank, an important presence in New York, with representatives on Wall Street from 1880–1914, did not return to the United States until 1979.

For almost 50 years the archives of major European banks were inaccessible, banking histories encased in time frames of 1900–1939 and 1946 onward. Slowly and painfully, the history of complicity and collaboration with wartime activities came to light through the opening of bank archives to American and German scholars, Volker Berghahn, Gerald Feldman, and Mary Nolan among others, allowing historical studies on wartime banking and industrial activity.

In literature there are very few references to the banks, therefore Irene Nemirovsky's recovered manuscripts, *Suite Française* (2006), offered rare insights on the role of banks and bankers in the exodus from Paris in 1940. A converted Russian Jew living in France, Nemirovsky, captured and killed in 1942, described the hierarchy and arrogance of social conventions between bankers and bank employees in the flight of refugees from Paris She described lower-level bank employees, entrusted with administrative duties trying to follow instructions and reach Tours, who, upon returning to Paris, are blamed and sacked after years of loyal service by the arrogant and devious bank director Corbin: "an uncouth individual who had begun his career in a lowly and almost vile manner, in a loan establishment" (2006: 170). "The Accounting Department was in Cahors, the executives in Bayonne; the secretaries had headed for Toulouse but had got lost somewhere between Nice and Perpignan. No one seemed to know where the banks papers had ended up" (2006: 171). Witness to the chaos, Nemirovsky minutely rendered the confluence of latent Jewish interests, displaced patriotism, and naïve belief that the German occupation would restore order and stability.

In the late 1930s, Swiss banks, having established confidentiality rules since 1934, promising neutrality in case of conflict, inspired confidence. Jewish bankers, professionals, and art dealers across Europe, especially Germany and Austria, established accounts in the belief that their funds would be safe and available. When tens of thousands of account holders never returned, Union des Banques Suisse, Swiss Bank Corporation (UBS since 2003), and Credit Suisse, in the following half century never opened the accounts, strove to locate survivors or made the information public. Switzerland's neutrality was also compromised, as it was revealed in law suits of the late 1990s that the banks had served as conduit for Third Reich funds.

Wars were initially fought for land and power, but wars also increased taxes, the production and distribution of goods, and the arms needed to wage war. World War II added another dimension to this infernal bargain, as the destruction of civilian populations, and a state ordained policy of genocide was carried out with the implicit support of financial institutions. The direct involvement of German industry, banks, insurance houses, and commercial enterprises in the undertakings of Nazi Germany, as well as the involvement of Italian insurance companies, and the tacit complicity of French and Swiss banks, refuted the notion of compartmentalization and separation of powers between warring governments and institutions which helped fund genocides and destruction of civilian societies, from Africa's "blood diamonds," to Chinese investment in Sudan, and terrorism funding.

5.9 Weirgild, Weidergutmachung, and the State of Israel

On March 12, 1951, the Israeli government sent a note to the four powers which had occupied Germany after World War II, and demanded German payments of 1.5 billion dollars for the integration of 500,000 Jewish refugees (three thousand dollars per person). One billion dollars were claimed from the Federal Republic and 500 million from the GDR ... November 1952, the Federal Republic of Germany and Israel concluded the Luxembourg Agreements, which were the basis for German payments to Israel in the form of goods and services valued at three billion D-marks delivered over a period of fourteen years ... An additional amount of 450 million D-marks was paid to the Conference of Jewish Material Claims Against Germany (Claims Conference), which had been established in 1951 by the major Jewish organizations throughout the world to negotiate agreements with Germany concerning property restitution, individual compensation, and global payments for the benefit of Jewish victims of Nazi persecution.

(Lehman 1991)

Since the earliest texts on money as "Weirgild" (originally established in legal reforms under Alfred the Great in the ninth century as money to reimburse family murders), compensation or reparation money for an honor killing or murder, still relevant in Albania and, Afghanistan, the concept of money for a human life is abhorrent, yet integral in primitive societies revenge and honor systems. The creation of the State of Israel in 1948, and its desperate need of international support was the basis for accepting massive German aid, justified as war reparation and reconstruction as well as personal compensation to the survivors of the Holocaust. The term

Wiedergutmachung – though the most suitable word in German – sounds helplessly naïve and out of place. Jews and Israelis used a number of terms for their material claims from Germany, since it was still quite unclear at the time what exactly they were demanding. English terms such as indemnities, reparations, recompense, compensation, restitution, collective reparations, recovering of property, or rehabilitation did not correctly express the nature of these claims.

(Lehman 1991)

The term may appear inadequate, but in fact it carries deeper connotations: Wieder = again, gut = good, machung = doing, juxtaposing moral and physical interaction, it underscores the moral responsibility of having to pay for the privilege of once again being considered worthy of good actions. It is a term of shame as it does not carry root or connotation of money, but rather of moral atonement to define the largest ever war reparation in response to genocide.

The biographies of and interviews with survivors such as George Soros and Felix Rohatyn, reveal how their attitudes toward money remains forever scarred, extremely cautious, defensive, pessimistic, and wary of its ephemeral and fragile nature. Rohatyn, former ambassador to France in the Clinton administration, senior partner at Lazard, and savior of New York in the 1970s, escaped from Vienna with his family in 1935, arriving in New York in 1942, via Paris, Marseille, Oran, Casablanca, Rio de Janeiro, and Miami. This trajectory, shared by mainly the most privileged and wealthiest of German and Austrian Jews, defines him: "He is at once preternaturally pessimistic about the outcome of events, extremely conservative financially, and far less prone to excessive ostentation than most of his extremely wealthy investment banking peers" (Cohan, 2007: 14). He always recalls:

Stuffing gold coins into toothpaste tubes. We had been well off, but that was all we got out. Ever since, I've had the feeling that the only permanent wealth is what you carry around in your head ... a theory of wealth which is that of a refugee.

(Cohan 2007: 14)

5.10 Bretton Woods: the Americanization of financial culture

So America is the undisputed world capital of stuff ... to them it was bizarre and funny to be confronted with twenty seven different brands of soap powder.

(Sante 2003: 71)

The significance of Bretton Woods, the July 1944 meeting at the Mount Washington hotel in Bretton Woods, New Hampshire, where delegates from 44 countries met to create a global financial framework under the aegis of the United States, was much more than an economic summit. In a near totally devastated world, by establishing fixed exchange rates with 1 percent parity bands pegged to the dollar, the dollar as reserve currency, the International Monetary Fund, and the International Bank of Reconstruction (World Bank), it formally granted the United States, the dollar, and the American Treasury undisputed hegemony over global financial systems and culture. Following John Maynard Keynes' and Harry Dexter White's blueprint, it established America as guarantor of economic security. Through August 1971, when Nixon expediently decided to decouple the dollar from gold and set free foreign exchange markets (formalized in the December 1971 Smithsonian Agreements), the conditions set out in Bretton Woods would guide all financial decisions. Money and markets, whether tangible, abstract, symbol, or representation, functioned in relation to the American dollar.

In 1955, a devastated, Europe, Eastern and Central Europe behind the Iron Curtain, Austria just freed from Soviet domination, Britain's economy a wreck, the British Empire, like the French, in tatters, barely contemplated the start of the Common Market. In the next 30 years, despite the economic miracle in Germany, the exceptional recovery of Western Europe under the Marshall Plan, and sound, cautious economic policies, there was very little interest in the culture of finance. The terms corporate culture and financial culture had not been coined and would have appeared to be oxymoronic. Whether under center right, the Christian Democratic Union in Germany, the Gaullist right in France, socialist regimes in the Nordic countries, or revolving doors governments in Italy, Europe turned to variations of socialism as psychological and economic safety nets. The "welfare" state provided a sense of security to a war ravished, bitter, hardened, and risk averse society. Fortunes were made, retrieved or re-established, but business and banking class kept a low profile.

> In a French survey conducted in 1947, when asked what mattered more love or money, 47 percent of men and 38 percent of women said money [...]. In 1953 72 percent of French men and women believe that real estate, jewels, and paintings are the safest investments, while 16 percent prefer stocks and other negotiable securities.
>
> (Prost and Vincent 1971: 153)

There was a fascination in the tabloid press, novels, and films with the "jet set," the few very wealthy who could afford air travel, described in Francoise Sagan's *Bonjour Tristesse* and Ian Fleming's James Bond series, but in reality, this group consisted largely of aristocrats, entertainment figures and heiresses, especially Americans like Barbara Hutton and Doris Duke. The press and television reveled in the fairy tale story of the American actress Grace Kelly and Prince Rainier of Monaco. Society pages in newspapers and magazines, on both sides of the Atlantic, would offer details of the lavish balls thrown by European aristocrats: the most sumptuous through the 1980s by Baroness Marie-Helene de Rothschild, recreating fantasies in the Proust Ball, the Surrealist Ball, in the seventeenth-century Hotel Lambert, where Voltaire had lived (Petkanas 2008). The expenditures and life style of the rich were of great interest, but their actual sources of income, business dealings, and financial holdings were kept out of the public and media. The purpose of bankers was to maintain stability in policy and institutions, of stockbrokers to carefully invest in safe companies for small groups of institutional clients and wealthy individuals. Only in the United States had shareholder culture begun to resurface, marketed to the middle classes (see Chapter 6). When bankers were depicted, they were elegantly dressed gentlemen engaged in esoteric activities, such as Cary Grant, a dashing American "international banker," engaged in "hard currency" negotiations in London that incongruously involved NATO and the British home office in *Indiscreet* with Ingrid Bergman (1958). Bankers were eminently respectable, cautious, important, and once again trustworthy.

For most of the twentieth century, money, consumerism, materialism, and finance were intrinsically associated with America. The American myth prevailed as it was unattainable, yet almost within reach. Most of the world wanted American products without American ideology, accepted American ideology but sought to retain higher moral ground in disdaining American products, or forcibly condemned American ideology while using American products. As Volker Berghahn showed, the industrial, managerial, mass culture, and consumption of America was imposed on Germany (Berghahn 1986 and 2001). America alone could decide how to present its culture, as benign consumerism, inculcated capitalist philosophy, or in large amounts of aid which improved conditions, while incurring moral and psychological indebtedness. European intellectuals could feel superior and ignore material reality in their works, but their disdain was tinged with bitterness, as economic progress and the revival of a material culture was the only salvation, a salvation entirely under American control and hegemony.

The only governments acceptable in the first decade after the war were left-wing with indisputable anti-Fascist credentials, socialist in tenor and philosophy, and intrinsically anti-capitalist. Governments understood that a strong stable public sector alone could guarantee a return of faith and confidence. Outside of Germany, prohibited to engage in any government takeovers of financial and industrial sectors, European countries were largely state run structures. In the 1960s, the French economy was nearly 80 percent state run, with the top three banks nationalized since 1946. Up until 1979, large sectors of the British economy were nationalized; Italy revived its multilayered state, local, and regional ownership of banks, industry, and press. Financial institutions, returned to the role of safe keeping, lending, and judiciously investing a small client base's often inherited fortunes. The public had limited interaction with financial intermediaries other than postal accounts, savings accounts, and pawnshops. John Le Carre, in *The Spy Who Came in from the Cold* (1963), debunked the James Bond fantasy of elegant spies in bespoke suits offered the following exchange:

> "We always ask for a banker's reference before giving credit" he said and Leamas lost his temper. "Don't talk bloody cock!" he shouted, "Half your

customers have never seen the inside of a bank and never bloody well will."
This was heresy beyond bearing, since it was true.

(Le Carre 1963: 50)

Postal accounts, savings and loans, thrifts, and credit institutions were sparingly
used for specific loans, deposits, and cashing services. Through the 1980s, the
four big British banks, Barclays, National Westminster, Midlands, and Lloyds,
were star global players but domestically catered to a limited client base.

> In 1980 less than sixty percent of Englishmen had bank accounts and most
> factory workers would not go near them: "The real challenge for us over the
> next few years," said Sir Anthony Tuke of Barclays in 1980, "will be our
> ability to create the necessary modern banking systems and facilities to
> attract the eleven million wage and salary earners who today have no active
> clearing bank accounts."

(Sampson 1981: 229)

After World War II, European bourgeoisie's standards of affluence, taste, propriety, and good manners, locked in a time capsule, *circa* pre-war Vienna, Berlin,
and London, survived, despite or perhaps because of decimation, insecurity, and
deprivation. In the homes and apartments of the well to do middle class, whether
in Paris, New York, Istanbul or Buenos Aires, refugees, emigrants, or re-
established fortunes observed the same standards of appropriateness and
decorum verging on the repressive, in dress, décor, manners, standards of enter-
tainments, codes of proper behavior, and class conscious respect and formality.
Above all, there was a sense of discretion imbued with fear and fragility; "As the
new rich came with good reason to fear the state, these timid families had only
one way to advance themselves and that was to show themselves to be more
European than they really were" (Pamuk 2005: 191). Well made, elegant, yet
modest and long-wearing goods recreated a sense of solidity, an illusion of
stability and order. Europe was not a consumer society. Europeans saved,
scrimped, bought durable consumer goods, and spent relatively little on non-
necessary purchases.

Faith and optimism in the progressive trajectory of capitalist societies had
been replaced by bitter ambivalence between dependency and fascination with
American financial power: economies under the tutelage of the Marshall Plan,
the almighty dollar as official and black market currency. America's image of
consumption, availability, and choice loomed in countries plagued by all encom-
passing shortages and rationing, American soldiers seen as liberators, but also as
crass, uncouth victors, offering chewing gum, silk stockings, and cigarettes in
exchange for women and liquor. The powerful Hollywood studios, given special
status in the 1947 General Agreement on Tariffs and Trade (GATT), saw movies
as a lucrative American export that could serve as subtle propaganda in the guise
of entertainment. For the next decade, Hollywood presented Americans abroad,
in a permanent transactional cycle, either seducing or being seduced, exploiting

or being exploited for their money. In the 1953 film *Gentlemen Prefer Blonds*, American showgirls, played by Marilyn Monroe and Jane Russell, sail to Europe to snare, persuade or lure American, British, or any men, away from their money: "He's your guy when stocks are high/But beware when they start to descend, It's then that those louses/Go back to their spouses/Diamonds are a Girl's Best Friend" (Styne 1949). *An American in Paris* presents American expatriates as the older rich woman trying to buy the young American painter, Gene Kelly, who in turn falls in love with the naïve shop girl Leslie Caron (a rare exception to the stereotype of French and Italian seductresses). *It Started in Naples* (1960), with Clark Gable as the rich, uptight American who comes to Technicolor Capri (geography tended to be vague in these films) to rescue his nephew, a street urchin. In a scenario reminiscent of the 2008 more socially condemnatory Oscar winner, the Anglo-Indian movie *Slumdog Millionaire*, featuring Indian slums and feisty street urchins, the nephew, under the care of his aunt, Sophia Loren, a quasi-prostitute and cabaret singer, begs, steals, and cajoles rich Americans. The American assumes that money alone will suffice to buy up the boy and his family under the guise of providing a better life. The other end of the spectrum was the high society spoof *The Grass is Greener* (1961), with Cary Grant and Deborah Kerr as a proper aristocratic but impoverished English couple, where one day an American businessman appears who wants to buy the wife. As in all these films, happy endings allow the Europeans to stay in place, somehow enriched by American generosity, bemused by the American lack of guile and misplaced good intentions. The premise is simplistic but persuasive in its sexual and financial dichotomy: the honest, rich but naïve American man is seduced by the clever, beautiful, poor French or Italian woman. When American women go to Europe, they in turn will be seduced by European men who at first profess love in order to get their money.

The extraordinary literary, theatrical, and cinematographic output in England, France, Italy, Germany, and Sweden in the late 1950s and 1960s, was political, depressive, psychoanalytic, representative of "culture." Infused with intellectual content, the visual was over-laden with complex political discourse in the Cahiers du Cinema school, religious political symbolism in Fellini, Antonioni, and De Sicca (although Italy produced light comedies readily exported, often starring Sophia Loren), torturous guilt in Ingmar Bergman, social outrage and nihilism in Osborne, Beckett, and Pinter. Historical literalism, realism, and naturalism were totally rejected as insipid bourgeois genres. The stigma, silence, and horror of World War II remained omnipresent and omnipotent, only America was unscathed, victorious, happy, and innocent.

In 1955, Alfred Hitchcock captured the paradox of high and low culture in *To Catch a Thief*. Grace Kelly, a wealthy American heiress, and her mother, a vulgar rich American widow from Montana, come to Monte Carlo and discover Cary Grant, former resistance fighter, cat burglar, who in a complex mystery plot is trying to escape the French police, an English insurance man, and to find the real cat burglar. The American women see him as a great "catch," which American money can buy. The French Riviera presents a France of lush luxury for foreigners, bitter militant working class, and hated police, pitting new and old money, culminating in an opulent ball with Grace Kelly garbed in gold as Marie Antoinette.

In 1978, the German director Fassbinder transferred the dialectic to the newly prosperous Germany in the iconic *The Marriage of Maria Braun*:

> The eponymous heroine picks up her life in the rubble of defeat, in a Germany where "all the men look shrunken" and coolly puts the past behind her ... Maria then devotes herself with unflinching single mindedness to the national preoccupation with making money, at which she proves strikingly adept. Along the way the heroine ... exploits the resources, affections and credulity of men – including a (black) American soldier – while remaining "loyal" to Herman, her German soldier husband incarcerated in the Soviet Union and whose wartime exploits are left studiously vague.
>
> (Judt 2005: 276)

Here the end is horrific and ironic, as in the new apartment, with all modern amenities including a gas stove, on the day the husband returns, the stove explodes killing them both.

5.11 International banking: the good, the bad and the ugly

Until 1930, Swiss banking focused on small private banks, founded since the 1760s, to represent French interests through Geneva, and German Austrian interests through Zurich and Basel. Bank Julius, Bank Sarasin et Cie, Bank Frey and Co., Banque Piguet, Valiant Privatbank, and Hottinger et Cie, with offices in Geneva, Zurich, Basel, Lugano, Luxembourg, London, and New York, catered to wealthy families with total discretion. Following the creation of Union des Banques Suisses, Switzerland entered international banking, but only after the creation of the Bank of International Settlements (BIS), established to help administer German reparation payments in 1930, and the Swiss Banking Act of 1934, assuring total confidentiality on numbered accounts, did the myth of the Swiss banker emerge. By the 1950s, with tales circulating of American gangster Myer Lansky buying a Swiss bank to hide Las Vegas casino holdings for tax evasion purposes, the image of Swiss banks took hold in popular literature and film. Switzerland, Monaco, Andorra, Liechtenstein, and Luxembourg, the small neutral, border principalities and republics of Europe became the conduit states of international finance, combining fairy tale settings with tax haven status, total discretion with political neutrality, and large fees in return for excellent services and no questions asked. With difficult geography, few natural resources and porous borders, banking became a national and highly lucrative source of income. The crisis of 2008, like the exposure of the Holocaust accounts a decade ago, has destabilized the image of Swiss banks. Luxembourg, Liechtenstein, Swiss, and Cayman Island banks held accountable in fiscal fraud and evasion, and UBS' involvement in the Bernard Madoff fraud, has highlighted the need for standardized disclosure practices and the vulnerability of secret accounts.

In March 2009, for the first time in their history, Swiss banks under global pressure agreed to adhere to European Union imposed standards of transparency and definitions of tax fraud.

From the 1750s to the 1950s, financial decisions were made in London, then Paris, Berlin, and New York and accounted for on the balance sheets and account books of these nations. The recipients were part of vast colonial empires or smaller foreign countries, which did not participate in the decision making process. When Barings nearly went under in 1890, which cost the bank nearly 21 million pounds, President Celman of Argentina, who had in part provoked the crisis by mismanaging his newly enriched economy, was not present at the final negotiations to bail out the bank. Credit in Argentina collapsed, trade with South America suffered, there was a mini panic in Germany and a run on gold, but all decisions were made and sealed among the lead European banks.

In the 1970s, the wider proliferation of Anglo-American financial institutions, practices, and behavior dramatically changed the relationship between bankers, nations, and specifically developing countries. International banking, limited to a few large multinational banks with centralized home office decision making, based on the East India Trading Company, Medici, and Fugger banks, was replaced by the transplantation of banks from home to host country. Once these branches became among the most profitable (European banks' American and Asian operations in the 1980s), they developed their own hierarchy and lines of reporting. Universal banks took on split identities, between home office traditional retail and corporate functions, imbued in a culture of caution and customer loyalty, versus foreign subsidiaries which functioned as corporate and investment entities, often pursuing more aggressive, competitive deals. Even when the top tier of senior management remained indigenous, as in French and Japanese banks, profitable foreign centers and home offices often differed on procedures and business practices.

American banks, limited at home by firewalls and interstate interdictions, began to expand retail and corporate activities abroad. Citicorp and Chase became brands, consumer entities with recognizable logos, identity, and architecture:

> Citibankers presented themselves as the forerunners of a relaxed and impersonal style of consumer banking, proclaiming each move with a salvo of publicity; like Mobil among the oil companies, they were compulsive communicators.
>
> (Sampson 1981: 214)

A generation later, Citibank would still have a global presence, but with far less operational, management, and identity cohesion. Functioning around the world, Citibank dominated Latin American markets, rivaled only by HSBC and Spanish giants, Santander and Banco Bilbao. In Japan in 2003, insensitive to cultural ramifications of collusion and overpricing products, Citibank was forced to officially apologize and withdraw all private banking activities from Japan.

The collapse of the French in Indochina, the growing instability in South America between communist influence and military dictatorships, and the liberation and creation of new countries in Africa forced a re-evaluation of the role of European banks and monetary policy. European banks kept former colonies under a dual banking system in which official trade and currencies flowed back to Europe, and indigenous development of markets was left outside of formal banking channels. French and British banks kept a presence in West Africa, in 1965 Standard merged with Bank of West Africa with presence in Cameron, Gambia, Ghana, Sierra Leone, and Nigeria. French banks maintained control over banking, trade, and monetary policy, until the decoupling of the French franc and the Communauté Financière Africaine (African Financial Community) (CFA) in 1994. "Tontines," informal banking and insurance groups, offered small loans, arranged repayment, and worked within market towns usually led by women. Corruption was endemic, and only through forms of micro financing was the local populations able to access alternate financing.

After the oil crisis of 1973, triggered by the Organization of the Petroleum Exporting Countries (OPEC), and the role of petro wealth, the Brandt Commission, set up by German Chancellor Willy Brandt, called for the then named "Third World" countries to become more involved in the process of their economic welfare. Through the 1970s and 1980s, Latin America, Africa, most of Asia, and all of the former Soviet Union fell into that category, despite vast natural resources. The wealth of the Saudis and their ability to integrate into the global financial community was already on the table: "it was about the money of religion, not the religion of money" (Sampson 1981: 25). Although not yet defined as risk management and categorized as political, commercial or structural risk, the issue of political interference and intersection was very relevant during the Cold War. The crisis in Iran in 1979, and the crisis in Mexico in 1982 made it clear that the distinctions between institutional lending and government lending had to be re-examined. When Chase suffered massive losses on unpaid loans to the Shah when Ayatollah Khomeini came to power, and large scale propaganda presented American banks as tools of capitalism which had sponsored the repressive police state, the stage was set for the irreconcilable intellectual conflict between perceived American capitalism as exploitation and fear of Iran as an anti-capitalist theocracy. Political and country risk returned with a vengeance to the forefront of international banking: By 1979, *Euromoney* magazine began grading countries by statistical country risk, based on economist Irving Friedman's models. Chief Executive Officer of Citibank, Wriston, introduced credit risk which included political intelligence.

5.12 Dangers and pitfalls: rogue banks, bankers, traders

But internationalization also opened the floodgates of deregulation, corruption, and political collusion between banks and governments in emerging, volatile nations. Chairman of Barings, Sir Edward Reid, in an address to the Institute of Bankers on "The Role of the Merchant Banks Today," in London (1963), expressed the following concern: "merchants banks is sometimes applied to banks which are not merchants, merchants who are not banks and sometimes to houses who are neither merchant nor banks." The scandals at Banco Ambrosiano and BCCI, from diametrically opposed cultures, epitomized the dangers in ethical, regulatory, and procedural laxity and negligence.

Banco Ambrosiano, a small Italian bank created in 1896, expanded into a Luxembourg holding company in 1963, with direct patronage and capital from the Vatican. Roberto Calvi, promoted to chief executive officer in 1971, in the spirit of the times, began aggressively buying offshore companies in the Bahamas and South America, selling stakes to Italian businessmen, and intersecting with a French offshore clearing house, ClearStream, implicating French and Italian politicians. In 1978, the Bank of Italy opened an investigation into Ambrosiano's complex interlinked regional Church, Masonic, and Mafia enterprises. By 1982, it was discovered that the bank had lost or siphoned US$1.2 billion. Roberto Calvi, fled to London where he died, hanged from Black Friars Bridge on June 18, 1982. The case exploded into the headlines with all the trappings of a Grand Guignol drama, invoking conspiracy theories last mentioned on the demise of the former Catholic Vatican funded bank, Union Generale, which folded exactly a century earlier in 1882. The ramifications and investigations prompted the Italian banking sector to begin to consolidate and slowly attempt to unravel incestuous interlinkages between finance, government, and Church.

BCCI, Bank of Credit and Commerce International, became the symbol of the dangers of international stateless banks with no clear regulation, managerial hierarchy or levels of accountability. After nearly two decades of investigation, information on the multilayered dealings of BCCI, the largest bank fraud until 2008, are so complex and disparate, that the clearest documentation comes from the official US congressional investigation: BCCI, "A Report to the Committee on Foreign Relations," United States Senate, December 1992. Founded in Pakistan in 1972 with capital from Abu Dhabi, United Arab Emirates, and the Pakistani Abedi fortune, BCCI was incorporated in Luxembourg, conducted operations out of London, and within ten years had established branches in 70 countries. By proclaiming itself a counterweight to Western European banks, it claimed to offer more culturally compatible services to Third World, and specifically Muslim leaders, seeking discrete banking services. What it offered in fact, was a global scale money laundering service which functioned through layers of entities, holding companies, affiliates, and subsidiaries, "fractured corporate structures" providing support for arms trafficking, smuggling, terrorism, and other criminal activity. Receiving siphoned deposits from central banks and political payoffs, it had contacts across South America, Panama, Pakistan, India, Nigeria, Cameroun, Senegal, Congo, Lebanon, Saudi Arabia, United Arab Emirates, Kuwait, Iraq, and finally the United States. Through former President Carter's Director of the Office of Budget and Management, and close friend, Bert Lance, the bank, in return for paying off his loans in 1977, "infiltrated the U.S. market through secretly purchasing U.S. banks which opened branch offices of BCCI throughout the U.S. and eventually merging with these institutions." By fraudulently purchasing Financial General Bank shares and contributing to Carter's foundations, BCCI implicated the National Bank of Georgia, prominent politicians, former Secretary of Defense Clark Clifford, and Bank of America. For the first time in its history, the Bank of England was indirectly involved in criminal activity when, cognizant of the problems, it allowed reorganization and recapitalization to proceed through Abu Dhabi, with the implicit agreement of Price Waterhouse, which had proven negligent in reporting auditing, accounting, and regulatory violations. Manhattan District Attorney, Robert Morgenthau, broke the case in 1989, when an investigation into the purchase of the American bank revealed huge losses, lack of compliance with state or federal disclosure rules, and political bribery charges. The American and British operations shut down in 1991, the losses were never recouped. The ensuing investigation implicating the Central Intelligence Agency (CIA), Treasury, and the highest levels of the British, American, and developing countries governments, led to the Foreign Bank Supervision Enhancement Act of 1991, which has required far more stringent oversight of foreign banks in the United States.

These scandals continued to reverberate over decades, as investigations continued and further corruption and illegal deals were discovered. In 1994, the first indications of the extent of Crédit Lyonnais' losses, which required a 50 billion French franc bailout, called "The Banking Scandal of the Century" (*Le Point* 1994), revealed connections to Banco Ambrosiano and BCCI through Paretti and Fiorini, shady Italian financiers who received and defaulted on huge loans to buy out MGM studios in California. In 2000, Marc Rich, international oil trader, convicted of tax evasion and pardoned by President Clinton in 2000, caused uproar when it was revealed that he had connections to BCCI. A United States Treasury Department investigation into terrorism funding in 2002, uncovered Bin Laden connections to BCCI through Saudi Arabia. In 2009, a thriller *The International*, modeled on BCCI, presented a mysterious, evil international bank with offices in Luxembourg, Berlin, Istanbul, and New York that acted as enabler for arms deals, corrupt African dictators, and generally evil people. However, in politically correct times, its bankers were all white, middle-aged, and vaguely European with a nasty older German thrown in for good measure. The heroes were an American and a British agent, who uncovered the plot and tried to bring the culprits to justice. The movie played well into the ethos of banking perceived again as amoral, esoteric, and conspiratorial. But beyond novelistic and cinematographic entertainment, the lessons of BCCI are relevant because these frauds proved that when financial institutions engage in activities outside of their borders, regulatory oversight has to take place at every juncture, and in every host country. Evasive and negligent reporting, closed books, and lack of disclosure allowed collusion between governments, banks, and criminal interests to pass undetected for years. The crisis of 2008, the Bernard Madoff and Allen Stanford fraud schemes again underscored the global impact of unregulated and unsupervised financial instruments and operations.

For a generation, despite serious political setbacks, disasters, and financial crashes in 1987, 1989, and 2000, recession in 1991–1993, corporate scandals in

2002–2003, and banking scandals, Banco Ambrosiano and BCCI, were judged as country or institution specific cases. Yet by the 1990s, the levels of banking scandals, trading frauds, liquidity and currency crisis, and country insolvencies increased at an alarming rate. However, as they did not have a long-term effect on the recovery of major bank sectors, and as economies rapidly recuperated, Crédit Lyonnais, Barings, the Peso Crisis in 1995 (truly an "annus horribilis" of international banking), were still viewed as isolated cases of aberrant behavior and gross negligence. Ironically, as technology within 20 years went from the telephone to the telex, fax to the internet to instantaneous communication, the availability and rapidity of information reduced rather than augmented transparency. Major bank foreign operations aggressively grew in size and personnel, without necessarily putting in place additional supervisory or monitoring mechanisms. Fiscal incentives and easing of tax laws in various American states, opportunities in Singapore, Hong Kong, and Taiwan encouraged European, American, and Japanese banks to increase foreign subsidiaries. Once banks in England and the United States turned from banking to trading culture as primary profit centers, bankers in management positions were not necessarily aware of or versed in the operations and innovative instruments of the trading room, and traders in turn had little background in the history and methodology of traditional banking practices. The outrage in the United States at huge bonuses paid to derivative traders at AIG (after it had been bailed out twice by the US government) was symptomatic of a more serious problem: why and since when had the main profit center of a global insurance firm, depended on derivative trading? The analogies between the debacle at Barings in 1995 and the Société Générale scandal in 2008, illustrate the dangers of merging trading and banking cultures without sufficient firewalls, supervision, and regulatory oversight.

Between 1991 and 1995: "Barings Securities was to be merged with parts of the merchant bank, to create an integrated investment banking business, combining the self discipline of the banking culture with the freewheeling entrepreneurialism of the securities arm" (Martin 1995). Asian operations grew from 15 to 1,000, without additional monitoring. Nick Leeson, a young trader, judged too coarse and uneducated for the London office, was shipped off to Singapore, where, in less than three years, he took charge of back office operations and trading for numerous accounts: Barings Security Japan, Barings Futures Singapore, and Barings Securities HK. In 1993, in an attempt to cover losses, he created a fictitious account "8888," and falsified back office records. Hoping to recoup his losses, he took very large long positions on the Japanese Nikkei futures Index. Unfortunately, nature was not in accordance with his plans and an earthquake in Japan in late 1994 provoked a precipitous drop in the Nikkei, causing Leeson to singlehandedly lose US$1.4bn of the banks money. Peter Baring, last of the original Barings on the Board, blamed the "rogue trader." London management did not understand the instruments or the methodology and were, therefore, unable and unwilling to exercise any oversight. Matrix management meant decentralization to the point in which the Singapore branch went unsupervised. In January 1995, the Bank of England, within hours of being informed of the magnitude of the problem, decided that contagion in the City was unlikely as the issue was solvency not liquidity. The response occurred in a global crisis environment barely a year after the Spanish bailout of Banesto, which had to be folded into Santander, the ongoing losses at Crédit Lyonnais, and the Peso Crisis in full force, with Mexico threatening to default, risking potential international meltdown. Barings was sold for one symbolic pound to the global Dutch bank ING, which absorbed its £660 million loss. In 2000, "Barings, the oldest name in London investment banking is set to disappear in a rebranding exercise. ING, its Dutch owner intends to phase out the local identities of subsidiaries worldwide" (Lex 2000). Leeson, fleeing Singapore in February 1995, was captured, tried, and jailed. Released in 1999, he became a sports consultant and manager, regaining notoriety in 2008 as a paid expert on the Société Générale copycat scandal. Historically, major losses rarely occur in the home office: The Barings loss of US$1.4 billion occurred in Singapore; John Rusnak lost Allied Irish US$691 million in Atlanta in 2002; Sumitomo's Hamanaka, "Mr. Cooper," was discovered in 1996 to have lost US$2.6 billion in fake trades in copper over 11 years in the New York office; Daiwa's chief government bond trader, Igushi, lost US$1.1billion in 1997 in New York. In fall 2007, a rogue trader at CALYON, the corporate and investment banking division of Crédit Agricole, lost 250 million euros on an unauthorized trade in New York.

Jerome Kerviel and Nick Leeson were both cases of extravagant positions taken, vast amounts of the banks money made available to junior traders, collusion between the back office and the trading floor, creation of fictitious accounts, and benign complicity on the part of management. But where Barings failed or turned a blind eye to the doings of profitable traders in their Singapore office, Société Générale's lack of oversight was part of a larger cultural and historical hierarchy in which Jerome Kerviel was culprit as well as the scapegoat. Once caught, he made it clear that in this business model of derivative trading:

> It is impossible to generate that much profit with small positions, which leads me to say that so long as I was in profit, the superiors closed their eyes to the way I did it and the amounts I took on. From day to day, in the normal course of trading and taking normal sized positions, no trader can generate that much money. As long as we were earning and it wasn't too visible, it was fine and nobody said anything.
>
> (Arnold 2008)

Where Leeson had been relegated to the "colonies" rather than London, Kerviel, hired in 2000 at the Paris office as middle office support staff, was smart enough to be promoted to the floor in 2005, as part of the elite, high power Delta One trading team. With degrees from second tier universities in Nantes and Lyon, he was ambitious, hardworking, and a loner. In order to prove himself, he immediately began taking large unauthorized positions and won big on some bets. Kerviel's expertise with computers allowed him to enter false contracts under different names, creating false emails to confirm accounts, and decode computer passwords. When caught he: "admitted inventing the false trades and said that he thought he had discovered a 'martingale,' an eighteenth century betting system based on doubling a bet after every loss. But as bettors realized, martingales works only with unlimited funds" (Sage 2008). His head of division, Mustier, claimed he was mythomanical and Société Générale CEO, Daniel Bouton, expressed shock and horror insisting through 2009 that this was the work of a lone criminal mind. Jerome Kerviel, son of a seaside hairdresser and metalwork shop teacher, respectable, hard working, and lower middle class, was "desperate to prove that he was the equal of the highly educated members of the Parisian elite who dominated SocGen's senior ranks". In his little town of Pont l'Abbe (population 8,000), within a few weeks he became a local hero, a cult figure of everyman: "In keeping with the country's deep rooted suspicion of capitalism, he is viewed as a little guy who has struck a blow against the fat cats of the global financial system." The deputy mayor said, "It is Paris or the big people ganging up on the small Breton, we don't like it" (Sage 2008).

In 1987, Société Générale, the first of the big three state run banks to be privatized in the initial Mitterrand Chirac co-habitation, was judged the soundest in productivity and risk coverage, compared to Crédit Lyonnais and BNP. Under the leadership of Marc Vienot from 1987–1998, the bank specialized in commodity financing and investment banking. Under Bouton, chief executive officer since 1997, Société Générale fended off BNP's hostile takeover in 1999, derailing the Société Générale–Paribas merger. He retained the bank's independence, despite American style pressure and tactics from BNP, and warded off potential takeovers in the next decade. Instead of focusing on more traditional cash equities business and advisory mandates, as lead banks for mergers and acquisitions, Société Générale specialized in equity derivatives, quickly gaining a reputation as lead expert in European Union markets. The bank combined two diametrically opposed sets of values: cautious, disciplined, risk averse, yet in order to earn huge profits in a hyper-competitive environment, innovative, risk taking, and creative. In 2007, it received the award for "Equity Derivatives House of the Year" from the *Banker*.

Société Générale has 120,000 employees in 77 countries and 22 million retail banking customers. A global player, it is the leading French bank in former East Central European countries, with a presence in Poland, Serbia, Romania, Moldova, Bulgaria, Croatia, Czech Republic, and Slovenia, as well as Morocco, Ghana, Brazil and with a stake in Rosbank, Russia's second largest retail bank. France did not address the problems at Société Générale; it merely absolved and internalized the crisis. Britain allowed Barings to fail, adopting an attitude of greater pragmatism and inevitability. In the crisis of 2008, the issue of which institutions are too big or too interconnected to fail has not been resolved. Should Lehman, rather than Bear Stearns have been salvaged?

5.13 Democratization of banks and markets

BCCI originally defended itself as an alternate source of funding for Third World projects. This assumption, albeit false, underscored the financing of projects in underdeveloped or emerging markets. Historically, accusations of lack of fair treatment for poor countries have been consistent, since the failed attempt in the Havana Charter to create the International Trade Organization (ITO) in 1948: "In the 1940s, less developed nations and colonies accused the advanced countries of perpetuating an unequal system of commerce. New nations as India supported cartels and high tariffs to keep out what they looked on as predatory capitalist powers" (Kreinin 2000).

McNamara, when head of the World Bank (1968–1981), became an advocate for developing countries and the transfer of wealth to post-colonial Africa, Asia, and emerging markets. The Brandt Commission report, as well as Mitterrand's Nord Sud (North South) policy, were attempts by socialist or left leaning world leaders to bring about improvement in the living standards, infrastructure, and governance of the poorest nations. The dream of a repeat Marshall Plan for Africa, India or South East Asia was understood to be essential to global stability in response to the multilateral financial and trade policies which favored rich countries. One of the most fervent advocates was Sir James Goldsmith, former corporate raider and financier, turned reformer. In *The Trap* (1993), Goldsmith, member of the European Parliament, viewed GATT as a worldwide market, run by a supra-national regulatory body, which would savagely increase inequality and wage differences. He envisaged that technology, seen as a leveler, would also create dual societal systems of computer literate and illiterate societies, which could not effectively compete. Goldsmith's anti-globalist, utopian worldview was of small self-sufficient nation states, which benefit from trade and investment, but are not beholden to multilateral institutions or supranational governments. Between 1990 and 1996, political scientists such as John Newhouse, and economists such as Martin Feldstein refuted the justification for monetary and political regionalization. There was concern that the nation state would be replaced by cross-border, economically compatible, regional blocs: a Lyon–Barcelona–Geneva axis, or a virtual if not actual secession between Northern and Southern Italy, in which economic compatibility would replace historical allegiances.

In 2002, the World Trade Organization (WTO) designated Supachai of Thailand, "the first poor country national to head a global economic institution," therefore, trying to counteract the myth of the WTO, promulgated since 1999 by anti-globalization protesters, as a secretive outfit biased toward large multinationals ("Globalization's New Cheerleader" 2002). In 2009, when for the first time in nearly half a century, the International Monetary Fund (IMF) is called upon, in coordination with major central banks, to rescue European nations, Iceland, Hungary, Latvia, and Ukraine; the grave concern is whether the poorest nations in Africa and Asia will continue to garner the attention they need. Can these countries achieve any level of self sufficiency if foreign governments and multilaterals can no longer offer aid whenever necessary? Will the poorest countries again risk becoming the forgotten countries in a crisis of globalization and global proportions?

The good news is that a new generation of Western educated bankers is in place in many of the most isolated and previously closed countries. They have the knowledge, contacts, and, more importantly, the philosophical leanings toward stabilization and cooperation. In Ulaanbaatar, Mongolia, there is a Mongolia International Capital Corporation (MICC), the first investment bank in Mongolia. There is now a generation of community banks and bankers based on the principles of the Grameen Bank, created in Bangladesh in 1976, of community lending and community responsibility. Following the leadership of Muhammed Yunus, granted the Nobel Peace Prize in 2007, built on the role of women as safe keepers of family savings and household expenses, these banks offer loans which allow investment and funding of small ventures increasing community productivity and income: 97 percent of these loans are granted to women across India, Bangladesh, and other emerging markets. These banks also serve as educational and societal intermediaries, by requiring that the recipients promote better sanitary, health, educational, and women's rights conditions in their communities. The achievement has been to combine economic and social power in rural and urban disenfranchised environments' communities, by giving women the means and the support to improve the community. Like tontines in Africa, community based lending, under the larger rubric of "microfinance" and "microcredits," is an incremental process which respects the traditions and standards of its recipients, without imposing on them the intimidating and often discriminatory criteria of anonymous commercial domestic or foreign banks.

5.14 Americanization of global finance

> His job has nothing to do with anything except money, the stuff itself. No f***ing around with stocks, shares, commodities, futures. Just money.... Equipped with only a telephone, he buys money with money, sells money for money. He works in the cracks and vents of currencies, buying and selling on the margin, riding the daily tides of exchange. For these services he is rewarded with money. Lots of it. It is beautiful and so is he.
>
> (Amis 1984: 115)

In 1984, Martin Ames published an outrageous, hilarious satire of the Thatcher–Reagan years of excessive consumption and fascination with all financial matters: *Money* subtitled *A Suicide Note*. The hero, John Self, advertising man and unredeemable drunk, finds himself in New York ostensibly to make a feature film entitled "Good Money and Bad Money":

> "With money, double-dazzle New York is a crystal conservatory. Take money away and you're naked and shielding your Johnson in a cataract of breaking glass." Back in London, dead drunk and dead broke "I want money again, but I feel better now that I haven't got any."
>
> (1984: 372)

If the 1970s redefined the government-financial global landscape, the 1980s redefined domestic government–financial relationships. Post-1986, the Anglo-

American financial model became the blueprint and goal for developed countries and transitioning economies. A symbiotic relationship evolved between socialism and capitalism, in which profitability, innovation, investment, and increased consumerism could be validated as benefiting the state and the individual. But more importantly, under Thatcher, Reagan, Kohl, Mitterrand, and, at the end of the decade, Gorbachev, capitalism returned with a vengeance, its excesses, greed, risks and rewards.

In 1983, London international finance was still divided among old discreet firms who advised governments, N.R. Rothschild, Samuel Montagu, and Schroder: "banks that hang on prince's favors avoid publicity where they can" (Ferris 1984: 213), its competitors being Lehman in New York, and Lazard in Paris. At the height of the Eurobond market between European investors who owned dollars and European borrowers who wanted dollars, S.G. Warburg (who had created the market in 1963 with a US$15 million issue for the Italian state highway authority) competed with Credit Suisse lead manager for 1.8 billion Eurobond issue by European Economic Community. Benefiting from lax tax rules in Luxembourg, clients sought to enact their transactions in Switzerland and Luxembourg banks. In order to remain competitive, US banks established branches in Switzerland, led by the Credit Suisse's First Boston connections. First Boston started as White Weld brokerage house in Boston in 1890 and during World War II helped liquidate British money from the colonies, moving their client's money out of Canton and Shanghai to Switzerland. Acquired by Credit Suisse, Credit Suisse White Weld changed its name to First Boston in 1974.

The incursion of American firms, offering larger salaries and aggressive marketing tactics, forced European, especially British markets and banking institutions, to modernize, culminating in Big Bang in 1986, at the tail end of the Thatcher corporate and industrial privatizations.

> Jacob Rothschild ... says that his search of published figures in 1983 showed that the highest paid financial services executive in Britain received £126,000 in a year while the chairman of Merrill Lynch was paid $1.5 million.... N.M. Rothschild paid seven directors between £85,000 and £100,000 a year... A comparable executive at Salomon Brothers or Morgan Stanley who wasn't earning five or ten times as much would feel underprivileged. Securities traders and salespersons on Wall Street can be paid hundreds of thousands of dollars.
>
> (Ferris 1984: 202)

Although Hambros, Barings, and Warburg wanted to maintain the tone and pace of the old boy network of clients, under which merchant bankers conducted trading through stockbrokers and jobbers under fixed commissions, by 1984 the closed world of investment banking had been breached, as merchant bankers began to buy stakes in brokers and jobbers. The banking establishment, run by a core of old elite merchant banks, the "Accepting House Committee," had never allowed foreign or commercial banks until the privatization of British Telecom in 1984, when S.G. Warburg, Kleinwort Benson was appointed along with Morgan Stanley. Sigmund Warburg, member of the Warburg family, exiled from Germany in 1933, arrived in London and in 1946 opened S.G. Warburg and Co. More aggressive, accused of American style tactics, he turned his bank into the premier investment bank in London. Under Big Bank 1986, Warburg became involved in major infrastructure and media deals, EuroTunnel, EuroDisney, hoping to match Salomon, although the "staff blamed executives whom they saw as stuck in the past, culturally and intellectually" (Gapper 1995b). The bank anticipated a merger with Morgan Stanley in 1994, but talks collapsed before completion. In 1995, in the ripple effect of the Barings collapse, Warburg suffered large losses in bond trading and began to lose top managers, forcing Warburg to agree to a bid from Société de Banques Suisses, under Marcel Ospel, in May 1995 (Gapper 1995c). The ramparts had been breached.

From 1950 to 1980, the "Trente Glorieuses," France, under De Gaulle and the center-right, regained economic, military and cultural clout. Yet France entered the modern economic age tentatively and with reservation. Rejecting the corruption and materialism of the Giscard era, France elected the Socialist party and Mitterrand in 1980. But unlike the government of Leon Blum, Mitterrand, a middle class, former-right-wing Gaullist, "converted" to Catholic Socialism center-left, brought a unique historical perspective to socialism and capitalism in his 15 year reign. The success of the French economy, as in Germany's Mittelstand, focused on rebuilding small and medium sized corporations, and encouraging individual investors to return to the banking sector through state owned deposit institutions. From 1976 to 1986, the number of checking accounts grew from 33 million to 71 million. Disdaining American culture, but quickly learning and integrating American technology, between 1980 and 1985 French banks became the most computerized in the world (monetique), adapting to high technology and retraining their personnel. The initial 1981–1983 period of nationalization of all private and semi-private banks with assets of over one billion francs encouraged modernization but restricted competitiveness and expansion. By 1983, the end of austerity and nationalization was justified as a necessary pragmatic move towards American type capitalism with growth in the Stock Market, the opening of the Second Market modeled on NASDAQ (MATIF in 1983), promoting the first ECU issues and an aggressive push for investment abroad under a revitalized Ministry of Foreign Trade. By 1984, the motto of French banks was: "profitability, security and liquidity" (Beaudeux 1984). Crédit Agricole, Crédit Lyonnais, BNP, and Société Générale remained in the category of top ten banks worldwide by market capitalization, despite government changes, the market crashes of 1987 and 1989, and the incursion of Japanese banks after 1980. Under Mitterrand's "cohabitation" government with Jacques Chirac as prime minister, France underwent a period of pro-American capitalism, similar to the first period of financial capitalism under Napoleon III.

In March 1987, Jacques Maisonrouge (former Minister of Industry under Chirac and former head of IBM) could declare to an American audience at

Harvard University: "The French now like business and understand what it takes to be successful in world markets" (Frommer and McCormick 1989: viii). French bankers and businessmen became instrumental in re-educating their colleagues, creating new programs and orientation for French business schools, with an emphasis on marketing, investment, and international studies. Privatization between 1985 and 1988 was more a rhetorical device to explain partial denationalization since, in practice, the largest numbers of shareholders in privatized companies including Société Générale, the first state owned bank to be privatized in 1987, remained state banks, and major state companies. Through the 1980s, the state could retain a 51 percent stake in any denationalized company (this stake was reduced to about 25 percent in the 1990s and finally reached 10 percent in the privatization of Crédit Lyonnais in 1999). In 2009, BNP was again 17 percent state owned, following the capital injections imposed by the state. The complex legal distinction between state owned, private, and privatized became less important than a government policy of a high profile financial presence in Europe, Asia, and the United States, and a major role in large bank syndications. A French banker in 1987 commented that French banks have not had a single bankruptcy in over 20 years:

> Not because they are better managed than any other banks in the world but because there is a system of solidarity organized by the French Treasury Department that makes it very difficult for a bank to go bankrupt even if it wants to.
>
> (Ange quoted in Frommer and McCormick 1989: 52)

Under the second right center cohabitation, Prime Minister Balladur (1993–1995, during which time BNP was privatized) encouraged a wave of privatized industries, yet retained control over the leadership ranks and shareholdings proving again such that:

> France still has a long way to go out of state capitalism. The long incestuous relationship between the state and the big companies results in a business elite with a very narrow base and a sort of "closed shop" system to get in.
>
> (Ries 1994)

The major changes in Europe, vastly increased flows of international investment and brought Japan into the ranks of top seven universal banks. Articles on both sides of the Atlantic heralded a new economic era: " The New Global Top Banker:Tokyo and Its Mighty Money" (Chira 1986b); "The Tokyo Summit has laid the first cornerstone of a new international economic regime" (*L' Expansion* 1986). Within a year "investment fever" hit Japan:

> "For years," Mr. Kyu said, "Japanese considered it shameful to talk about money. Now," he said, "I'm in the center of money-crazy Japan," as the country re-evaluated its economic identity and relations with western

powers ... "Money fever," as the Japanese call it, is rampant here as an increasingly affluent society discovers that there are other ways of amassing savings than simply depositing money in the bank.

(Chira 1986a)

As described in a *New York Times* article of April 27, 1986, "Japan's emergence as a leading capital exporter is relatively recent" (Chira 1986). In five years, Japan enthusiastically embraced the precepts of consumerism, focusing on luxury products, simultaneously creating and imitating the latest fashion trends. Japan went on a spending spree across Europe and the United States, buying up French chateaux and vineyards, the Rockefeller Center, and the most prestigious golf club in America, Pebble Beach in California, where US presidents have played. In 1991, the nine top world banks were Japanese followed by Crédit Agricole. In Japan, banks financed credit unions, lending for housing, industry, and manufacturing, but once the global economy weakened in the recession of 1991–1993, locked into incestuous keiretsu structures of industrial financial holdings, Japan was unwilling to unravel bad loans, force reforms in inefficient banks or close down insolvent banks. Reverting to its traditional formula of very high savings rate, wariness of foreign incursion, closed hierarchal management structures, and embedded cultural xenophobia; Japan for a decade would become a very wealthy, modern consumer society with inefficient insulated financial sectors and practices.

Around the world, a new phenomenon appeared in rich developed countries: the middle class suddenly discovered international bond and currency markets. This new middle class professional investor became known as "The Belgian Dentist" (Macleod 1984). This conservative bourgeois placed his carefully earned funds in safe, government-backed securities. In the United States the counterpart was the American pediatrician, who also turned toward foreign investments:

> Dr. Marvyn D. Cohen decided last year to try something new with some of the $200,000 he had saved for retirement. After hearing a lecture given by an investment specialist at Shearson Lehman Brothers Inc., the pediatrician from Columbus, Ga., decided to put a portion of his money into a mutual fund specializing in foreign investments ... "This economist said it was logical for Americans to be more world-minded, that we're not an isolated group," said Dr. Cohen, who at the time had exclusively invested in various United States equities. "It made good sense to me."
>
> (Bronstein 1986)

5.15 European Monetary Union: inventing Europe

We shall no more be spared Europe than shall we be the Internet, the single currency or the chains selling deep frozen foods: these things happen come what may. They follow their course in spite of any opinions to the contrary.

(Baudrillard 2002)

The vast bureaucratic apparatus of the European Union, often seen as unwieldy and ponderous, underlies an extraordinary historical mission and redefinition of European political and economic identity. De Gaulle and Konrad Adenauer understood that France and Germany could only be resurrected through economic necessity, the only formula which could sublimate history.

Through the Common Market, the Treaty of Rome (1957), and the Single European Act (1988) culminating in the Maastricht Treaty (1992), the principle objective was to achieve progressive "deepening" and "widening" of the community of states, from six to 12 to 27 in 2007, through simultaneous economic, legal, social, and cultural policies. The ability to integrate wealthy, stable European Free Trade Area (EFTA) countries in 1995, and fragile, transitional post-Soviet countries in the 2004–2007 expansion, coupled with the special conditions allotted to England, Denmark, and Sweden (membership without obligation to join Economic and Monetary Union) was achieved efficiently and relatively painlessly. The principles of monetary harmonization, laid out in the Delors Plan in 1988, first formulated in the Werner Plan in 1970, went through various permutations to establish a European Community central bank and single currency, to equal the United States and the dollar. Despite serious obstacles (the currency crisis of 1992) and volatility in the dollar–euro relationship, the European Economic and Monetary Union (EMU), as codified in the Maastricht Treaty, has been an unmitigated success. The three stages of development have been the creation of a single currency from ecu to euro, the creation of the European Central Bank, and regulatory harmonization of the banking sectors of member countries. The last part has been a work in progress since 1994, leaving national banking sectors under domestic regulatory regimes proving that issues of sovereignty, institutional identity, and history cannot be readily resolved or absolved on a balance sheet.

5.16 The euro

No more wars, no more borders, one continental money, all freedoms and Paris, the capital of this Europe, home to an Assembly elected by universal suffrage.

(Victor Hugo, Correspondence, 1855)

To paraphrase Pirandello: In 1992, Europe was an identity in quest of a currency, after 2002 the euro has been a currency in quest of an identity. The euro, account money for government and market transactions since 1999, was launched as "real" money on January 1, 2002, becoming sole legal tender for 12 nations. The transition was surprisingly smooth, even in Germany, which expressed the greatest insecurity at giving up the powerful Deutschmark. Robert Mundell, the euro's most optimistic and influential advocate in the United States, offered a realistic view of the impact: "It will be a much more efficient money for Europeans, not only will they be able to compare prices across the continent, but they will possess a world-class money, second in importance in the world, only to the dollar" (Mundell quoted in Devitt 2002).

> The euro will not resolve the EU's inbred resistance to institutional change nor will it displace or weaken the hegemony of the dollar. But, it will validate on a more profound level the idea of Europe and the ability to harmonize and consolidate economic, commercial, monetary policies and regulations, in turn creating a greater sense of communality and reinforced solidarity.
>
> (Finel-Honigman 2003)

Since 1998, under the European Central Bank, the challenge was to build and maintain political confidence under stringent economic guidelines, to educate the public, and to produce the currency on time. A boom economy, stable governments, and technology learned in the "Y2K" build-up helped meet the challenge (the change in all ATMs). The Mitterrand–Kohl–Delors vision was realized, now the hard work began to create a legislative, regulatory, institutional, and oversight framework. Despite the creation of one currency, the EMU continues to lack fiscal harmonization. There is no equivalent of the Securities and Exchange Commission (SEC) or the Office of the Comptroller of the Currency (OCC). The European Central Bank (ECB) is still debating whether it will assume a larger supervisory role in relation to the national central banks. One of the biggest drawbacks in the rejection of the latest attempt at political unification, the Lisbon Treaty in 2008, has been the lack of a European Union Treasury, putting the entire burden on the European Central Bank. Within both the public and private sector lack of fiscal and regulatory harmonization has been an impediment to large scale cross-border mergers.

> If Europe is to have a truly integrated financial market under a single currency in which capital is continuously allocated to the most productive uses (and equally important denied to the least competitive) a uniformed approach to corporate control will ultimately have to emerge from the highly divergent systems that have traditionally existed in the national economies.
>
> (Walter and Smith 2000: xvi)

But the real challenge was whether the euro would help accelerate cultural adaptability. The naming and implementation of the European Currency Unit (ecu) in 1979, the result of European monetary coordination in the post Bretton Woods environment, was an economic and market watershed, but it had little impact on the public at large.

Naming a European currency, which would supersede the Deutschmark and 12 or more other currencies, caused a huge debate in the media and press in 1995. The choices, franc-mark, franco, europa, and ecu all had cultural, linguistic, and historical connotations that were deemed offensive, arrogant or distasteful to one or more members. The *Financial Times* charming editorial suggesting the florin (December 15, 1995), seemed to offer a better solution, at least cognizant of history. The final decision was a neutralized, ahistorical semantic remnant: the prefix "euro" (as in eurochecks, eurobonds, and eurodollar), devoid of any atavistic or symbolic resonance. The notes designed with imaginary monuments, gates, archways, and porticos, representing openness, could have been created by Borges or Calvino as part of imaginary cities or civilizations.

In 1996, European Union officials understood that the process of implementing this instrument required much more than a government edict and organized a "Round Table on the Euro: Communication Challenge." The panel, consisting of Delors, Lamfalussy, Lord Jenkins, and even Pierre Werner (the original architect of the single currency plan), called for a public information campaign to help "accept this unprecedented step in the course of European history." There was a concerted effort to focus on consumers, women (under-represented in political decisions), the young, teachers, merchants, and clergy (in Portugal). Children's books were published on the euro with illustrations. Banks were to be engaged as "ambassadors for Euro." By 1998, the issue gained momentum, as it was clear that older pensioners, the rural population, less educated, and disabled were scared and anxious whether they would lose their welfare benefits or suffer reductions in pensions. As an article in *The Economist* entitled "Work in Progress, A Survey of European Business and the Euro" (2001) made clear, the problems for the consumer were price differentials and lack of fiscal harmonization. Initial responses involved fears of price gouging, false conversions, and spike in daily goods. Studies conducted in 2003 to 2004 proved that these fears had been unfounded.

But the other issue was more complex: trust in a new currency in a continent scarred by memories of hyperinflation and worthless currencies. The real test of the new currency was not that it functioned smoothly at Alcatel and Allianz, but at the corner pharmacy in Mainz, the local hardware store in Lyon, and the shoe store in Cordoba. Corporate balance sheets dealt in euros since 1999, but invoices and salary slips had to adjust. For the consumer and citizen, a real euro was no longer the realm of politicians and Brussels or Frankfurt Eurocrats, but the reality of the paycheck, the pension, and the monthly bills. In a referendum on September 14, 2003, Sweden soundly defeated joining by 56 percent. Denmark rejected joining in 2000 and 2002. Referendums were discussed, but never took place in the United Kingdom.

Although Slovenia quietly joined the Economic and Monetary Union in January 2007, the population expressed nostalgia for the tolar. Despite boom economies and positive effects, a 2005 survey in Germany (Forsa Poll) showed that 58 percent preferred the Deutschmark, in France 52 percent expressed regret at losing the franc (SOFRES Poll). In June 2005, the strongest reaction was in Italy, where the right-wing Northern League suggested that Italy would benefit from leaving the Eurozone. The concept of a single currency, set out in Maastricht, did not present any blueprint for leaving the single currency zone. In moments of panic or economic uncertainty, when countries have seen potential advantages in devaluation, as Italy in 2005 and in the crisis of 2008, there have been rhetorical rumblings, but in reality the euro offered a safety anchor in times of national unrest or crisis. In France and the Netherlands in summer 2005, following the rejection of the European Union Constitution, the riots in Paris in

November 2005, and the government strikes and shut down in April 2006, the euro was minimally impacted. As proven in the "petit oui," near rejection of the Maastricht Treaty ratification in September 1992, which instigated furious speculation against the French franc and the ensuing currency crisis of 1992, individual currencies were far more prone to market volatility than a regional currency with one monetary policy.

At their entry into the European Union, the new countries were expected to join in 2007–2009; these dates have been pushed back to 2010–2012 at the earliest. Under the strain of the crisis of 2008, the endemic weakness of all emerging market currencies, fear of inflation, and inability to stabilize their economies, their entry is far from certain. All signals seem to indicate that the euro, like the dollar, will gain in reputability and strength once the worst of the crisis subsides. At present the worst financial crisis in the post-World War II period has not become a currency crisis. The euro has proven a strong anchor, the European Central Bank has maintained stable monetary policy, while being forced to assume additional functions as lender of last resort for euro and non-euro European nations. National central banks have seen a restoration of greater power, as they have the sole ability to monitor their respective sectors. The dollar remains primary safe haven, but the "gallant little euro," a bit too feisty at times and in need of some bolstering, has more than held its own. In 1868, Walter Bagehot, in a work entitled *A Practical Plan for Assimilating the English and American Money, as a Step Toward a Universal Money* again proved prescient although the world was not yet ready for one code of commerce and one money: "But I believe we could get as far as two moneys, two leading commercial currencies, which nations could one by one join as they chose and which, in after time, might be combined" (Bagehot 1868).

5.17 European Central Bank

The debate over the functions and objectives of the European Central Bank (ECB) must be examined. It is extremely relevant in the present crisis when a greater scope of activities are allotted to the Federal Reserve, and there is a call in the European Union and "G8" countries for an international regulatory body, and in the United States for an umbrella regulatory agency to assume oversight functions of the financial sector including insurance, mortgages, and private equity.

The origins of the Bank of France, the Bundesbank, and the Bank of England reveal that historical criteria and the public perception of the institution's role in society define each country's interpretation and practice of independence as much as microeconomic regulations and policies. Margaret Thatcher's categorical rejection of the European Monetary Union, dissolution of sterling, and her alternate plan on 13 currencies with a hard ecu cast doubts on the purpose of an independent super-banking structure. "We do not accept that a European system of central banks or Eurofed should be wholly independent" (Smith 1990). Despite constant discussion and the promise of referendums on the issue of joining the Economic and Monetary Union (EMU), through the tenures of John Major and Tony Blair, the United Kingdom has remained steadfast to the principles of Thatcherism on monetary independence for the Bank of England and the pound. Britain has headed the small group (Denmark, Sweden) of non-Eurozone core economies benefiting from divergent business cycles, an artificially strong pound, and a booming financial sector prior to the crisis of 2008.

A 1991 United Nations Interaction Council report on "The Role of Central Banking in Globalized Financial Markets," chaired by Valery Giscard d'Estaing, stressed that the role of central banks must be to "enhance their capacity to deal with any such crisis in the new financial environment," a need for agreed capital adequacy requirements (an issue where France and Germany disagree), coordination of responses to a liquidity crisis, and a key role in controlling inflation. The report foresaw a tripolar monetary world, dollar–ECU–yen, with equal power. In 2009, this scenario is still in play with Asian currencies augmented by the Chinese yuan.

The European Monetary Union was the result of the unique French–German partnership under President Mitterrand (1981–1995) and Chancellor Kohl (1982–1998), reinforced by the solid relationship between the Governor of the Bank of France, Trichet (Head of the ECB since 2003) and the President of the Bundesbank, Tietmeyer. Trichet saw the European Central Bank as the finalization of monetary union and a single currency, largely under French influence and guidance. Tietmeyer, a far more pragmatic, intellectually subtle Europeanist than his immediate predecessor Schlesinger, saw a European Monetary Institute (the preliminary institution established on January 1, 1994) as a testing ground for a potential European central bank but not necessarily an ecu currency, although granting the importance of currency convergence: "'We at the Bundesbank do think European,' he said at the October 1 ceremony. 'But we cannot be a central bank for Europe,' and later added: 'The EMI's task is to facilitate but not to promote the ECU'" (Whitney 1993). Since 1991, the Bundesbank dictated European monetary policy and was instrumental in global monetary policy, this based on historically influenced stringent anti-inflationary and high interest rate policies. Yet in 1991, the Deutschmark had been more severely hit by the global recession and far more wracked by internal disorder and long-term vulnerability than the French franc.

The decision to establish the European Central Bank in Frankfurt was a peace offering from Mitterrand to Kohl, in gratitude for Kohl's support of a strong franc. The European press and media played on the Frank furt = franc fort. President of the European Commission, Jacques Delors, suggested the term EuroFed in a period of Europtimism, when it was assumed that a three stage timetable for Economic and Monetary Union would be on target, without snags, and that a fully integrated 12 nation economic community would be in place by 1993. From 1990 Delors proclaimed his faith in the power of monetary union as catalyst for political unification. A constant balance of French–German interests permitted the resurrection of Economic and Monetary Union after the currency crisis of 1992, which forced all other currencies out of the European Monetary

System (EMS), requiring realignment of the parity bands and a re-evaluation of currency convergence in August 1993. After the EMS crisis, the issue of controlling market attacks and cooperation with the all powerful trillion dollar foreign exchange market was viewed as crucial in order to avoid future reoccurrences. Fighting off a move by the Clinton administration to limit the powers of the Federal Reserve and to meld it into a larger, more diffuse regulatory agency, Chairman Greenspan specified that in a period of volatility the need was not to extend government interference, but to coordinate independent policies and to allow central banks to retain responsibility for monetary policy. The currency crisis of 1992, in a recessionary environment caused by the aftershocks of market disruptions and the crashes of 1987 and 1989, brought central banks, for the first time in history, to the attention of the general public not as esoteric forums of economic theory housed in splendid architecture, but as epicenters of financial decisions which affect their daily lives and sense of national security.

The Maastricht Treaty mandated that all central banks had to become totally independent as of January 1, 1993. The Maastricht Treaty officially conferred total independence on the European Central Bank, declaring that all central banks of member countries had to be independent of any and all government control or influence.

> When exercising the powers and carrying out the tasks and duties conferred upon them by this Treaty and the Statute of the ESCB, neither the ECB, nor a national central bank, nor any member of their decision making bodies shall seek or take instruction from Community institutions or bodies, from any government of a Member State or from any other body.
> (*Treaty on European Union, The Maastricht Treaty* Article 107 1993: 221)

Under the provisions of the Maastricht Treaty, on January 1, 1998 all central banks of the European member countries, had to renounce sovereignty and become part of a new entity, the European Central Bank. "The prime objective of the ESCB shall be to maintain price stability" (*Maastricht Treaty* Article 105: 218). This mandate was not only seen as sound economic policy, but as the legacy of the Bundesbank, leader of European monetary policy which, since its inception in 1957, understood that minimal or zero inflation alone would guarantee renewed faith in the post-war German economy haunted by the specters of 1921 to 1922, and the near disasters of 1946 to 1947 until the creation of Deutschmark on June 20, 1948.

From their inception until the 1930s, central banks were independent, private organizations under the jurisdiction of boards of directors, cautious, highly respected, collegial group of bankers, merchants, and ministers who could be entrusted with the wealth management of the nation. "Revolution, depression and another world war between them led to the subordination of central banks almost everywhere to governments.... The logic of nationalization was that the private ownership of central banks was incompatible with their macro economic responsibility" (Ferguson 2001: 157–158). Gerard Corrigan, head of the New

York Federal Reserve from 1985 to 1993, wrote: "The single theme of a contemporary central bank's functions is to provide stability – stability in the purchasing power of the currency of the country and stability in the workings of the financial system, including the payments system" (Deane and Pringle 1995: 2). Since its inception in 1998, the European Central Bank has attained exceptional credibility, stability, and prestige. Willing to chart an independent course from the Federal Reserve on interest rate policy, often assuming a far more cautious stance in the 2002–2006 period, it has also worked closely in cooperation with the Federal Reserve in the period following September 11, 2001, to help stabilize world markets and to maintain coordination with the dollar. In the fall of 2008, and as the crisis worsened in 2009, the European Central Bank under Trichet has been forced, like the Bank of England, to engage in more dramatic rate cuts. The European Central Bank, despite unclear guidelines, has judiciously chosen when to intervene in country bailouts and to work in close cooperation with the International Monetary Fund and the Federal Reserve.

5.18 Banking harmonization

> Countries typically experience slow and sometimes painful integration of monetary and banking institutions by regions.
>
> (Kindleberger 1999: intro)

In 1993, the 1989 Single Banking Market Program implemented the Second Banking Directive, which meant that cross-border banks would be regulated under the legislative framework of the home country. The single banking passport meant that any bank licensed to do business in one European Union state was entitled to do business in any other European Union state. Under the provisions of the directive, specified by the European Commission on Competitiveness decision of July 1995 on state subsidies and privatization of state banks, any bank in a European Union member state could set up a branch, subsidiary or take over any bank in another member state. These principles were to guarantee mutual recognition, national treatment, and lay the groundwork for European Union-wide regulatory harmonization. It was projected in 1992 that within a decade Europe would have five to eight megabanks, led by Deutsche Bank and Crédit Lyonnais. By 1999, the European Union had not created a pan-European bank and the market was fragmented and inefficient: "The blame lays largely with European governments outdated notions about the link between ownership and national sovereignty. But banks have also been at fault for their timidity in challenging such notions" ("Meddling With European Banks" 1999).

If the United States since the end of the 1980s promoted and promulgated deregulation in the financial sector, the mantra in the European Union, under the new euro since 1999, was privatization, consolidation, and mergers. The sector underwent a complex evolution, achieving large scale domestic consolidation, privatization, substantially increased efficiency, transparency, and profitability. However, open cross-border integration through mergers, acquisitions, and consolidation, as well as regulatory harmonization, has only been partially successful. The Financial Services Action Plan (FSAP), first conceived in 1994 under Alexander de Lamfalussy, and revised in 2000 and 2004, has still not been finalized and only partially implemented. The original blueprint, which called for across the board harmonization of retail, commercial, and investment sectors, as well as supervisory and monitoring rules and regulations, has been considerably diluted. In 2007, Charles McCreevy, European Union Commissioner for the Internal Market, called for greater flexibility in the retail and commercial spheres, taking into account national requirements, cultural, and societal factors. European Union harmonization has also had to work in coordination with the implementation of Basle II and US opposition to full accounting standardization. The global banking environment has been further complicated by post-September 11, 2001 concerns of money laundering, "terrorist funds," control, and transparency of cross-border capital flows. The end result was that in case of an endemic crisis, it remained unclear who was responsible as lender of last resort and what functions remained under national central bank versus European Central Bank jurisdiction. In September 2007, the images on the front page of the *Financial Times* of Northern Rock customers lining up to withdraw funds and the subsequent bailout by the Bank of England proved that European Union banks need far clearer legislation on bailouts, responses to national and regional contagion risks, and "lender of last resort" definitions. There are "no fixed rules on cross border rescue ... culturally some EU governments are not prepared to regard larger domestic banks as simply another form of business which should be allowed to fail" (Giles 2007).

After a century of banking sector privatization–nationalization cycles, national governments across the European Union are no longer majority shareholders. The elimination of state subsidies to the German Landesbanken between 1999 and 2007, created a competitive European Union market on a level playing field with United States, Japan, and emerging markets. However the influence of governments remains strong and the fine line between influence and interference is not always clear. In 2006, the governor of the Central Bank of Italy was forced to resign after he tried to block the potential buyout of Antonveneto by ABN Amro, in favor of a rigged bid by a weak Italian bank (BPI). In 2006, the Polish government fired the head of the Central Bank when he approved the European Union decision to allow Unicredito (which had absorbed Hypoverein) to complete its takeover of the Polish branches of Hypoverein, claiming that Polish sovereignty was at stake. In the late 1990s Italy, most open and pragmatic on foreign shareholdings, allowed ABN Amro to acquire a stake in Banca di Roma. Italy's banking sector, plagued by fragmentation, inefficiency, and corruption, with nearly 80 percent of its banks controlled by the public sector in a century-old structure of regional, municipal, and former church holdings, finally consolidated into five major banking groups. Unicredito, the largest international group, is a dominant presence in the new European Union member countries, with only 33 percent of its revenues in Italy. In the wake of the Crédit Lyonnais scandal and state bailout for 50 billion francs, a 1996 Goldman Sachs report described the French banking sector as unprofitable, lagging in technology and efficiency. Within a decade, the sector morphed into a powerful, highly efficient global network led by BNP Paribas and CALYON. Yet this merger was imposed by the French government, which prolonged the privatization of Crédit Lyonnais from 1999 to 2003 in order to ensure that Deutsche Bank, HSBC or any other foreign entity will never be able to take a majority stake. Until 2007, Germany never achieved cross-border mergers or large scale domestic consolidation. In 1997, the merger of two Bavarian banks to create Hypoverein, was hailed by Helmut Schmidt as the start of "a bank of regions" seeking to emulate US super regional banks, but within a decade, weak and noncompetitive, it was bought out by Unicredito. The failed attempts at mergers between Deutsche Bank and Commerz Bank and Deutsche Bank and Dresdner in 2000 were symptomatic of the internal fragmentation and lack of efficiency of the domestic market where the largest banks only service about 35 percent of the retail market. Citibank's interest in Deutsche Bank in 2003 was immediately rejected and required that Chancellor Schroder intervene to placate the anger of German chief executive officers at such a suggestion. Finally, in 2007, regional former state subsidized banks began active consolidation and in summer 2008, at the start of the downturn, Commerz Bank and Dresdner Bank agreed on a merger which would create a new German mega bank. At present, the German banking sector, although having to reluctantly accept state injections of capital in October 2008, has weathered the crisis relatively well.

Consolidation and regional integration has been far more successful in smaller markets where mergers improved competitiveness and profitability, and where institutional and political history is less burdensome. The Spanish banking sector, after the 1994 bailout of Banesto and its takeover by Grupo Santander, evolved from basket case to the most profitable in the European Union. Banco Santander's bid for Banco Centrale Hispanoamericano in 1999 created BSCH, which took over major stakeholdings in Mexico, Chile, Brazil, and Venezuela. In 2005, Santander bought Scotland's Abbey National in one of the first and few cross-border mergers. After a drawn out battle in 2007 with Barclays, for the prestigious Dutch multinational ABN Amro, Santander led a consortium with Fortis and Royal Bank of Scotland to acquire the bank. This deal, touted as proof of further European Union banking integration, collapsed in 2008 once Fortis and RBS were declared near insolvent. In fall 2008, Santander could still claim better corporate governance than other European Union banks. However, a few months later, heavily exposed to major losses in the overinflated Spanish property market and the Madoff fraud scheme, Santander had been humbled in its aspirations, although still in a sound position as the Spanish economy struggles to regain equilibrium.

Since the 1995 failure of Barings, the United Kingdom has concentrated on the global market, focusing on the United States, Far East, and emerging markets, largely bypassing the European Union. Matthews and Norton in their report "The EU Single Banking Market Programme: Fit for Purpose" (2008), emphasize that British banks benefit from a long history of involving "shareholders, customers and employees in the management of the bank, they are traditionally better run and more profitable than European universal banks." The situation drastically deteriorated in late 2008 and the first quarter of 2009: Lloyds has had to be nationalized in return for full guarantees, RSB is insolvent, and London has suffered major job losses in a financial sector dependent economy.

Swedish banks served as a model of successful temporary nationalization. In the aftermath of the fall of the Soviet Union, market disruption, and bad property loans (1991–1993), the government had to intervene to recapitalize the banks, creating a "bad bank," the Securum, to sell off the bad loans. This program, planned for five years, was accomplished in three years under sound management, judicious valuation, and disciplined reforms. In 1996, the Swedish sector began a series of effective cross-border mergers between Swedish, Finish, and Danish banks, the merger of Merita and Nordbanken in 1997, followed by the incorporation of Dansk in Denmark and Christianson in Norway, creating a vast regional network which, since 2004, has established a key presence in the new member Baltic countries. Based on historical and political affinities, Swedish banks took large stakes in Baltic banks and provided the bulk of loans to the Baltic countries. They are now willing to assume responsibility for potential bailouts: "They are new democracies; they are part of our economic region" (Dougherty 2009). However, as Nordea and Swedbank have had to accept government aid and guarantees, and as bank bailouts worsen into state bailouts, how much of the burden will they be willing, and able, to assume in Estonia and Latvia, downgraded and needing International Monetary Fund and Swedish central bank aid?

Across Europe the question arises of whether the strong can carry the weak, whether the rewards of salvaging the new member nations are worth the sacrifices, and Europe can return to a two tier Europe of nations? According to European Union bankers in the United States, unlike the 1990–1991 period, when European banks, state owned or state controlled, offered assurances and stability in the wake of Citibank's near collapse, the crisis of 2008 has proven the interdependency of all banks and as independent institutions, the shared vulnerability of all transatlantic financial sectors.

5.19 Financial and commercial monoculturalism

> What the Anglo-Saxons want is a Europe without limits, a Europe which would no longer have the ambition to be itself. A Europe without borders. English style Europe. In reality, America's Europe. The Europe of multinationals. A Europe which in its economy, and more so in its defense and politics, would be placed under inevitable American hegemony. A Europe where each European country, beginning with ours, would lose its soul.
>
> (De Gaulle quoted in Peyrefitte 1994: 367)

Within 20 years, the American multinational model would be applied to European brands, equally guilty of American style monoculturalization. For centuries the poor were similar in every culture, the rich were unique to their culture. Since the 1980s, the poor are different, with vast gradations of misery between the developing and emerging markets, yet the rich are the same. In the 1980s, the internationalization of luxury brands helped create a homogeneous affluent consumer society. Starting with Benetton, the ubiquity of Italian and French fashion brands, Scandinavian design, German automotive: Gucci, Hermes, Ferragamo, Fendi, Marrimekko, Breuer, BMW, and Mercedes, the same logos, products, and prices became available within a narrow range from Montreal to Martinique, Copenhagen to Lisbon, Geneva to Tokyo. Financial utopia, a cultural oxymoron, created on a world wide scale, depended on an endless stream of new investors from an expanding affluent middle class, innovative instruments, larger, cross-border and cross-regional, and more loosely regulated institutions, the competition of capital markets, and an endless appetite for wealth and material goods. It meant a new credit culture in which even the most money cautious countries would spend and charge.

In 1988, while Germany had one Visa distributor for all of West Germany, and the Japanese only used a debit card, the French enthusiastically adopted credit cards, although they tended to have only one card. In 1987, there were 16.5 million credit cards in France the most popular were Carte Bleue, Crédit Agricole, Credit Mutuel, AMEX, Diners Club, and Eurocard–Mastercard. Gaining ground over deeply embedded traditions of distrust and fear of speculation, financial capitalism returned to Europe. Worldwide economies recovered exceptionally well from the Crash of 1987. The assumption that the era of the American style "golden boys" and "raiders" had ended seemed premature as in April 1988 the Paris bourse gained 20 percent, with New York and Tokyo following suit. Money, as it had in the 1860s and 1880s, dominated the political discourse. In the French election of 1988, between Mitterrand, Chirac, and Barre, *Le Nouvel Observateur* devoted an issue to "Les Candidats et l'Argent" (*Le Nouvel Observateur* 1988), showing the three candidates against a 200 franc bank note. Mitterrand, solidly immersed in the tradition of Catholicism socialism remained ambivalent toward money and the market. The Mitterrand credo of "economie mixte," meant a system which would allow private and public sectors to compete on equal grounds, increasing capital gain taxes on large fortunes, promoting and creating incentives for export sectors, but retaining French control over key industries: "mitterrandisme" equaled "la democratie plus la moralisation du capitalisme" (*Le Nouvel Observateur* 1988). Jacques Chirac, in 1988 the most pro-American candidate, oscillated between aristocratic disdain for money and markets, and pragmatic interest in wealth generation. At ease with the business world, his cynical view was: "il est normal ... que les riches s'enrichissent, que les entrepreneurs entreprennent et que les travailleurs travaillent [it is normal ... that the rich get rich, that entrepreneurs undertake and that workers work]" (*Le Nouvel Observateur* 1988).

Once elected President of France (1995–2007), Chirac reversed course accusing America of capitalist excesses. Through the 1990s, European intellectuals and politicians begrudgingly admitted that by force of media, technology, CNN,

Hollywood, Silicon Valley, and Wall Street, the United States had become the sole economic, military, and cultural superpower. The 1993 adversarial General Agreement on Tariffs and Trade (GATT) negotiations, between the United States and the newly formed European Union, established the demarcation lines in the debate on globalization. Although the United States required "fair and free trade," it was the Europeans who made pragmatic distinctions between trade, culture, politics, and issues of human rights and the environment, echoing the Mitterrand interview on French television, *Antenne 2*, October 1993: "Nos cultures ne sont pas a negocier [our cultures are not negotiable]."

For politicians and intellectuals, the pursuit of money without validation, as prestige for the state or the betterment of society, retained a whiff of ill repute and danger. De Gaulle's contempt still resonated: "Au milieu de tout ce joli monde, mon seul adversaire, celui de la France, n'a jamais cesse d'etre l'argent [amid this nice little world, my only adversary, France's only adversary, never ceased being money]" (quoted in *Le Nouvel Observateur* 1988, author's translation). Finance, capital, and money remained totally outside of the sphere of literary or philosophical pursuits. History was denigrated; literature became a means of internalization, objectification, and rupture between text and context. The Nouveau Roman and film, the transmutation of object and subject in the works of Barthes, Robbe-Grillet, Duras, Butor, Resnais, and Godard, rejected traditional literary and linguistic norms, creating a new topos, semantic field, and set of critical norms. The French philosopher Derrida, fascinated with Marx's obsession with money, translated it as a psycholinguistic rather than sociological phenomenon. In the 1970s, Derrida, Man, the sociologist Goux, and the psychoanalyst Lacan discussed economic phenomenon as psychoanalytic abstraction, sign or symbol rather than manifestation of reality.

Structuralism, semiotics, hermeneutics, and post modern theory dissected economic principles, but had no direct relationship to its actual impact or reflection in society. Influenced by Dos Passos, William Gaddis creates a brilliant satirical mosaic, *JR*, in 1975, foreseeing the dotcom geniuses creating virtual companies. JR, an American teenager, creates a company based on negotiating profitable arbitrage operations on army surplus, and soon:

> With the money from these initial deals in plastic, JR builds an extensive financial empire which steadily expands until it includes factories in the United States and abroad, stock transactions, banking interests and even a cemetery and funeral home franchise.
>
> (Taylor 2004: 193)

Once JR's corporation finally comes to the notice of the Securities and Exchange Commission (SEC), like all Ponzi schemes, it collapses having existed only in the realm between rumor and information, between reality and faith in the unattainable.

In 2009, the vision of this phantasmagoric Americanized world of an eternal bazaar of goods and money still intrigues novelists and artists around the world:

[New York] was much newer or rather more awash with new products, new toothbrushes.... In a world where every object was thrown away at the slightest sign of breakage or aging, at the first dent or stain and replaced with a new and perfect substitute, there was one false note, one shadow, the moon.

(Calvino 2009)

5.20 Art of finance – finance of art

If literature deflected and derided monetary global culture, in the last decade the art world has embraced it with a new enthusiasm, blurring distinctions between art, commodity as art and art as commodity. In the first Gilded Age, collecting Old Masters and antiquities was sign and symbol of taste; in the second Gilded Age, art became symbol and proof of wealth. In America, new money bought prestigious art to enhance their new social status, but from the 1930s art also enhanced commerce. The clothing store magnate Gimbels (rival to Macy), bought Cézannes, Picassos, Braques, Old Masters, Turner, Titian, Warhol, and Rauschenberg. Since the 1960s, New York luxury stores on Fifth Avenue show-cased American artists. From Hogarth and Daumier to Thomas Nast, money has been the subject of social commentary and condemnation in etchings, cartoons, and drawings visualizing and popularizing the economic issues of the day. After World War I, Dadism, Surrealism's transposition of daily objects from the toilet to the pipe onto the canvas, interpreted money as one other object. Marcel Duch-amp's Tzanck Cheque (1919) recreated a check on an American bank in dollars, an imaginary check for an imaginary amount. "The Teeth's Loan and Trust Company Consolidated" (Droit 1992: 125), was a dare to the public to enter the joke and pay for ownership of a replica of fake money. In the last three years, American artist David Heatley's cartoon collages of fake currency, Mike Rollins deconstructions of financial operations depicting a stock market ticker; Fame Theory, a young artists duo's fake electronic ticker tape used as indicator of market value of art broke down the barriers between art and money as finance became the subject of their art. "The current market ... is so invasive that it forces artists to regularly consider issues of celebrity, status and money in their studios" (Salz quoted in Honigman 2009).

In the 1960s, Warhol, whose revival in price and popularity soared in the last decade, best understood the subversive nature of art imitating and sublimating objects of literal and figurative consumerism. Mark Taylor in his analysis of Rauschenberg, Jasper Johns, and Warhol emphasizes the symbiotic relationship between American creativity and consumerism, art = money and vice versa. For five years at the height of the bubble, art prices, art fairs, and auctions expanded globally. The few biannual art fairs in Venice, New York or Basel were quickly rivaled by additional fairs in Miami, Dubai, and Berlin. Offering opportunities to more artists to take advantage of the glut of money and buyers, and for artifi-cially constructed economies like Dubai, the art fair served as validation of its new economic clout. Prices reached their apex in 2007, when Jeffrey Koons'

Technicolor sculptures, including gigantic plated animals and party favors, and Damien Hirst's mummified animals, pill paintings, and diamond encrusted human skull sold for millions of dollars. Hirst, extremely attuned and top art world star, had the last laugh as his Golden Calf with 18 karat gold hooves and horns and suspended in formaldehyde, was sold at Sotheby's on September 15, 2008 for US$18.6 million.

In retrospect, artists were far more prescient than bankers, as shown in Adam Dant's *The Art of Hedge*, "showing the heads of the whiz-kids popping out of a bubble bath of clouds. Profits zag off a chart. Hedge fund heaven. But here the whizzes are being shot at by rabbits. Hedge fund hell" described as "comic visual language for the financial world." Based on Dante the work is a detailed diptych: "It's a short trip from heaven to hell" says Dante. "Just read the financial pages" (Haden-Guest 2007). Within one month, the art world reflected the sudden panic and downturn, even among the world's wealthiest as illustrated by Marc Titchner's humorous banner at the Berlin Art Fair in November 2008: "The World Isn't Working." "Sales were slow and many spaces lamented the excruciating trickles that replaced the easy flow of money that splashed around the Messe Berlin in previous years" (Honigman 2008). As retail sales slumped worldwide six months later, and as the luxury market in trendy items imploded, art appraisers and dealers in New York and London saw the art world shift. The principles of caution and sound investment, fueled by fear, returned to the most extravagant niche market.

5.21 Anti globalization, anti-capitalism: crisis of globalization

In 1967, *Le Defi Americain* by Servan-Schrieber (with an afterword by Jacques Maisonrouge, head of IBM France and Minister of Industry from 1986–1988) was a call to arms for a Europe about to be overrun by American investment, buyouts, and multinationals. Europe suffered from lack of initiative, state run enterprises, dearth of technical expertise, and immediate need for reforms, tax incentives, and new business schools and management training. A report by the Hudson Institute, part of the Rand Corporation in 1968, quoted by Servan-Schreiber, forecast global growth and expansion for 1980, predicting that a new European Community, multicultural and multinational, could come about only when Europe could define "an economic and technological personality" (1967). The question was how quickly could European nations realign their economic priorities, energize their industrial policy, and develop human capital and management skills able to create companies, which could compete with the United States. In the last century, each financial crisis and each boom period has been attributed to the influence of American capitalism. If the crisis of 2008 can be called "a crisis of globalization" (Ferguson 2008: 339), its roots are in anti-globalization, anti-American movements. Capitalism and globalization become code words for Americanization. In the 1990s, European right-wing factions translated globalization, open trade, open borders, immigration, the euro, and a larger European Union into loss of national values, and identity, a surge of illegal (translated as criminal) aliens, and a loss of control of national institutions. For the left-wing, the same principles connoted wealthy foreigners and corporations exploiting the workers, ruining the environment, and destroying traditions and local way of life. Anti-globalization, like anti-capitalism because of its eclectic nature, tends to foster theories of conspiracies, attributing to supra national governments, organizations or multinational corporations, an unrealistic level of power, control, and autonomy. At its most sordid globalization transformed all activity into gain for the greatest profit, exemplified by Michel Houellebecq's nihilistic novel *Plateforme* (2001), which defines global sex tourism in developing countries as the most logical result of American-style efficient capitalism.

The psychocultural dichotomy between exploitative bankers and conspiratorial foreign bankers, regardless of all the virulent stereotypes attached, were transferred to the issue of trade, trade financing, and multilateral banks. Riots in Seattle and Genoa at World Trade Organization and "G8" meetings; disruptions in Washington at the International Monetary Fund and World Bank meetings; European Union anti-globalization became part of a larger protest movement against financial institutions, originally created to protect and provide aid to disenfranchised nations. The World Bank, World Trade Organization, and International Monetary Fund, which at their origin were meant to inspire unity, cooperation and stability in a post-World War II world were contorted to represent anonymous economic totalitarianism. In a rather vicious historical twist, the crisis of 2008 has evoked the hatred, fear, and prejudices against bankers, all the while depending on Central Banks, the International Monetary Fund, and the Bank of International Settlements to rescue banks, markets, and governments.

Since the New Deal hearings (see Chapter 6), the American public has expressed little outrage at the excesses of capitalism. The direct correlation of morality and capitalism were left to Europeans, American wanted capitalism without being lectured about moral implications. In 2009, populist fury in the United States against bonuses paid to banking executives in institutions that received "tax payer" bailouts, especially the global insurer AIG whose London derivative trading branch brought about debilitating losses, underscored the shock of the revelations on wage differentials between top executive and workers. Although chief executive officer level compensation across the European Union greatly increased, in 2004, the average chief executive officer in Sweden earned 13 times the salary of average blue-collar worker as opposed to 15 times in Germany, 24 times in the United Kingdom, but 475 times in the United States! As long as the economy was surging ahead and these companies were in the private sector, the American public accepted these wage differentials with complacency. Months before the debate in the United States, Dexia and Caisses d'Epargne, two banking groups hit by the crisis and in need of government funds, were obliged to "waive their severance packages" following a model set up by the Swiss banks which dropped all bonuses, in turn followed by Goldman Sachs. A smart marketing move, it generated favorable press and calmed some shareholders as to how government rescue packages were put to use, but in the case of France it further elucidated the issue of financial morality. President Sarkozy announced that in an attempt "to moralize French capitalism" (Betts 2008), he planned to introduce legislature to limit or even outlaw exorbitant salaries, specifically golden parachutes. Jean-Francois Revel in *L'Obsession anti-americaine* (2002), in one of the most balanced analyses of the European anti-globalization, anti-capitalism dilemma, explained how historically France and Europe could only truly accept globalization as a political and ideological "civilizing mission."

5.22 Bond, James Bond: to the rescue of Anglo-American capitalism

The longest global film franchise, the James Bond series, traces the political and financial cultural trajectory from the 1962 to 2008. The plots are never mere theft of global riches, but very sophisticated plans to subvert and, in effect, destroy value rather than tangible wealth. From Goldfinger's plan to capture the global gold market by making Fort Knox radioactive, the heroin trade (*Live and Let Die*, 1973), stealing a priceless Russian Faberge Egg (*Octopussy*, 1983), a post-Soviet Union scheme to steal the reserves of the Bank of England by erasing all financial records with the computer program Golden Eye, thereby incapacitating the British economy (*Golden Eye*, 1995), to *The World is Not Enough* (1999), which opens at a Swiss Bank in Bilbao receiving a large sum of cash belonging to British oil tycoon with shady post-Soviet connections linked to Azerbaijan oil, banks proliferate as agents of suspicious payments, transactions, secrets, and evil conspiracies. In 2006 and 2008, the films become darker and more existential, but the plots still circle around money in a poker game among global villains (*Casino Royale*, 2006) and the ecological culprit, Le Chiffre. The persona of the agent, represented by possessions more than self, the bespoke suits, expensive watches, pens, elegant hotel suites, martinis, cars, and accoutrements, have allowed entirely different actors to assume the role with expertise and flair. Every time James Bond, with an equally prototypical side-kick from the Central Intelligence Agency (CIA) saves the world from SMERSH, Communism, insane billionaires, and ecological fiends, he is also safeguarding and guaranteeing Anglo-American capitalism with all its flaws and all its glories.

6 American financial culture

Myths and models of American capitalism

In 2007, at number 48 Wall Street, on the former site of the Bank of New York, the Museum of American Finance opened. An affiliate of the Smithsonian Institute, it is "the nation's only independent public museum dedicated to celebrating the spirit of entrepreneurship and the democratic free market tradition ... to better the financial lives of individuals, companies and nations" (Museum of American Finance 2007).

A museum dedicated to the history and artifacts of money and finance is the quintessential expression of American financial culture. Deconstructing the credo of the museum reveals slogans from the 1890s (capitalism), the 1950s (free enterprise), and the 1990s (entrepreneurship). It respects and justifies finance in the name of betterment of society, in which the individual, the corporation and the state play equal roles. It also reinforces the predominance of the private sector in finance, which, despite the encroaching role that the government is being now called upon to assume, with injections of capital, buy-ups of preferred stock, and partial nationalization of the banking sector in the crisis of 2008, remains the fundamental principle of financial capitalism and has done so throughout American history. Washington may be asked to regulate, oversee and provide guarantees for the financial sector, as it has since the crisis of 1907; it may assume responsibility and demand accountability, as it did in the 1930s, and, to varying degrees, post-1987, but it cannot assume a permanent role of decision maker as to the types of loan, to whom credit is extended, the level of compensation, and how investments are allocated, without impinging on the basic separation of the public and private sector, which is at the heart of American financial culture. The extent and severity of the banking crisis in 2008 has demanded a re-evaluation of the functions and identity of American and European global banks. It has called for a total reform of the American regulatory system, established in the 1930s, and superficially modified in the 1970s and 1990s, and it has forced the American public to re-examine its attitudes toward the role of government in financial and industrial policy. However, despite the shock to the system, and the need for radical surgery, fundamental faith in American financial ingenuity, innovation and independence will survive, as it has during the previous 200 years. An examination of American financial culture proves the resilience, constant renewal, and ability to reconcile capitalism and populism. Faith in Wall Street and East Coast financiers had been shattered again and again: 1825, 1857, 1866, 1873, 1893, 1907, 1929, 1987, 2000, yet each time the market and the banking sector have rebounded and new, consolidated or merged banks resurface. The present crisis is complicated by the global connectivity of Asian, American and European Union markets, but overall there has been little currency volatility, unlike the 1930s when monetary, economic and trade policies were totally asymmetrical and desynchronized. As in previous crises, the press, media, literature, arts, cinema and, now, the internet has lent their voices to condemn or praise Wall Street, to exonerate Main Street, to seek out scapegoats and to keep the public interested. Money in America is fun, virtuous or evil, it fascinates and entertains. To understand its role in American financial history, it is necessary to delve into commentary, news articles, novels, plays, movies and television shows that reflect and transform economic analysis into popular culture.

6.1 Resilience and renewal

"When I was a student, we learned about the three Gs; God, Gold and Glory. They all mattered, but the greatest of all was Gold, because gold paid the bills, armed the fleets, lured and consoled the flesh" (Landes 2003: 393). Witty and provocative, this commentary underlies Anglo-American ideology: the separation of church and market place, acceptance of the inevitability of the market, and the removal of morality from practicality. As history proves, and scholars corroborate, nations where God and glory, alone or in unison, dominate the collective social and political discourse, economic development is far more erratic and vulnerable. In America, these principles went further as financial success was a source of pride and resilience.

American financial history is strewn with failed investment, wholesale and retail banks, corporate bankruptcies, Wall Street booms, busts, recessions, and speculative frauds. Although Bernard Madoff's US$50 billion Ponzi scheme is the largest, there are numerous precedents in American history. Andrew Dexter's real estate and financial fraud in Boston in 1809, entailed major losses in the business community when Dexter used as collateral, worthless paper notes issued by bankrupt rural banks to construct a vastly expansive Exchange Coffee House. Charles Wyman Morse, overleveraged banker worth US$60 million in 1900, with a fleet of coastal and Hudson River steamboats, sought to buy a steamship line with non-existent funds and was convicted of "misapplication of funds and sentenced in 1910 to 15 years in prison" (Stevenson 2007); Richard Whitney, the former head of the New York Stock Exchange, was arrested in 1938 for embezzlement, check kiting, and hiding fraudulent assets in his wife's name. Beep Jennings, the genial president of Oklahoma Penn Square bank, whose gas and oil lease Ponzi scheme in 1982, almost destroyed Chase Manhattan, and brought down Continental Illinois (see Kamensky 2008; Stevenson 2008).

Thousands of small and large American banks have failed over the past two centuries, with more than 1,000 banks failing between 1987 and 1992 (Congressional Budget Office 1994). Yet over two centuries the dynamism, flexibility and resilience of American markets and financial institutions remain unsurpassed. Charles Dickens, often accused of disdaining American capitalism as coarse and brutal, understood the strength and vitality of American initiative and ability to rebound, admiring the unique capacity for "love of smart dealing which gilds over many a swindle and gross breach of trust; many a defalcation, public and private and enables many a knave to hold his head up with the best" (Dickens 1842: 242). American capitalism and the culture of profit and money is so unique because it is fundamentally devoid of moral content, it is self perpetuating, renewable, deemed essential rather than existential in the collective psyche, what H.W. Brands called the "aristocracy of capital" (Brands 2006: 192). Even when there is popular outcry against abuses, whether in 1893 against tycoons and the gold lobby, in 1907 against trusts and monopolists, "fat cats" in the post-Depression era, or the oblivious heads of the "Big Three" automobile companies who arrived in Washington, in November 2008, by private jet to ask for taxpayer funded bailouts, Americans profoundly believe in the principles of a market economy. Built by escapees and convicts from debtors' prisons, religious and economic persecutees, Protestant merchants and tradesmen, pirates and renegades, there is a deep seated tolerance for financial failure and recovery. More than any other nation, bankruptcy in America does not entail immediate social stigma, dishonor, or expulsion from the community.

Tocqueville, in his prescient analysis of the American character wrote in 1835:

> Americans, who see in commercial audacity a type of virtue, could never under any circumstances, condemn the audacious. From this derives in the United States, the unique tolerance for the merchant who declares bankruptcy; the honor of such an individual is in no way affected. In this, Americans are different, not only from European nations, but from all contemporary trading nations; thus by their attitudes and needs do they stand apart from all others.
>
> (Tocqueville 1981: 292)

Historically, American financial swindlers and fraudsters are punished, fined, even jailed, but are often able to resurrect their fortunes and reputation. Charles Wyman Morse, pardoned for reasons of health by Taft, regained a fortune, and profiteered during World War I, dying a wealthy man in 1933 (Stevenson, *New York Times*, December 6, 2008). Beep Jennings was indicted but never convicted in Oklahoma; Ivan Boesky and Michael Milken, the faces of the 1987 crash, insider trading and failure of Drexel Lambert, were jailed, released, and went on to redeem their reputations and wealth. America invented the Ponzi Scheme (see Chapter 2), the concept of white-collar crime, and redemption for financial sins. In 2008, the culprits were the heads of investment banks: Richard Fuld at Lehman Brothers, for his failure to disclose losses in time to salvage the bank; and John Thain, the highly respected former head of the New York Stock

Exchange (NYSE), and head of Merrill Lynch, for the lesser, but more visible transgression, of spending millions to redecorate his office, while his firm needed a government bailout amid large layoffs.

6.2 Land of opportunities

Unlike other cultures, where sources of wealth are limited to a few sectors and profound psycho historical uneasiness remains in place concerning profit, gain, and the ostentatious display of wealth, American wealth is neither static, dynastic, nor organically linked to one area or domain. Enormously dynamic, fluid and adaptable, after the crash and recession of 2008, as following the severe crash and aftermath of the crisis of 1987, Wall Street, although geographically more symbolic than real, retains power and global prestige. Americans are not universally rich, or even well off, but money, luxury and excess retains its vast appeal in the collective American conscience. Wealth generation is a basic part of American values and system of cultural norms. Therefore, even when decried as a sign of moral deprivation and societal destruction, it remains an engine of inherent dynamism and progress.

Geographic, labor mobility and demographic shifts across the West, South and South West in the nineteenth and twentieth century created endless opportunities. Real and fictional financiers and speculators, Jay Cooke, Jim Fiske, Daniel Drew, and Jay Gould, like their fictional counterparts in the novels of Dreiser, Norris, and James, made fortunes in railroads, steamships, and speculation between greenbacks and gold during the Civil War, and then moved into the world of respectable banking and high finance.

Jay Cooke started as bond salesman for the Republic of Texas before annexation in 1848. Like medieval traders in the Bruges to Seville to Genoa routes, Cooke learned to sell across the country, taking advantage of the time lags, distances and different rates of interest in different regions of the country. Surviving the boom and bust of mining speculation during and after the Gold Rush, in 1861, at the start of the Civil War, he opened the firm of Jay Cooke and Co. in Philadelphia. Caught in the financial panic of 1873, after speculative trading and loss of liquidity in railroad bonds, the firm closed in September 1873 causing a run on banks and the failure of thousands of smaller institutions. Within a decade he opened another firm, joining forces with Indiana banker and former Secretary of the Treasury and Comptroller, Hugh McCulloch, with offices in New York and London.

Devoid of the aristocracy, monarchies, and Church which incubated European culture, built its palaces, mansions, universities and fostered its manuscripts and works of art, America had to turn to its merchant financiers to assume the role of benefactor and mécène. From the onset, it was clear that neither the federal government nor state governments were going to set aside a percentage of revenues for culture, higher education or scientific research. Unlike France, where 1 percent of gross domestic product is devoted to state sponsored cultural projects, under the Ministry of Culture, the concept of such an institution or arrangement was always seen as somewhat effete and discretionary in American politics. In each crisis, financiers and bankers are decried as "fat cats" who only seek personal enrichment, yet in each period of prosperity, the arts, universities, libraries, medical and research facilities (outside of the military) have vastly benefited from the generosity of individual benefactors.

In the first Gilded Age, Morgan, Frick, Belmont Lehman, Harriman, Warburg, Hellman, Carnegie, Vanderbilt, Rockefeller, Astor, and Peabody, thriving through close business and familial alliances (with linkages to the major British and German financial dynasties) set the standards for American philanthropy. Able to access the boardrooms as easily as the treasure troves of Europe, their endowments, donations and subsidies justified their wealth for the betterment of the community. In the second Gilded Age, former Chief Executive Officer of Citigroup, Sandy Weill, who compared himself to Andrew Carnegie, as patron of the arts, ballet, music, and medical research; Kenneth Griffin; Steven Schwartzman; and Jacob Ezra Merkin, all derided in 2008 as exploitative, vulgar money men, but who, in the past decade contributed substantial sums to cultural institutions.

Americans tolerate exorbitant wealth if it is used to benefit others, but this benevolent paternalism is best given and received under a unique American caveat of "no strings attached."

6.3 Wall Street

Steven Fraser, in his exhaustive study, *Every Man a Speculator, A History of Wall Street in American Life* (2005), establishes a time line:

> For nearly a century from the time of the Civil War through the Great Depression, Wall Street had been an essential element of the country's cultural iconography, nearly as omnipotent as Uncle Sam or the Western cowboy. For the next forty years, roughly from 1940 to 1980 it vanished from the front page and lived out its life in the business section of the daily newspaper.
>
> (Fraser 2005: intro.)

The resurgence that occurred in the 1980s was rapid, spectacular and began a pattern of large scale crises, recoveries, panics and volatility, which finally came to a brutal end in 2008. In the past two decades, faith in the street reached proportions unheard of since the late 1920s, as the market, not only produced ever higher level of returns, but demonstrated extraordinary resilience, to rebound within a year in the aftermath of severe downturns in 1987, 1989, 2000, after endemic abuse of corporate power in the Enron and World.com scandals in 2003, and even after the devastation and tragedy of September 11, 2001.

The ability of the market to recover after large scale losses was first tested in the Crash of 1857, which severely hit French and English exchanges. The crisis, which impacted Europe, hit American wheat prices, railroad shares, banks, and land speculation. More than 1,400 banks failed in October 1857, resulting in New York in large scale unemployment, and homelessness and riots, but the economy revived quickly and by 1859 order was restored, and a new wave of money poured in.

Henry Clews, in his memoirs *Fifty Years in Wall Street* (1908), and in another work, *The Wall Street Point of View* (1900), presented first hand perspective of American business and financial dynamism: "Any man or woman may become wealthy if he or she begins aright." In chapter VI, "Art of Making and Saving Money" he advocated "hard work, thrifty habits, good investment" and the need to consult conservative men for sound advice, such as Vanderbilt, George Peabody, Wannamaker, Drexel, and Morgan. Clews, a dry goods broker turned investor, bought a seat on the NYSE in 1857 for US$500 (the same seat selling in 1908 for $35,000). After the Crash of October 1857, in which shares lost 50 percent of their value, he recouped his losses, founding Livermore, Clews and Co. in 1859, which made a fortune in federal bonds during the Civil War. A staunch supporter of gold, he deplored Bryan's call for silver, judging the crisis of 1893 to have been a currency crisis: "production, financing and credit was as a rule, in a perfectly sound, conservative and fairly profitable condition when the tidal wave struck us" (Clews 1908), provoked by depletion of gold. A firm believer in American capitalism and initiative, against class distinctions and injustice, aware of the opportunities and dangers of the market, he wrote a chapter on "Panics and their Indicators" (chapter X): "We have a ceaseless stream of new issues of stocks, mortgages and commercial paper, comprising a large amount of outstanding obligations, liable, from the uncertainty of their basis, to wide fluctuation in value" (Clews 1908). He defined panics as a "descending wave of activity and rising prices" followed by "hesitation and caution," a "contraction by lender and discounter" as prices fall, "at which point credit becomes more sensitive and is contracted, transactions are diminished" followed by depreciation of property (Clews 1908). Praising American ingenuity and youth, he wrote: "In America only does the youthful element predominate in financial affairs, and results have justified the selection, which perhaps in no other nation is justified" (Clews 1908: 5).

Early on Wall Street became site and symbol of financial activity. The area nearly burned down in 1776, and again in 1835 and 1845. Each time it was quickly rebuilt with little impact on active trading. Already in the 1780s, it was a vibrant and well established "home to its flourishing mercantile aristocracy" (Fraser 2005), with the Merchant's, and later Tontine's coffee house, at the corner of Wall and Water street, and Trinity Church, the most prestigious church in the city, surrounded a few blocks north by the active, boisterous seaport. It was perfectly situated to receive goods, exchange information and to circulate rumors among the merchants, tradesmen, stock jobbers and speculators congregating within the network of narrow streets, lanes, alley ways and coffee houses adjacent to the port. The Tontine Coffee House became the center of activity and the first exchange in the 1790s as New York was rife with information on the French Revolution between 1789 and 1791. Wall Street and the seaport for the next half century was a rowdy, dangerous area, where rooming houses, bordellos, taverns, and depots which serviced ships and sailors, cohabiting with brokers and merchants offices.

Charles Dickens, the century's foremost chronicler of financial foibles and moral drama, even before his first visit to America in 1848, understood the dangers of Wall Street's speculative schemes. *Martin Chuzzlewit* (1843) portrayed the typical foreign dupe: "seduced by the huckstering riffs of New York land promoters – an irresistible rhetorical blend of high falutin democratic egalitarianism and un blinkered covetousness – even before he gets off the boat from England" (Fraser 2005: 44). Bamboozled into investing in a fictitious land deal, he ventures out west to discover that he has lost all his savings in swamp land, a fictional portent of the real estate schemes which would destroy capital and trust in markets through the 1920s, and resurface in the notorious subprime mortgage deals of 2005–2008. Herman Melville's last novel adapted folk tales and Chaucerian allegories to speculative ruses and business dupery. Published in April 1857, a few months before the crash, *The Confidence-Man: His Masquerade*, revealed the cunning of a financial fraudster and the credulity of his victims on a Mississippi steamboat. Chapter IX, entitled "Two Business Men Transact A Little Business," describes all the tactics of the classic con game, in which the confidence man lures in the young man by feigning indifference, mentioning in passing excellent returns on a fictitious company, Black Rapids Coal Company, presenting seemingly genuine paper certificates, and later pushing a land investment, so blatantly false, a "water lot in city of New Jerusalem," assuring the victim that they are indeed on "terra firma" (Melville 1857: 71–78).

6.4 Anti-Wall Street confederacy

The dichotomy in financial culture between France and England replayed in the United States between the industrial North and the rural, slave labor Southern economy. Thomas Jefferson, while ambassador to France, was inspired and delighted by aristocratic disdain for commerce and bankers, which Benjamin Franklin, as ambassador, regarded with caution and disapproved of. Southern plantation owners had a deep aversion toward stock jobbers and bankers on Wall Street, seeing them as foreigners and philistines. Southern planters hated bankers and banks as Yankee tricksters, and "one Virginia planter swore that he would no more be caught going into a bank than into a house of ill fame" (Chernow 2004: 350). By the 1840s, the tax structure and fiscal needs of north and south deviated, as large landowners in Virginia rejected property taxes, and invested very little revenue, while Massachusetts merchants accepted a sophisticated system of taxation on industry and corporations, and even an initial income tax.

Abraham Lincoln, like Napoleon, had the political genius to understand that political and military transformation was not sufficient without economic and administrative policies. Before and during the Civil War, Lincoln pushed forward support for the banks, embraced monetary reforms to bolster the low stock of gold under Treasury Secretary Chase, issuing "greenbacks" notes as legal tender in February 1862. Once the South seceded, it became clear that, "According to Jefferson Davis, the Confederate president, two thirds of the entire taxable property of the area at the outbreak of the war was in land and slaves" (Myers 1970: 166). Desperate for income and unable to raise sufficient taxes, it also tried to issue paper money in 1863, which quickly depreciated, provoking inflation with its corollary of high food prices and food shortages. During the course of 1863, the price of a gold dollar "rose from 3 dollars in paper to 20 in paper" (Meyers 1970: 166). Washington was accused of manipulating the price of silver, creating in the rural West, a distrust of banks and Northern bankers. At the end of the Civil War, Southern contempt for finance and bankers had turned to hatred and fear.

This myth of the rural, anti-capitalist South remained ingrained in American imagination long after the Civil War, its most famous representations in the hugely popular movies *Jezebel* (1938), and *Gone with the Wind* (1939), based on the Margaret Mitchell's best selling 1936 novel. *Jezebel*, a melodramatic tear jerker, directed by William Wyler, with Bette Davis as headstrong New Orleans Southern belle, Julie Marsden, and Henry Fonda as the young banker, Preston Dillard. After breaking off his engagement, the young banker moves North on business, later returning before an outbreak of yellow fever with his Northern wife, Amy, who epitomizes the sharp contrast between the attractive, sensible city style of the North and the emotional lavishness of the South. *Gone with the Wind*, an American epic, reinforced the image of the inability of the South to convert to economic modernity. After the Civil War, Southern grace and gentility deteriorated into passivity and victimhood, as Southerners brutally clung to segregation and a property based economy. The characters of Ashley Wilkins, Rhett Butler and the heroine, the implacable Scarlet O'Hara, personify the cultural and economic battle of the South, oscillating between quasi feudalism and modern capitalism until the 1970s. William Faulkner, descendent of a prominent Confederate military family, disgusted by the greed and corruption of the New South, elaborated the mythology of post-bellum decay, vulgarity, and social dissension in his trilogy of Yoknapatawpha County, Mississippi, dominated by the Snopes family. In *The Town* (1957), Flem Snopes, sharecropper turned property owner, town water works manager, and banker through fraudulent deals, bribery, and profiteering, represents the forces of capitalism, sacrificing moral and social virtues in the name of money and profit.

6.5 Gold, silver and the Wild West

The economy of the Western territories and states, initially based on gold and silver mining, expanded into copper, railroad, construction, trade, and shipping within a generation. Linkages, through family or business connections with established East Coast banks and investment houses, helped stabilize and civilize the Wild West. The Gold Rush (1849–1855), provoking huge volatility in the price of gold and silver, followed by erratic currency fluctuations, led in part to the Crash of 1857. The California Gold Rush and the Klondike, Alaska Gold

Rush, in 1896, became part of the lore and legend of the American West. From Jack London, Frances Brett Hart, Mark Twain, to Charlie Chaplin's *The Gold Rush* (1925) and American television shows, popular literature and media recaptured actual accounts, sagas and folklore of prospectors, brutal mining camps, prostitutes, swindlers, and the love of gold lost and found.

The discovery of gold at Sutter's Mill in Coloma, California in 1849 incited the Gold Rush, aptly named for the wave of emigrants from the East and Europe, especially France, but also from across the Pacific, as Australians and Chinese poured into California. The transformation of the sleepy Mexican hamlets of San Francisco and Los Angles into booming, lawless frontier towns accelerated California's application and acceptance of statehood in 1850. Although banknotes could be exchanged for gold by 1854, the state constitution banned banks from operating until after the Civil War. The economy ran on gold, with huge fortunes quickly acquired, and often just as quickly spent in the bars, saloons, brothels, and proliferating swindles. Longer lasting fortunes were made in providing services for the miners, the best known, Levi Strauss, who opened his dry goods emporium in 1853, and Isaias Wolf Hellman, who opened the Farmers and Merchant Bank in 1871, provided much needed credit for the new wave of emigrants, moving West in the aftermath of the Civil War. Hellman was prominent in the development of the Los Angeles electricity grid; trolley and rail system; newspapers; he was a founder of University of Southern California. It took nearly two years for the panic of 1873 to reverberate in weakening silver and gold prices, but in 1875 Hellman was able to quell a run on the bank with bank guarantees from Lehman and other East Coast financiers. In the panic of 1893, Hellman single handedly took on the role of Morgan. As president of the Nevada Bank of San Francisco (created by silver fortunes in the 1870s, it had failed and was bought by Hellman and a consortium of East and West Coast investors in 1890) Hellman personally oversaw the transfer of US$500,000 of gold coin from the Nevada Bank to Farmers and Merchants in Los Angeles to reassure depositors and restore confidence. Hellman, a German Jew from Bremen, was related to Mayer Lehman, founder of Lehman Brothers. In his purchase of Nevada Bank,

> Hellman was soon oversubscribed. Lehman Brothers bought $250,000 worth of stock and Levi Strauss & Co. bought 150,000 in stock. Other investors included members of the Haas family ... Isaac Van Nuys from Los Angeles and capitalists Antoine Borel and Christian de Guigne.
>
> (Dinkelspiel 2008: 26–30)

In 1905, Hellman bought the banking unit of the Wells Fargo Express company, merging it into Wells Fargo Nevada National Bank. This time the shareholders included "Edward H. Harriman, the owner of the Southern Pacific and other railroads; Jacob Schiff, the banker from Kuhn, Loeb; Levi Strauss & Co; and Phoebe Hearst, the widow of mining magnate, George Hearst" (Dinkelspiel 2008: 30).

There were a few women like Margaret Tobin from Missouri, who worked in steamboats, moved West, marrying Jimmy Brown who made a fortune in silver and later gold in the rugged mountains of Leadville, Colorado. Rejected by Denver society where she built a lavish mansion, she charmed Europe, survived the sinking of the Titanic, and became a philanthropist, going down in American legend as the "Unsinkable Molly Brown," retold in immensely popular musical theater and film in the 1960s.

The next boom in commodities would come with the discovery of oil in California in the 1870s, the Kern River fields in early 1900, and East Texas in 1901, followed by Oklahoma. Big Texas oil fortunes resurfaced in the mid-1930s, until the 1960s wedding of ostentatious wealth to political power, giving Texas money a special cachet in American culture. A state since 1848, Texas remained proudly independent and deeply conservative, wary of cosmopolitan East Coast values and Wall Street institutions.

The major oil fortunes, by the mid-1970s diversified into commodities, including the Hunt brothers, who nearly cornered the silver market in 1979 (personally owning one-third of the world supply). On March 27, 1980, when silver shares, reaching an apex of nearly US$50 in January, dropped precipitously to US$11, the Hunts could not meet their margin calls, causing a panic on Wall Street. Their brokerage firm, predecessor to Bache, had to be rescued with a US$1.1 billion loan through a consortium of banks. The Hunts filed for bankruptcy and were indicted for stock manipulation.

Legends and folklore surrounding oil barons and "black gold" are ingrained in literature, media, film and television, epitomized in *Dallas*, which became the most watched soap opera worldwide in the early 1980s. A decade after Saudi wealth rivaled US oil fortunes, and in the midst of the oil and gas scandals in Oklahoma, the lavish spending, corruption, wheeling, dealing, and personal travails of the fictional Ewing clan assuaged America's loss of prestige in the early Reagan years before the next boom.

6.6 American old and new money

In the decade after the Civil War, the North South dichotomy evolved into an Eastern Western bi-polarity between old moneyed interests of New York and Boston society, and the new railroad, mining, gold, silver and commodities fortunes from Chicago, Denver and, after the Gold Rush, California. Jay Cooke in railroads; Andrew Carnegie and Collis Huntington in steel and railroads; Isaias Hellman in California and Nevada banking; Vanderbilt, Drew, Fisk and Gould in the Erie canal and steam boats speculation; Guggenheim and Henry Clay Frick in coal and steel; and Guggenheim in copper mining, invested and circulated immense amounts of wealth. German Jewish bankers settled in New York, with the Kuhns, Loebs, and Shiffs opening in 1867 the firm of Kuhn Loeb (which merged with Lehman Brothers in 1977).

Historian Theresa Collins' exhaustive studies of Thomas Edison and Otto Kahn; Nicholas Fox Weber's work on the Clarks and Singers upstate New York fortunes in industry and real estate; Ron Chernow's conclusive study of the Morgan dynasty; and Annie Cohen-Solal's work on American painting, its mentors, and institutions, describe how vast fortunes, earned through innovation, investment, speculation, and pragmatic business skills, financed the civilizing mission of American capitalism. The Metropolitan Museum in New York opened in 1880 as a bastion of culture against the philistines of Wall Street, exemplifying the tension between old money, ensconced in the closed society of old Dutch and English families, the Knickerbockers, the Boston Cabots, and Lodges, described in the works of Edith Wharton and Henry James, and new money, which financed and built universities, museums, private residences, clubs, and hotels. Morgan, a descendent of prominent old money and creator of new money, straddled both worlds. He funded the Metropolitan Museum, the Metropolitan Opera, the New York Botanical Garden, and Madison Square Garden. Yet, when older traditional clubs were loath to admit bankers and financiers, J.P. Morgan, in 1893, commissioned the most ostentatious monument to unbridled American finance, the Metropolitan Club. Gilded and ornate, dripping with gold leaf decorations from its extravagant golden gateway and courtyard off Fifth Avenue, it did not just declare wealth, it screamed it. By 1880, the 400 families of established society had already been bypassed by the wealth and power of Morgan, Harriman, Stillman, Loebs, and Seligman as New York society evolved from linear to concentric patterns of wealth and prestige among the different ethnic groups.

Spanning 40 years of economic growth in Philadelphia and Chicago, Theodore Dreiser's hero Frank Cowperwood in *The Financier* (1912) and *The Titan* (1914), traces the trajectory from bookkeeping, to brokering, to note brokerage (the selling of municipal notes), and then to investment banker (a new and more prestigious occupation than commercial banking because of its power to create and direct financial undertakings). Success is followed by the downward spiral of misappropriation of city funds, desperate financial scheming, and inability to meet loans called in the panic that followed the Chicago Fire of October 1871. This leads to bankruptcy, trial, and imprisonment, but in the unique American fashion, culminates in his pardon and return to the market in 1873, with new ventures in land and lease speculation in Chicago. Dreiser's portrayal of the financier combines respect for the skills and adaptability needed to create fortunes, with tolerance for the amorality that permeates his political, business, and sexual standards. In Dreiser's portrayal the financier can be a noble figure, "He was a financier by instinct and all the knowledge that persisted to that great art was as natural to him ... as the subtleties of life are to a poet" (Dreiser 1912). But it is Henry James, the archetypal European elitist among great American novelists, who captured the post Civil War American financier in *The American* (1883), focusing on his physiognomy, his strength, and virility, "a powerful specimen of an American" (James 1877: 34). Unlike European bankers in Dickens, Flaubert, or Zola, Christopher Newman is a new hero, young, forthright, ambitious and generous, yet totally unapologetic in his devotion to money. James endows him with unique American business acumen, the ability to gamble and speculate successfully, and a total commitment to gain and profit. Reconciled to his identity and persuaded that he provides an important social function in a growing country; he is frustrated and confused by the rigid social conventions of Europe, and the inbred disdain toward money and commerce:

> He had known what it was to have utterly exhausted his credit, to be unable to raise a dollar, and to find himself at nightfall in a strange city, without a penny to mitigate its strangeness ... It must be said, rather nakedly that Christopher Newman's sole aim in life had been to make money; what he had been placed in the world for was, to his own perception, simply to wrest a fortune, the bigger, the better, from defiant opportunity.
>
> (James 1877: 53 and 54)

Henry Clews as first generation financier saw an endless pioneer spirit with new lands, mines, railroads, banks, and corporations to be created: "The future will be brilliant in inventions and discoveries and in the advancement of gigantic business enterprises without limit as to sphere" (Clews 1908: 183). Fearing socialists, communists, anarchists, and nihilists after the assassinations of the late 1890s, he saw their objective to destroy the foundations of American economic life:

> Some now want to see fortunes demolished by terrible and destructive forces ignorant or unmindful of the fact they constitute the chief fund from which capital is drawn for the development of all great enterprises and for the advancement of civilization.
>
> (Clews 1908: 183)

6.7 Civilizing wealth

In New York, Chicago, Philadelphia, Atlanta, Saint Louis, Nashville, Milwaukee, and San Francisco can be found magnificent buildings housing banks, exchanges, universities, museums, art galleries, concert halls, opera houses, hotels, and private clubs built by banking, land, mining and railroad fortunes between 1880 and 1917. Similar to the donations of bankers and hedge fund managers from 2002 to 2008, the accumulated fortunes of the first Gilded Age philanthropists were so vast that "the sums that these wealthy men lavished on their philanthropic campaigns, though enormous, usually accounted for a minute fraction of their total worth" (Cohen-Solal 2001: 217). These buildings enhanced cities, helped create new neighborhoods, and democratized access to culture, but they were also monuments to validating and honoring individual fortunes. By 1919, wealthy American women became leaders in cultural patronage: Bertha Honore Palmer in Chicago; Gertrude Vanderbilt Whitney in New York; Isabella Stewart in Boston; followed in the 1920s by Peggy Guggenheim; Abby Aldrich Rockefeller; Lilly Bliss; artists and collectors Florine and Etta Stettheimer; were instrumental in the creation of America's foremost museums, galleries and art collections (see Cohen-Solal 2001: 258–268).

The Yale Club of New York, on Vanderbilt Avenue opposite Grand Central Station, named in honor of Commodore Vanderbilt, was completed in 1915. Its elegant neo-classic design with its ornate carved marble ceiling in the vast second floor lounge, its library and dining halls, built to mirror similar halls and reading rooms on the Yale campus, was sign and symbol of American material as well as intellectual superiority. The goal of the neo-Georgian Harvard Club and the Renaissance Revival University Club was not only to imitate or recreate the glory of various European imperial styles in art and architecture but, in stone, marble, and gold, to pass on to America the mantle of European civilization and wealth. Rivaling and then surpassing England, early twentieth-century American universities, museums, as well as stock exchanges, and banking houses would mold their identity on Europe as proof of pedigree and prestige, but aggressively move forward in their own unstoppable quest of money and economic power. The Guaranty Trust Company of New York, under Morgan, opened in 1913 in a grandiose building on Liberty and Broadway (now occupied by Brown Brothers Harriman). The bank had a "temple like dignity. In the bank solemnity was demanded of employee and visitor alike" (Hunt 2008: 32). The bank was instrumental in financing American imports from Europe during World War I, providing international loans to France and England, and domestic loans to Bethlehem Steel, and Remington Arms. The building was majestic, with a 100-foot banking main floor with Corinthian columns, French marble, incorporated mosaics, and "massive doors facing the street contained elaborate carvings of Greek coins" (Hunt 2008: 33). The vault held a fortune in gold and securities, the bank catered to wealthy clients, handling deposit accounts, notes, bond coupons and commercial paper, and international banking through overseas offices. It sold trust services, trustee duties for corporations, employing by the 1920s more than 3,000 people with a wide range of benefits for employees including medical care, educational courses and activities, social clubs, an employee cafeteria, and a pension system instituted in 1914. In France, Crédit Lyonnais, the most profitable bank with a global network in 1910, began a similar program of benefits and services for its employees. Social welfare programs often originated in the large corporate financial institutions which created the best workers wages and work conditions, all in the name of capitalism. In 1958, the bank merged with J.P. Morgan, creating the Morgan Guaranty Trust Company of New York. The Bowery Savings Bank of New York, completed in 1894, a Greek revival building with magnificent marble columns, stucco paneled ceiling and carved inlays, was the bank of robber barons as well as struggling emigrants in the twentieth century, as the Lower East Side deteriorated into tenements and sweat shops.

By 1914, American capitalism, in its quest to buy up European treasures, titles and properties, was already tainted as crude, corrupt and potentially destructive. Europe seemed to be for sale, and put on display in the newly built, great museums in New York.

The Fifth Avenue palaces ogled by New Yorkers were lived in disproportionately by families enriched by the Street. Papers never tired of titillating
the taste for society's prodigality, providing detailed accounts of James
Hazen Hyde's $200,000 ball at Sherry's in 1905.

(Fraser 2005: 261)

During World War I, the Great War, Fraser explains, old and new money finally
reached mutual respect in the name of patriotism, another unique American
trait. Sons and fathers among the Aldrichs, Rockefellers, Warburgs, and
Stimpsons all volunteered, served, and helped finance the war effort for the
Allied cause, universally seen as a fight to save democracy and civilization.
Fraser illustrates this new partnership in the description of the "Silk Stocking
Regiment" who trained at the sumptuous 107th Infantry Regiment on Park
Avenue. Its members were the elite of society and Wall Street money, who
together manned the front lines, fought in the trenches, and returned as heroes.
After 1918, American capitalism and American virtues were no longer adver-
sarial as the United States was represented at the Treaty of Versailles by
Bernard Baruch, Thomas Lamont, and Norman Davis, Morgan's partners. Wall
Street moved from the domestic to the global realm where America exerted its
new financial and political clout.

6.8 The New York Stock Exchange

If the Stock Exchange were abolished, great enterprises would soon be paralyzed. Without its medium it would be impossible to raise the capital for
conducting our great railroad and industrial corporations.

(Clews 1908)

Although the first American stock market was created in Philadelphia in 1790,
the New York Stock Exchange was officially founded in 1792, following over-
speculation in the bond market by an unscrupulous colleague of Alexander Hamilton, William Duer, causing a crash in stock and newly issued government bond
prices. A group of 24 merchant traders signed a document, named the Buttonwood Agreement, on May 17, 1792:

We the Subscribers, Brokers for the Purchase and Sale of Public Stock, do
hereby solemnly promise and pledge ourselves to each other that we will
not buy or sell from this day for any person whatsoever any kind of Public
Stock at a less rate than one quarter per cent Commission on the Specie
value and that we will give a preference to each other in our Negotiations.

(Museum of American Finance 2009b)

This private trading association became the New York Stock Exchange. During
the nineteenth century, in periods of speculative frenzy, other exchanges
opened:

Among them were the Open Board, the Mining Exchange, and the Gold Room. For a period during the Civil War, traders could trade at the Board during the day and then head over to Gallagher's' Evening Exchange on 23rd Street and get in on the action there.

(Akhtar 2008: 6)

The war of 1812 fueled speculation in war bonds, followed by excessive speculation and volatility that culminated in the panic of 1819. On March 8, 1817, coinciding with the completion of the Erie Canal, the New York Stock and Exchange Board was founded, with a constitution, officers and rules of business, essentially basically following the model of the Dutch and English East India trading companies. In 1825, the exchange traded about 100 stocks and was still a "semi rusticated 'financial district', not far from open fields and masticating cows" near the Battery (Fraser 2005: 35). By the mid-1830s, the start of the international railroad boom, and the construction of canals increased the number of shares traded a day to 600. Totally unregulated markets in currencies, stocks, and commodities gave rise to counterfeiting, speculative fraud, and confidence games in fictitious land and stock investments. By 1830, the exchange listed nine companies, including two banks, a canal company, four insurance firms, a coal, and a gaslight company. Renamed the New York Stock Exchange in 1863, it built a headquarters at Broad Street, until 1900, when the majestic Greek revival building opened at 100 Wall Street.

During the railroad boom after the Civil War, speculators entered the market, bringing in untested tactics such as short selling, which contributed to greater volatility. Daniel Drew and Cornelius Vanderbilt were accused of creating bear markets, a term first used in Chicago in 1884. By 1886, daily trading broke the one million shares a day barrier, and "the universe of individual investors nearly doubled between 1900 and 1910, growing from 4.4 million to 7.4 million" (Fraser 2005: 172).

In May 1896, the market information sheet published by Edward Jones, a broker, and Charles Henry Dow, a financial journalist became the *Dow-Jones Newsletter*, with information on 12 major stocks. Financial journalism was booming at the time, from stock tip sheets, and counterfeit warning sheets, to respectable newspapers carrying financial information. The original Dow 12 reflected America as a commodity (sugar, cattle, cotton, rubber, and leather) and gas and oil power house. Financial institutions, despite their prominence, were not listed in the original Dow. Of the 12 stocks, only General Electric, created by Thomas Edison, remains. The other 11 stocks were American Cotton Oil; American Sugar Company; American Tobacco Company; Chicago Gas Company; Distilling and Cattle Feeding Company; Laclede Gas Light Company; National Lead Company; North American Company; Tennessee Coal, Iron and Railroad Company; US Leather Company; and United States Rubber Company. By 1916, the index rose to 20 stocks, reaching the Dow 30 in 1928. GM (1925), Exxon (formerly Standard Oil) (1928), Proctor and Gamble (1932), DuPont (1935), and United Technologies (1939) are the only companies in place since before World War II. These stocks reflected the shift toward pharmaceutical and diversified industrial sectors as in 1999 Microsoft, Intel, SBC Communications, and Home Depot replacing Chevron, Goodyear, Union Carbide, and Sears, reflected the new communication technologies. AIG (which was dropped following its November 2008 bailout) joined the Dow in 2003 with Pfizer and Verizon. A comparative study of the Dow-Jones Index and major European Stock Exchanges blue chip stocks reveal a striking degree of fluidity, change, and integration of new industries and sectors in the Dow compared with an equally striking degree of continuity despite certain brand and name changes through mergers and consolidation across European financial, industrial, and corporate sectors.

The New York Stock Exchange shut down only twice in its entire history. The first time was July 30, 1914, following the Austro-Hungarian and German declaration of war against Serbia, Russia, and France. On July 31, 1914, the London Stock Exchange, fearing a panic, decided not to open, causing the NYSE directors, anticipating a contagious drop in prices, to remain closed until December 12, 1914. The second time was the destruction of the World Trade Center and the devastation of the adjoining Wall Street area, on September 11, 2001. Reopening less than a week later, on Monday, September 17, 2001, in extremely difficult and hazardous conditions, the Dow lost nearly 1,300 points that week, but quickly rebounded and closed above the 10,000 mark at the end of December 2001.

The largest one-day percentage gain prior to 2008 occurred on March 15, 1933, following the Roosevelt's inauguration and his first fireside chat on the bank rescue plan March 12, 1933. The market had the largest one day percentage drop on October 19, 1987 – Black Monday – when it fell 22 percent. The Dow reached 3,000 in 1989, and 5,000 in November 1995. On March 29, 1999 the average closed above 10,000 and on May 3, 1999 it passed 11,000, in the huge dotcom boom and bubble, reaching 11,700 in January 2000, achieving a 499 point jump in March 16, 2000. Again on January 9, 2006 it broke 11,000 – despite signs of hyper volatility. February 27, 2007 the market lost 415 points, caused by a global selloff after a mini-crash in Chinese stocks, but by April 2007 the Dow topped 13,000. On October 9, 2007 the record was reached at over 14,000. On July 8, 2008, gas prices soared to US$140 per barrel, and US$4 a gallon, and the bear market began with unheard of volatility, starting with the 500 point drop on September 15, on the news of Lehman Brothers' failure. On November 20, the market hit a six-year low of 7,500, and again rebounded to finish the year in the vicinity of 8,500. By the end of 2008, for the first time since 1931, the NYSE lost 34 percent of value.

The NYSE, modeled on London, which opened its opulent exchange in 1801, and its new ultra modern building in 2004, became in turn the model for the Tokyo Stock Exchange in 1878, Hong Kong in 1914, Nairobi in 1954, Kuwait in 1963, Tehran in 1967, and Sao Paulo in 1986. Despite vast differences in political, gender, and social norms, the physical layout, mechanisms and methodology of trading, reconciling, and back office are strikingly compatible with any New York or Chicago trading floor.

6.9 Debtor to creditor nation: new banker to the world

The American Revolution initiated the shift of European currencies toward the new continent. Before 1776, England kept a strict control over the colonies' economy in order to eliminate trade competition and maintain dependence on British loans. However, after the Revolution, there began a shift of currencies toward the United States, with Holland as the largest subscriber to overseas loans. Throughout the eighteenth century, Amsterdam was inundated by German sovereigns, French gold louis, and British silver after 1776. The Dutch invested in English funds and state loans, and in American shares. Braudel quoted the papers of Louis Greffulhe, head of a "counting house" and broker in 1778 in Amsterdam:

> "Your former clerk Bringley," wrote Greffulhe to A. Gaillard in Paris, "is up to his ass in Americans." As for himself, Greffulhe, who had a finger in every promising pie, went in for speculation on the Stock Exchange in a big way, on commission. He acted for himself and for others, for Rodolphe Emmanuel Haller ... for Jean-Henri Gaillard, the Perregaux, the ubiquitous Panchauds, bankers in Paris and Geneva, for Alexandre Pictet, Philibert Cramer, Turrettini – all names written in gold in the ledgers of Protestant banking. The game was difficult and risky, with very large sums of money at stake. But in the end, if Greffulhe played it with such aplomb it was because he was staking other people's money. If they lost, it annoyed him, but it was no tragedy.
>
> (Braudel 1982)

The American Congress of 1778 established a continental currency (paper money) and began issuing short-term treasury obligations. Currency legislation of July 3, 1789 defined the dollar's par value against British Sterling, £1 = US$4.44. The ratio remained steady from 1792 to 1830, encouraging active export of American dollars through London. The French consul to New York described a very modern economic community in 1810: "New York can be described as a permanent fair in which two-thirds of the population is always being replaced, where huge business deals are being made, almost always with fictitious capital and where luxury has reached alarming heights" (Braudel 1982).

An influx of Dutch and French money helped finance the railroads. However the widespread financial crisis of 1856–1857 on Wall Street and on the Paris Exchange, frightened many Europeans, who divested themselves of American securities and curtailed the flow of capital to the United States. In 1865, despite this active market in foreign exchange and close connections between banking houses in London, Boston and New York, including the Kidder Peabody Barings partnership, "Most Americans knew little and cared less about what was happening in European counties" (Myers 1970: 206). Domestic concerns, geographic distance and basic distrust of foreigners lent to this perception. In 1867, the United States sent representatives to the Latin Monetary Union conference in

Paris, in order to have a voice in global currency issues. The Latin Monetary Union, led by France to rival the hegemony of the pound, pegged most continental currencies to the franc and set the parity at 5 francs = 2 US half dollars or US$1. Foreign exchange operations opened in 1873 at First National Bank of Chicago, in Bank of New York in 1893, and National City Bank in New York in 1897. National City Bank, which represented the interests of Rockefeller and Standard Oil (two Rockefellers married daughters of Stillman, president of National City) was the first major bank to establish branches abroad. By 1905, National City directors were on the boards of railroads, insurance, Western Telegraph, and utility companies, which all favored foreign investment. Yet, outside of New York and San Francisco, American banking remained parochial and wary of foreign commitments.

An American Bankers Association conference, in October 1901, emphasized the need to combat "American banking provincialism," hoping to persuade Washington that "authorizing the establishment of international banks with headquarters to be in New York" would facilitate international trade and benefit the US economy (*New York Times*, October 17, 1901). Mira Wilkins, author of *History of Foreign Investment in the United States* (1989), pointed out how throughout the nineteenth century, state restrictions required foreign banks to go through London for transactions denominated in foreign currency, and for commercial transactions with European counterparts. These limitations created opportunities for Barclays and Barings, which had partnerships with banks like Morgan, Kidder Peabody, but made it costly and impractical for French banks such as Crédit Lyonnais, to maintain an office in New York in the 1880s. By 1904, there were suggestions by American bankers to set up a Russo-Chinese bank for Far Eastern commerce, and in 1910, to create a Russo-American bank to facilitate investment in the Russian fleet. Only once the dollar became convertible currency, under Teddy Roosevelt in 1905, did America begin to flex its competitive muscle in global markets dominated by the French and British banks. By 1912, New York was a major banking center and San Francisco had offices of 15 foreign banks, centered on trade with China. The Hong Kong Shanghai Bank (HSBC), which had opened a branch in California in 1865, had branches in Chicago and New York by 1880.

In the late 1890s, retail banks opened in emigrant communities to service urban ethnic communities and businesses. Bank of America began as Bank of Italy, founded in 1904 by an Italian immigrant in San Francisco to cater to the Italian small businesses community. Historian Rebecca Kobrin, in her 2007 study "The Almighty Dollar: East European Jews, Money and Speculation in Gilded Age America," explores how, in New York, poor Eastern European Jews settled on the Lower East Side, having no contact with the established German Jewish banking elite, founded their own bank, Jarmulovsky Bank, to deposit savings to send back home. The outbreak of World War I in August 1914, provoked a run on the bank, but when the depositors learned that the bank had lost most of its assets through real estate speculation by the owner's son, they marched on City Hall, causing riots. New York Jews "disbursed over one hundred million dollars they raised over the course of the inter war period to reconstruct life in Eastern Europe" (Kobrin 2007).

By 1919, "the country shifted from its former net debtor position and became a net creditor to the world" (Myers 1970: 270). Foreign holdings of American securities declined from 5.4 billion in 1914 to 1.6 billion in 1919. "When their securities had been liquidated, the Allies had to borrow and by the end of 1920, Great Britain owed the United States 4.2 billion dollars, France owed 3 billion and Italy 1.6 billion" (Myers 1970: 270).

Within a decade the Allied powers who had won the war, dismally lost the peace. Europe, in economic and geographic disarray, faced with the rise of the Marxist state in Russia, could no longer claim global financial hegemony. World War I gave the United States a new role as international arms, steel, and capital supplier as Wall Street financed the war with foreign loans and war bonds under the guidance of Bernard Baruch and President Woodrow Wilson. In reality, the United States was not prepared to become guarantor of the financial health of a disrupted world. It had the capital, but did not have the institutions, the regulations, or the political interest in place. The Edge Act of 1919 allowed corporations to carry on commercial banking activities abroad and issue foreign securities. As American banks opened foreign branches, during and after the war Americans jumped into foreign securities indiscriminately. There was massive traffic of buying and selling Latin American securities. Between 1914 and 1916, American banks opened branches in Buenos Aires, Rio de Janeiro, Santiago, and Havana. National City opened an office in Petrograd (formerly St Petersburg) in 1916, forced to close in 1917. On December 14, 1917, all banking assets were appropriated by the state and the bank, in a first case of sovereign risk, lost nearly US$26 million.

In 1927, National City Bank had branches across China in Canton, Hankow, Harbin, Hong Kong, Peking, and Shanghai, with the largest amount of loans, assets, overdrafts in Shanghai to the amount of US$8.7 million. In 1929 the bank opened an opulent office at 60, Champs Elysees in Paris. Between 1920 and 1929, "the total of American foreign investment, direct and portfolio, increased from US$7 to 17 billion" (Myers 1970: 96). As Americans invested abroad between the wars in the geopolitical chaos of new countries, borders and laws, transactions went unregulated, and fraudulent or shady schemes abounded, as depicted in Christine Stead's *House of All Nations* (1966 [1938]). By 1930, "European firms and governments were far and away the largest borrowers underwritten by National City" (Miler 1993). In 1933 National City Bank had a presence in 20 countries with 76 branches (*Annual Reports of the Comptroller of the Currency* 1927–1929).

The dollar and sterling became rival currencies until 1939, despite the devaluation of sterling once Britain went off the Gold Standard in 1931. Following the Bretton Woods Agreement of July 1944, America set the rules and the dollar set the standard for the global economy until 1971:

> These rules were quite strict, and enforced by a new world economic policeman, the International Monetary Fund. Countries had to declare a "par

value" – an exchange rate – of their currency in terms of the American dollar and/or gold and change it only after consultation with the IMF.

(Deane and Pringle 1995: 77)

Creating a system of fixed exchange rates, America dictated monetary policy and controlled the international money markets, helping to accelerate the recovery of Europe and Asia. The dollar was based on gold, but in reality the American dollar replaced the Gold Standard after World War II. However, by the 1960s, recovery across Europe and especially in Germany was progressing far faster than anticipated, and the Deutschmark was chaffing against the rigidity of American rules, soon to be followed by the recently realigned French franc under De Gaulle (1958).

Although America went through periods of inflation, political and monetary instability in the 1960s and 1970s, the prestige and mythology of the US dollar remained intact (see Chapter 5).

6.10　J.P. Morgan: America's banker

That only Midas and Morgan and Maecenas knew.

(Fitzgerald 1925: 4)

J.P. Morgan (1837–1913), combined in one individual the prestige of the Barings and Rothschild families, the power and influence of the Bank of England, and the myth of the omnipotent banker. Unlike self-made men, Pierpont Morgan inherited wealth and the calling of banking: "The banker's calling is hereditary. The credit of the bank descends from father to son; this inherited wealth brings inherited refinement" (Bagehot quoted by Chernow in *House of Morgan* 1990: 163). The elder Morgan started a firm in Boston with George Peabody, an American merchant banker in London. Pierpont, educated in England and Germany, came to Wall Street in 1857 and opened J.P. Morgan and Company in 1861. Cautious, yet willing to invest in new scientific and industrial ventures in the late 1870s, he funded Thomas Edison and Andrew Carnegie. Morgan, not personally affected by the Crash of 1873, orchestrated a compromise between the battling railway interests, establishing himself in the public and press as the mediator in financial rescues. By the 1880s, Morgan already stood for stability, power as well as philanthropy, and mentor of the arts. In 1893, in order to calm the markets during the bimetallism currency crisis, President Cleveland called on Morgan to rescue Treasury's gold supply by setting up a special bond issuance, guaranteed by Morgan. Taking on the mantle of central banker, Morgan was seen as savior of the Gold Standard, revered on Wall Street, in Washington and Europe, but the American populist movement saw him as arch villain:

Ruthless predator robbing American farmers and workers to line his own pockets.... Morgan spent most of the decade reorganizing bankrupt railroad and industrial companies. When the government all but ran out of gold in

1895, he raised sixty-five million dollars and made sure it stayed in the Treasury's coffers.

(Strouse 1998: 66)

Upton Sinclair's novel, *The Money Changers* (1908), "portrayed a Morgan like figure orchestrating the financial crisis to devastate ordinary people for his own gain" (Strouse 1998: 66). Morgan capped his career and his legend in the crisis of 1907, where he singlehandedly orchestrated the large scale bailout of Wall Street brokerage and commercial banks.

Without interstate or federal regulation, banks functioned haphazardly across the country using New York as clearing house. New York's big banks, although solvent, were heavily invested in the Stock Exchange and did not have sufficient liquidity to meet sudden large redemptions. Trust companies, which functioned as combination commercial deposit and investment banks, were the most vulnerable. Failed commodity ventures in October 1907, caused a run at Knickerbocker Trust, which could not meet its obligations, with US$60 million on deposit, but only US$10 million in cash. Morgan returned to New York and began the fabled marathon session in the Morgan library in his mansion on Park Avenue, bringing together the heads of all major New York banks, First National and National City (the Rockefeller Bank, associated with Standard Oil which in 1955 would merge into Citibank), Bankers Trust, and Morgan's partner, George Perkins. The purpose was to arrange a loan to Knickerbocker in order to quell the panic and stop capital flight of gold out of New York, staunching a potential crisis in London and Paris. Awash in rumors, the press created a new panic by announcing the failure of other trust companies, requiring Morgan to reconvene Henry Clay Frick, E.H. Harriman, and John D. Rockefeller to lend US$25 million to the Exchange. Panic spread across the country in the next week as banks increased withdrawals from New York. By the end of October, New York City was so short of funds it could not meet its payroll. Morgan set up a system issuing bonds, which the banks in the syndicate would turn over to the Clearing House, which in turn would pay for them by issuing certificates credited to the city's account at First National and National City banks, keeping the banks afloat until Treasury stepped in and issued bonds and certificates to back the notes. Again confidence was restored, but on November 1, 1907, Moore and Schley, a large brokerage house, heavily overleveraged, owed millions of dollars to New York banks. The firm had put up as collateral, shares from Tennessee Coal, Iron and Railroad Company in Alabama, an enterprise with less than sterling credentials. Once the market weakened, the shares lost value, inciting fear of another major default. Again Morgan had to intervene, organize a consortium and bailout. On Monday, November 4, the panic died, and the market soared.

As America did not have a central bank, the image of the omnipotent banker solidified the reputation and prestige of bankers, but caused concern in Washington that they could wield power to control, manipulate and function as an entity equal to the government. In the congressional hearings under Taft in 1913, questioned by Samuel Untermeyer about the role of money and monopoly of money,

Morgan feigned naïvety as to his power. When asked if owning all the banks in New York would not guarantee him control over credit, he replied:

> "No, sir, Not at all"
> Untermeyer was mystified, "Is not the credit based upon the money?"
> "No sir."
> "...What then was credit based on?" Untermeyer asked.
> "The first thing is character," Morgan replied,
> "Before money or property?"
> "Before money or property or anything else. Money can not buy it"
>
> (Brands 2006: 195)

Morgan died in 1913, leaving an estate of US\$68 million, a very modest sum by the standard of the robber baron era. Andrew Carnegie was reputed to have said, "and to think he was not a rich man." His death marked the end of an era and the start of the regulation and codification of American finance in the establishment of the Federal Reserve and the income tax system.

J.P. Morgan and Company became the first bank since the Depression to win the authority to sell and trade corporate stocks. "The Federal Reserve's approval on Thursday was the largest breach in the Glass-Steagall Act of 1933, which divorced commercial from investment banking" (Hansell 2000).

Ironically in the first salvo of the 2008 financial debacle, history did repeat itself when the investment bank Bear Stearns failed and the Secretary of the Treasury, Henry Paulson, and the Federal Reserve Chairman, Ben Bernanke, called upon the new incarnation of J.P. Morgan in the person of the J.P. Morgan Chase Chief Executive Officer, Jaime Dimon, to intervene and stabilize the markets.

6.11 Wall Street to Main Street and back again

> But what strikes the most in the United States is not the extraordinary size of a few large industrial enterprises, but the multitude of small enterprises [mais ce qui me frappe le plus aux Etats Unis, ce n'est pas la grandeur extraordinaire de quelques enterprises industrielles, c'est la multitude des petites enterprises].
>
> (Tocqueville 1981: 197)

What impressed Tocqueville in 1835 is still relevant in 2009 America, where small businesses, defined as a payroll with 500 persons or less, create 75 percent of all jobs. Wall Street generates optimism, fear, pride, and projects American power, but in American collective culture, Main Street conveys security, confidence, and a return to virtues and values. The debate on American values, small town versus urban centers, the working man and small business owner versus the financiers and industrialists, recurs in every presidential campaign and deteriorates into the worst clichés from "bailing out the fat cats of Wall Street" versus "Joe the Plumber," the everyman. Whereas in France, the merchant sought to be ennobled and the worker to overthrow the exploitation of the bosses, and in England the merchant sought to become a gentlemen farmer, and the worker a respected small business owner, in America it was not a question of changing the system, even in the worst of times, but rather to demand that their voices be heard in Washington and Wall Street, that the "average Joe" be treated with equal respect and allowed to pursue his or her own version of the so called American dream. In the 2008 crisis, the issue resurfaced in the debate between extending massive injections of capital and bailout money to the banks (majority of the US$700 billion TARP money) versus the initial decision to force the automobile sector into bankruptcy. Under pressure and media coverage that bankruptcy would cause nearly two million workers to lose their jobs, pensions and benefits, the decision, in December 2008, to extend a US$14 billion bridge loan to the "Big Three" automobile companies was a compromise toward restoring faith in the government's equal treatment of Wall Street finance and Detroit industry, bankers and blue-collar workers. The rhetorical and philosophical appeal of the Obama candidacy in 2008, was the belief that, because of the historic opportunity to elect the first African-American president, representative of the most disenfranchised of all minorities, all social classes and ethnic groups would benefit. Elected in the worst economic crisis in decades, the assumption was that he alone could resolve the mortgage crisis, emblematic of Main Street, and rescue the failing banks, emblematic of Wall Street. Political allegiances have shifted along demographic and regional lines since the 1990s, as large banks and corporations tend to split their political donations and voters have chosen their representatives based more on specific issues than part affiliation. Unlike Europe, whose leaders still retain the invisible mantle of the monarchy, America requires its presidents to be "the guy you want to have a beer with," common man, and world leader.

Since Andrew Jackson, bringing the values and comportment of the frontier states to the White House, the Washington–Wall Street–American rural and industrial heartland relationship has been fraught with tension and ambivalence. The sudden losses in the market in 1873, caught the country by surprise, as thousands of small businesses, farms factories, mining concerns, and textile mills, directly or indirectly linked to the vast railroad and manufacturing industries, affected by the international drop in prices and demand, failed or had to lay off workers. Hundreds of thousands were unemployed, unprotected, and made homeless or destitute, setting off riots from 1873 to 1877 in major cities, including New York's Upper East Side. Gold and Wall Street became the culprit and the scapegoat.

By the 1880s, the interests of the West, farming states, and small towns differed widely from the interests of the East Coast and New York. The urban poor, small farmers and ranchers, railroad workers, miners, small businessmen, and labor, which increased industrial and agricultural production enriching Wall Street, began to express their sense of disenfranchisement. After 1886 and the Haymarket riots, cartoons in *Harpers Weekly*, *Puck*, and Thomas Nast's depictions of corrupt financiers and politicians influenced ambivalent feelings for Wall Street, and amused tolerance turned to outrage. The populist movement of the 1890s leading to the riots of 1897, combined the rhetoric of religious fervor against greed and speculation, espousing sound Protestant values ingrained in Victorian England with a strong American message of hard work and frontier virtues.

Although rich East Coast owners often guaranteed employment and provided better living and working conditions than independents, the perception of Wall Street monopolies against the interests of the common man, dominated popular culture and sentiment. Conflicts between Western miners with labor union support and Eastern owners culminating in strikes and horrific repression at the Rockefeller-owned coal mines in Ludlow, Colorado, in 1914, came to symbolize the bitter antagonism between the people and the plutocrats.

6.12 "Follow the Yellow Brick Road"

Sinclair Lewis' sardonic take on Flaubert's small town boring shopkeepers and bitter housewives, presented the ordinariness and pettiness of the American affluent middle class. *Main Street* (1920) and *Babbitt* (1922) transformed the mythology of the American capitalist hero into the lives of a partner in a modestly successful real estate firm and the wife of a small town doctor.

> This is America – a town of a few thousand, in a region of wheat and corn and dairies and little groves. (Gopher Prairie, Minnesota). Main Street is the climax of civilization ... What Ole Jensen the grocer says to Ezra Stowbody the banker is the new law for London, Prague, and the unprofitable isles of the sea; whatever Ezra does not know and sanction, that thing is heresy, worthless for knowing and wicked to consider.
>
> (Lewis 1920: foreword)

Underneath the gentle sarcasm, Sinclair Lewis created an American Madame Bovary in Carol Kennicott, romantic wife of small town doctor in 1920s Minnesota. But where Emma Bovary, emotionally and financially bankrupt, has no other recourse than suicide, leaving behind an impoverished husband and a child who ends up in a work house, Carol Kennicott, despite her attempts at romance, adventure and disdain for small town mores and platitudes, keeps her good sense, propriety, and thriftiness, and returns home to hearth, family and solid middle class values.

Nineteenth- and early twentieth-century American literature divided along lines of tolerance and exoneration of wealth in James, Wharton, and Dreiser, versus contempt and condemnation in Melville, Norris, Dos Passos, and Jack London. Mark Twain, ever pragmatic and cynical, combined bemusement with satire. Three works of popular literature, Frank Baum's fantasy series, *The Wizard of Oz* (1900), Frank Norris' moral tragedy *The Pit* (1903), and George McCutcheon's humoristic tale *Brewster's Millions* (1903), reflected the impact of these monetary and political battles on the American cultural land-scape. Frank Baum and the illustrator W.W. Denslow had been involved in populist movements in the 1890s, and although Baum supported McKinley and sound money, as best for small businessmen, and may have based the Wizard on his own dubious business ventures, readers and critics through the 1930s attributed political allegory to the work. Images of the Wizard, Lion, Tin Man, and Yellow Brick Road had appeared in cartoons during the tumultuous years of the bimetallism crisis and the election of 1896. Dorothy was seen as the archetypal naïve young American, Tin Man as the industrial worker, Scarecrow as the farmer exploited in the price wars, Lion as William Jennings Bryant, and the Wicked Witch as McKinley, with the Yellow Brick Road as the Gold Standard. The movie, *The Wizard of Oz* (1939), at the end of the Depression, symbolized the virtues of the America heartland. In Kansas, Dorothy's aunt and uncle, hardworking struggling farmers, are threat-ened with dispossession of their land by the rich hoarders, in the figure of the evil spinster Miss Gulch, who morphs into the Wicked Witch of the West. Dorothy, portrayed by Judy Garland, is the epitome of good, solid American virtues, unfazed by the outside world. Along with the Tin Man looking for a heart, the Scarecrow, a brain and the Lion, courage, Dorothy vanquishes the Witch and the forces of evil, including a field of opium poppies (nefarious foreign trade entering American markets), unmasks the falsehoods of the Wizard, and can achieve her only wish, to return home to Kansas. Whether allegory of populist monetary theory, post Depression populist empowerment, or American heartland values, the work continues to be aired on television during the holidays every year, maintaining its emotional resonance after six decades.

George Barr McCutcheon's comedic *Brewster's Millions* (1903), had huge appeal and garnered even greater success as a play in 1906 (inspiring seven cinema versions since 1914). A charming young man, Monty Brewster, inherits from his grandfather US$1 million, but within a few days another mysterious rich relative has apparently died and bequeathed him US$7 million from gold mines and ranches in Montana, under condition that on his twenty-sixth birth-day, "Montgomery Brewster was to have no other worldly possession than the clothes which covered him" (McCutcheon 1903: 29). He was to prove that "he was capable of managing his affairs shrewdly and wisely – that he possessed the ability to add to his fortune through his own enterprise" (McCutcheon 1903: 31). The problem is that he has to dispose of US$1 million in one year. He begins by lavishly spending, he "leased one of the most expensive apartments to be found in New York City. The rental was $23 thousand" (McCutcheon 1903: 49), giving lavish dinners, and investing in what seem like losing stocks on Wall Street. But the more he tries to lose by selling stocks, the more he arouses the interest of the market, and his stock picks become winners, thereby increasing rather than decreasing in value. He becomes "the Napoleon of Finance" (McCutcheon 1903: 89). But then "one of the banks in which his money was deposited failed and his balance of over 100,000 was wiped out" (McCutcheon 1903: 115). There is a financial panic with "short wild runs on the banks" (McCutcheon 1903: 114). Only by removing his money and placing it all in the larger, failing "Bank of Manhattan Island," where his presumed fiancée's father is the banker, does he restore confidence in the system by making the bank solvent again. In this take on the Morgan model, he also saves the fortune of Mrs. Grey and her daughter Peggy. Finally realizing that only by going abroad and being willingly swindled by unscrupulous Europeans will he be able to spend all his money, the story plays into the popular stereotypes of naïve Americans duped by impoverished and dishonest foreigners. Peggy, as others unaware of the conditions of these wills, still loves him and is willing to marry him even penniless. All ends well as the executor of his uncle's will returns, gives him the US$7 million and invites him out to Butte where "we have real skyscrapers and they are not built of brick. They are two or three miles high and they have gold in 'em" (McCutcheon 1903: 324).

In each subsequent movie version, the amount of the bequeath goes up as a sign of the times. In 1985, the updated movie version, with African American comedian Richard Pryor, makes Monty an aging baseball pitcher who inherits US$300 million on condition that he spends US$30 million in 30 days. The attempts include a failed political campaign, other prototypical New York adventures, and again with an honest young woman's help, the hero retains the fortune.

Part of the "muckraking" newspaper and literary criticism of the excesses of speculation and the temptations of "easy money," Frank Norris in 1903 published *The Pit, A Story of Chicago*, a scathing attack on the dangers of the Chicago commodities markets, where the very buildings, like Zola's Exchange in *L'Argent*, become mythological beasts, "the pile of the Board of Trade Building, black, monolithic, crouching on its foundation like a monstrous sphinx with blind eyes, silent, grave" (Norris 1928: 37). Chicago, "the Great Grey City," is the site of animalistic urges and battles, where the hero Curtis Jadwin, already wealthy – "He was very rich but a bachelor (about 35 or 40) and had made his money in Chicago real estate," decides to become a grain broker. Initially trading in commodities seemed safe, with commission trading uninfluenced by fluctuations in the market, but he soon falls prey to the dangers of speculation in the Pit: "a dozen bourses of continental Europe … a dozen old World banks firm as the established hills, trembled and vibrated" (Norris 1928: 37). Although knowing that wheat speculation is actually futures selling and buying, Jadwin is lured into buying a seat on the Board of Trade. Once a speculator, totally caught in the obsession, when the market crashes, his firm is suspended, he loses everything and is disgraced. The woman he loves and nearly loses, Laura, stays by him as they decide to leave Chicago bankrupt, ready to start anew.

6.13 Bimetallism and the roots of populism

Since Alexander Hamilton's decision to allow minting of both gold and silver coins, bimetallism provoked constant battles between gold and silver interest groups. Establishing the Bank of New York in 1784, "one of Hamilton's motivations in backing the bank was to introduce order into the manic universe of American currency" (Chernow 2004: 201). Passage of the Sherman Silver Act of 1890, after the Silver Convention of 1889, represented the growing power of mining interests in the West with four new states admitted to Union in 1890. The strong silver lobby in Congress, from Iowa, Nevada, and Colorado, pushed increased purchases of silver, but the 1893 Wall Street crash, gold hoarding in New York banks, and rising unemployment forced the repeal of the Sherman Act in 1893. The animosity between North and South in the 1850s now was transferred to East West polarization over monetary policy and currency wars, leading to a severe recession between 1893 and 1897, with withdrawals from US securities, drop in railroad shares, fueled by rumors of machinations on Wall Street and Washington against Western mining, farming and ranching interests.

Until 1890, America pursued the Gold Standard, redeeming greenbacks in gold, but under this policy the economy remained more vulnerable to currency fluctuations in Europe, instigating the depression of 1893. The depression had far greater political impact than the previous Crash of 1873, as over 100 small banks failed, putting at risk farmers and small town business owners. In this environment a young Chicago man, William Harvey, exploited the mood of the country in 1894 when, under the name of Coin, he established a "school of finance" in the Art Institute in Chicago. His premise was that gold was to blame for the weakness in the economy, extolling a return to silver and bimetallism. He declared that following the British Gold Standard, American monetary policy had lost its inability to have greater control over domestic wages, victimizing the American worker. He set up a new paradigm, pitting Wall Street's cosmopolitan interests against true American values incarnated in silver coinage. His book "Coin's Financial School" (1893), was a huge success, inciting heated debate and numerous books on bimetallism. The election of 1896 was framed by vehemence against President Cleveland's policies, with the support of J.P. Morgan and Wall Street bankers "gold lobby" provoking the Democrats to seek as candidate the most "radically anticapitalist of the credible contenders" (Brands 2006: 180), William Jennings Bryan, former Congressman from Nevada, who called for unlimited bimetallism and coinage of gold and silver at ratio of 16 to 1. A brilliant orator, Bryan's "Cross of Gold" speech at the presidential convention in Chicago in July 1896, electrified the audience, setting up the original principles which would define the two parties' approach to monetary policy: the people against big business. Bryan's oration against gold redefined the term businessman, in which the laborer, small merchant, and farmer:

"Is as much a business man as the man who goes upon the board of trade and bets upon the price of grain ... We come to speak of this broader class of business men." Ending in a thunderous denunciation of the gold standard only benefiting the wealthy: "You shall not press down upon the brow of labor this crown of thorns! You shall not crucify mankind upon a cross of gold."

(Brands 2006: 184)

In the *Age of Betrayal: The Triumph of Money in America, 1865–1900* (2007), Jack Beatty wrote that democracy, redeemed in the Civil War, was betrayed in the Gilded Age. By 1889, the unregulated monopolies in commodities, oil, copper, iron, steel in collusion with Washington (brutally caricatured in the "Senate of the Monopolists by the Monopolists" cartoon in *Puck*, Fraser 2005: 129), and the Chicago and New York coalition of exchanges and chambers of commerce, accepted or ignored horrific working conditions, huge increase in urban poverty, and disenfranchisement of the poor. Bryan's speech became part of American political folklore, but in reality the country wanted stability, order and sound business management more than populist rhetoric.

The Republicans, choosing as candidate a Midwestern Governor, William McKinley, easily won the election with the support of Northwest and Ohio Valley commercial, mining, and regional banking interests. McKinley's slogan, "Prosperity at home, prestige abroad, commerce, civilization," resounded across the country. His inauguration was celebrated with a ball of "criminal opulence" (Beatty 2007: 373) at the Waldorf attended by Vanderbilts, Morgans, Drexels, Cunard, Rockefeller, Belmont, Fisk, and Astors. In office he immediately passed the Gold Standard Act of 1900. But the triumph of the gold and trust lobby was short lived, as President William McKinley was assassinated on September 6, 1901 by a self-described anarchist of Polish origin, bringing to power Theodore Roosevelt, the perfect combination of Republican prestige, policy, and Democratic reforms. Justice Louis Brandeis, reverting to the French phrase "l'Argent des Autres" (see Chapter 4) in a pamphlet in 1914 entitled *"Other People's Money,"* established the distinction between finance capitalism and industrial capitalism, a dialectic which reverberated in the bailout of 2008, when the Federal Reserve had to justify why financial institutions were more deserving of a bailout than the automotive sector, heart of American industrial production since the 1920s:

> Other people's money was a damning apercu. It lent an air of illegitimacy to all the deliberations and weighty decisions taken by the distinguished directors and trustees of the country's most formidable financial institutions, but it also set up a difference between the investors and the directors. They were stakeholders – or sought to be – in a market economy that they claimed the "money trust" was ruining for everyone but itself.
>
> (Fraser 2005: 286)

6.14 Wall Street spends, Main Street saves

Philosophically the role of banks after the Great Depression was to guarantee the safety of deposits, the creation of the Federal Deposit Insurance Corporation (FDIC) was a fundamental covenant between the government and its citizens to secure their savings. The concept and rate of savings in various countries differs widely, with very low rates in the United States and very high interest rates in Italy, Germany, and Japan, and the highest rate of savings in China. Savings constitute an economic category, but are also an indicator of profound societal attitudes, reflective of fear and insecurity within social groups. The rate of savings has dramatically decreased in the last 30 years in the United States and in the last 15 years across Europe. Despite rising consumer confidence index in European Union countries, Europeans overall continue to save far more than Americans.

The sudden loss of confidence in banks in 2008 provoked a new pro-savings movement seen in billboards, advertisements, media and press trying to encourage renewal in consumer spending and use of credit cards by encouraging sound spending habits and saving accounts. The message is now that the country needs to return to traditional values ensconced in savings in order to regain confidence to spend.

In 1900, America strongly advocated virtues of thrift, abstinence and perseverance. Jesse Stiller, historian of the OCC writes of an early film reel in 1914, made for the American Bankers Association, *The Reward of Thrift*, a morality play of the ant and grasshopper variety in which two construction workers, one "thrifty teetotaler" who after a work accident caused by his friend, "a hard drinking bachelor," is able to recover thanks to his savings. Filled with remorse, he renounces his bad habits and at the end of the reel "he is being escorted into a bank to open a new savings account" (Stiller 2008). This film shown in nearly 2,000 theaters was seen by 1.7 million people by mid-1915. A sequel, the five-reel *The Dollar and the Law* (1916), featured "ten attractive co-eds who set up a thrift club to help fund their tuition" (2008: 29).

The tradition of children saving a coin into a school account was turned into a large enterprise. The press, community organizations and clubs and even bankers such as A.P. Giannini, founder of Bank of America, had an agent traveling throughout California to work with teachers and administrators to encourage this savings movement. "To that end some banks set up Home Savings Departments, staffed by female employees" (2008: 30)" in the lobby of banks to encourage housewives to come in to open a savings account. By 1910, following the model in Europe, postal saving banks were set up and by 1914 nearly 400,000 Americans had opened postal accounts. The sixteenth Amendment instituting federal income tax in 1913 sought to encourage sound fiscal discipline on the basis that paying taxes would necessitate saving. In the Western states, strongly against the increased role of government in personal finances, a culture of saving and thriftiness demonstrated that upstanding citizens did not need that much regulation. After the crisis of 1907, banks wanted to encourage new accounts and expand their client base. Encouraging savings as a virtue became a patriotic duty during World War I, as the country needed more capital.

America in 1900 was a leader in industrial innovation, but above all it led in products and services which appealed to the middle class from electricity to vacuum cleaners, new pharmaceuticals to makeup, refrigerators to phonographs and cars. Many of these new industries of household goods and the burgeoning automobile industry worked on the installment plan and on loans for such purchases: "But bankers saw themselves as guardians of American values first, and so determined that the bar would be set high to help people differentiate between their needs and their desires" (Stiller 2008: 28). Americans were taught to save in order to spend, the perfect solution for expanding credit and insuring a flow of savings The working class was seen as uneducated and prone to lack of control: Workers in a mill town in Massachusetts were accused of poor sense of values, having even in the poorest homes "a player piano and a phonograph – the most expensive makes. Over their gingham gowns the housewives … wore fur coats the cost anywhere from 150 up" (Stiller 2008: 29).

Martin Mayer judged the demise of the Savings and Loans in the late 1980s, as a breakdown of confidence, "the saddest story in the long history of the relationship of American government and American banking is the collapse of the savings and loan industry in the 1980s and early 1990s" (Mayer 1997: 361). These institutions were basically community pools of money in which members bought negotiable shares, "not 'banks' which took deposits" (Mayer 1997: 363). Associated with the housing reforms of the early 1930s, part of the Federal Home Loan Bank system, and directly associated with mortgages and the housing market, they had nearly gone bankrupt many times. In the 1970s, these institutions were allowed to engage in market activity, to develop property, make commercial loans, buy junk bonds, and invest in non financial business. By relaxing regulatory standards and allowing Savings and Loans to dabble in other ventures, there was bound to be room for scams and misuse of funds.

The principle at stake was guarantee of deposits. The concept of deposit insurance dates back to 1829, in New York State, where protecting deposits meant protecting the hard working farmers, mechanics and laborers against insolvency due to bank failure. But the issue in 1987 was that in order to protect deposits, it was necessary to control the use of these deposits by the banks. Mayer quotes Milton Friedman and Anna Schwartz: "Federal insurance of bank deposits was the most important structural change in the banking system to result from the 1933 panic." The FDIC was the most important piece of legislature from the Roosevelt era as it was "the most conducive to monetary stability" (Mayer 1997: 387).

America has progressed, or regressed, from a savings to a spending society, from international and domestic creditor to debtor. Reversing the trend in the aftermath of the market and credit crisis of 2008 will be very difficult, as an entire generation has been encouraged, and in fact inculcated, by politicians, advertisers, media and newspapers to spend, shop, invest, and consume. Since 1990, there are few remaining Savings and Loans, savings accounts yield low dividends, the US tax structure encourages investment rather than savings. All the conditions put in place to protect the American public in the 1930s, immediately reinforced in the first few months of the 2008 crisis, including increasing bank deposits from $100,000 to $250,000, bankruptcy laws, and protection on mortgage foreclosures, are crucial bulwarks against further deterioration of the economy. These are essential steps, taken worldwide to avert the danger of a global recession, but they will also insure that, in all likelihood, there will not be a radical shift in American financial culture.

6.15 How do you regulate American finance?

> Experience over the past decade [1983–1993] is consistent with a long history of repeated banking difficulties that indicate supervision and regulation are not reliable techniques for sustaining the safety and soundness of banks.
>
> (Shull 1993: 13)

One of the most complex issues facing the Obama administration in the aftermath of the banking crisis of 2008 was the degree of government intervention, partial ownership, and control of the banking sector. Under the aegis of government aid, whether bailouts, capital injections, preferred shares or even majority shareholding, the various government agencies in charge of the banking sector have to recalibrate their role as shareholder, overseer, and policing agent. In January 2009, members of Congress tried to impose guidelines on chief executive officer salaries, an attempt to appease small town America's justified outrage at revelations of huge bonuses, extravagant expenditures, and average annual salaries of US$10 million. In a need to identify scapegoats, bankers are blamed for the economic crisis, but in reality Jimmy Cayne, Richard Fuld, Chuck Prince, and John Thain, as cavalier, arrogant, secretive, and oblivious to the perception of their dereliction of duty, functioned within an institutional, socio-cultural, and political environment which fostered these very traits. "The legislative response to the rash of financial failures since the mid-1980s has been consistent with the 'bad bankers' theory of banking system mal functioning. Congress' response to the crisis has increased the power and number of regulators" (Bernard Shull 1993: Introduction).

Immediately after the announcement of the rescue plan to recapitalize, stabilize and restructure the banks, in October 2008, Republican members of Congress accused the Treasury and Federal Reserve of "nationalizing" the banks. Whereas British partial nationalization, European Union guarantee of all liabilities, and in many cases re-nationalization was greeted with trepidation, but overall acceptance, the concept of the US government taking partial control of the financial system was judged as anathema to the core principles of American capitalism. Politicians, in the fall of 2008, threw out accusations of socialism and even communism, in an excess of rhetorical outrage at the level of the government's intervention.

The Federal Reserve has been praised for the rapidity and efficacy of its response to the crisis, in contrast to the disastrous policies executed in 1929, but beyond lender of last resort, the expanding role of the Federal Reserve as overseer and provider of endless bailout packages has generated heated political debate and concern. The American regulatory system, more layered and decentralized than in other large economies, was developed in stages during the Civil War, at the creation of the Federal Reserve, and following the Great Depression. The partitioning of responsibilities has been very effective in chartering and defining functions of financial institutions, but not in coordinating the supervisory role of the various bodies.

Since the creation of the first American banks, Bank of North America in Philadelphia in 1781, and Bank of New York, founded by Alexander Hamilton in 1784, the bank–government relationship was consistently uneasy until the mid-twentieth century. The initial division of powers in Washington favored government oversight of finances: September 2, 1789, the Treasury Department was established, providing for a comptroller, auditor, treasurer, and register, and the need to make reports to Congress. Hamilton, inspired by the Bank of England, advocated creating a bank to encourage merchants to deposit or invest money "in the stock of a bank" in 1790 (Chernow 2004: 345). He strongly believed that American merchants needed good credit rating, and wanted to assure that the federal government took responsibility for state notes and consolidating the national debt. As described in the Federalist Papers and in his report on public credit, Hamilton wrote that "the proper handling of government debt would permit America to borrow at affordable interest rates and would act as a tonic to the economy. Used as loan collateral, government bonds could function as money" (Chernow 2004: 297).

Hamilton also favored taxation and, in 1787, tried to create a cohesive tax structure. Named first secretary of the Treasury in 1790, Hamilton called for a central bank to bring order to currency, national debt, and monetary policy. On January 20, 1791 the 20-year charter of the Bank of the United States passed the Senate, and would be situated in Philadelphia. It "exerted the influence of its position as the depository for federal taxes and duties by refusing to accept the notes of state chartered banks that did not convert them to gold or silver on demand" (Shull 2005: 19). Unpopular from the start, pitting the Federalists, attuned to the needs of commerce and finance, against the Republicans, advocating the interests of the rural South and farmers, its charter was not renewed and the First Bank closed on March 3, 1811. The Second Bank of the United States, chartered in 1816 with 25 directors including Nicholas Biddle, who became president of the bank in 1823, was granted authority to make loans, accept deposits, and issue bank notes. Under his tutelage "The Bank's policy of restraining state bank note issues ... helped maintain convertibility, stabilized the value of the currency, and promoted economic stability and growth" (Shull 2005: 20). The relationship between the bank and the Federal government was cordial until the advent of 1828 when, as the country went through a period of instability, high inflation, a fall in land prices and hoarding, loss of confidence in the currency increased. Andrew Jackson, wary of the bank's authority over states, made it clear that in 1836 he would oppose renewing the charter. In 1842, Charles Dickens in *American Notes* described the bank as follows: "It was the Tomb of many fortunes, the Great Catacomb of investment, the memorable United States Bank." Whether an internal battle between Wall Street and Philadelphia, or as "Jacksonians implied, a contest between the humble agrarians and the moneyed aristocracy" (Myers 1970: 90) the United States rejected central banking for the next 75 years.

As the country grew and expanded between 1812 and 1850, there was a need for note issuing, deposit, commercial, and investment banks. Canal, road and rail projects from Chesapeake and Delaware Canal Company, chartered in 1799, to larger canal construction from the Great Lakes down the Atlantic seaboard, the Erie Canal in 1817, the Cumberland Road in 1818, and railroads from the 1840s, all required private and public joint financing. Barings, partnering with Morgan in New York and Peabody in Boston, was key in advising and securing loans guaranteed by the cities of Washington, Georgetown, Alexandria. Traders and merchants opened small investment firms like Astor and Sons, and Brown Brothers and Company, alongside brokers, and security dealers. New York became the undisputed financial center as notes, even from Boston, were often sent to New York institutions for redemption. As the Union expanded, state banks were chartered on the local level by state legislatures: the Bank of Indiana in 1834 and Bank of Missouri in 1837. But in some states "there was great fear and dislike of banks, especially after the unhappy experience of the late 1830s ... Texas in its constitution of 1845 prohibited banking altogether, Iowa and Arkansas followed suit in 1846" (Myers 1970: 124). Prior to the Civil War, banks proliferated with very little supervision and were allowed to print their own notes. In the West "wild cat" unregulated institutions, calling themselves banks were issuing nearly 7,000 different kind of notes, many totally worthless, with no way to prove if they were backed by gold or silver. By 1860, there were about 1,600 banks with capital of more than US$400 million and bank note circulation of more than US$200 million.

Lincoln, upon taking office, was facing a banking crisis, with increased loss of confidence in a totally unaccountable system. In 1863, during the Civil War, working with Treasury Secretary Chase, they established the Office of the Comptroller of the Currency under the auspices of the Treasury, which would serve as the sole chartering, supervisory, and monitoring bank regulator until 1913. A small agency, not part of the Cabinet (although the Comptroller is a presidential appointment requiring Senate confirmation), its function is to regulate, supervise, and charter all national banks and agencies of foreign banks and to guarantee "the safety and soundness of the national banking system" (*Annual Reports of the Office of the Comptroller of the Currency* 2007).

Hugh McCulloch, highly respected banker and President of the Bank of Indiana, was named the first Comptroller, setting a precedent for bankers or attorneys specializing in banking law in this position. From 1864, a state or federal charter would be required to open a bank, harmonizing state and federal standards for banks and other financial institutions.

Major investment houses and large New York banks, Morgan, Chase (the largest commercial bank in the country in 1877) and National City, were totally independent and accountable to none other than their closed, incestuous boards. After the crises of 1873 and 1893, American presidents had to plead with J.P. Morgan to take charge and rescue the economy. By 1907, it became clear that the lack of organization and regulation over New York banks had become untenable: "the New York banks were holding not only the reserves of the country's banks, but also large amounts of deposits of state banks and trust companies, many of which had quite inadequate reserves against their own customer's liabilities" (Myers 1970: 245). Trust companies were not under the jurisdiction of the Superintendent of Banks in New York, nor the Comptroller. As non members, but users of Clearing House facilities, they did not even have to provide reports until 1899. By 1912, the level of corruption and unregulated activity in stocks, bonds, and "interlocking directorates of railroads and financial institutions, misuse of funds by insurance companies, relation of bank and securities markets" (Myers 1970: 253) and industrial and railroad corporation finances was so great that the Arsene Pujo, Head of the House Committee on Banking and Currency, called for hearings led by Samuel Untermeyer, the Committee's legal counsel. Despite enormous publicity and pressure, witnesses were reluctant to testify against any of the lead banks. The power of these institutions was nearly impossible to regulate as their interests overlapped. In New York, First National Bank and National City Bank, and in Boston, Kidder Peabody and Lee Higginson were linked with Morgan, in Philadelphia, Drexel, and in Chicago the three largest banks were associated with Morgan. The country was under monopolistic control of the bank and the largest industrial trusts, which were also Dow-Jones Index stocks. US Steel, organized from 228 small companies in 1901, had assets of US$676 million, American Tobacco had monopoly over all tobacco products, International Harvester over all farm equipment, and GE over water power plants in 18 states.

Yet the great irony of American regulation is that it was "the very same bankers who most feared regulation who wrote the regulatory framework, whether to protect their interests or to exonerate themselves is a topic debated by economic historians ever since" (Shull 2005: 47). The Democratic Wilson administration wanted to establish a central bank within the Treasury with 25 branches. A consortium of bankers from Morgan, Paul Warburg (who had written a manuscript, revised in 1907, which appeared in the *New York Times* on January 6, 1907, entitled "Defects and Needs of Our Banking System"), Vanderlip, President of National City Bank, Benjamin Strong of Bankers Trust, and Nelson Aldrich convened at Morgan's private domain on Jekyll Island and formulated the Aldrich bill. Professor Seligman invited Warburg to present "A Plan for a Modified Central Bank" at Columbia University Academy of Political Science in 1907, where he had met Nelson Aldrich. The Federal Reserve Act of 1913 was a compromise between the Wilson administration and the Aldrich plan. Achieving compromise between Washington and state rights: "The Federal Reserve, then was a regionally diversified joint venture ... that affiliated the banking community with the federal government" (Shull 2005: 57) with one member elected from each district for its Reserve Board. It also set out a complex relationship with the Comptroller of the Currency, partitioning chartering and supervisory functions.

America now had a Central Bank with large independent executive level powers. In 1913, Federal Income tax was levied for the first time and "from a population of about 100 million, returns were filed by 368,000 individuals or families; only 44 of them reported incomes of more than 1 million dollars" (Myers 1970: 267). From here on the Federal Reserve Bank would be responsible for the country's monetary policy, bank supervision, and overall financial health as lender of last resort. It would be largely ignored for the next decade, blamed for having aggravated and mishandled the Crash of 1929, denigrated through the 1930s, returned to prestige and trust in the 1970s in aiding the economic recovery in the late 1970s and 1980s under Paul Volcker (now advisor to President Obama), exalted and revered for managing the Crash of 1987 and, for the next 20 years under Alan Greenspan, guiding the economy to unsurpassed prosperity through September 11, and the technology bubble of the late 1990s. In the crisis of 2008, the Federal Reserve under Bernard Bernanke has received high marks for restoring confidence, containing the crisis, and acting swiftly to lower interest rates. As Alan Greenspan admitted, the Bush administration and the Federal Reserve had seriously underestimated the depth and scope of the weakness in the housing market and the potential domino effect. Could they have reined in the market sufficiently without taking emergency steps of renationalizing the largest mortgage brokers, and requiring the banks to reveal the extent of their bad loans? Would the public and their congressional representatives have accepted that much government intervention in a non emergency environment?

For a country that so vehemently refused federal paternalism in the form of control or even oversight of its banking sector, that reluctantly and belatedly accepted a Central Bank, it is debatable to observe in the crisis of 2008 how much additional power has been allocated to the Federal Reserve. Is it being asked to not only set monetary policy, supervise and monitor, but to become lender, printer and bailout agent of last resort? Is it time to reorganize and streamline the entire regulatory agency system, granting these powers to the Federal Reserve?

6.16 The Crash of 1929 and the Great Depression

In 1925, in *The Great Gatsby*, America's first and foremost nihilist novel, Scott Fitzgerald captures in the narrator Nick Carraway, the virtues of the Middle West, in opposition to the corrupt materialism of the East Coast, embodied in Jay Gatsby: "My family have been prominent well to do people in this Middle Western city for three generations" (Fitzgerald 1925: 2). After the war, aware that finance rather than commerce is the wave of the future, he decides after Yale "to go East and learn the bond business. Everyone I knew was in the bond business, so I supposed it could support one more single man" (Fitzgerald 1925: 3). "[Every night] I took dinner usually at the Yale Club – for some reason it was the gloomiest event of my day – and then I went upstairs to the library and studied investments and securities for a conscientious hour" (Fitzgerald 1925: 57). Taking a job like all other ambitious, well bred, and well educated young men at "Probity Trust ... I bought a dozen volumes on banking and credit and investment securities, and they stood on my shelf in red and gold like new money from the mint, promising to unfold the shining secrets" (Fitzgerald 1925: 57).

Fitzgerald conveys a sense of nostalgia in these descriptions for the values of small town America and the sound principles of a well regarded financial career, hinting that, perhaps, had the narrator returned home all subsequent tragedies could have been avoided. Nick Carraway, once entering the magic realm of Gatsby bridges the gap from respectable, staid banking to shady, glamorous speculation. Gatsby, nee Jimmy Gatz of Chicago, self-made mythomane, who invents his identity, his family, his fortune, and in the end loses it all, is symptomatic of the flip side of the Roaring Twenties; the callousness, shadiness, and large fortunes at play on Long Island. Fitzgerald barely conceals his pernicious anti-Semitism in the persona of Meyer Wolfsheim, who started Gatsby in business, but exactly in what business the reader never learns, other than references to bootlegging, shady bets, and back door deals.

Colette in *Cheri* and *La Fin de Cheri*, Aldous Huxley in *Point Counterpoint*, and Fitzgerald understood that after the horror of World War I, the tormented "heroes" wanted an endless sybaritic existence of parties, liquor, and luxury. The raging bull market of the 1920s reflected America's new momentum worldwide. In 1922, there were 62 commercial banks dealing in investment banking, by 1929 there were 285, and,

> The annual total of new domestic industrial securities tripled from 1920 to 1929. "Financial department stores," integrated financial services enterprises pioneered by National City Company, (the brokerage/investment offshoot of National City Bank) opened up branches with securities subsidiaries all over the country to cater to the new retail investment market.
>
> (Fraser 2005: 385)

Nearly two million Americans were invested in the market, including a new breed of lady investors (55 percent of original investors in AT&T were women), and women brokers. A few intellectuals like H.L. Menken expressed some doubts, but overall academics, experts like Clarence Barron of *Barron's Financial Weekly* and Richard Whitney, head of the Stock Exchange, all persuaded the American public that the fundamentals were sound. As in 1986 and 2007, Wall Street was where the best and the brightest went to seek their living, "Back in the good old days in 1928, 17 percent of the graduates of Harvard Business School started careers on the Street; in 1941, only 1.3 per cent did" (Fraser 2005: 473).

> American bank failures between 1925 and 1933 were mainly "small independent banks ... Eighty percent of the failed banks had a capitalization of $25,000 or less; another 10 percent had capital of $25–50,000. Only 32 failed banks, less than one third of 1 percent had a capital of 1 million or more."
>
> (Myers 1970: 310)

Despite flaws in the analogy, the financial meltdown and global recession of 2008, requiring massive government bailouts and intervention, has entered the

American consciousness as a sequel of the Great Depression. As in 1929, the United States provoked the crisis, inciting and encouraging excessive speculation in dubious instruments, overheating in the property markets, and lack of legislative oversight. As in 1929, European countries and emerging markets readily gave in to temptation and have had to take radical measures to stabilize their economies. Unlike 1929, these governments and the body of central banks led by the Federal Reserve, the European Central Bank, and the Bank of England have at their disposal instruments, policies, and knowledge of lessons learned, which have allowed them to contain the crisis in deep recession rather than a full blown depression. Yet again, as under Roosevelt's guidance in the decade following the Crash of 1929, the United States, under the careful stewardship of the Obama administration, is leading the recovery.

The Great American Depression had different symptoms and very different political, economic and cultural repercussions than the depression which hit Europe in 1932. As Europe descended into the horrors of totalitarianism, America turned protectionist, reactionary and populist, but despite discrediting and rejecting financiers, bankers, Wall Street and any form of speculation associated with banking, fundamentally America did not lose faith in the potential of capitalism. Main Street would dictate the conditions of financial activity based on solid assets and cautious, long-term profits.

Published in 1954, John Kenneth Galbraith's *The Great Crash* remains one of the most lucid, entertaining and perceptive analysis of American culture before and during the Great Depression. America's new found wealth and prestige in the immediate aftermath of World War I was reinforced by the instability in Europe. Despite the reinstatement of the Gold Standard, the English economy did not recover. The fragile state of the Reichsmark and the devaluation crisis of the French franc in 1924–1926 encouraged gold transfers to the United States. Although European central bankers tried to work in unison and persuaded the Federal Reserve to ease monetary policy, there was a boom in stock speculation. Broker's loans, which were in the range of US$1 billion until 1926, reached over US$5 billion in the winter of 1928. As more people bought stocks, the banks increased lending and money kept on pouring into the United States in order to benefit from this wealth. In 1920, "American capitalism was undoubtedly in a lively phase" (Galbraith 1954: 9). But there was a get rich quick mindset, seen in the land boom schemes in Florida, based on future speculation where land was sold at increasingly high prices for smaller lots in more isolated areas. Charles Ponzi started a scheme on imaginary developments in 1925–1926, until two major hurricanes hit, and it became clear that the ability to actually develop and make good on these land deals was hugely reduced. Value dropped nearly 90 percent in three years as the bubble burst and the prices settled. "The Florida boom was the first indication of the mood of the twenties and the conviction that God intended the American middle class to be rich" (Galbraith 1954: 12). A.M. Sakolski wrote in 1932, *The Great American Land Bubble: The Amazing Story of Land Grabbing, Speculation and Booms from Colonial Days to the Present Time*, describing the frenzy and despair of speculative schemes, the last chapter

"Florida, the Latest Phase," deriding the ridiculous projects to built hotels and casinos in Coral Gables and Boca Raton in 1925–1926. Ridiculed at the time, land speculation in Florida would prove to have been the soundest of all investments.

As corporate earnings increased, stock prices steadily rose in 1924–1925, but by 1927 they often shot up on a daily basis. By the winter of 1928, stocks began to rise often 15–20 points in one day. The newspapers carried market news on the front pages, as the volume of shares traded in March 1928 rose from 3,875,000 to 4,790,000 and, by June, over five million shares changed hands. Sudden fluctuations were seen as dramatic, but each time the market rebounded and increased (Galbraith 1954: 17). In 1928, Hoover won by a landslide, causing the number of stocks traded to reach 6,503,000 on November 20, 1928. But the largest numbers of transaction were bought on margin:

> Margin trading must be defended not on the grounds that it efficiently and ingeniously assists the speculator, but that it encourages the extra trading which changes a thin and anemic market into a thick and healthy one.... Wall Street in these matters is like a lovely and accomplished woman who must wear black cotton stockings, heavy woolen underwear and parade her knowledge as a cook because unhappily her supreme accomplishment is as a harlot.
>
> (Galbraith 1954: 25)

Although Charles Mitchell had some reservations, as head of National City Bank and director of the New York Federal Reserve, he reassured the markets, taking a bullish stance. The market stabilized and the National City monthly letter declared:

> The National City Bank fully recognizes the dangers of overspeculation and endorses the desire of the Federal Reserve ... to restrain excessive credit expansion for this purpose. At the same time, the bank, business generally, and it may be assumed the Federal Reserve Banks ... wish to avoid a general collapse of the securities markets such as would have a disastrous effect on business.
>
> (Mitchell 1933: 42)

Galbraith stresses that Secretary of the Treasury Andrew Mellon "was a passionate advocate of inaction" (Galbraith 1954: 31) and "the Federal Reserve Board in those times was a body of startling incompetence" (Galbraith 1954: 32). "Had it been determined to do something, it could have for example have asked Congress for authority to halt trading on margin by granting the Board the power to set margin requirements" (Galbraith 1954: 36). An increase in margins from 40 to 50 percent to 75 percent could have stopped the boom and contained the markets. President Hoover, by late March 1929, was told that something should be done about speculation, but he assumed that the New York Governor,

Franklin D. Roosevelt, would be responsible for regulating the market. Everyone followed a laissez faire policy as manuals came out with schemes for beating the market.

The Dow 20 reflected the consolidation of major industrial sectors, dominated by US Steel, International Harvester, International Nickel, and American Tobacco. Montgomery Ward and Woolworth, which became retail chains, led a booming retail sector. Investment trusts originated in England and Scotland in the eighteenth century where it was understood that trusts guaranteed better information and long-term return for small and medium investors as well as large companies. United States Trusts held securities of typically 500 to 1,000 operating companies. Regarded with suspicion in New York, after 1907, and attacked in Roosevelt's anti-monopolist legislation, they were first listed in 1929 on the NYSE. Goldman, Sachs and Company, investment and brokerage partnership, entered the investment trust business in November 1928. Organized as the Goldman Sachs Trading Corporation, selling publicly 90 percent of its stock, by merging with smaller firms, it issued more stock, buying back its own stock and splitting shares further by August 1929. Galbraith called the summer of 1929 "the twilight of illusion" (1954: 66), as individual stocks like Westinghouse and GE gained nearly one-third in value. The volume of speculation rose as "brokers loans during the summer months increased at a rate of about $4 million a month" (Galbraith 1954: 70). Levels of loans were defended as proof of the strength of the market and there was no room for pessimism when, in June 1929, Bernard Baruch told the *American Magazine* "the economic situation of the world seems to be on the verge of a great forward movement" (quoted by Galbraith 1954: 73). A few voices called for restraint, like Paul Warburg, who expressed anxiety at the "unrestrained speculation." But in reality, out of a population of 120 million in 1929, 29 exchanges had about 1.5 million customers (Galbraith 1954: 80). About 600,000 accounts were on margin and the rest were based on cash transactions. As Marquand and Bromfield would describe in their novels, traders would stand around watching the blackboard, just like in 1999–2001 at the height of the dotcom bubble, day traders would stayed glued to their computer screen, and the CNBC financial network.

On September 5, 1929, there began to appear ominous signs when blue chips US Steel and Westinghouse began to drop. "Thursday, October 24 is the first of the days which history ... identifies with the panic of 1929. Measured by disorder, freight and confusion, it deserves to be so regarded" (Galbraith 1954: 101).

> The crowds on Broad Street outside the Exchange began to panic, "Rumor after rumor swept Wall Street and these outlying wakes. Stocks were now selling for nothing. The Chicago and Buffalo Exchanges had closed. A suicide wave was in progress and eleven well known speculators had already killed themselves."
>
> (Galbraith 1954: 102)

As discussed in Chapter 2, these rumors were false, but very dramatic and fear mongering. By noon, the chairmen of National City, Chase, Guaranty Trust, Bankers Trust, and Thomas Lamont, senior partner at Morgan, met. As in 1907, it was assumed that order would return and indeed by the end of the day the market more or less stabilized with losses of an average of 12 points on the blue chips. But by October 28, it was understood that the damage could not be contained. Tuesday, October 29 was "the most devastating day in the history of the New York stock market" (until October 19, 1987, and September 15, 2008), selling was extremely heavy, canceling all the gains of the previous year. The bankers not only did not find a solution but had to counter rumors that the wealthiest were selling stocks and aggravating the crisis. New York banks increased loans in order to avert a money panic, as banks outside of New York reacted "by calling home two billions" (Galbraith: 1954: 117).

By November, the values of all stocks and investment trusts (many of which were trades among themselves) continued dropping dramatically. November 5, 1929 was Election Day and the market was closed. James Walker won a second term by a landslide over Fiorello LaGuardia (accused of being a Socialist), but the debacle continued. Finally, by mid-November, President Hoover became involved, as the economic fundamentals began to be seriously affected. "Prices of commodities were falling. Freight car loadings, pig iron and steel production, coal output and automobile production were also all going down" (Galbraith 1954: 139).

Despite all signs to the contrary, Hoover insisted by the spring of 1930 that the worst was over and that the economy would recover by the fall. Professor Irving Fisher, guru of optimistic forecasting insisted that "psychology of panic ... mob psychology" (quoted in Galbraith 1954: 149) had provoked the crash. Goldman Sachs would become a bastion of conservatism. National City and Chase National suffered huge losses in money, prestige and credibility. Charles Mitchell, head of National City was finally arrested on tax evasion in 1933. Although Mitchell, accused of stock manipulation and insider trading (he sold his stock to his wife to avoid taxes) was acquitted, he became the symbol of the evil dissolute banker. "In his inaugural address on March 4, Roosevelt had promised to drive the moneychangers from the temple. Mitchell was widely regarded as the first" (Galbraith 1954: 156). Within three years, the American political landscape shifted as Wall Street became the scapegoat for all economic ills: "And the center of immorality was not the banks but the stock market ... with its promise of easy riches was what led good if not very wise men to perdition" (Galbraith 1954: 158). Thomas E. Dewey, Manhattan District Attorney on March 10, 1938 arrested Richard Whitney, former head of the NYSE, on charges of grand larceny. He had continued to kite operations through 1938 in order to keep his own firm afloat. Congress had enacted the Securities Act of 1933 and the Securities Exchange Act of 1934. Full disclosure was required on new security issues. Inside operations and short selling was outlawed. The Federal Reserve Board was granted authority to fix margin requirements. Commercial banks were divorced from their securities affiliates under the Glass-Steagall Act of 1934.

The American regulatory system, which would last unchallenged until 1999, was in place.

Galbraith, looking for causes to the crash, quoted Macaulay and Bagehot on the South Sea Bubble: "Speculation, accordingly, is most likely to break out after a substantial period of prosperity, rather than in the early phases of recovery from a depression" (1954: 173). The speculative bubbles of 1987, 1999 to 2000, 2003, and 2008 seem to fit the same pattern. It is not that people seek more money in times of scarcity, but rather that people seek even more money in times of prosperity, and become both greedy and careless. The danger signs in 1929 were weak investment and weak consumer spending, despite the froth in the market. Banking structures were weak, failures spread quickly, as "346 banks failed with aggregate deposits of \$115 million" (Galbraith 1954: 182). Foreign balances and debt repayment contributed to global instability, worsened by lack of cooperation between central banks and very poor economic intelligence outside of the *New York Times* and the *Wall Street Journal*. Galbraith wrote his work in 1954 (revised in 1961), when the market was in a deep slump and America was in the grips of McCarthyism. After accusations of pro-Communist market ideology, the book appeared in 1955. His final message resonates painfully in 2009:

> Yet in some respects the chances for a recurrence of a speculative orgy are rather good. No one can doubt that the American public remain susceptible to the speculative mood – to the conviction that enterprise can be attended by unlimited rewards which they, individually were meant to share.
>
> (Galbraith 1954: 191)

6.17 Transformation of American financial culture

During the years of the Great Depression, America not only went to the movies, it went into the movies, as illustrated in Woody Allen's tragicomic *Purple Rose of Cairo* (1985). America did not lose faith in the beauty and joy of wealth, it simply no longer believed it to be accessible as reality, so it sought it out as fantasy.

In *My Man Godfrey* (1936), Mr. Bullock, patriarch of the ditzy rich family loses all in the market, but is saved by Godfrey the patrician turned butler, who pawns a necklace, selling short and endorsing the transaction to Bullock, saves the family and makes a profit, allowing him to open a nightclub at the city dump in order to employ the homeless and give them food and shelter. Frank Capra's *Mr. Deeds Goes to Town* (1936), stars Gary Cooper who inherits US\$20 million in the tiny hamlet of Mandrake Falls, Vermont. The rube comes to New York, is duped by a smart reporter, and almost loses his money, but when attacked by dispossessed farmers and accused of being a "heartless, ultra rich man," he decides to give a huge tract of land to the poor farmers and have them work and repay their loans. Frank Capra's *It Happened One Night* (1934) stars Colette Colbert, a pampered heiress who has run out on an old rich husband, meets a reporter, played by Clark Gable, on a bus and discovers how the poor, and the homeless live across America. In the end she marries the reporter and will use her father's money to help the poor.

Musical comedies featuring lavish dance and costume sequences, gangster dramas (*Little Caesar*, *Public Enemy*), presenting feisty heroes and heroines, or ostracized lower classes pushed into crime, were immensely successful and offered solace to an impoverished and nervous society. But these movies also played into the American mythology of wealth being temporary, fragile, and not a given right, of basic equality in love and ability to redeem happiness in the face of disaster. They underscored strong undercurrents of growing populism, as bankers and rich men were presented as easily duped old fools. The comic strip *Little Orphan Annie*, by Harold Grey, starts in 1931, with Daddy Warbucks as victim of the Crash of 1929, having lost his first fortune and recovered his wealth, he is vindicated once he adopts the little orphan.

On stage, Archibald MacLeish's play *Panic*, offered a brutal take on a capitalist who loses all after the crash. Henry Luce created *Fortune Magazine* in 1930, featuring articles on fashion, money, and even the Rothschilds as a source of distraction and potentiality (Fraser 2005: 434).

In the early 1900s, a first version of the game Monopoly was created as a "Landlord's game" board (which by 1935 became the Charles Darrow board game, sold by Parker Brothers around the world). The character of mascot/dealer appeared in 1936 as jolly old "Rich Uncle Pennybags," bearing a physical resemblance to J.P. Morgan. The game, actually a middle class version of the subprime mortgage market, offers properties to buy, lose, pay income tax on, acquire, merge, get caught in a tax or fraud scheme, go to jail, get out, and start again. There were also games of Bankers and Brokers and other board games of chance, evoking the activities of Wall Street. For decades family pastimes would replicate the American dream scheme: making a fortune, losing money, acquiring property, going bankrupt, cutting losses and regaining entry to the game.

From the 1940s, American society was imbued in a multigenerational culture of money, where the average family could have its children and parents reading *Richie Rich* or *McScrooge* comics, watching funny millionaires on television, playing Monopoly as, in each subsequent generation, the number of programs, home entertainment, and illustrated magazines, devoted to financial activity increased. In the business world the emblematic American myth of rags to riches, played out from the mailroom to the executive suite. The 2007 Forbes list of the 15 richest fictional characters has 13 American cartoon, television or comic book characters, including two females, many dating back to the 1950s. Led by Scrooge McDuck described on Wikipedia as "a Scottish Glaswegian anthromorphic duck," having made his fortune in the Klondike, combining the stereotypical avarice and hoarding of the Scots and the innovative shrewdness of the American self-made man. Modeled in part on Andrew Carnegie, his only rival is John D. Rockerduck. With a fortune of "one mutiplujillion, nine obquatumatillion, six hundred twenty six dollars and sixty two cents" (Wikipedia: Scrooge McDuck), his fortune, all in gold bullion, would be about US$28bn, according to Forbes 2007 estimates. The core audience for these comic books, fantasy and television heroes and antiheroes are primarily American and English pre-adolescent male children. The characters vary from the somewhat villainous and sinister, to the heroic: Bruce Wayne, alias Batman; happily idiotic Thurston III from Gilligan's Island; Jed Clampett, the good hillbilly who strikes oil (*Beverly Hillbillies*) played by Buddy Ebsen; the country "Doc" character in the movie version of Truman Capote's *Breakfast at Tiffany's*, another apocryphal American tale of rags to riches in 1960s New York.

A quiz show, *Take it or Leave it*, ran from 1940 to 1947, offering cash prices which morphed into the television series *The $64,000 Question* (CBS), paving the way for *Who Wants to be a Millionaire*, with Regis Philby, and British and Indian counterparts. In the 2008 joint Indian American movie *Slumdog Millionaire*, the horrifically poor and abused low caste protagonist is suddenly transformed on the show from object of derision to national hero when, by luck and coincidence, he wins 20 million rupees. The philosophical premise is that every individual can be granted equal status once he earns by smarts, hard work or the roll of the dice, a sufficient amount of money. Even in the most caste, class conscious societies, every man (and it still remains a male referent) can attain through money a higher level of social rank and prestige.

6.18 Return to basics: banks and bankers, 1933 to 1983

The most succinct and lucid definition of banks and their function in the economy was provided in the speech that officially ended the panic of 1933, and inaugurated the recovery. On March 12, 1933, President Roosevelt gave his first radio broadcast "On the Banking Crisis," to explain why he had declared a bank holiday and what the government intended to do:

> I want to talk for a few minutes with the people of the United States about banking – with the comparatively few who understand the mechanics of banking but more particularly with the overwhelming majority who use banks for the making of deposits and the drawing of checks ... First of all let me state the simple fact that when you deposit money in a bank the bank does not put the money into a safe deposit vault. It invests your money in many different forms of credit-bonds, commercial paper, mortgages and many other kind of loans. In other words, the bank puts your money to work to keep the wheels of industry and agriculture turning around.

Roosevelt continued that banks do not have enough currency in reserve to cover the withdrawals of large number of depositors in a panic, that most banks would reopen once recapitalized and be able to again lend and extend credit. He exonerated the principles of capitalism, justified the new role that the state would have to take to restore confidence, and lay the blame on the few bad bankers: "Some of our bankers had shown themselves either incompetent or dishonest in their handling of the people's funds. They used the money entrusted to them in speculations and unwise loans (Roosevelt 1933).

In a quirk of history, the speech is totally relevant in 2009, Until the Depression, American banks and bankers thrived in a decentralized state structure that emphasized the individual's ability to create new markets and generate new wealth through speculation and investment. The image of the banker as adventurer and pioneer acquiring wealth through skill, daring, and shrewd financial manipulation was part of the American myth of the individual's power to transcend and control their origins and surroundings. "In the historic world of commerce, the bank was the city on the hill. In Calvinist America where many things were seen to have been pre-ordained, bankers enjoyed unrivaled autonomy" (Mayer 1997: 1).

The Senate Banking and Currency Committee hearings in January 1933, led by Ferdinand Pecora (a Sicilian born rough hewn attorney) on the causes of the Crash of 1929, not only vilified, denounced and indicted bankers and speculators but:

> For the next decade they were fair game for congressional committees, courts, the press and the comedians ... A banker need not be popular; indeed a good banker in a healthy capitalist society should probably be much disliked. People do not wish to trust their money to a hail-fellow-well-met but to a misanthrope who can say no. However, a banker must not seem futile, ineffective or vaguely foolish. In contrast with the stern power of Morgan in 1907, that was precisely how his successors seemed, or were made to seem in 1929.
>
> (Galbraith 1954: 118)

The hearings were cathartic as "the riveting confrontation between Pecora and the Wall Street grandees was so theatrically apt it might have been concocted by Hollywood. The combative Pecora was the perfect foil to the posh bankers who paraded before the microphones" (Chernow 2009). The result of the hearings was the passage of the Securities Act of 1933, the Glass-Steagall Act in 1934, which would establish firewalls between banking, investment, and trading activities, and the Securities Exchange Act of 1934, which established the regulatory oversight body (which has now been discredited and accused of total ineptitude in the bank failures and Madoff debacle).

In order to regain respectability, banking had to return to its basic functions, lending, extending credit, taking deposits, and protecting assets. Banks and bankers had to prove themselves to their communities and to the public at large. One of most popular comic novels and later film and television series over four decades was Thorne Smith's 1926 pre-Depression *Topper*, followed by *Topper Takes a Trip* in 1932, and the movie *Topper*, directed by Hal Roach in 1937. The character of Topper is a sweet, staid bored banker who suddenly is adopted by a couple of very high society feckless ghosts. Topper wants to have fun, but at heart he is very proud of his work and reputation as a banker: "A solid man, a good man" (Smith 1926), he is shocked by those for whom: "this bank isn't home, it's something they want to control through notes and money and chicanery" (Smith 1926). In the 1950s, the British actor Leo Carroll takes on the role, emphasizing the propriety and rectitude of Topper even in the strangest circumstances.

Historically, American small towns always depended on their banks as liaison to the outside world and as protector of the community's assets. American communities favored and benefited from local banks, which lent the community's money and lent to the community. The interconnection between bank and community was so great that, in fact, a bank failure could put at risk an entire small community. Before 1934 and the FDIC, if a bank was declared insolvent by the Office of the Comptroller of the Currency it simply closed and all savings and deposits were void. Between 1934 and the 1980s, bank failures were very rare as banks became purposely "stodgy," under tight regulation and public oversight.

6.19 Bankers and financers: redemption, discretion

Fear of scandal, implication in any dubious transactions, and above all any hint of illegality haunted bankers in fact and fiction, through the post-World War II period. The profession had become tainted and immoral, requiring constant justification and redemption. In Louis Bromfield's *Mrs. Parkington* (1942), the heroine, widow of Major P. of railway and mining fortune, epitomizes the conflict of old and new money. When son-in-law Armory is accused of embezzlement:

> It was like Armory thinking there was something distinguished in being a stockbroker, like automobile manufacturers who believed they were messiahs and had brought about the millenniums, like men believing that intelligence and humor, civilization and wisdom could be bought at so much a pound.

> (Bromfield 1942: 295)

In Robert Penn Warren's, *At Heavens Gate* (1943), the hero immerses himself in banking literature, and becomes vice president in a securities department, the plot detailing insurance firms, banks, bond houses, till the outside world intervenes with rape and murder, emphasizing the contrast of emotional havoc and the façade of respectability.

John P. Marquand, one of America's most popular novelists, in *Point of No Return* (1947), captured the depression and near paranoia in an old WASP bank, where all risk is forbidden, for the hero who must bear the stigma of his father's reckless dealings and behavior, having lost all in the Crash of 1929. Louis Auchincloss' *The Embezzler* (1960), is a psychological study of financial mores in 1936, attributing to capitalist amorality a populist justification, where Guy Prime, the playboy broker's embezzlement scheme can be rationalized as a reapportionment of available resources. Frank Capra's sentimental parable of small town America, *It's a Wonderful Life* (1946), sets up the dialectical tension between good and bad bankers. George Bailey (portrayed by America's favorite good citizen actor) James Stewart, sacrifices his own interests to take over his family's failing mortgage brokerage firm, Bailey's Building and Loan, which continues to provide loans, even to those with less than worthy credit. He is pitted against the town banker, mean stogy Mr. Potter, who refuses to extend further credit to Bailey and wants to repossess unpaid mortgages. George, on the verge of bankruptcy, is about to kill himself when an angel intervenes, showing him a Bedford Falls without his caring generosity where greed, sin, exploitation, and unfettered capitalism reigns. George goes back home, is rescued by kind neighbors and unfailingly patient family, promoting wholesome virtues in contrast to heartless profits and business. Relevant in the subprime mortgage crisis, which combined the values of Bailey and Mr. Potter, as bank and brokers lied about the viability of extending fraudulent or less than credit worthy mortgages in the name of the American dream of home ownership, but the bankers, instead of carefully judging the true value of these mortgages, transformed them into complex, multi-layered financial instruments, passing them on to the balance sheets of large and small banks, creating in their wake "toxic" loans and worthless assets.

Faulkner's *The Town* (1957), caricatures the profession and institution of banking. *The Town*'s debunking of hypocritical mores in the South incorporates grotesque characters as the child named Wall Street Panic by his mother (his teachers rename him Wall Snopes) whose life's ambition is "to learn how to count money" (Faulkner 1957).

6.20 "3–6–3 rule"

Traditionally in American history, bankers were "all male and all white of course and overwhelmingly Protestant and of northern European ancestry, but this categorization leaves room for great social, educational and geographic diversity" (Mayer 1997: 3) Through the 1970s, in the quest for sedateness and propriety, quotas were unspoken but imposed against foreigners and ethnic minorities in so called "white shoe firms." Dealings between prestigious Jewish and Protestant banking houses diminished or were carefully kept out of the public notice. Chase Manhattan, City Bank, Bankers Trust, and Bank of New York maintained unwritten rules, pushing non German Jewish, Irish, and Italian bankers into foreign banks, smaller establishments, brokerage firms, and trading floors.

Respectable bankers played golf, drank martinis and followed the "3–6–3 rule: Borrow at 3 percent, lend at 6 percent and tee off by 3 p.m." (Hughes and Mac Donald 2002: 417). The function of investment banks such as First Boston, Morgan Stanley, Kuhn Loeb (merged with Lehman), and Dillon Read "was to raise capital for companies on the basis of long associations and old friendships" (Hughes and Mac Donald 2002: 417). Trading and brokerage houses, Salomon, Goldman Sachs, and Merrill Lynch were slightly below in the pecking order of prestige and respectability. In 1955, Martin Mayer still distinguished between brokers and underwriters. As late as 1983, investment banking was a small exclusive club "between them in 1983 four of the five Bulge firms (the exception was Merrill Lynch, a special case) employed barely twelve thousand people …

with capital and reserves of the investment and broking business ... about $11 billion" (Ferris 1984: 94–95).

Emma Latham's mystery series (1961–1979) banker protagonist, John Putnam Thatcher, senior vice-president of the Sloan Guaranty Trust, perfectly captured the requisite culture of investment banks, and Wall Street's facade and reality:

> Wall Street is the greatest financial market in the world, and the function of a market is to provide an arena for smooth and orderly transactions. ... It is only in theory that competition and profit maximizing have a Doric serenity; in practice they entail one battle after another.
>
> (Latham 1971: 1)

However complex and, at times, involving crimes or corruption, these battles are still fought in wood panel boardrooms among well mannered gentlemen, out of view of the public and the press.

Overall between 1945 and 1965 "no radical changes occurred" (Fraser 2005: 384). The number of commercial banks declined slightly to about 13,800, under a regime of relatively few bank mergers conducted under strict supervision and with an increase in bank holding companies. Only a few large banks, led by Citibank expanded into foreign countries. By 1965, 13 large banks "had more than 200 branches in 50 countries scattered over four continents" (Fraser 2005: 386). Banks lent aggressively to domestic commercial, industrial, agricultural, and real estate sectors and consumers. Banks also began to see competition from other financial institutions, including mutual savings banks, savings and loans, life insurance companies, credit unions, and sales and personal finance companies. Martin Mayer in *The Bankers* (1975), narrates an anecdote about a banker honored for 50 years of service at a Virginia bank who, when asked what had been the most significant change, replied "Air conditioning" (Mayer 1975: 16).

America was affluent, middle class, conservative, and money conscious, proud of its living standards and value system, disdainful of impoverished, ravaged Europe, and fearful of the threat of the Soviet Union. Friedrich Hayek and Milton Friedman, professors at Chicago University's School of Economics, were the new voices of moral and economic authority, promoting the role of the individual and the free market in opposition to all central planning. Hayek's *Individualism and Economic Order* (1948), and *The Pure Theory of Capital and the Road to Serfdom* (1944) advocated a role for government in social welfare and monetary policy, combined with laissez faire capitalism. More marginal, but influential movements like Ayn Rand's theories of heroic capitalism in *The Fountainhead* (1943) and *Atlas Shrugged* (1957), attracted young intellectuals, including Alan Greenspan, with the vision of economic oligarchy and free enterprise. America in the post-World War II years, prided itself as the country of individual initiative, yet the role of the government expanded in the 1960s.

If banks had been signaled out, brokerage firms had been stigmatized. Mistrust of Wall Street continued through the 1960s. Cameron Hawley's *Cash McCall*

(1955), personifies the speculator as sexual and financial predator, engaging in secret transactions, making a fortune buying and selling companies. Brokerage firms were greatly reduced in size: Merrill Lynch in 1959 had 12.5 million less shareholders than in 1930. Merrill Lynch understood the mood of the country and carefully cultivated its brand, selling securities to average families. Often focusing on the housewife in the traditional one income family, which had become the norm in the post-war years, the firm created an image of American wholesomeness. Capitalism in the 1950s moved away from cosmopolitanism and sophistication, the trademark of the 1920s, to representing American values and traditions. In the time of McCarthy and the "Red Scare," money and market philosophy regained acceptance as antithetical to Soviet State socialism and anti-capitalism.

The market rose carefully and steadily in the prosperous 1950s without fanfare:

> Holdings of institutional investors ballooned from 11 billion in 1949 to 219 billion in 1971. Almost all of that was parked in blue chips, high capitalization Dow industrials, safe and sound companies like GE, GM, Proctor and Gamble. They were dubbed "one decision stocks" – you bought them once and held on to them forever.
>
> (Fraser 2005: 496)

Stock market activity almost quadrupled in 20 years, from 769 million shares in 1945 to 2.671 million shares in 1965 (Fraser 2005: 395).

The model of the American financier and banker, true to the values of the 1950s, yet successful in 2008, Warren Buffet, nicknamed "Sage of Omaha" remains emblematic of intrinsic American belief in the virtues of capitalism. In an interview on MSNBC in April 2008, he described himself at 78 as "having had the good fortune to have been born in America, white, male and wired for asset allocation." Chief Executive Officer of Vanguard (the largest mutual fund in the United States), John Bogle, reiterates these principles in *The Battle for the Soul of Capitalism* (2005). Of the same generation as Buffet, Bogle, representative of elite, urban Yale-educated bankers, defines soul, quoting Aquinas "vital power, shaping an individual," to explain how capitalism functions within the body politic. Bogle emphasises the role of fiduciary responsibility, the inherent relationship of trust: "a virtuous cycle of in which an everyday level of trustworthiness breeds an everyday level of trust" (Surowiecki quoted in Bogle 2005: 5). For Buffet and Bogle, bankers' fiduciary and moral responsibility must be to their clients and shareholders. Representative of the generation, educated in the post-Depression era and having achieved success in the years of caution and regulation, prominent financiers and investors such as John Bogle, Peter Peterson (former head of Lehman from 1973–1984), Warren Buffet, and Wilber Ross viewed with alarm the move from "owners capitalism" to "managers capitalism" (Bogle 2005) since the 1990s, seeing an erosion of a moral-societal obligation in the pursuit of capitalist activity. Hardly Keynesian, Bogle quotes Keynes: "When the capital development of a country becomes the by product of the activities of a casino, the job is likely to be ill done" (Bogle 2005). One of the unanswered questions is whether bankers, in the aftermath of 2008, can and will return to these principles, reinventing banking as a function defined by the needs of the community and depositors rather than the market.

6.21 Financial technology and innovation

From Samuel Morse's electrical telegraph in 1837, revolutionizing global communication, to the Morse code, from the first transatlantic cable in 1866 to the first stock ticker, invented by Edward Calahan in 1867 (replacing messengers running from office to office with prices: "by 1880 more than 1000 tickers were in use" (Storey 2002: 25), American financial innovation transformed the availability and rapidity of market data.

> The New York Quotation Company, a NYSE subsidiary, provided ticker service locally and to distant customers via the Western Union Company. Taking information from the trading floor, telegraph operators entered data on a circular keyboard activating the print wheels of tickers in subscribers' offices. By 1913 ... more than 1,000 tickers were in operation.
>
> (Storey 2002: 25–31)

By the 1880s in London, accounts were cleared through exchanges of clearing house gold certificates. New York banks served as clearing houses, until, in 1914, settlement became a transfer of money on the books of the Federal Reserve Bank in New York. CHIPS (Clearing House Interbank Payment System), introduced in New York in 1970, kept track of all dollar denominated foreign transactions by New York and correspondent banks worldwide. The first computerized global settlement system was further perfected to reflect real time settlement following the failure of Herstatt bank in 1974 (see Chapter 5).

Automated Teller Machines (ATMs) created in 1939 in New York (perfected by a British engineer, Shepherd-Barron, in 1965) quickly transformed retail operations in the United States, Europe, Canada, and Japan, reaching nearly 1.5 million machines in 2006. Eliminating the need for multiple tellers in each branch, offering deposit, cash, transferring accounts, and balance statements into one computerized set of transactions, by charging a fee for these services, ATMs proved a very simple way of generating profits and reducing costs.

As larger segments of traditional banking clients made less use of "brick and mortar" banking services, competitive demands called for widening the range of services and facilities, focusing either on low-end advisory services in competition with cash checking and remittance facilities, or expanding private banking, wealth management, custodial, and specialized investment advice for the wealthiest demographic. Kindleberger foresaw the trend in 1999:

> Securization of mortgages and export and installment credits are part of the movement from client banking to capital markets along with a weakening of

tight relations between bank managers and small business, although these links are likely to survive in reduced branch networks.

(Finel-Honigman 1999: foreword)

The next major leap in financial technology occurred in the 1990s: internet banking where Wells Fargo took the lead. America was not at the forefront, but followed suit after Sweden, Finland, and Germany. Cheap, accessible, well promoted, and readily distributed under government incentives and public private partnerships, internet banking facilities, similar to cell phones across Europe, were much better managed and more effective than in the United States. By the 1990s, in Belgium every bank account came with a debit card. Finland inaugurated the "ecard" as a central bank, health, and social security card. America, however, regained competitive advantage in electronic commerce and payment facilities with eBay and PayPal.

6.22 Credit card culture

Diners Club, the first credit card, introduced in 1949, was followed by the American Express Card in 1958, charging a higher fee to appear "a little upscale of Diners Club" (Mayer 1997: 113). American Express originated in Buffalo, New York in 1850, linking with Henry Wells and William Fargo to establish Wells Fargo. In the 1960s, it began marketing its credit card business under an image of exclusiveness, with the Gold Card in 1966, and the Platinum Card in 1984, feeding into the snobbism and nouveau riche culture of the Reagan boom years. By imposing a fee for these cards (US$450 yearly in 2008), the cards proved extremely lucrative, while appearing to offer exclusivity.

Bank of America created its predecessor to Visa in California in 1958, incorporating National Bank Americard in 1970. The card's appeal was its universality once it received the first electronic authorization in 1973. Known as Visa since 1976, it was recognizable and easy to pronounce in all languages. Visa established the first global ATM, 24-hour availability in 1983, and in 1999 Visa offered the first card transactions in euro.

MasterCard followed suit in 1966 in California, joining forces with banks in Kentucky, and New York and becoming the interstate United States card in competition with Visa. In 1994, Dee Hock, former CEO of Visa, defined his theoretical framework, set out as early as 1968: "Money had become nothing but guaranteed alphanumeric data recorded in valueless paper and metal. It would eventually become guaranteed data in the form of arranged electrons and photons which would move around the world at the speed of light" (Mayer 1997: 129). The credit card culture, indigenous to the United States at its inception, spread quickly to Europe, yet the extent and scope of the industry and its appeal remained unique to the United States. Through the 1990s, outside of the United States, purchases continued to be paid mainly in cash or by bank check. High-end businesses, hotels, transportation services, and retail accepted and used credit cards, but individuals rarely had more than one card, with greater use of debit rather than credit cards.

The credit culture, derivative of the installment plan culture, which originated in urban centers and emigrant communities in the 1920s, was rapidly exploited by banks and retailers alike in the 1970s. But by the 1970s, retailers such as Sears (the slogan for Sears financial services was "If you lose your shirt, we'll sell you another"), General Motors, and General Electric (GE), became self contained financing corporations, which no longer needed the bank as middle man. The appeal of credit cards further spread the fragmentation and pervasive influence of credit facilities in society at large, eliminating the need for personal relationships with a local bank or banker.

The amount of fees charged varied according to state and institution, leading to abuses and excessive surcharges. The amount of interest paid on credit card purchases, the major cards, retail store cards, and gas company cards rose from 5 percent to nearly 20 percent generating vast profits, in addition to late fees and extra interest on delayed payments. The psychological and physical lure of the cards rests in their ease of usage, interconnection with ATMs worldwide, safety factor (eliminating the need to carry large amounts of cash in unsafe or foreign loci), and false sense of financial security: paying by card removes the immediacy of spending cash, therefore inciting larger and more numerous purchases.

In the crisis of 2008, the issue of unpaid credit card debt is becoming one of the most complicated problems to resolve. As credit card companies scrabble to recoup losses and to consistently increase their client base, there are widespread examples of total absurdity: once an individual is under a tax lien for unpaid taxes, the information is in the public domain, yet individuals continue receiving "pre-approved" credit card solicitations by mail, based on their outstanding credit rating: "by consistently honoring your financial obligations, you've built a solid credit history" (DiscoverCard mail solicitation, February 2009). As Washington and Main Street attempt to find a balance between spending and saving, as banks need to regenerate credit facilities, and as public and private debt needs to be addressed, on a daily basis the American consumer is encouraged to resume the worst habits of the pre-crisis culture.

6.23 Return to basics

The gargantuan shock to the banking system in 2008 proved that banks could no longer take for granted their niche sectors or clients. In attempts to increase their appeal, there were examples of banks reverting to marketing ploys, combining the advantages of technology with the basic comforts of home spun Americana. Umpqua, a bank chartered in the Western states in 1995, grew to 140 branches by offering book, music, and coffee shop facilities on site, creating a Barnes and Noble Starbucks bank model. During the worst of the crisis in fall 2008, many small town banks continued to function and even thrive, having avoided the subprime mortgage fiasco and by maintaining customer loyalty: Country Bank in Greenwood, South Carolina, geared a marketing campaign based on southern biscuits, as in "business banking as you like it" bundled under "together under the name BNizkit. Biscuit. Get it?" based on the local specialty of "ham biscuits" and pitched as "fresh, simple business banking." As reported "it is surely better to have a bank bring you a hot biscuit than to have a bank land in hot water" (Elliott 2008). Whether viewed as crass or corny, these local institutions reverted to comfort and ingenuity, in the belief that marketing confidence could help regain confidence.

In New York there were 469 bank branches in 2002, and 631 in 2006, mostly in Manhattan. While bank charters decreased since 1984, with a sharp drop between 1994 and 2003, the number of physical bank offices steadily increased. During the height of the real estate boom in New York, there was a proliferation of new banks and bank branches opening (see FDIC 2004). This occurred during a period of rapid technological advance, including an increase of ATMs in banking venues that should have diminished the need for brick and mortar institutions, but as the *New York Sun* reported in July 2007, in the architecture section: "somewhat tautologically ... the main function of these banks is nothing other than to incarnate the message that they can afford to be there in the first place." It was assumed that banks were not going to default on the rent, a premise which will be sorely tested in a new era of forced consolidation and mergers (*New York Sun* 2007).

6.24 Consolidation and diversification

In the crisis of 2008, when, within six months, the major investment banks of Bear Stearns, Lehman Brothers and Merrill Lynch, the large retail banks – Washington Mutual and Wachovia, and the major insurer, AIG, have either failed, been absorbed or are in eminent danger, when the most important private partnerships, Goldman Sachs and investment bank Morgan Stanley, have been forced to change their status to bank holding companies in order to be eligible for public rescue funds, and when the world's largest bank and the core of American global finance for over a century, Citigroup, is being pushed into restructuring and divesting major assets, there is an understandable sense of panic and loss of faith in the American banking sector. But history is a reminder that drastic bank failures, consolidation, mergers, and absorption have occurred in recent memory in 1982, 1987–1992, and 1998 resulting in leaner, meaner, more competitive and more profitable institutions.

In 1945 there were 16 major banks in New York City, by 2000 there were four: Citigroup, Bank of New York (incorporating Irving Trust in 1988), Bankers Trust (bought by Deutsche in 1998), and the multiform merger of J.P. Morgan Chase (derived from Chemical, Corn Exchange Bank, New York Trust in 1959; Guaranty Trust Morgan in 1959; Manufactures Trust and Central Hanover Bank in 1961; Chase and Bank of the Manhattan Company in 1955). Across America there were 12,000 banks in 1980, reduced to 7,000 banks in 2000.

The tumultuous years of the Vietnam War, 1968–1972, riots, protests, and the dissolution of the entrenched value system of post-war America, followed by the end of dollar hegemony in 1971, the oil crisis of 1973, the loss of faith in the government under Watergate, and Nixon's resignation in 1975 left the country bitter, disillusioned and hungry for radical change. Wall Street conducted business quietly, as American financial interests became more global and as American corporations became far more aggressive abroad. Servan-Schreiber's *Le Defi Americain* [*The American Challenge*] (1967), see Chapter 5) was a wakeup call to Europe to fear, admire, and counterpunch America's corporate offensive. In 1970, US banks held 30 percent of the world's banking assets (by contrast, in May 1990 they had less than 10 percent, as Japanese, German, French, and Dutch banks had learned their lessons, consolidated, and reformed into universal mega banks).

The one-term Carter administration (1976–1980), offered very little relief, unable to control race riots, sweeping urban crime, and ghettoization at home, or to counteract the loss of American prestige abroad. Ronald Reagan became president in a demoralized country plagued by a weak dollar, low exports, and restrictive regulations. The recession of 1982, incited by the huge surge in oil prices following the Revolution in Iran, saw unemployment pass 16 percent (Leonhardt 2009). Reagan had an acrimonious relationship with Paul Volcker, head of the Federal Reserve, who favored maintaining tight regulatory firewalls and cautious monetary policy, all virtues in 2008 (Paul Volcker is presently economic advisor to President Obama), but seen as restrictive and detrimental to economic recovery, in the mid-1980s. In 1980, Wall Street began to slowly change as foreign banks were able to expand, thanks to more favorable New York State tax policy (foreign corporate banks would be allowed to open interstate branches or subsidiaries prior to the repeal of the McFadden Act restricting US interstate banking), and US banks became more aggressive and competitive in lending. Exports slowly rose, as South Carolina, New Jersey, Illinois, and even poor small rural states like Alabama and Arkansas began to offer tax incentives to bring in foreign corporations, producing goods with American labor and factories. By the end of the decade, German and Korean car manufacturers, German and Swiss pharmaceuticals, and French electronics would be manufactured in the United States.

Shocked by the oil crisis and dominance of Middle Eastern petrodollars, by 1983 "Reaganomics" policy encouraged the loosening of accountability and restriction on cross speculative activities from small banks, the search for revival of the US energy sector, and the start of "cowboy capitalism." The phrase, coined in the French publication *L'Expansion*, in 1983, became a global catch phrase for American tactics, practices, and style (Tendron 1983).

6.25 Penn Square and funny money

Between 1982 and 1989, America's financial landscape was strewn with the remnants of market failures, massive bankruptcies, huge fortunes made and lost, and venerable old firms destroyed and absorbed. It began on July 5, 1982, when a small bank in Oklahoma City, Penn Square Bank failed. Mark Singer's, *Funny Money* (1985) reads like a combination of the Beverly Hillbillies and a Securities and Exchange Commission (SEC) report on total supervisory failure. Penn

Square was symptomatic of the period's exuberance, hubris, the culture of Western independence and antagonism for Washington and Wall Street. It also serves as a precedent for the misplaced belief that:

> Held that a bank did not have to lend its own deposits, because it could lend other banks deposits. Penn Square could earn interest lending its own funds, but could generate far greater earnings, with very little risk by arranging loans and collecting fees as a middlemen.
>
> (Singer 1985: 19)

Penn Square, as a regional bank, was perfectly entitled to deal with large money center banks in order to guarantee its loans, "at its zenith Penn Square could legally lend up to three million dollars at one time," then engage in "over lines" through other banks (Singer 1985). Oklahoma saw various oil booms and busts since the first well was sunk in 1859. The chairman of Penn Square was an old line Oklahoman born and bred, a solid member of his community, generous and philanthropic. He was the ideal community banker, but the bank was faltering in 1976 when he decided to start an oil and gas department. He engaged in lending practices which passed along the risk and the guarantees based on the principle from real estate to oil and gas possibilities made available to

> The decent right thinking people who had gone to the trouble of owning or leasing mineral rights throughout Oklahoma, Texas and Louisiana did not have the capital that they needed to get the oil and gas out of the ground. The Yankee bastards, among others had the capital.
>
> (Singer 1985: 23)

Basically Penn Square became the 1980s soap opera *Dallas*, writ large. Normally, as undeveloped leases and drilling rigs and equipment have no real collateral value, traditional banks through the 1970s refused to lend unless individuals were in the business for a decade. For "Beep Jennings believed that 'character' could compensate for missing collateral." After the oil crisis of 1973, there was not only a fear, but a hatred of OPEC, the theme of American dependency on a bunch of Arab sheiks resonated from Washington to the West. Oil and gas exploration was seen as patriotic. The present crisis over the price of oil began in 1973, when there were predictions that oil prices could reach US$80 or US$90 a barrel by 1990 (by this account the US$130–US$140 in 2008 seems reasonable). Major banks were willing to lend in this market such as Continental Illinois National Bank and Trust Company of Chicago, in 1976 the eighth largest bank holding company. Eventually Continental began to shop off these loans to Michigan National and all the way to Chase Manhattan. As in each scandal, extraordinary optimism combined with sheer greed. Within a few years, Penn Square's loan portfolio and level of loan participations sold to out of state banks increased exponentially. Although banks auditors, Arthur Young, found dubious and substandard assets and by 1980, the Office of the Comptroller of the

Currency, who had examined the bank numerous times, issued warnings of "financial, operational or compliance weaknesses" (Singer 1985), yet bankers only saw a growing balance sheet: "Everyone was having an enchanting time" (Singer 1985: 73). Oil men were a unique type in Americana and as described,

> Once prosperity invaded Culpepper's life, the word "no" disappeared from his vocabulary. Along the way came the Learjet, then two more, then the jet helicopter, the second home in Cancun, the third home in Baja, the seaside estate in Santa Barbara, the eighty two foot yacht in Newport Beach.
>
> (Singer 1985: 93)

Once the bank collapsed, it was revealed at hearings that loans were granted upon request with almost no due diligence or collateral required. Deals were pushed through by word of mouth. At the end, as the bank was collapsing, Jennings and Patterson, head of oil and gas, went on a salmon fishing expedition in British Columbia along with other bankers and major customers. (Jimmy Cayne was at a bridge tournament as Bear Stearns folded). When it was declared insolvent, Penn Square had US$37 million in capital and identifiable losses of US$20 million, but as the story unraveled there were no assets left. Chase's role was so difficult to unravel that it took weeks to figure out the actual exposure through all the other correspondent banks. The bank was taken over by the FDIC. Within a few months, over 25 banks in Texas, Tennessee, Kentucky, and across Oklahoma had failed, or were listed as problem banks. By 1984, "the FDIC's list of problem banks had risen to 617, a post Depression record" (Singer 1985), Chase wrote off its Penn Square portfolio, but "bad news in banking does not breed confidence" (Singer 1985: 155) and there were massive layoffs and litigation. In 1983, the chairman of Chase, Willard Butcher, told shareholders that the experience had been "difficult and certainly a source of acute embarrassment" (Singer 1985: 157). Bill Patterson was seen as the main culprit and was indicted. During the investigation, Beep Jennings continued to insist that "if given a fair chance by the Comptroller of the Currency, Continental Illinois, Chase Manhattan and Seattle First would have taken over Penn Square" (Singer 1985: 195). The bank was liquidated, Jennings was indicted in Chicago, but never convicted in Oklahoma, and acquitted on all charges as not having intended to defraud.

6.26 Trading transactions: futures, FOREX, NASDAQ

N.R. Kleinfield in *The Traders* (1984), wrote one of the first accounts of the revitalized commodity trading in 1983 at the Chicago Board of Trade, the world's largest futures exchange: increasing from 9.3 million contracts in 1968 to 118 million contracts by October 1983. By 1986, a year before the crash, the action was mainly on Treasury bond futures.

The description of soybean futures and Treasury bond traders in 1983 is applicable to FOREX traders in 1985, Nick Leeson in 1995, Jerome Kerviel in 2008:

They have an affinity for money. Money is their fix and rush. Presented with the opportunity to coin a plenitude of money quickly, they are never timid about taking risks that would send shivers through the bones of most people. They look on themselves as the last individualists in America.... Nowhere though is the action so hot, nowhere are the stakes so high, as in the wilds of the futures pits, where traders speculate on what beans or corn or some other commodity will sell for months before the crops actually come to market. ... There are hedgers and speculators, private investors and professional traders who buy the contracts and assume the risk.

(Kleinfield (1984)

Similar to the first futures traders, dealing in "windhandel" in seventeenth-century Amsterdam described in Braudel (see Chapter 3):

For them, commodity trading is a game of buying and selling things they never actually own or care to own. The physical strain was very real, permanent hoarseness, loss of hearings from the decibel level, sore backs, injured ribs, high blood pressure. The hours are short, 9 to 3, the pace grueling, risks and rewards are huge. Like gamblers they believe in totemic articles of clothing, jewelry or habits. In 1982 the government already sensed problems and was ineffective in quelling or controlling the market, sensing potential problems.

(Kleinfield1984)

"In Congress, more than 100 bills designed to banish futures trading have been introduced though none have got terribly far along in the legislative process before being scuttled" (Kleinfield 1984). The cultural paradox was that despite all the negative images of machismo, sexism, and turning the market into a high stakes poker game, traders' culture revitalized the banking sector. The short hours, corny deal making and restricted personnel policies were no longer possible in a brutally competitive internal and external environment.

The National Association of Securities Dealers Automated Quotations (NASDAQ) System, opened in 1981, offering electronic over-the-counter trading, led by Frank Zarb of Lazard (one of its directors was Bernard Madoff). Within a few years it would start to specialize in technology stocks, becoming the model for the short lived Neue Markt in Frankfurt in (1999–2003), and Nouveau Marche in France (1999–2004).

In the 1970s, Leo Melamed and Richard Sandor, traders on the Chicago Mercantile Exchange, started the futures market. On May 16, 1972, under the umbrella of the Mercantile Exchange, trading of foreign currencies began in Chicago, barely a year after Nixon broke the dollar-gold link. Foreign Exchange (FOREX) trading would dominate US, European, and Japanese bank profits until 1993. Complex arbitrage operations on small variations in the value of major currencies, led by the US dollar, Deutschmark, French franc, Swiss franc, British pound sterling, and the Japanese yen, led to massive global currency speculation, provoking the collapse of the European Monetary System in 1992, the collapse of Barings in 1995, on falsified yen transactions, and the fortune of George Soros.

6.27 Trading culture: a ride on the wild side

The work force on Wall Street was also changing, with the incursion of women into banking and more so into trading rooms (see Chapter 2: it would be another decade before minorities were hired and accepted). The combined culture of bankers and traders, of different ages and backgrounds, colleagues and rivals (by the mid-1980s traders could earn substantially more) fueled a competitive, brash, and tense environment. Bankers had to be reflective, to consider the deal and the client; traders had to be extremely fast and aggressive. Foul language, coarse behavior, overt sexism, and alcohol and drug consumption became part of the culture of trading rooms. These patterns of behavior were not encouraged, but they were never seriously curtailed as long as the profits rolled in.

Interest and awareness of what occurred on Wall Street began to permeate the broader culture once again. As the economy began to recover, Wall Street generated excitement and glamour, with new gleaming skyscrapers, restaurants, the rebuilding of South Street Seaport, and the sudden surge of profits, salaries, and bonuses, feted by elaborate Christmas parties in luxury hotels. The most popular and prescient movie of 1983 was *Trading Places*, starring Eddie Murphy as a street smart black delinquent, suddenly catapulted onto Wall Street to switch places with an arrogant young investment banker. This scheme is concocted by the senior partners at the bank, on the Pygmalion premise that the thug will become a banker a lot sooner than his counterpart will take to life on the crime ridden streets of New York. Groomed, dressed, and given basic instructions, his gut assessments are much more valuable and make the firm's elderly partners rich until the perfunctory happy ending and resolution. Emblematic of the Reagan era was the weekly soap opera, *Dynasty*, which aired from 1981 to 1989, and attracted a worldwide following. The truest form of "camp," it offered every plot line, stereotype, and accessory reflective of the period's materialistic narcissism, and obsession with money. Set in Denver, Colorado, oil tycoon Blake Carrington, living in an ornate mansion, marries his secretary, the blond Krystle, who will have to battle with a slew of relatives and adversaries, including the former wife, Alexis. Joan Collins, resplendent in large shouldered couture, full length furs, sequins, and diamonds, playing an English socialite turned business woman, epitomized in Alexis Carrington the glitter, vulgarity, and rapaciousness that, combined with business acumen and newly declared feminist power, embodied in the Reagan White House.

6.28 Traders take charge: Lehman Brothers

The demise of Lehman Brothers on September 15, 2008, was lamented as the end of a noble 158-year history. The actual story is more complex and less distinguished. The managerial, strategic, and philosophical changes that took place at Lehman in 1984 epitomized the vast sea change that Wall Street was about to experience. Like so many firms, Lehman started as textile merchants, moving from Alabama to New York, and into banking in the 1860s.

In the 1930s, Herbert Lehman, who would become governor of New York, chose to have the firm become an investment bank, which stayed under family leadership until 1969. In 1973, management appointed Peter Peterson, a former Secretary of Commerce, as Chairman, as the firm modernized, expanded, and began to integrate trading activities in stocks and bonds. Merging with its former colleagues, Kuhn Loeb, in 1977, the firm grew under the joint management of the chairman and a president, Lewis Glucksman (a dangerous precedent which never works: consider John Reed–Sandy Weill and Robert Rubin–Vikram Pandit at Citigroup), seeking to integrate two entirely separate corporate and managerial styles. Ken Auletta, in *Greed and Glory on Wall Street, the Fall of the House of Lehman*, and Paul Ferris captured the personality differences, which moved from benign compatibility to antagonism within a year. The assumption was that an investment bank had to integrate underwriting with trading in securities, and the concern that the bank would lose "the mystique, the elegance, the legacy, the history whatever words you want to use to describe the essence of this business" (Ferris 1984: 101) had to be surpassed, in order to remain competitive. Within six months, Lewis Glucksman was named sole chairman.

> When Lew Glucksman arrived at Lehman Bros. Kuhn Loeb Inc. in 1962, the Ivy League-educated gentlemen investment bankers who ran the old-line firm looked down on his forte: trading securities. ... Today, Lew Glucksman is the top man at Lehman – and the personification of the forces reshaping investment banking. The once scorned traders are taking charge, giving Wall Street a more frenetic and hard-bitten mien.
>
> ("The Traders Take Charge" 1984)

In April 1984:

> The directors sold Lehman Brothers for $360 million to one of the new Wall Street conglomerates, Shearson/American Express, which had combined Shearson, Loeb and by acquiring Lehman combined insurance, property, credit cards, stockbroking, underwriting, becoming one of the first financial supermarkets ... The old Lehman ceased to exist.
>
> (Ferris 1984: 104)

American Express would divest of Lehman in 1994, where the firm would recoup its name under Richard Fuld, a protégé of Glucksman, until September 2008. Morgan Stanley (created in 1935 as the separate investment arm of Morgan), First Boston, and Salomon Brothers under John Gutfreund (the world's most renown government bond trader until his downfall in 1991), put star traders front and center in the push for profits and in the redefinition of investment banking. In *Business Week*, Gutfreund defined investment banking as "a business of creating ideas that move people to action. It is not just brute force. The market is much bigger than any one dealer" ("The Giants Retrench" 1989). The strength of Salomon through the 1980s was to seek out the best financing for complex deals, advising international clients, and using the firm's aggressiveness to undertake more deals and create interdependency between corporations, investment banks, and traders.

Joe Perella and Bruce Wasserstein at First Boston, specializing in mergers and acquisitions (which took hold in 1974 in a depressed environment, still considered in the 1980s as crass and unethical but necessary); the impersonal, disciplined traders at Merrill Lynch, specializing in equities, with the largest work force (45,000 across the United States); Bache which merged with Prudential Insurance in 1981, combining stockbrokerage, underwriting, and insurance to become sole rival to Merrill by the end of the 1980s; were all components of the reconstituted Wall Street culture. Trusts in all but name, these firms flourished under the scrutiny of the SEC and Glass-Steagall by maintaining separation of banking and speculation, but by engaging in all other cross over activities.

6.29 The road to deregulation

A pro-business Reagan White House moved toward "recent emphasis on deregulation and a move toward an open global economy [which]can be viewed as a reaction to overly stringent controls which are now judged as counterproductive to natural growth and discordant with international communications and electronic networks" (Beidleman 1987: 36).

> The quantum increase in trading of financial instruments of all kinds, and the speed at which information on which trading decisions are based is supplied to institutions and individuals everywhere, has emasculated governments' powers to regulate their domestic money and capital markets from behind barricades that were established to protect them from events elsewhere. As a result, entire financial systems, and the regulations wrapped around them, that were built in the depression era of the 1930s (in the case of the United States) and in the postwar period (as in Japan) are swept by change.
>
> (*Euromoney* 1984)

If "Reaganomics," and Wall Street were in search of a solution to the firewalls, Britain provided it on October 27, 1986 with "Big Bang," the all in one deregulation of the financial markets which abolished distinctions between stock jobbers and stockbrokers on the London Stock Exchange. The end of fixed commission charges, eliminating the elite closed network based on connections and social alliances became the cornerstone of Margaret Thatcher's reforms, setting off an economic boom and expansion in London as New York firms could now compete on a level playing field. Merrill, Salomon, Goldman, and

Morgan Stanley rapidly opened or expanded London offices. Low profile presence was replaced by extravagant architecture, décor and furnishings. Salomon's vast space near Buckingham Palace Road boasted "a space age escalator, ... To British clients coming off the street, the place was simply amusingly American" (Lewis 1989: 199). The *New York Times* assured its readership that "New Rivals Aside, Wall Street Still Calls the Tune" (Sterngold 1986) stressing that, although sharing the spotlight with "revitalized London and an emerging Tokyo as financial market centers but.... The American capital markets with headquarters in New York continue to be the largest by far and the envy of the rest of the world." John Gutfreund was quoted saying that "The style in the U.S. is that everything is negotiable. That is the source of our greatness" (Sterngold 1986).

"Big Bang" and the shift from banking to trading profit centers on Wall Street proved that, once capital was mobile, institutions would become equally mobile and create new profit generating units outside of regulatory barriers. Michael Lewis' scathing, witty portrayal of American traders in London and the Salomon culture emphasized the "rules do not apply to us" mindset:

> Never before have so many unskilled twenty four year olds made so much money in so little time as we did this decade in New York and London. There has never before been such a fantastic exception to the rule of the marketplace that one takes out no more than one puts in.
>
> (Lewis 1989: preface)

In the 1980s, banks still had separate units for corporate finance and investment banking, known as sales and trading. Trading was seen as the toughest, meanest and most respected part of this game of testosterone. The dream job was Wall Street analyst: "Forty percent of the thirteen hundred members of Yale's gradating class of 1986 applied to one investment, First Boston alone" (Lewis 1989: 24).

John Gutfreund, called, "The King of Wall Street" by *Business Week*, was the legendary chairman with his omnipresent expensive cigar, having sold Salomon in 1981 for US$40 million and earning the highest salary on Wall Street in 1986 – US$3.1 million. Gutfreund and John Meriwether, one of the best bond traders, were also inveterate poker players. Meriwether, known for his cool at winning and losing, was the King of the Game, hence the challenge for a matchup for the million dollar game of Liars Poker, in which each player attempts to fool the others about the serial numbers printed on the face of his dollar bill. "Each player seeks weakness, predictability and pattern in the others and seeks to avoid it in himself" (Lewis 1989: 17). "People like John Meriwether believed that Liar's Poker had a lot in common with bond trading" (Lewis 1989: 16). Comparing financial operations to high risk gambling made it sound dangerous, sophisticated and exciting, but it also subliminally accepted crossing lines between following the law and interpreting laws and regulations, in the name of profit.

6.30 Savings and loan debacle

If investment banks were doing battle abroad and at home, domestic commercial banks and credit institutions began to see deterioration in profits, which would steadily worsen following the savings and loan (S&L) debacle and the Crash of 1987. The failure of Home State Savings Bank in 1985 set in motion a chain reaction of S&L failures, 747 failed with charges of political manipulation in Washington. Starting from a simple premise that by allowing savings banks and thrifts (the backbone of the banking industry in the American heartland) to invest in commercial paper, they could increase their assets and benefit their communities. Complex legislation and different set of rules for various S&Ls gave some institutions that were supposed to protect the savings of their clients, the right to use insured deposits for non regulated ventures, which included junk bonds. As in 2008, banks persuaded noncreditworthy buyers to purchase mortgages, regardless of whether they could pay or not, by promising that the properties themselves would serve as ever increasing assets to cover their payments. West Coast bankers, led by Michael Milken, lured in small and medium sized thrifts to invest in below credit rating instruments, which were in fact high yield but very high risk. The government had to intervene in emergency measures under which Congress created the Financial Institutions Reform and Recovery Act and Trust Resolution in 1989, forcing taxpayers to pay the costs of shutting hundreds of insolvent savings and loans. The Resolution Trust Corporation, established under emergency provisions, set out the guidelines for the good bank/bad bank model which is being considered under the TARP and 2008 recovery plan.

6.31 The Japanese are coming

Since the mid-1980s, beneath the bravado, there was also fear and nervousness over the reach of Japan as global economic powerhouse. In 2008, the ambivalent relationship with China is a replay of the fear of Japan buying up America assets and cultural icons. In 1987, Japanese investors had put US$80 billion in Treasury bills and bonds, and nearly US$16 billion in real estate, including the Rockefeller Center, Tiffany, and Pebble Beach golf course. ("Rising Sun on Wall Street" 1987).

Although the system was revealing cracks, with problems in the Savings and Loans (S&Ls): "Treasury Now Favors Creation of Huge Banks," the Treasury decided that ""the Government should encourage creation of very large banks that could better compete with financial institutions in Japan and Europe" (Nash 1987). Alan Greenspan, nominated by Reagan to head the Federal Reserve, endorsed efforts by large industrial corporations to acquire banks, creating vast pools of capital, favoring mergers – although regulations were still officially in place. In 1986, GE bought Kidder Peabody and Goldman sold a minority interest to Sumitomo Bank of Japan. As foreign banks were allowed to expand, Hans Angermueller, vice chairman of Citicorp stated that "we need to get leaner, meaner and stronger. We don't do this by preserving the heartwarming idea that 14,000 banks are wonderful for our country" (Nash 1987).

In 1990, out of the ten largest banks in the world, seven were Japanese, two French and one, Deutsche Bank, was German. Citibank and Chase were no longer among the top ten. The United States was overbanked with 12, 300 banks. In the summer of 1991 it seemed that the only winners of the Wall Street debacle were bankruptcy lawyers: "Amid the Ruins a Ball for the 90s" (Cowan 1991) described 100 or so bankruptcy lawyers and investors feasting on shrimp and cocktails in the Hamptons.

Although American banks, led by Citi, J.P. Morgan, Goldman Sachs, Morgan Stanley, and Bank of American continued to perform very well in FOREX markets in 1991, currency markets, under the impetus of the new European Union and the upcoming currency harmonization, were about to undergo major changes.

6.32 The Crash of 1987

> You are on a roll, enjoy it while it lasts because it never does.
> (Wall Street, 1987, the older trader's advice to the young go-getter)

Tom Wolfe's novel, *Bonfire of the Vanities* (1987), Caryl Churchill's play *Serious Money* (1988), Oliver Stone's movie, *Wall Street* (1987), and Michael Lewis' journalistic expose, *Liar's Poker* (1989), came to personify the Zeitgeist of 1987 before and after the market Crash of October 1987. October 19, 1987 the Dow hit a peak of 2,700 and dropped 508 points, losing in one day 22 percent of its value. The reverberations were heard around the world as in the next two days: the CAC, FOOTSIE, DAX, AND NIKKEI crashed in turn, only to recover within six months.

Despite the scandals, merger and acquisition mania of the next decade would consolidate the role of investment banks as markets makers and breakers. Between 1987 and 1992, nearly 1,000 banks would close, due to the domino effect of the Crash and S&L failures, insolvency, mergers, and consolidation. Barely a year after the Crash, Kohlberg, Kravis, Roberts, led by Henry Kravis, star "raider," bought RJR Nabisco in a leveraged buyout for US$40 billion, following an acrimonious hostile takeover battle. Between 1987 and 1991, Wall Street was dominated by M&A activity, providing new life to investment banks as advisors to huge domestic and international mergers, and creating in its wake a new topology and terminology. Junk bonds, corporate raiders, green mail, and hostile takeovers were the instruments and tactics employed by a new class of financial agent.

The warning signs had been recorded since 1985 (just as the collapse of the housing bubble in summer 2008 had been predicted since 2006), the Crash of 1987 was the culmination of a slow erosion of confidence in the banking sector, fear of foreign buyouts led by Japan, and a deepening sense that underneath the veneer and glitz of the era, bankers and traders were crooks in tailored suits.

The Wall Street firm of Drexel Burnham, Lambert (with impeccable pedigree in investment banking), encouraged Milken to engage in "subprime" bond trading, earning him the name of "junk bond king," with a salary of US$500 million in

1986. However, the dealings at Drexel, Kidder Peabody, and even Goldman Sachs entailed the exchange of confidential information on prior knowledge of corporate transactions, mergers and buyouts which went under the heading of "insider trading," a practice specifically prohibited under the Security and Exchange Commission rules. The indictment and trial of California financier and Milken colleague, Ivan Boesky, in 1986 (he turned state witness and received a reduced sentence) became the first case of "insider trading" prosecution. The SEC (maligned in 2008), along with the US Attorney's office in New York under Rudy Giuliani, became the heroes of the three-year battle between Wall Street firms and the government. Giuliani, who would become Mayor of New York, conducted his investigations under media scrutiny and insisted that executives were arrested and hauled out of their offices in handcuffs, fueling the image of corrupt bankers being brought to justice by a working class, first generation son of Italian immigrants (like Ferdinand Pecora in 1933), underpaid public servant. Connie Bruck in *The Predator's Ball: The Inside Story of Drexel Burnham and the Rise of Junk Bond Raiders* (1989), and James Steward in *Den of Thieves* (1991), conveyed the cathartic dichotomy between Wall Street hubris and disregard for the average citizen with Washington's ethical rectitude. The subsequent indictments and convictions of insider traders, culminating in the trial and imprisonment of Milken in 1989, introduced the concepts of "white-collar crime," corporate defendants, and minimum security prisons into American financial culture.

Reactions abroad to the insider trading scandals were analogous to Watergate and the Monica Lewinsky political scandals, varying from amusement to incomprehension of American mores. Although insider trading interdictions were on the laws of most developed countries (Mexico had some of strictest laws on the books), it was seen as almost impossible to enforce or prosecute. In most societies, a much smaller and homogenous financial elite, closely interconnected by family and social ties, was naturally assumed to partake of the same sources of information. Elevating political and sexual indiscretions to the level of impeachment, or financial indiscretion to the level of criminal behavior worthy of conviction is unique to the paradoxical American ethos of Puritan morality and free market amorality.

The 1991 movie *Other People's Money* set up a visual parable of thesis and antithesis of corporate mergers: Gregory Peck, the tall elegant, soft spoken, iconic, all-American hero, plays a New England family-run factory owner, the backbone of small town values pitted against Danny de Vito, short, tough, megalomaniacal, brilliant, New York tycoon, who decides to buy out the company, dissect, and restructure the products and management, and provide outstanding dividends to the shareholders, who then, ideally, can help resurrect the town's dying economy.

6.33 Masters of the Universe

In the global game of financial chess, bond trading was much more than a financial transaction in the 1980s. Tom Wolfe's work meticulously recorded this transformation as the sedate, profitable, but obscure bond market exploded in the 1980s: "Markets of all sorts became heaving crap shoots: gold, silver, copper, currencies, bank certificates, corporate notes – even bonds" (Wolfe 1987: 61). McCoy, top bond salesman, has the sophistication, knowhow and contacts to deal in complex international bond issues such as:

> The Giscard, French gold backed bond ... The deal would bring Pierce and Pierce a 1 percent commission up front – 6 million – for conceiving the idea and risking the capital. Sherman's share including commissions, bonuses, profit sharing and resale fees would come to about 1.75 million.
>
> (Wolfe 1987: 64)

Michael Lewis in Liars Poker establishes the difference:

> A commercial banker wasn't any more a troublemaker than Dagwood Bumstead. He had a wife, a station wagon, 2.2 children and a dog that brought him his slippers when he returned home from work at six ... The investment banker was a breed apart, a member of a master race of deal makers.
>
> (Lewis 1989: 27)

Wolfe's hilarious, kinetic Bildungsroman takes the hero, Sherman McCoy, from the heights of Park Avenue and Wall Street wealth and prestige through the netherworld of New York's crime ridden outer boroughs, corrupt judiciary and political machine, and through the press to a state of quasi redemption for his sins of perceived invulnerability, arrogance and greed. Wall Street was frenetic, viciously competitive, juvenile in its extreme vulgarity, sexism and racism, demanding instant gratification as fortunes were made and lost almost instantaneously. But it also meant that there was a massive flow of liquidity which translated into vast consumption, consumer spending and generation of income. Michael Lewis documented behavioral shifts, as firm loyalty, a key component of the banking profession, vanished in the name of profits. Turnover was enormous as profits alone counted and the pressures were infernal: "If he could make millions of dollars come out of those phones, he became the most revered of all species: a Big Swinging Dick" (Lewis 1989: 53).

Tom Wolfe coined the phrase "Masters of the Universe," which would embody the power; Oliver Stone's Wall Street would create the character, Gordon Gekko, who in a parody of Ivan Boesky says, "Greed is good, greed is right, greed works." The phrase and the character has become a cliché, but in 1985, Ivan Boesky was so respected that he was invited to deliver the Commencement Address at University of California, Berkeley where he made similar comments.

> The "Masters of the Universe" were a set of lurid, rapacious plastic dolls that his otherwise perfect daughter liked to play with ... Yet one fine day, in a fit of euphoria, after he had picked up the telephone and taken an order for

zero coupon bonds that had brought him a 50,000 commission, just like that, this very phrase had bubbled up into his brain. On Wall Street he and a few others –how many – three hundred, four hundred, five hundred? – had become precisely that ... Masters of the Universe. There was ... no limit whatsoever!

(Wolfe 1987: 12)

Sherman McCoy, educated at Buckley, St Paul and Yale, part of "old line well fixed Protestant families in Manhattan" (Wolfe 1987: 276), sees himself as venerable old money, contemptuous of his wife's part Jewish and mid-Western academic background, but compared to his neighbor, Pollard Browning, law partner at a top law firm and descendent of the true blue Knickerbockers, he was the parvenu. The levels of ostentation and pseudo aristocratic décor and furnishings in vogue set the stage for the immense manors, yachts, and lavish art collections of the 2006 hedge fund managers: McCoy's bond trading room filled with Yale, Harvard, and Stanford graduates who have been promised: "By age 30, 500,000 – and that sum had the taint of the mediocre" (Wolfe 1987: 59). Wolfe, like Lewis, emphasizes American obsession with faux British architecture, decor, and mythologized life style, from the pseudo gothic buildings on the Yale campus to New York's exclusive private clubs to Ralph Lauren's country squire fashion empire.

In every period of great prosperity, there is an underlying sense of insecurity in which wealth has to be reaffirmed by taking on the trappings of English or French taste. Russian oligarchs in the 1990s reverted to the excesses of pre-Revolution Russia, the Chinese in the 2008 Olympics, to prove economic ascendancy, presented the opulence of imperial power, France is imbued in the glory of its heritage, but American wealth in the first Gilded Age, the 1980s, and the second Gilded Age very rarely seeks authenticity but rather perfect reproductions of a mythical foreign past. In times of crisis, the psycho historical reversion to Populism brings back the elements of American mythology invoking apple pie, the great outdoors, self-made heroes and "true grit."

Oliver Stone's *Wall Street*, which reappears on television and in theaters in every period of financial turmoil, is in discussion for a sequel in the aftermath of 2008. The movie's appeal was not only the portrayal of the ultimate "raider," Gordon Gekko, played by Michael Douglas, the "corporate" hero of the era (complicit victim of female sexual and corporate predators), but the juxtaposition of Wall Street and populist prototypes. The young trader, enthralled by Gekko, is the son of a failing airline's honest union leader who wants to salvage his company. Betrayed by his son, who uses insider knowledge to offer the company for dissection and liquidation to the "raider," he will be redeemed (after a heart attack), as the young trader is caught and convicted of insider trading, and turns government witness to implicate Gekko. The Faustian bargain is absolved and redeemed as the trader learns true values and has to relinquish all the perks of ill gained wealth and power. The trader, played by Charlie Sheen, exposes all the corruptive force of new found wealth, the luxury apartment, art work, glamorous girlfriend, and glittering life style. Gekko's spurts of wisdom between deal making: "I am a liberator of companies," "it's a zero sum game," "illusion becomes real," "it's a free market," "no nobility in poverty," and "money never sleeps" become the totemic code words of a culture, steeped in self illusion, before the fall.

In London, a month after the crash and in January 1988 in New York, Caryl Churchill's vicious caricature of post Big Bang capitalism, *Serious Money*, was a huge success. Frank Rich, drama critic of the *New York Times*, titled his review "The New Greed Takes Center Stage," Depicting the antics of traders and raiders as vulgar money grubbing Thatcherites, who welcome the assault of American money, the message is anti-capitalist as the "old generation of financial aristocrats is being devoured by the new generation of sharks" (Rich 1987).

The crash was over; the market had not collapsed, despite the unique gravity of the drop in value. Optimism returned very quickly, Leonard Silk wrote "Is Wall Street as Bad as It Is Painted?"

> And crowds of money people from the City of London and Wall Street have flocked to see themselves pilloried in Serious Money. Wall Street is a hit in movie houses all over the country and Bonfire rides high on the best seller list. The stock market and its fall was the story of the year for all those, inside and outside Wall Street who sincerely desire to be rich or richer.
>
> (Silk 1988)

6.34 Lessons learned

Michael Lewis met with John Gutfreund again in 2008, Gutfreund's rage at the scathing attack in Lewis' book had not diminished, but Lewis had mellowed, and understood that

> The public lynching of Gutfreund and junk bond king Michael Milken were excuses not to deal with the disturbing forces underpinning their rise. Ditto the cleaning up of Wall Street's trading culture. The surface rippled, but down below in the depths the bonus pool remained undisturbed.
>
> (Lewis 2008–2009)

Wall Street was forced to adapt to societal changes in the late 1980s and 1990s, aided by technology which depersonalized and suppressed some of the raucousness and demeaning behavior of the trading rooms. Firms, under threat of lawsuits from female employees and under political pressure from African American politician and civil rights leader Jesse Jackson's Rainbow Coalition, and other groups, began to superficially address problems of discrimination and gender bias. Management followed all the rules, but by the mid-1990s, the dotcom bubble and a renewed bull market, traders across Wall Street remained largely young, white, and male. There was more diversity among bankers, as women attained senior positions but progress was slow and often painfully won (see Chapter 2).

In 2007, Dana Vachon, a former Morgan Stanley broker, wrote a well received first novel reprising *Liars Poker* and *Bonfire of the Vanities*. *Mergers and Acquisitions* (2007) was a ribald, morbid satire of an investment bank, no longer on Wall Street but on Park Avenue (where many banks had migrated after the commercial real estate collapse in the mid-1990s), specializing in mergers and acquisitions:

> On each floor teams of men and women do everything possible to make money, and when they are done, they go on to do everything possible to take credit for the money made. This is how you prosper as a banker, and that is why a career in banking beats out even corporate law as the most risk free way to make a fortune. ... The lure of easy money was enough to make even privileged young men and women afraid to complain as we sat, day after day in the windowless basement, not far from the nuclear-bombproof vault where the banks' gold reserves had been kept in the sixties, spending our first fall after college graduation puzzling over financial equations and corporate earnings statements.
>
> (Vachon 2007: 19)

The composition of the recruits from the Ivy League and Wharton is much more diverse, with foreigners from India, Brazil, and Japan, as well as true WASPs, but the same ethos prevails as the work load and pressure can cause fatalities, older managers are sadistic, alcohol, drug use and failed relationships abound, salaries are enormous, and the firm proves its competitive edge. The risks and rewards are identical to those in previous boom years under other headings. Vachon illustrates to what degree women and history had not civilized Wall Street, but rather how embedded norms of behavior coarsened, ingested, and destroyed all who dare enter.

6.35 Too big to fail

Coinciding with the cataclysmic global changes in 1989–1991, the American financial sector felt vulnerable and at a loss for solutions. Following the market Crash of October 1989, caused in part by the collapse of Drexel Burnham Lambert and its subsequent demise in February 1990, large banks sought to downsize and return to their regional roots: "The Giants Retrench, After Major Losses Banks No Longer Want to Be Money Centers but Regionals" *Business Week* 1989). Bank of America returned to California; Citicorp, already weakened, sold its trademark building in Manhattan to a Japanese insurer and relocated its retail headquarters to a rundown area in the outer borough of Queens; and Chase moved back office operations to Brooklyn.

The largest commercial banks were losing lenders and deposits, as corporations discovered they could save money by issuing securities rather than borrowing from banks. The stock market had recovered and money flowed out of banks and into stocks and mutual funds. This was brought into focus in the liquidity crisis at Citicorp in 1991, which required an injection of foreign capital from the Saudis for US$1.8 billion. The *New York Times* ran a long article under the banner "The Risks and Benefits of Letting Seriously Ill Banks Die" (Nasar 1991). Although top economist, Milton Friedman, and banking scholar, George Kaufmann, felt that bank failures were not necessarily destructive to the economy, the concern was that there could be "silent runs" with flight of capital from weak to strong banks. The principle would also come under the rubrique of "too big to save," enounced by William White, whose concern was whether imposing on the taxpayers the burden of rescuing huge institutions was cost effective. In 2009 this dilemma is again on the table for federal regulators and politicians to resolve.

The "too big to fail" principle advocated by Greenspan, first coined in 1991 meant that if necessary the government could intervene to avoid contagion and asymmetrical shocks to the system as a whole. Harmonization and reforms in clearing house procedures following the Herstatt failure in 1974, led to greater awareness of global contagion. In 1991, the combination of market incertitude and the need to protect the financial industry promoted the sentiment that American banks had to streamline, merge, and achieve domestic consolidation in order to regain competitiveness. There were still 12,000 banks, where Germany, France, Britain, and Japan all together had 1,240, and still were judged over-banked. Bigger banks meant loss of client relationships and risk of loss of jobs but efficiency and regaining profitability was deemed more important: "Bigger Banks Are Better" (Editorial, *New York Times* 1991).

The era of large banks and mergers had begun: the July 16, 1991, *New York Times* headline on page one was "Big Bank Merger to Join Chemical, Manufacturers" (Quint 1991). The largest bank merger, orchestrated by Chairman and Chief Executive Officer of Manufacturers Hanover, John McGillicuddy, between Manufactures Hanover Corporation and the Chemical Banking Corporation in 1991, became a way to save the banks reeling from heavy exposure to bad loans in real estate at Chemical and to emerging markets at Manufacturers.

6.36 End of Glass-Steagall

> In Largest Deal Ever, Citicorp Plans Merger With Travelers Group: For two decades Washington has tried and failed to update the Depression-era laws governing the rapidly changing financial services industry. Today the industry took matters in its own hands.
>
> (Stevenson 1998: 1)

The transaction, at US$70 billion in stock, pushed the Dow for the first time over 9,000. It created a behemoth with a new logo: Citigroup with a market capitalization of US$166 billion, 161,700 employees, and 100 million customers in 100 countries. Before 1999, First Union–Core State; Nations Bank–Bank of America; BancOne–First Chicago; and Norwest–Wells Fargo had merged. The era of mega banks and frenetic merger and acquisition activity had returned.

The *Financial Times* editorial "Wall Street's Unreal World," on April 7, 1998, was the sole voice expressing qualms: "The two merging institutions have undeniable strengths. But it could plausibly be argued that these strengths are more likely to be diluted than enhanced by a merger." The editorial focuses on the joint leadership under a chairman and chief executive, whose "motivation [is] to engage in diversification to enhance stock performance rather than interests of investors."

These concerns would prove unfortunately prescient and accurate, as proven in the immediate failure of joint management, with the departure of John Reed within two years; the inability of the bank to maintain profitability and cohesion without Sandy Weill, who departed as CEO in 2005; the inability to maintain a clear international strategy; a lack of oversight over bad loans in the housing market; internal dissension; and poor management under Chuck Prince, leading to the need for a US$25billion bailout from the government in December 2008.

Sandy Weill, started his career at Shearson Loeb, became president of American Express when it merged, bought Travelers in 1993, and began the trajectory toward Citibank by acquiring Salomon for US$9 billion in stock, in September 1997. Travelers, which specialized in insurance and mutual funds, owned the Smith Barney brokerage, and by acquiring Salomon it rivaled Merrill and Citicorp.

> "He's decided to build the greatest financial services company in the history of this country and the history of the world," said Joseph A. Califano Jr., a member of the Travelers board and Secretary of Health Education and Welfare in the Carter Administration.
>
> (Truell 1997)

Weill's decision to push through the Travelers Citicorp merger singlehandedly brought down the firewalls which had been weakening, but could not withstand the market pressure. Within a year the Gramm-Leach-Bliley Act was passed in 1999. Alan Greenspan defended the decision in 2007, saying: "Fortunately, Gramm-Leach-Bliley, which restored sorely needed flexibility to the financial industries, is no aberration. Awareness of the detrimental effects of excessive regulation and the need for economic adaptability has advanced substantially in recent years. We dare not go back" (Greenspan 2007: 376).

6.37 Long-Term Capital Management: missed warning

In 1998, America, enthralled with President Clinton's personal problems, barely cognizant of the dangers posed by the Asian currency crisis and the warnings issued by the British on Taliban activity in Afghanistan, enjoyed complacency and prosperity. In this environment it was assumed that American technology could "go where no man had gone before," including conquering the volatility and incertitude of markets.

Long Term Capital Management, a hedge fund established by two Nobel laureate economists (1997), Robert Merton and Myron Sholes, and led by former Salomon trader John Meriwether, based its success on sophisticated mathematical models, formulated on the absolute belief that risk could be quantified, that markets were inherently efficient, and that liquidity would always be available. As discussed in Roger Lowenstein's *When Genius failed: The Rise and Fall of Long Term Capital Management* (2000), the premise was that investors acted rationally and that extreme market shifts were infinitesimal. Oblivious to the political reality and the irrationality of currency fluctuations in poorly run fledgling democracies in Asia and Russia, they specialized in high risk arbitrage deals in US, Japanese, and European bonds. Leveraged to banks for US$120 million, and carrying US$1.25 trillion in financial derivatives and other exotic instruments, they were caught completely off guard by the Russian default. On August 17, 1997, Russia devalued the ruble, defaulting on Treasury bills. The International Monetary Fund (IMF) refused a bailout, causing investor panic. Within four days, LTCM lost US$553 million, and by the end of August the amount reached US$1.9 billion in assets and 45 percent of their capital. "Practically overnight, its stunned founders watched the nearly $5 billion in capital they'd built up drain away" (Greenspan 2007: 194). With the blessing of Greenspan, the New York Federal Reserve, under William McDonough, repeated the Barings (1890) and J.P. Morgan (1907) scenario, bringing together J.P. Morgan, Merrill, Morgan Stanley, Goldman, Salomon Smith Barney, Bankers Trust, Chase, Lehman, Credit Suisse, Deutsche, Barclays Capital, UBS, Société Générale, and Paribas to form a consortium creating a bailout package of US$3.6 billion. The LTCM case did not affect taxpayers, but the headlines, "Seeing A Fund as Too Big to Fail, New York Fed Assists its Bailout" (Greenspan 2007: 194), gave the impression that the Federal Reserve had decided to help out a group of careless millionaires at the public's expense. LTCM's inability to integrate geopolitical factors into its risk assessment, a total disregard of the potential ramifications if the models failed, and hubris in trying to corral market volatility, counter to 250 years of crashes and panics, should have served as a warning.

6.38 Irrational exuberance

> But how do we know when irrational exuberance has unduly escalated asset values, which they become subject to unexpected and prolonged contractions as they have in Japan over the past decade?
>
> (Greenspan 2007: 177)

Greenspan went on to explain that, although the impact of 1987 had been fairly mild, there were larger risks in an unfettered and bubble-prone economy. The message became his catch phrase, but the subtle warning was ignored by the expansion, and huge increase of participants in a seemingly permanent bull market. Under Secretary of the Treasury, Robert Rubin, the economy was booming, the deficit was reduced, exports had increased, and the world at large was relatively at peace, engendering unequaled faith and enthusiasm in the market. In reality, the Peso Crisis of 1995, the start of the Asian currency crisis in fall 1997, and endemic internal instability in Russia under Yeltsin, revealed cracks in the facade of democratic market economies in emerging markets.

American capitalism was very appealing, but hardly applicable to most transitional and developing economies. The 1990s saw two interlinked phenomena which fueled this sense of euphoria: day traders and the financial media.

A small financial network created in 1989 at CNBC, an affiliate of NBC, decided to expand programming in 1993, bringing in new anchors and direct reports from Wall Street, including on site coverage of the NYSE. A young New York financial reporter became anchorwoman, covering the afternoon on the floor of the Exchange. Photogenic, extremely knowledgeable, and assertive, Maria Bartiromo became the face of the new generation of financial journalism. Nicknamed "The Money Honey," she reversed all sexual innuendo in the term, and in 2007 trademarked the term. CNBC increased coverage, adding diverse reporters offering short segments of information, analysis, and commentary, with a constant rolling ticker with all exchanges and bourses indicators. In alliance with Dow-Jones in 1997, the program became one of the most watched in offices and homes. In 2002–2005, two conservative analysts Jim Kramer, a former Harvard educated lawyer, and Lawrence Kudlow, a journalist, joined forces to present loud, rambunctious critique of the economy. By 2005, Jim Kramer's "Mad Money" in the evening, offered vaudeville style spectacle. Money had always been entertaining, but now money was entertainment.

Accessibility, consumer friendly financial television, and increased availability and price reductions in computers synchronized with the dotcom bubble:

> August 9, 1995, will go down in history as the day the dotcom boom was born. What set it off was the initial public offering of Netscape, a tiny, two year old software maker in Silicon Valley that had almost no revenues and not a penny of profits.
>
> (Greenspan 2007: 164)

The stock skyrocketed on its first day of trading and "the Internet gold rush was on" (Greenspan 2007: 164). The explosion of IPOs by small and medium sized technology firms had all the right criteria in place: young, well educated, computer literate entrepreneurs rushing to California, home of Microsoft, to find venture capital (bypassing the cumbersome processes of traditional bank loans), listing their stocks on the invigorated NASDAQ exchange, and watching prices rise exponentially, as new investors poured into the market, looking for the next opportunity. There was one problem: very few of these start-ups had an actual product, based on the assumption that any product or set of services could be offered on line, very few had an actual supply and distribution chain to meet demand. The bubble lasted until March 2000 when the market peaked at over 11,000 and NASDAQ, which had listed most of the dotcoms, reached over 5,000. Suddenly, the economy and the enthusiasm for innovative enterprises sharply contracted. Computerized trading at home, moving from stocks to currencies to bonds, provided with too much information and too little knowledge, began to look less appealing and far more risky as the dotcoms collapsed and the market became volatile through 2001.

6.39 The bubble and the analysts

When the bubble burst in 2000, millions of small investors lost a substantial part of their earnings in the market. Unlike 2008, this did not affect the large banks, which actually increased their profitability, and nor did it impact the economy at large. It did however reveal the role of unscrupulous analysts, who worked in collusion with banks and corporations:

> They gave credibility to the overvalued markets to millions of new investors who were largely unaware that the analysts had taken on a more conflicted role of recommending stocks and helping their firms win the lucrative investment banking deals from the same companies that helped pay their own outsized salaries.
>
> (Gasparino 2005: 8)

The 1990s boom had benefited average people "barbers, mechanics and house-wives who became millionaires overnight by investing in technology stocks and mutual funds pumped during the bubble. Now that the party was over, Spitzer became intrigued by the victims of Wall Street's unabashed bullishness" (Gasparino 2005: 216). In the investigations and indictments in 2003, as in 1987, the culprits were the Wall Street insiders, experts in technology and communication industry, Jack Grubman, Henry Blodget, and Mary Meeker, propagating tainted information to inflate stock prices, regardless of the true value of the companies, regulators paying too little attention, and the heroes were civil servants, like US Attorney Elliott Spitzer, who prosecuted Wall Street, becoming a champion of the average investor (before his own downfall while governor of New York in 2008). Although there should have growing wariness of Wall Street, the public continued to look for the next opportunity in an amazingly resilient market. The next sure investment would be concrete, traditional and safe: the housing bubble had begun.

6.40 Wall Street and 9/11

On September 11, 2001, in attacking the World Trade Center, Osama Bin Laden's knowledge of American finance and financial culture was accurate, but far too literal. The assumption was that simultaneous attacks on the Pentagon and the World Trade Center would destroy American military and financial might. The reality is that the World Trade Center was not the center of world trade nor of United States financial power, although tragically some of the greatest losses incurred in brokerage companies on the top floors. However, the press, media or history will judge Richard Grasso, then Chairman of the New York Stock Exchange or Alan Greenspan, Chairman of the Federal Reserve, in September 2001, their immediate responses convinced global markets of the strength of the dollar and the stability of the Federal Reserve, and more dramatically, by reopening the NYSE on Monday September 17, manifested the power, resilience and courage of American finance. Almost all of the 3,000 victims were workers of all social and ethnic backgrounds, employed in the Towers at all levels of service and financial industries.

On that Monday, within a few hours, in the most chaotic conditions, with almost all phone lines down, horrid dust, stench and debris, sirens wailing and the area under military lockdown, the traders on the floor, who had all lost colleagues and friends, stabilized global markets as the CAC, DAX, and FOOTSIE responded, and the initial losses of 600 points began to be recouped. The performance of the NYSE proved that the depth, liquidity, fundamental strength and confidence had survived. The impact of 9/11 on American politics, economic strategy, civil society and culture has long lasting implications, but Wall Street came back with a vengeance. Mayor Giuliani and Mayor Bloomberg's injunctions to New Yorkers to spend, shop, rebuild, and continue with their lives has often been interpreted as callous and overly materialistic, but it was also fundamentally healthy and in adherence with American spirit of resurgence and dynamism. Physically Wall Street seems the same, yet the concrete barriers, extremely tight security required to enter the Exchange, Federal Reserve or most banks, are constant reminders. The site of the World Trade towers remains a construction site; the surrounding area reveals entirely new neighborhoods, hotels, and office buildings near the Hudson River.

6.41 Second Gilded Age

In 2007, in an interview in the *New York Times*, Sandy Weill said that "the whole world is moving to the American model of free enterprise and capital markets" (Uchitelle 2007). By the late 1990s, and in the endless binge before the Crash of 2008, finance, money, transactional culture regressed back to the elite, the initiated, the select few, after having reached a level of democratization in the mid- to end twentieth century.

Mutual funds (US$8 trillion mutual fund industry, with 95 million bond holders, the nation's largest financial institution) based on the contractual relationships between financier and investor to protect assets, were replaced by the allure of hedge funds, "under the hedge" unregulated, esoteric, almost alchemic activity between financier, banks, and markets to strip and speculate in assets. The American model, applied globally led the expansion as "unfettered finance is fast reshaping the global economy" (Wolfe 2007). Although dictated by a new set of circumstances, globalization, technology, computing, communications, 24-hour trading activity, creation of complex instruments, and short-term turnover rather than long-term custody of assets, "the new banking system is dominated by institutions that trade in assets rather than hold them for long periods on their own books" (Wolf 2007). By 2005, equity securities were six times greater than bank deposits in global financial assets. Private equity companies, hedge funds are perfect examples of pure capitalism, where the purpose of money is above all to make money.

Proud of the legacy of ruthless, innovative, trans-border European, British, and post-Civil War American bankers and financiers, moneymen in 2007 designated themselves as "The Richest of the Rich, Proud of a New Gilded Age" (Uchitelle 2007). The press, media, and politicians tried to emphasize the vast discrepancies in salaries, income distribution, and the gap between labor and management reminiscent of the 1910–1917 period, and late 1920s, but quasi populist rhetoric was a thin veneer to cover or justify the fascination, envy, glee and pride in the accomplishments of the wealthiest. In 1918, the largest fortunes belonged to Rockefeller in oil, Frick in coal and steel, and Carnegie in banking. In 2008, the largest American fortunes belonged to Gates in technology software, Buffet in investments, Adelson in hotels and casinos. However, globally the wealthiest are still in the traditional sectors of energy and finance.

In the midst of the real estate and hedge fund bubble, Conde Nast launched a new business publication, in 2007, *Portfolio*, featuring articles on Greenwich Connecticut (home of so many hedge fund billionaires that it was nicknamed Hedgistan), and an amusing portrayal of their culture by Tom Wolfe. Rupert Murdoch, after buying out the *Wall Street Journal*, launched a new FOX Business Channel, where afternoon market analysis took place in the bar of the Waldorf Astoria, provided by heavily made up anchorwomen in tight, low cut, bright dresses, and flashy baubles. It seemed as if *Dynasty* and the financial channel had merged to appeal to Middle America, the core audience of FOX television. ABC had a new show, *Dirty Sexy Money*, and Donald Trump planned to come out with his own publication. These gossipy, superficial publications and shows professed to simultaneously glamorize and simplify wealth, the market, corporate deals, financial instruments, and operations by focusing on the individuals, the new buccaneers as well as the old dynasties. James Traub, in the *New York Times* defined as "a new phenomenon in New York and no doubt elsewhere: the merely well-to-do's envy of the rich." According to Traub, the very rich "had their money as of right, by virtue of their birth into a self enclosed and self regarding class (Traub 2007). The wall between classes was almost impermeable." In the new, or second Gilded Age, the amounts of money, visibility, and impact of exceptionally wealthy individuals reached new levels across the globe, by vast purchasing power, consumption and excess. The American model became the aspirational standard setter for the bankers in the Putin years (Martinuzzi and Prince 2007 "Moscow bankers get $7 Million Payday, Double New York Average"), and billionaires in Hong Kong, Shanghai, and Dubai.

The art market, art fairs, old line auction houses, and galleries became the beneficiaries of these new fortunes quest for investment and status. America celebrated what the art world critic Jerry Salz named "monism," in discussing whether the art market is defined by its monetary value and whether the role of the market directly impacts on art criticism. It was often unclear whether the most elitist of pursuits, the buying and selling of art had been transformed into a commodities exchange of art as one more luxury good? Was art marketed rather than critiqued, or can the two be compatible? In a constant quest for novelty, provocation, and art as status, Jeffrey Koons, Damien Hirst, Cindy Sherman, and Terrance Koh could demand and receive higher prices for their conceptual, provocative "art" than Old Master prints. Commentators and participants in this glut of riches, Tom Otterness' large bronze statue of a Plutocrat devouring industry and workers, sitting on a gold bag of cash ("The Public Unconscious" exhibit, October–November 2007); Jeffrey Koons' gigantic caramelized puppies, balloon dogs and gift ribbons on the roof of the Metropolitan Museum; and Damien Hirst's conclusive statement of the period: the diamond encrusted skull, were the modern masters of this already bypassed era.

Yet once the financial crisis hit, auction houses had to decide whether art would have to serve as a security investment, like gold and jewels, rather than a vanity investment. Wall Street's direct linkage to the art world was revealed in the *Wall Street Journal*, which reporting that, as early as July 2008, Richard Fuld, while assuring investors that Lehman was sound, was selling "a group of 16 post-war drawings owned by the Fulds that were quietly put up for sale by Christies last month, including Gorky, de Kooning" (Craig and Crow 2008).

6.42 The lure of hedge funds

In the wake of the Bernard Madoff scandal, the interconnections between unregulated hedge funds, private equity firms, and major global banks has revealed the degree of opacity, lack of risk management and potential fraudulent activity. As hedge funds face increased calls for redemptions, will there be additional LTCM fiascos?

Just two years before the meltdown of large bank and hedge fund portfolios in 2007–2008, Roger Lowenstein could write in the *New York Times*:

> Markets were less worrisome, when they were simpler, when they confronted us with fewer choices; hedge funds seem an embodiment of complexity. Also the last near market meltdown was occasioned by the implosion in 1998 of Long Term Capital Management, a Greenwich, Conn. bond trading firm that was, indeed, a hedge fund. That is hardly reason to indict such funds for the next collapse.
>
> (Lowenstein 2005)

Created in 1949:

> Today a hedge fund is whatever one wants it to be, any combination of long positions and short, bonds and stocks, unleveraged and leveraged (often by ratios that would curl one's hair) relying upon sophisticated quantitative methodologies or basic security analysis and in some cases following merger arbitrage strategies or "event driven" strategies. As a result, risk levels vary from extremely low to truly awesome.
>
> (Bogle 2005: 121)

Basically "hedge funds are privately owned financial companies that raise cash from very wealthy individuals and institutional investors, such as pension funds and charitable endowments" (Cassidy 2007). However as they are largely unregulated, their number grew from 500 to about 10,000. The formula, based on fees of 2 percent of the amount invested, and 20 percent of any profits generated, allowed managers to earn more than US$1 billion. At its peak, seen as another feat of American financial ingenuity, hedge funds promised the rich a sure fire way to get richer. By 2009, they appear vulnerable and liable to investigation and closure.

6.43 American wealth distribution

According to a *New York Times* survey in 2006, between 1980 and 2004, the annual salaries of chief executive officers (CEOs) increased 1,147 percent, and workers salaries 136 percent! These outrageous statistics barely caused a ripple when the doubling of stock market valuation between 1997 and 2000 brought a shift from stock owners to stock traders, which seemed to validate excessive CEO salaries and executive perks. As each financial scandal and subsequent crash shows, the financial community is rarely, if ever, able to be its own gatekeeper as long as profits flow. After Enron and the analyst scandals of 2003, there was a call for a re-evaluation of the role of investment banks in the biggest deals, the role of analysts and the closed incestuous relationship between managers of mutual funds and retirement plans and large financial conglomerates. The question becomes who are the actual owners and who has the most power to influence decisions that affect the shareholders. By 1998, the 13,000 richest families in America had as much income as the 20 million poorest households, their income 300 times more than the average family. In 1985, there were 13 billionaires in the United States, in 2008 there were 1,000. America has nine million millionaires, and a new term has emerged, "middle class millionaires." It is not that they lack for anything, but in comparison to those richer, and in order to maintain a lifestyle seen as worthy of their work, effort or status, they do not see themselves as very rich.

For the past decade the average salary in America is about US$30,000. The paradox is that for the world at large this is a princely sum ($16,000 a year is considered middle class in India), so that the poor in America are indeed wealthier than most of the world, but they are also absurdly less well off by a ratio of 1: 450 to their wealthiest co-citizens (Faber 2008).

In 2009, the United States, despite the recession of 2008, is far richer than in any previous decade since World War II, yet the wage differentials are getter larger. Where the salary differential between a CEO and a worker is 10–15 percent in Nordic countries, 25 percent in Germany, 40 percent in France, the figure in the United States in 2007 was nearly 425 percent!

6.44 Financial patriotism

John Bogle, Wilbur Ross, Peter Peterson, Warren Buffet, John Gutfreund, Alan Greenspan, Robert Rubin, and Sandy Weill epitomize American financial culture, in all its glory and all its squalor. Unabashed in their belief in the ability of the individual to become wealthy, to increase profits of their institutions, and in turn to improve their community and their country, these men (sadly in 2009 the old guard remains very much male) express a type of quintessential American financial patriotism. They understand and suffer the role of government when and wherever absolutely necessary, but they are unabashed advocates of free markets, unfettered but respectful of its own code of behavior. Direct descendents of the "robber barons," "plutocrats," and "capitalists," of other eras, they are convinced of their generosity to their community and their business acumen in protecting their own interests, removing stigma, and moral interdiction from financial activity. They still judge themselves as worthy citizens and human beings, true Calvinists, regardless of their background or faith. In spring 2008, a conversation with Gutfreund, recognizable and respected in Manhattan, showed a judicious cautious manner. Judgmental, astute and critical of every little detail, he expressed doubts about the monopolization of financial sectors following the dissolution of Glass-Steagall, opening the door for the government to step in and return once problems recurred. He firmly believed that the dollar would bounce back, mergers would resume, and presciently noted that Citibank was too big and no one seemed to be in charge. He urged greater caution and concern combined with a warning that crises come and go and as always the market recovers.

Endowed with immense hubris, generators of great wealth are fundamentally pragmatists, desirous to promote their institutions yet, when necessary, willing to accept the loss of their firms and the opportunities to start anew.

> Artists, sportsmen surgeons, plumbers and the rest of us have secret voices of doubt, inner reservations, but if you go to work with money, and make money, you can be proved right in the most inhumanly pure way. This is why people who have succeeded in the world of money tend to have such a high opinion of themselves.
>
> (Lanchester 2008)

Scapegoats and objects of derision in cartoons, films, media, and the press, American money men feed into the crux of anti-American propaganda, for at the heart they really like money. T. Boone Pickens, Texas oilman, now advocate for wind energy, interviewed on CNBC when asked about his plan to build the worlds largest wind farm: "Is it about money or the environment" answered: "Money! First thing it's about money!"

Money Should be Fun by *New Yorker* cartoonist of societal foibles, William Hamilton (1980) centered on money in this totally relevant book of cartoons, capturing the middle aged, heavy set, beautifully tailored, arrogant, slightly lecherous, sedentary banker in the clubs, restaurants, boardrooms, and cocktail parties of New York: The man on a date discussing life with an elegant woman: "Oh, if I hadn't got into stocks, I suppose I might have got into something completely different. Bonds, maybe warrants, options, futures ... who knows" (Hamilton 1980: 68).

In early 2009, the Morgan Library, a museum on the site of J.P. Morgan's mansion, incorporating the original study, library and reading room with its magnificent Florentine marble pillars, Renaissance and medieval works of art and collection of first editions, had a show entitled "On the Money: Cartoons from the New Yorker," including the Mick Stevens drawing of a former Wall Street type with the caption, "I was at a high powered investment firm for seven years and a high powered penal institution for a year and a half" (Stevens 1997). The Museum of Financial History, in its role as archivist of Wall Street "hedging its bets, has already started collecting mementos from the current crisis."

Conclusion

The economic enemy of capitalism has always been its own self generated dynamics, not the presence of an alternative economic system.

(Heilbroner 1989)

The relations between capitalism and culture are even more ambiguous because they contain a contradiction: culture is both support and challenge, guard dog and rebel ... Almost invariably, culture becomes the mainstay of the existing order and capitalism derives not a little of its security from it.

(Braudel 1982)

Within one year, from March 2008 to March 2009, the shocks suffered by the American financial system reverberated globally at precipitous speed, as every country and region with few exceptions (Canada, Finland, Israel, New Zealand, China, India and Latin America have been affected, but to a to a lesser degree) declared recession amid a cascade of bank and industrial failures, massive fraud scheme losses, increase in unemployment, and manifestations of political and populist anger. The definition of capitalism as a force of evil, or social destruction, counteracted by profound fears of government intervention associated with Marxism, fears of nationalization and surges of nationalism, societal determinants thought to have been submerged and de-fanged have resurfaced. The worst repercussions were felt in the post-2004 EU member countries, far more economically fragile and politically volatile than presumed. Although analogies with the Great Depression are very premature, and have to be carefully dissected, the referential context of the crisis of 2008 will be as pervasive and far reaching as 1929. Has international capitalism undergone a seismic shock, a period of upheaval of such proportions that it will force transformative institutional, regulatory, economic and cultural changes inaugurating an era of responsibility? As for two generations after the Great Depression, will the excesses of unfettered capitalist activity, having been made so public and having aroused such levels of anger, translate into a more austere, discrete and cautious shift in operations, agents, instruments, and institutions, or will it result in short-term prescriptions and punishments under the aegis of new rules and regulation? Will the center of global finance, as Braudel predicted in 1986, shift from West to

East with the rise of China, as occurred in the 1980s with Japan and the yen as superpower? Will it then cyclically revert to a stronger concentric Europe with focus on the core Euro countries as lead financial powers? Will the United States and the United Kingdom reassert their financial prestige, albeit more cautiously, under far more stringent regulatory systems with greater dependence on public–private financial partnerships?

This work explores the political and socio-economic factors which determine fallibility and resilience in financial cultures, periods of crisis, transition, and recovery based on cyclical rather than linear historical progression. Examining the roots of financial capitalism, and financial crisis in Europe and the United States proves that cultural and psychosocial reactions to financial success, endeavor, and calamity transcend specific periods or events. The crisis of 2008 inserted into the economic discourse references to morality, guilt, fear, "witch hunts," and the specter of stereotypes thought to have been long repressed and eliminated. Distrust and misperception of esoteric financial instruments, the trauma of past market panics and bank runs, anti-Semitic commentary incited by the collapse of Lehman Brothers and the Bernard Madoff scheme, the invisibility of women in the echelons of high finance (images of top British bankers interrogated by a Treasury panel in the British Parliament, top American bankers testifying to the United States House of Representatives Financial Services Committee in February 2009, revealing the total lack of gender diversity) resurfaced with a vengeance. The age of irony and post-modern relativism gave way to profound atavistic responses.

Technology and instantaneous communication accelerated the impact of the crisis from America to Europe to Asia, but despite standardization of information, cultural homogeneity, pragmatism, regional rather than national identity in Europe, post-modern, and post-ethnic discourse, in times of extreme stress, proved unable to mute or transform age old prejudices and the search for scapegoats.

Aristotle's basic principle that money has a purpose as medium of reciprocal exchange is inherently acceptable, but activities involving self generation or interest have always been judged condemnable to the fabric of society. As money becomes more and more abstract, moving from tangible to non tangible, it becomes harder to trace, quantify or justify, the distinction between transactional and speculative activity blurs. In the past 20 years, as the center of profit moved from banking to trading, as larger segments of the population engaged in the stock market, and as pension funds and savings were anonymously invested in market operations and instruments, the relationship between the individual, the banker, and money became abstract and depersonalized. In the most basic terms, "where has the money gone" is more and more difficult to answer. Billions and trillions no longer have real attributes, and cannot be visualized or considered as material objects.

In 2006, world output was in the amount of US$47 trillion, stock markets of US$51 trillion, "derivatives outstanding was US$68 trillion" (Ferguson 2008: 4). In 2008, banks lost about US$500 billion, the first US rescue package (TARP) was US$700 billion, the British government injected almost £40 billion into banks. The figures become imaginary, as fictional as Scrooge Mc Duck's "mega zillions." Populist rage against AIG and the Royal Bank of Scotland, and government demands in France and Switzerland that bonuses be annulled or returned, revealed the depth of anger at the incomprehensible, suddenly made accessible. Ordinary citizens could viscerally and intellectually react to US$1 million given to bankers, who were accused of malfeasance and seemed implicated in the losses that had necessitated government intervention. Before the crisis, the salaries of hedge fund managers had become incoherent, outside of any comprehensible context or realm of justification similar to the US$1 million Damien Hirst diamond encrusted skull where death, art, and money are all equally priceless and worthless.

For a generation, since the mid-1980s, financial culture was driven by a belief in the power and ultimate good of the market. The fall of the Soviet Union and the creation of the European Union led to pro market, pro capitalist optimism. If American and European economies were not consistently accelerating, the periods of deceleration, bank, currency crises and recessions were relatively short and mild. Recovery after the Crash of 1987 occurred within six months, the recession of 1991 was far more severe, but large banks continued to grow and expand, recovery after September 11, 2001 was exceptional. There was a deep seated belief in the power of the private sector to self correct which led to a belief in self regulation.

In 1992, in this period of Euro optimism following the Maastricht Treaty, on the belief that Europe under one currency would have pan European banks, markets, press, and media, *Le Monde* organized a forum entitled "Comment Penser l'Argent" (How to contemplate Money), bringing together bankers, philosophers, essayists, and journalists to decipher the mysteries of money, its immutability, its virtual and tangible nature, its psycho-cultural, and economic constructs. It also focused on the "new" obsession with money opposed to: "there was once a world where money was discrete, and almost silent. It was very much present – this world was industrialized, urbanized, and productive – but money was rarely mentioned" (Droit 1992: 5).

In 2009, in a world where money is shouted everywhere, even in countries and societies where it had been utterly silenced for decades, the questions are the same: how to balance emotional, visceral, atavistic responses to an all pervasive, yet abstract concept with the reality of markets, economies and governments that have to regulate and corral these forces?

When this book was first conceived in 2004, American capitalism and financial culture, while understood that after the currency crisis and financial scandals of the 1990s it had to be applied judiciously to post-communist and developing countries, rather than in sudden surges of short-term investments and imposed standards, was viewed as the global standard for economic progress. The booming economies of the European Union, whose number had increased from 12 in 1992 to 25 in 2004, provided a model of universal banking, adapted by the United States after the deregulation reforms of 1999. After decades of post-World War II government control, privatization, deregulation, and mergers incited global financial sectors to expand, and banks to create and disperse innovative, complex financial instruments that promised high yield, high risk returns. The American–European financial model, despite discrepancies in philosophy and methodology, offered a sound socioeconomic paradigm for financial institutions and markets in transitional economies, and especially in the newly named BRIC countries (Brazil, Russia, India, and China). Extreme economic volatility had been relegated to the "black swan" theory of very low probability, yet in hindsight the collapse of LTCM and Barings, the large scale bailout of Crédit Lyonnais, the Peso Crisis in 1995, and the currency crises in Asia and Russia in 1997–1998 should have sounded warning signals. Minsky, Shull, Kaufmann, George Soros, Martin Wolf, and John Kay expressed doubts about the combination of ever larger financial institutions dependent on regulatory structures established in the 1930s, but other renowned economists, academics, central bankers, market experts, and heads of government held onto the belief that, as in the previous decade, each crisis was an isolated incident and could be resolved on a case by case basis. The greatest risk was judged to be political destabilization through terrorism and fundamentalism, not economic or financial cataclysms.

In that environment, scrutiny and research was devoted to "corporate culture," management tactics, and market theories, but the concept of culture as motivator in financial decision making had been relegated to academia, as global financial institutions prided themselves on having overcome national, regional, and historical barriers in the name of efficiency, global strategies, and profitability. Sanford Weill, CEO of Citigroup from 1998 to 2004 epitomized the disdain, declaring "culture is for yogurt" (as quoted in Paine *et al.*, 2008).

The Hofstede management matrix from the 1980s, and corollary studies at INSEAD in 1992 on the banking sector, studied cultural determinants, measuring relationship to power/distance, individualism/collectivism, centralization/decentralization, long/short-term strategy planning (Hofstede 2001).

American resilience, British pragmatism, French ambivalence between order and individualism, German caution, consensual oligarchy, and efficiency in relation to risk, failure, and individual initiative, the Nordic/French/Japanese approach to the role of the state as benign paternalism, Anglo-Nordic decentralization, personal initiative, flexibility, entrepreneurship versus Asian centralization, paternalism, and strong collective identity are not universally applicable traits (specific cases of financial scandals and fraud warn against generalization). However in times of economic crisis provoking societal and political transformations, when citizens seek reassurance and a return to order, inherent country and culture specific responses systemically recur throughout financial history.

The themes explored in this work: the progression of financial semantics, numeric and economic knowledge, the interplay of social and financial determinants in transforming cultural norms, consistent characteristics of financial crises and panics since the 1720s, the role of governments as mediators and stabilizing forces through central banks and regulatory systems, prove that the forces of desire, greed and the quest for material goods, which instigate the worst excesses and its repercussions in bubbles, panics, and busts, are simultaneously elemental to innovation, initiative, wealth generation, and the democratization of prosperity. Landes argues that conditions for wealth generation, or the lack of, are not political or moral issues, but economic and cultural determinants. It is not a question of favoring one area over another, the accusations of Eurocentricism versus universalism in economic history: "If we learn anything from the history of economic development, it is that culture makes all the difference" (Landes 1999: 516). Financial activity must be propelled not only by secularization, but by the belief that, although a necessary evil, it needs to be integrated into the fabric of society. The genius of Dutch merchants, English traders, goldsmiths, economists, French philosophers, American politicians, Gresham, Newton, Smith, Say, Ricardo, Guizot, Hamilton, Greenspan, and Bernanke has been to seek a point of equilibrium between the state and market forces, both in times of growth and in times of crisis, from the South Sea Bubble to the subprime mortgage crisis. More than in any other sector of the economy, as finance touches on all sectors, civil society must have confidence in its governing authority to reestablish stability. The breakdown of this relationship, due to extreme market volatility, hyper inflation, rampant corruption, or the lack of sound regulation, carries the danger of the greatest destabilization and far worse. "Governments of capitalist economies are also charged with the need to oversee, restrain, adjudicate, and correct tendencies of the economic realm that may arise from the uncoordinated or shortsighted or simply harmful operations of its individual members" (Heilbroner 1989).

Financial culture implies collective pride in economic accomplishments. From the burghers in Bruges and Antwerp, to the bankers in London and New York, whether Japan, Finland, or France, wealth and financial success reflected on the prestige of the community and the nation. Germany could only reassume statehood through economic achievement after the Nazi era, when the Deutschmark and the Bundesbank were the only acceptable sources of national identity.

Heilbroner, Landes, Braudel, Kindleberger, Galbraith echoing Adam Smith, and Tocqueville, who presciently judged the American colonies even surpassing England, understood the fundamental distinction between "being rich and thriving" (Landes 1999: 553), between viscerally accepting the process of making money, rather than having wealth. Since the eighteenth century, America and Britain have benefited from the least tormented relationship to money, profit, speculation, and business.

Financial dynamism demands that individuals and institutions can fail if necessary, without sentiment or fear of societal or political repercussions. Over centuries, as wealth mutated from immediate gain or value to future yield, from absolute to potential, it became more difficult to assess and more difficult to justify. The fate of bankers, traders, and financiers throughout history, in fact and fiction, has often been to lose their souls in the name of profit, to gain redemption by losing their money, but to be able to rise again and earn for another day. Some suffer a far more colorful fate such as John Law, dead in exile, disgraced and impoverished, Roberto Calvi, murdered by hanging at Black Friars Bridge in London, Nick Leeson, imprisoned, ill, released, and working as a consultant, Bernard Madoff, jailed for consecutive life terms. Institutions likewise fail, are dissolved, merged, incorporated or closed down. The demise of major investment in 2009 has caused consternation, but in the United States there is a long history of banks failing, while in Europe and Japan, banks have been maintained long after they are cease to be efficient or profitable.

Since the Renaissance, growth and progress in England, France, the Low Countries, and Italy occurred in periods of increased trade and merchant mobility. Major firms with diversified portfolios, in metals, spices, textiles, and currency trading, with subsidiaries in all the market places in Europe, bypassed political boundaries. The house of Jacob Fugger, the Buovisi family's holdings from 1575–1610 in London, Antwerp, Frankfurt, Paris and Milan, the Medici Bank in the 1400s met the definition of a conglomerate with diversified holdings. Banking dynasties Rothschild, Barings, Warburg, Morgan, Botin in Spain and Latin America, play a significant role in financial history as pillars of stability and continuity, often better able to withstand periods of crisis.

Capitalism, the integration of finance within the cultural framework of a nation or region, requires a spirit of competitiveness, which may presume levels of inequality in the name of dynamic evolution. However, where inequality is embedded in anachronistic caste, class, ethnic, or religious structures, economic progress remains stifled and limited to a small part of the political body. Financial culture thrives when all may not become wealthy, but opportunities for economic advancement are made available and, above all, acceptable to all. It also requires political will to invest and reinvest in order to spread the wealth and eventually democratize the benefits, which include international transactions, inherent in the progression of capitalism, and financial institutions expanding from the domestic to the international arena, from home to host countries.

Since antiquity, when guilt, hatred, self loathing, and fear of the outsider dominate attitudes toward money, economic evolution is thwarted. If those who earn are seen as less worthy than those who inherit, if those who deal in international trade, deals which may require bypassing religious interdiction, are ostracized or worst, if financial initiative is not allowed to flourish, monetary activity continues to be seen as inferior, unworthy, unclean, or even antithetical to the interests of society at large. In the crisis of 2008, politicians have had to balance the outrage of the public at financial abuses with warnings not to demonize financial innovative or profits.

Marxism failed, in part, when incentives to produce and innovate were repressed, and the ability of the collective to replace the individual became less and less successful. The eradication of markets, banks, bankers, monetary instruments, agents, and even money itself as convertible exchange, could be forcibly imposed under Marxist and Maoist ideology, but the underlying assumption that all remnants of financial culture, its roots and manifestations, the temptations of materialism and consumption, could also be erased from the collective consciousness proved false and illusionary. By the early 1980s, the Soviet Union had become porous and economically untenable. In the information age, the culture of capitalism and consumption can only be kept at bay by reversion to theological interdiction, rather than isolation or ideology. Post-Marxist societies, Russian and Chinese tycoons, testing out the perimeters of capitalist activity, have, in many ways, followed the path of the American capitalist evolution. Wanting to show and spend their newly acquired wealth, they bought luxury goods rather than reinvesting in their national heritage, communities, or industries. But similar to nineteenth-century European industrialists, they embrace the principles of materialism and consumption, yet turn to the state for investment, infrastructure, and policy directives. Marxism is comatose, but anti-capitalism and anti-Americanism is alive and well, as seen in the responses to the crisis of 2008.

Flexibility, innovation, "toleration," and pragmatism are the cornerstones of successful economic progress, epitomized since the eighteenth century in Nordic and Anglo-American culture. Non democratic regimes, theocracies, dictatorships or other authoritarian governments can maintain economic stability and generate wealth, but cannot generate renewal or competitiveness. If dominant ethnic or religious groups cannot reconcile their basic system of values with economic, monetary, commercial activities, then most often outsiders, marginalized foreigners or expatriate minorities within the society, will undertake and succeed at these activities: Huguenots in pre-Revolution France prior to the revocation of the edict of Nantes, Jews in Spain and, after the inquisition, in German states and Poland, Chinese in East and South East Asia, and Armenians in Russia.

Totally unregulated "cowboy capitalism" has been proven dangerous to society and the market, but regulation has to be balanced with innovation and commensurate reward structures. The huge surge of wealth, consumption, and corruption in sixteenth-century Spain, in late eighteenth-century France, in the 1850s United States post gold rush, in czarist Russia in the 1890s, in Africa in the post liberation decade of 1960 to 1970, in Mexico and the Asian Tigers in the 1990s, in oil rich Arab countries, like market bubbles and manias, from the tulip mania to dotcom, the hedge funds of 2006–2007 is not sustainable. In each case the government or power structure was not in control, rule of law, the basics of sound governance, and management controls were not in place. "Inebriating rates of profit and spectacular capital gains" (Greenspan 2007: 526), gild a balance sheet or a country's cumulative assets, but have short-term benefits and immense long-term risks.

Islamic banks can function successfully within the confines of Islamic states, but can they be adapted to the needs of foreign, non-theologically defined societies; communist regimes can establish profit generating semi public banks and markets, but can they continue functioning in times of crisis outside of the demands of state policies? History proves that one system, methodology, structure or ownership of finance is not viable long term. Cycles of private and public sector control and influence, despite the volatility and risk of temporary chaos, engenders far more overall dynamism. Ideology, like theology, in its best and worst forms becomes restrictive.

In 2008, economic and political discourse used and misused financial terminology, as neutral economic terms were politicized and laden with historical signifiers. Depression, nationalization, capitalism, socialism, terms fraught with psycho-cultural trauma figured front and center in the media and political debate. The cover of *Newsweek* on February 16, 2009, heralded "We Are All Socialists Now, the Perils and Promise of the New Era of Big Government." The use of the term "nationalization," prevalent in the American and British press since the start of 2009, conjured visions of "European socialism" at best, shades of Communism at worst, provoking fear and anxiety. A firestorm was caused in American politics, especially in the disgruntled conservative faction of the Republican party, where on the same day as a Citigroup announcement, Rush Limbaugh, the most popular conservative radio host in America, at the Conservative Party Convention in Washington said "We cringe to watch capitalism insulted" (Limbaugh 2009). Adhering to the definition of temporary partial nationalization:

> The US government agreed to become the biggest single shareholder in Citigroup yesterday, ... The partial nationalization will give the government a stake of 36 per cent in a troubled lender, capping a spectacular fall from grace for what was one of the world's largest financial institutions.
>
> (Guerrera and Beattie 2009)

Where reactionary movements in America revert to capitalism as a cultural icon of American folklore, the parallel emergence of reactionary movements across Europe (as too often in past history) look at capitalism as cause and effect of social corruption and loss of national values. A cartoon in the *Boston Globe* shows Chairman Bernanke and two colleagues around a table at the Federal Reserve, with the caption that:

> "Nationalization" sounds too Socialist..., too Swedish.
>   Suppose we call it something more "All-American?"
>   Looking happy, they announce, "We declare the Patriotization of the Banks"
>   They stand up, Bernanke waving a flag, all pledging allegiance say, "Operation Enduring Finance."
>
> (Wasserman 2009)

In Europe and Russia, the term "American capitalism," already heavily tinged with negative historical resonance, was the subject of similar misperceptions immediately following the collapse of Lehman Brothers. Politicians' recriminations against the United States included Steinbruck, German finance minister, who stated that the "US will lose its status as the superpower of the world financial system," and President Sarkozy of France, who stated that the "crisis was not born in Europe. This crisis was born in America" (Erlanger 2008). However, this attitude belied the depth and scope of European bank exposure to the sub prime mortgage instruments and overvalued property assets on and off European

Union bank balance sheets. In 2009, even the oldest bank in Europe, Monte Dei Paschi di Siena, intact since 1472, part of the third largest consolidated Italian banking group, and the proprietor of magnificent art collections, has had to request, for the first time in its history, a €1.9 billion capital injection.

At the 2009 World Economic Forum in Davos, attended by few bankers and many heads of state, Prime Minister Putin of Russia and Premier of China, Wen Jiabao, were explicit in their criticism of American capitalism. The Islamic Economic Forum in Jakarta railed against "irresponsible, unregulated western financial markets," and touted sharia banking as a framework for a more stable global financial system, as banks in Malaysia, Singapore, and the Gulf states have been relatively unscathed by the crisis. However, this is still very limited in scope, and it is unclear how effective or flexible these institutions could be. President Lula of Brazil accused "white bankers" of inciting the financial crisis (Wheatly 2009).

Initial responses to government rescue packages revealed the deeper implication of government intervention within national and institutional culture. Despite the tradition of government intervention and ownership of financial institutions in continental Europe, and a more sporadic history of bank nationalization in England, a decade of privatization, consolidation, and efficient reforms had created significant resistance to government bailouts, even in times of crisis. Chief Executive Officer of Deutsche Bank, Joseph Ackerman, is "reported as having told an internal meeting ... he would be ashamed" if the bank had to use the rescue fund (Benoit 2008). Editorials in the *Financial Times*, "In Praise of Free Markets" (2008), and "Why Free Markets Must Be Defended" (2008), stressed that, while some intervention is inevitable, it must be minimized. Europe struggles with redefining the architecture of its financial system on the regional level; America offers a blueprint for immediate rescue. The fundamental dichotomy of long-term versus short-term strategies remains intact.

In societies where theology or ideology dictates that money, profit, wealth discrepancy, excessive consumption, choice of consumer goods, speculative activities, in short the culture of the market, is consistently stigmatized, can these societies accept a culture of finance, and a financial culture free of all moral and political trauma? Can governments that are still run by hard line Communists in China, mid-twentieth-century Socialists in India, or entrenched theocracies in the Middle East reconcile the basic tenets of faith with the principles of capitalism, including open markets, free trade, labor mobility, globalization, and technology? As traditional socialism fades, as a new generation born in post-Marxist Russia or post Tiananmen Square China, reach maturity and engage in Western style capitalist activity, will participatory democracy alone be the most conducive engine of economic progress?

China's unique case of authoritarian government and free market economic ideology, collective and individual market impulses, represents the great experiment of this century.

The exceptional literary output in China, including Hua, Ma Jian, and Chi Li whose works follow the trajectory of Chinese history from the Cultural

Revolution to the dual system of commercialism, markets, and capitalist activity within the strictures of an authoritarian state, present in one decade a Chinese version of Naturalism, Realism and Existentialism where, similar to nineteenth-century France and England, the novel becomes mirror and critique of a society in economic transition. The fundamental conditions of freedom of action, flexibility, adaptability, individual action, non-restrictive movement of individuals, institutions, and instruments are intrinsic to long-term financial evolution, yet the interplay between democracy and capitalism is still a work in progress.

After the crisis of 2008, as the American model, even once reformed will not be universally applicable, when America and China are inexorable interlocked in trade and currency interdependency, in a partnership of mutual economic deterrence, what Ferguson dubbed "Chimerica" (2008: 12), when China can demand a new role as partner rather than recipient, the paradigm presented by Heilbroner, in 1989, again best describes diametrically opposed financial cultures seeking a symbiotic core: "Transformation of socialism into capitalism; this is to ask how closely capitalism, under its most democratic impulse could approach socialism under its most economically open arrangements" (Heilbroner 1989).

And finally, examining parallel and intersecting trends, reactions, and controversies in the cultural history of finance, one consistent factor has been humor: from Aristophanes to Molière, street ditties in 1720 London and Paris, Defoe's to Tom Wolfe's satires, Daumier, Nast, and Hamilton's caricatures, "*My Man Godfrey*" to "*Other People's Money.*" Each successive economic crisis engenders brittle, sharp, downright funny reactions to deflect, reflect, and perfectly illustrate the moment. Irrepressible *Financial Times* journalist Lucy Kellaway's Martin Lukes, epitome of the insane excesses, insider trading, management abuses, semantic, attitudinal and cultural shenanigans which characterized the last days of "irrational exuberance," was sentenced to two years in jail on December 23, 2007. Upon his release in December 2009, will he be chastised, a reformed man ready to adapt the new frugality, will he be a recessionista, seeing in the downturn new opportunity for flagrant abuses, can and will he be resurrected at all?

Bibliography

About, E. (1856) *Ces Coquins d'agent de Change*, Paris: Dentu.

Adhémar, J. (ed.) (1983) *Daumier, Business and Finance*, New York: Vilo.

Aftalion, A. (1927) *Monnaie, Prix et Change*, Paris: Editions Sirey.

Ahamed, L. (2008) *Lords of Finance*, New York: Penguin.

Akhtar, L. (2008) "Trading on the Street: Exhibit Features Buttonwwood Agreement," *Financial History*, fall 2008

Alcott, L.M. (1947) *Little Women*, New York: Grosset and Dunlap.

Aldcroft, D.H. (1977) *From Versailles to Wall Street (1919–1922)*, Berkley: University of California Press.

Allen, R.C. (2005) "Capital Accumulation, Technological Change and the Distribution of Income during the British Industrial Revolution," *Economics Series Working Papers* 239, University of Oxford.

Almeras, H. d' (1927) *La Vie Parisienne Pendant Le Siège et Sous La Commune*, Paris: Albin Michel.

Amis, M. (1984) *Money*, New York: Penguin Books.

Amstad, R. (1949) *Des Conceptions Monétaires et Bancaires en France et à Lyon (1960–1720)*, Geneva: Droz.

Andersen, J. (2006) "Six Women at Dresdner File Bias Suit," *New York Times*, January 10.

Andreau, J. (1999) *Banking and Business in the Roman World*, Cambridge, UK and New York: Cambridge University Press.

Annual Reports of the Comptroller of the Currency (1927–2007) Washington, DC: US Government Printing Office.

Antoine, N. (1973) *Le Conseil Royal des Finances au 18eme Siècle*, Geneva: Droz.

Apter, E. (2007) "Translation as a Genre of Literary Labor," *PMLA*, October, vol. 122, no. 5, pp. 1403–1415, Modern Language Association of America.

Aragon, L. (1934) *Cloches de Bâle*, Paris: Denoel et Steele.

Ardant, G. (1976) *Histoire financière de l'Antiquité a nos jours*, Paris: Gallimard.

Aristophanes (c. 1931) *The Plutos, the Lysistrata*, trans. B. Rogers, London: William Heinemann.

Aristotle (1938) *Politics*, trans. B. Jowett, Oxford: Clarendon Press.

Arnold, M. (2008) "Kerviel Challenges SocGen over Dismissal," *Financial Times*, April 3.

Arnould, A. (1791) *De la balance du commerce et des relations commerciales extérieures de la France dans toutes les parties du globe*, 3 vols., Paris: Seligman Collection.

Aron, R. (1983) *Mémoires, 50 Ans de Réflexion Politique*, Paris: Juillard.

Ash, T.G. (1993) *In Europe's Name, Germany and the Divided Continent*, New York: Random House.

Attali, J. (1992) *1492*, Paris: Fayard.

—— (1994a) *Un Homme d'Influence*, Paris: Fayard.

—— (1994b) *Europe(s)* Paris: Fayard.

Aubert, F. d' (1993) *L'Argent Sale*, Paris: Plon.

Auchincloss, L. (1966) *The Embezzler*, Boston: Houghton Mifflin.

Auletta, K. (1986) *Greed and Glory on Wall Street: The Fall of the House of Lehman*, New York: Warner Books Edition.

Austen, J. (1813) *Pride and Prejudice* in *The Complete Novels of Jane Austen*, New York: New York Modern Library, first edition.

Bagehot, W. (1897) *Lombard Street: A Description of the Money Market*, New York: Scribner's Sons.

—— (2008 [1889]) *A Practical Plan for Assimilating the English and American Money, as a Step Toward a Universal Money*, Germany: Kolthoff Press.

Baird, H. (1873) "The Bank Check and not the Circulating Note, the Great Monetary Instrument of the Age," *Philadelphia Telegraph*, October 15.

Baker, H. (1854) *Banks and Banking in the United States*, Boston: Ticher, Reed & Feld.

Balzac, H. de (1855–1863) *Oeuvres Complètes*, Paris: A. Houssiaux.

—— (1961a) *Les Illusions Perdues*, Paris: Editions Garnier Frères.

—— (1961b) *Père Goriot*, Paris: Editions Garnier Frères.

—— (1961c) *Eugénie Grandet*, Paris: Editions Garnier Frères.

Banco do Brasil (2009) *March 2009 Report*, Banco do Brasil.

Banque de France (1905) *Célébration de Jubile de la régence de M. le Baron Alphonse de Rothschild*, Paris: Dupont.

—— (1916) *Les opérations à Paris et dans ses succursales*, Paris: Dupont.

Barber, B. (1996) *Djihad versus McWorld, mondialisation et integrisme contre la democracie*, Paris: Fayard.

Barbier, A. (1886) *Pierre d'Amours: Commissaire des Finances a Poitiers sous Henri IV*, Poitiers, Le Poiré sur Vie: Imprimerie générale de l'Ouest.

Barres, M. (1902) *Scènes et Doctrines du Nationalisme*, Paris: Juven.

—— (1954) *Les Deracines*, Paris: Plon.

Barrie, J.M. (1911) *Peter Pan or the Boy Who Wouldn't Grow Up*, London: Hodder & Stoughton.

Bartholomy, F. (1875) *Coup d'oeil sur l'avenir financier de la France*, Paris.

Battilossi, S. and Cassis Y. (eds.) (2002) *European Banks and the American Challenge: Competition and Cooperation in International Banking Under Bretton Woods*, Oxford: Oxford University Press.

Baudrillard, J. (1990 [1987]) *Cool Memories I & II*, Paris: Editions Galilee.

—— (2002) *Screened Out*, trans. Chris Turner, Paris: Verso.

Baum, F. (1900) *The Wonderful Wizard of Oz*, Chicago: George M. Hill.

BCCI (1992) *"A Report to the Committee on Foreign Relations,"* United States Senate by Senator John Kerry and Senator Hank Brown, 102d Congress, 2d Session, December, Senate Print.

Beatty, J. (2007) *The Age of Betrayal: The Triumph of Money in America (1865–1900)*, New York: Knopf.

Beaudeux, P. (1984) "Les Banquiers a la Rose," *L'Expansion*, May 24.

Beaumarchais, P. de (1869–1871) *Les Deux Amis ou le négociant de Lyon, Théâtre complet de Beaumarchais*, 4 vols., Paris: Academie des bibliophiles.

Beauvoir, S. de (1954 [1953]) *The Mandarins*, trans. L. Friedman, Washington, DC: Regnery Gateway.

Beidleman, C. (ed.) (1987) *Handbook of International Investing*, Chicago: Probus.

Bellanger, S. (1986) "La Déréglementation dans le secteur bancaire et financier," *Banque*, no. 460, April.

Bellet, R. (1983) "La Bourse et la littérature dans la seconde moitie du XIXème siecle Romantisme," *Revue du Dix-neuvième siecle*, no 40.

Beltran, A. and Griset, P. (1988) *La Croissance Economique De La France, 1815–1914*, Paris: Armand Colin.

Benoit, B. (2008) "Germany Responds to Stigma Fears by Softening Conditions for Rescue," *Financial Times*, October 21.

Bergeron, L. (ed.) (1978) *Les Capitalistes en France (1780–1914)*, Paris: Julliard.

Berghahn, V. (1986) *The Americanization of West German Industry 1945–1973*, Oxford: Oxford University Press.

—— (2001) *America and the Intellectual Cold Wars in Europe: Shepard Stone between Philanthropy, Academy and Diplomacy*, Princeton: Princeton University Press.

Bernigaud de Granger, J.L. (1792) *De l'état des finances et des causes principales de leur délabrement*, Paris.

Betts, P. (2008) "Effects of Sarkozy's Push to Moralise French Capitalism," *Financial Times*, December 15.

"Bigger Banks Are Better" (1991) Editorial, *New York Times*, July 7.

Bigo, R. (1927) *La caisse d'escompte et les origines de la Banque de France (1776–1793)*, Paris: Presses universitaires de France.

—— (1947) *Les Banques Françaises au Cours du 19eme Siècle*, Paris: Editions Sirey.

Bilan Economique et Social 1992 – Crises – 20 Ans de Monnaies Européennes (1993) Le Monde Dossiers et Documents no. 9301.

Bloch, J.R. (1917) *Et Cie…*, Paris: Dentu.

Bodin, J. (1568) *La Reponse de Jean Bodin au Paradoxe de M. de Malestroit sur le faict des monnoyes*, Paris.

—— (1955) *On Sovereignty: Six Books of the Commonwealth* (abridged and trans.) M.J. Tooley, Oxford: Basil Blackwell.

Bogle, J.C. (2005) *The Battle for the Soul of Capitalism*, New Haven: Yale University Press.

Boorstin, D.J. (1983) *The Discoverers*, New York: Random House.

Bordo, M. and Schwartz, A. (1984) *A Retrospective on the Classical Gold Standard, 1821–1931*, Chicago: University of Chicago Press.

Bordo, M.D. and Cortes-Conde, R. (eds.) (2001) *Transferring Wealth and Power from the Old to the New World: Monetary and Fiscal Institutions in the 17th through the 19th Centuries*, New York: Cambridge University Press.

Bosher, J.F. (1970) *French Finances, 1770–1795*, Cambridge, UK: Cambridge University Press.

Bouchard, L. (1891) *Systeme Financier de L'Ancienne Monarchie*, Paris: Guillaumin.

Bouchary, J. (1939) *Les manieurs d'argent à Paris à la fin du XVIII siècle*, Paris: Marcel Rivière & Cie.

Bourgoin, J. (1623) *Recherche des abus, mal-versations et peculats commis es finances de sa Majesté*, Paris.

Bouvier, J. (1961) *Le Crédit Lyonnais de 1863–1882*, Paris: SEVPEN.

—— (1968) *Histoire Economique et Histoire Sociale*, Geneva: Droz.

—— (1973) *Un Siècle de Banque Française: Les contraintes de l'Etat et les incertitudes des marches*, Paris: Hachette Littérature.

Bowen, H.V., Lincoln, M., Rigby, N. (eds.) (2002) *The World's of the East India Company*, Rochester, NY: Boydell Press with the University of Leicester.

Brancati, A. (1969) *Le Istituzioni Bancarie Nell' Antichita*, Firenze: La nuova Italia.

Brandeis, L.D. (2009 [1914]) *Other People's Money and How the Bankers Use It*, Louisville: University of Louisville Louis D. Brandeis School of Law.

Brands, H.W. (2006) *The Money Men, Capitalism, Democracy, and the Hundred Years' War Over The American Dollar*, New York: W.W. Norton & Company.

Brathwait (1641) *The English Gentleman*, London: John Dawson.

Braudel, F. (1979) *Civilisation Materielle et Capitalisme*, Paris: Colin.

—— (1982a) *The Structures of Everyday Life, Civilization and Capitalism*, vol. I, trans. Sian Reynolds, New York: Harper & Row.

—— (1982b) *The Wheels of Commerce, Civilization and Capitalism*, vol. II, New York: Harper & Row.

—— (1982c) *The Perspective of the World, Civilization and Capitalism*, vol. III, New York: Harper & Row.

—— (1985) *La dynamique du capitalisme*, Paris: Arthaud.

Brecht, B. (1967) *Die Dreigroschenoper*, Frankfurt: Suhrkamp Verlag.

—— (1972) *Gesammelte werke*, Frankfurt: Suhrkamp Verlag.

Breuer, R. (1998) *Financial Times*, September 11.

Brewer, E. III, Genay, H., Hunter, W.C. and Kaufman, G.G. (2002) "The Value of Banking Relationships during a Financial Crisis: Evidence from Failures of Japanese Banks," working paper series WP-02–20, Federal Reserve Bank of Chicago.

Broder, E.G. (1989) "Are Banks Ready for 1992?," *International Economy*, March–April, pp. 78–89.

Bromfield, L. (1942) *Mrs. Parkington*, New York: Harper & Brothers.

Bronstein, S. (1986) "Americans Finding Buyers Overseas," *New York Times*, June 1.

Brooks, J. (1984) "Fiction of the Managerial Class," *New Yorker*, April 8.

Bruck, C. (1989) *The Predator's Ball: The Inside Story of Drexel Burnham and the Rise of Junk Bond Raiders*, New York: Penguin Books.

Bruguiere, M. (1969) *La première Restauration et son Budget*, Geneva: Droz.

Bruhat, J., Dautry, J. and Tersen E. (eds.) (1970) *La Commune De 1871*, Paris: Editions Sociales.

Buissière, E. (1992) *Paribas, L'Europe Et Le Monde, 1872–1992*, Antwerp: Fonds Mercator.

Burkhardt, J., Koopman, H. and Krauss. H. (1993) *Wirtschaft in Wissenschaft und Literatur*, Augsburg: Pressestelle der Universität Augsburg.

Byron, G. (2004 [1823]) *Don Juan*, New York: Penguin Classics.

Calvino, I. (2009 [1968]) "The Daughters of the Moon," trans. Martin McLaughlin, *New Yorker*, February 23.

Camus, A.G. (1791) *Au Nom de la Commission Nommée Pour la Surveillance de la Tresorie Nationale Dans la Séance du 12 Floréal*, Paris.

Carosso, V.P. (1979) *More Than a Century of Investment Banking: The Kidder Peabody and Co. Story*, New York: McGraw-Hill.

Cassidy, J. (2002) "Striking It Rich," *New Yorker*, January 14.

—— (2003) "Annals of Finance," *New Yorker*, October 6.

—— (2007) "Annals of Finance", *New Yorker*, July 2.

Celine, L.F. (1932) *Voyage au bout de la nuit*, Paris: Gallimard.

Cepiene, I. and Jasiene, M. (2001) "Savings Banks in Lithuania," *EABH Bulletin*, Vilnius: Vilnius University.

Chamberland, A. (1904) *Un Plan de Restauration Financière en 1506 Attribue à Pierre Fouquet De Fresne*, Paris: H. Champion.

Champmeslé, C.C. de (1682) *La Rue St Denis*, Paris.

Chancellor, E. (1999) *Devil Take the Hindmost: A History of Financial Speculation*, New York: Farrar, Strauss, and Giroux.

Charmat (1789) *Sur la Finance, la Banque et l'Agiotage*, Paris: Seligman Collection.

Chaucer, G. (1912) *The Complete Works*, Oxford: Oxford University Press.

Chernow, R. (1990) *The House of Morgan*, New York: Penguin Books.

—— (1997) *The Death of the Banker: The Decline and Fall of the Great Financial Dynasties and the Triumph of the Small Investor*, New York: Vintage Books.

—— (2004) *Alexander Hamilton*, New York: Penguin Books.

—— (2009) "Where is our Ferdinand Pecora?" *New York Times*, January 6, A25.

Chira, S. (1986a) "Investment Fever is Sweeping Japan," *New York Times*, 29 March, p. 29.

—— (1986b) "The New Global Top Banker: Tokyo and Its Mighty Money," *New York Times*, April 27.

Choury, M. (1970) *La Commune Au Coeur de Paris*, Paris: Editions Sociales.

Chown, J.F. (1996) *A History of Money: From AD 800*, London: Routledge.

Cicero (1999 [68–44 BC]) *Ad Atticum*, vol. 3 of Loeb Letters to Atticus, Books 8.16–12.40, Cambridge, MA: Loeb Classical Library, Harvard University Press.

Claretie, J. (1882) *Le Million*, Paris: Dentu.

Cleland, J. (1985 [1748]) *Memoirs of a Woman of Pleasure*, Oxford: Oxford University Press.

Clews, H. (1900) *The Wall Street Point of View*, New York: Silver, Burdett and Co.

—— (1908) *Fifty Years in Wall Street*, New York: Irving Publishing.

Cohan, W. (2007) *The Last Tycoons: The Secret History of Lazard Frères & Co*, New York: Doubleday.

Cohen-Solal, A. (2001) *American Painting, The Rise of American Artists, 1867–1948*, New York: Knopf.

Colette (1920) *Cheri, La Fin de Cheri*, Paris: Fayard.

Collins, T. (2002) *Otto Kahn: Art, Money and Modern Times*, Charleston: University of North Carolina Press.

Conant, C.A. (1896) *A History of Modern Banks of Issue: With an Account of the Economic Crises of the Present Century*, New York: G.P. Putnam's Sons.

Condorcet (1772) *Discours sur les finances, Discours sur la nomination et la destitution des commissaires de la trésorerie nationale et des membres du bureau de comptabilité*, Paris.

Congressional Budget Office (1994) *The Changing Business of Banking: A Study of Failed Banks from 1987 to 1992*, Washington, DC: Congressional Budget Office.

Coppons, De (1785) *Critique de la théorie et pratique de M. Necker dans l' administration des finances de la France*, Paris: in Columbia University: Lindsay French Political Pamphlets, 1547–1648 Collection.

Corneille, P. (1961 [1633]) *Théâtre Complet*, 3 vols., Paris: Classiques Garnier.

Cossigny (1797) *Réflexions sur le plan d'une banque territoriale par le citoyen Ferrieres*, Paris.

Coullet, M.P.J. (1865) *Etudes sur la Circulation Monétaire, la Banque et le Crédit*, Paris.

Courtois, A. (1875) *Histoire de la Banque de France et des Principales Institutions Françaises de Crédit depuis 1716*, Paris: Guillaumin.

Coville, G. (1987) "Les Financiers Dérangent," *L'Expansion*, June 5–18.

Cowan, A.L. (1991) "Amid the Ruins A Ball for the 90s," *New York Times*, August 15.

Craig, S., Crow, K. (2008) "Fallen Tycoon to Auction Prized Works," *Wall Street Journal*, September 26, p. W1.

Crouzet, F.M.J., Chaloner, W.H. And Stern, W.M. (1961) *Essays in European Economic History, 1789–1914*, London: E. Arnold.

Dana, R.H. Jr. (1872) "*Usury Laws. Speech of Richard H. Dana, Jr., in the House of Representatives of Massachusetts, February 14, 1867, On the Repeal if the Usury Laws,*" New York: Cowan, McClure & Co.

Dancourt, F.C. (1710) *Les Agioteurs*, Paris.

Dante (1994) *The Inferno of Dante*, trans. Robert Pinsky, New York: Farrar, Strauss and Giroux.

—— (1961) *Dante's Purgatorio*, trans. John D. Sinclair, New York: Oxford University Press.

Darragon (1795) *Plan ou projets de finance*, Paris.

Daudet, A. (1877) *Le Nabab*, Paris: Lachaud.

David, J. (1985) *Crise financière et relations monétaires internationales*, Paris: Economica.

Deane, M. and Pringle, R. (1995) *The Central Banks*, New York: Viking.

Defoe, D. (1701) *Villany of Stock-Jobbers Detected*, London.

—— (1719) *Anatomy of Exchange Alley*, London.

—— (1726) *Complete English Tradesman*, London.

—— (1965) *Moll Flanders*, London: The Folio Society.

Delany, P. (2002) *Literature, Money and the Market*, New York: Palgrave.

Delors, J. (2004) *Memoires,* Paris: Plon.

Denhem, R. (1985) *Histoire de la pensée économique des mercantilistes à Keynes*, Paris: Presses de l'Université Laval.

Denizet, J. (1985) *Le Dollar: Histoire du système monétaire international depuis 1945*, Paris: Fayard.

Dermine, J. (ed.) (1993) *European Banking in the 1990s*, Oxford, Blackwell.

Devitt, J. (2002) "Nobel Laureate Robert Mudell Sees Bright Future for the Euro," *Columbia News*, Columbia University, January 25.

Dickens, C. (1842) *American Notes for General Circulation, In Two Volumes*, London: Chapman and Hall.

—— (1848) *Dealings with the Firm of Dombey and Son, Wholesale, Retail and for Exportation*, London: Oxford University Press.

—— (2000) *Martin Chuzzlewit*, New York: Penguin Classics.

—— (2001) *American Notes for General Circulation*, revised edition, New York: Penguin Classics.

—— (2004) *Little Dorrit*, New York: Penguin Classics.

Dickey, C. (2009) "French Roast," *Newsweek*, February 2.

Dimock, W.C. (2007) "Genres as Fields of Knowledge," *PMLA*, October 2007, vol. 122, no 5.

Dinkelspiel, F. (2008) "Towers of Gold, How One Jewish Immigrant named Isaias Hellman Created California," *Financial History*, fall 2008.

Dos Passos, J. (1937) *USA*, Boston: Houghton Mifflin.

Dostoevsky, F. (1989) *Crime and Punishment*, trans. R. Peavear and L. Volokhonsky, New York: W.W. Norton Critical Edition.

—— (2004) *The Gambler*, trans. R. Pevear and L. Volokhonsky, New York: Everyman's Library.

Dougherty, C. (2009) "Sweden Aids Bailout of Baltic Nations," *New York Times*, March 13, p. B7.

Drakulic, S. (1997) *Café Europa, Life after Communism:* New York: W.W. Norton & Company.

Dreiser, T. (1912) *The Financier: A Novel*, New York: Harper & Brothers.

—— (1914) *The Titan*, New York: John Lance Co.

Droit, R.P. (ed.) (1992) *Comment Penser L'Argent*, Paris: Le Monde Editions.

Drumont, E. (1892) *La France Juive*, Paris: Flammarion.

Duby, G. (1991) *France in the Middle Ages, 987–1460* trans. J. Vale, London: Basil Blackwell.

Ducrocq, T. (1887) *Etudes d'Histoire Financière et Monétaire*, Paris: Corvée.

Duhamel, G. (1945) *La passion de Joseph Pasquier*, Paris: Mercure de France.

Dumas, A. Fils (1857) *La question d'argent*, Paris: Charlieu.

Dunbar, C. (1891) *Chapters on the Theory and History of Banking*, New York: Putnam.

Dyer, G. and Anderlini, J. (2008) "The Vanishing Billionaire," *Financial Times*, November 29–30.

Edict du roy contre les banqueroutes et cessionnaires (1618) Rouen: In Columbia University Lindsay French Political Pamphlets 1547–1648.

Eichengreen, B. (1998) *Globalizing Capital: A History of the International Monetary System*, Princeton: Princeton University Press.

Eichengreen, B. and Flandreau, B. (eds.) (1997) *Gold Standard In Theory and History*, London: Routledge.

Einaudi, L. (2001) *Money and Politics: European Monetary Unification and the International Gold Standard, 1865–1873*, Oxford: Oxford University Press.

Einzig, M. (1935) *World Finance 1914–1935*, New York: McMillan.

Elliott, S. (2008) "With Banks Feeling the Heat, One in South Carolina Goes to the Kitchen," *New York Times*, November 12, p. B.5.

Elon, A. (2002) *The Pity of It All, A History of Jews in Germany 1743–1933*, New York: Metropolitan Books, Henry Holt.

Emmett, B. (2003) *20:21 Vision, Twentieth Century Lessons for the Twenty First Century*, New York: Farrar, Strauss and Giroux.

Erlanger, S. (2008) "Sarkozy Stresses Global Financial Overhaul," *New York Times*, September 26.

Espinas, G. (1933) *Les Origines du Capitalisme: Sire Jehan Boinebroke, Patricien et Drapier Douaisien*, Lille: Bibliothèque de la société d'histoire du droit des pays flamands, picards et wallons.

Euromoney (1984) "The Great Deregulation Explosion," *Euromoney*, October, p. 55.

"Executive Pay Survey" (2006) *New York Times*, Sunday Business Section, April 9.

Faber, S. (2008) "The Super Rich," *CNBC Report*, July 20.

Fabricant, G. (2008) "When Citi Lost Sallie," *New York Times*, November 16, p. BU1.

Fair, D. and Raymond, R. (eds.) (1994) *The Competitiveness of Financial Institutions and Centers in Europe*, Boston: Klower Academic Publishers.

Fairbanks, J. K. (1992) *China, A New History*, Harvard: Harvard University Press.

Falkner, W. (1957) *The Town*, New York: Random House.

Fanfani, A. (1933) *Le origini dello spirito capitalistico in Italia*, Milano: Vita e Pensiero.

Fatouville, N. (1687) *Le Banqueroutier*, Paris.

Fay, S. (1996) *The Collapse of Barings*, New York, Norton and Sons.

FDIC (2004) *An Update on Emerging issues in Banking*. Online, available at: www.fdic. gov/bank/analytical/fyi/2004/030104fyi.html.

Fear, J. (2008) *Making Capitalism Respectable: The Political and Cultural Origins of German and American Corporate Governance 1873–1914*," Conference on Transatlantic Capitalism: Financial and Intellectual Flows, April 2–3.

Feiertag, O. and Margairaz, M. (eds.) (2003) *Politiques et Pratiques des Banques d'émission en Europe: XVIIe-XXe siècle*, Paris: Albin Michel.

Feinstein, C.H. (1995) *Banking, Currency and Finance in Europe between the Wars*, Oxford: Oxford University Press.

Ferguson, N. (1999) *The House of Rothschild: The World's Banker 1849–1999*, New York: Viking.

—— (2001) *Cash Nexus*, New York: Basic Books.

—— (2008) *Ascent of Money*, London: Penguin Press.

Ferris, P. (1984) *The Master Bankers' Controlling of the World's Finances*, New York: William Morrow.

Ferry, J. (1888) *Comptes fantastiques d'Haussmann*, Paris: Le Chevalier.

Feuilhade de Chauvin, T. de (1958) *Une Grande Banque de Dépôts: Le Crédit Lyonnais*, Paris: Editions de l'Epargne.

Fielding, H. (1999) *History of Tom Jones, A Foundling*, London: Wordsworth Editions Ltd.

"Financial Times Special Anniversary Issue" (2002) *Financial Times*, November.

"Financial Times Survey of Most Respected Companies" (2007) *Financial Times*.

Finel-Honigman, I. (1987) "A Historical Perspective of International Investors and Investments," in C. Beidleman (ed.) *The Handbook of International Investing*, Chicago: Probus Publishing.

—— (1988) "The Theme of the Banker, Financier, and Usurer in Literature," in J.C. Seigneuret (ed.) *Dictionary of Literary Themes and Motifs*, New York: Greenwood Press.

—— (1993a) "Popular Culture in the Global Economy: Antithesis or Reconciliation," in R. Dennehy and R. Sims (eds.) *Diversity and Differences in Organizations: Issues and Perspectives*, Westport, CT.: Quorum Books.

—— (1993b) "Socio History of French Banks and Banking: Role Model for Global Banking," in D. Ghosh (ed.) *The Changing Environment of International Financial Markets: Issues and Analysis*, New York: McMillan.

—— (ed.) (1999) *European Monetary Union Banking Issues: Historical and Contemporary Perspectives*, Stamford: JAI Press.

—— (2003) "Le Petit Euro Deviendra Grand, Happy Birthday Euro," *Council for European Studies Newsletter*, February.

Fitch Ratings (2007) *Country Report: Russian Banking System and Prudential Regulation*, New York and London: Fitch Ratings.

Fitzgerald, F. Scott (1925) *The Great Gatsby*, New York: C. Scribner.

Flandreau, M., Holtfrerich, C.L. and James, H. (eds.) (2003) *International Financial History in the Twentieth Century: System and Anarchy*, Cambridge, UK: Cambridge University Press.

Flaubert, G. (1951 [1869]) *Œuvres Tome I, II*, Paris: Bibliothèque de la Pléiade.

Flobert, P. (1716–1720) *Recherches sur les billets de la banque de Law*, London: Seligman Collection.

"Forbes Rich List" (2008) *Financial Times*, March 10.

Forrestier, V. (1996) *L'Horreur économique*, Paris: Fayard.

—— (2000) *Une étrange dictature*, Paris: Fayard.

Fovier, J. (1971) *Les Contribuables Parisiens à la Fin de la Guerre de Cent Ans*, Geneva: Droz.

France, A. (1908) *L'Ile des Pingouins*, Paris: Calman-Levy.

Fraser, S. (2005) *Every Man a Speculator: A History of Wall Street in American Life*, New York: Harper Collins.

Friedman, M. and Schwartz, A.J. (1971) *Monetary History of the United* States, 1867–1960, Princeton: Princeton University Press.

Frommer, J. and McCormick, J. (eds.) (1989) *Transformations in French Business, Political, Economic and Cultural Changes from 1981 to 1987*, New York: Quorum Books.

Furet, F. and Ozouf, M. (eds.) (1989) *Cultural Dictionary of the French Revolution*; trans. Arthur Goldhamme Jr., Cambridge, MA: Harvard University Press.

Furetiere, A. (1868 [1666]) *Le Roman Bourgeois*, Paris: E. Picard.

Galbraith, J.K. (1954) *The Great Crash, 1929*, New York: Time Incorporated Books.

—— (1975) *Money: Whence It Came, Where It Went*, Boston: Houghton Mifflin.

—— (1994) *A Journey Through Economic Time*, Boston: Houghton, Mifflin Company.

Gapper, J. (1995a) "Year that Killed the Global Dream," *Financial Times*, May 22.

—— (1995b) "Inspectors Ask If Top Staff Knew About the Problems," *Financial Times*, July 7.

—— (1995c) "Industry Lessons To Be Learned From Saga," *Financial Times*, July19.

Gasparino, C. (2005) *Blood on the Street*, New York: Free Press.

Gaxotte, P. (1938) *Le Siècle de Louis XV*, Paris: Fayard.

Geisst, C. (1997) *Wall Street: A History*, New York: Oxford University Press.

—— (2004) *Wall Street: A History: From Its Beginnings to the Fall of Enron*, New York: Oxford University Press.

Gellman, M. (2008) "A Letter to Madoff," *Newsweek*, December 31.

Germain, M. (1915) *L'Histoire du Crédit en France Sous Louis XIV*, Paris: Editions Sirey.

—— (1929) *Histoire Economique de la Nation Française*, Paris: Plon.

Gide, A. (1949) *Les Caves du Vatican*, Paris: Gallimard.

—— (1958) *Romans, Récits et Soties*, Paris: Bibliothèque de la Pléiade.

Gilbart, J. (1837) *The History and Principles of Banking*, London: Seligman Collection.

Gilbert, F. (1980) *The Pope, his Banker and Venice*, Cambridge, MA: Harvard University Press.

Giles, C. (2007) "UK Watchdog Faces Flak over Northern Rock," *Financial Times*, September 27.

Gille, B. (1967) *Histoire de la Maison Rothschild, Tome 1, 2*, Geneva: Droz.

—— (1970) *La Banque en France au 19eme Siècle*, Geneva: Droz.

Gloaguen, J. (1984) "Nationalisées: des Banques Trop Encadrées," *Le Nouvel Economiste*, April 2.

—— (1986) "Les Banquiers au Charbon," *Le Nouvel Economiste*, January 17.

"Globalization's New Cheerleader: Face value: Supachai Panitchpakdi, the WTO New Boss" (2002) *The Economist*, September 7.

Goallier, J.P. (1967) *Le Systeme Bancaire Français*, Paris: PUF.

Godechot, J. (ed.) (1970) *Les Constitution de la France depuis 1789*, Paris: Garnier-Flammarion.

Goethe, J.W. von (1879) *Faust Part II*, trans. B. Taylor, New York: Crowell-Collier Co.

Gogol, N. (1997) *Dead Souls*, trans. R. Pevear and L.Volokhonsky, New York: Vintage.

—— (1999) *The Collected Tales of Nicolai Gogol*, trans. R. Pevear, New York: Vintage.

Goldsmith, J. (1993) *The Trap*, New York: Carroll and Graf.

Goux, J.J. (1973) *Freud, Marx, Economie et Symbolique*, Paris: Editions du Seuil.

Gower, A. (1982) *Cashing In*, New York: Houghton Mifflin.

Graham, B. (2003) *The Intelligent Investor*, revised edition, New York: HarperBusiness.

Gray, F. du Plessix (1985) "The French Portrait of a Country through a Family," *New York Times Magazine*, October 13.

Gray, P. and Richards, S. (1994) *International Finance in the New World Order*, London: Pergamon Press.

Greenhouse, S. (1988a) "Making Europe a Mighty Market," *New York Times Sunday Business Section*, May 22.

—— (1988b) "On to 1992, the World Watches Europe, the Powers that will be," *New York Times Sunday Week in Review*, July 31.

Greenspan, A. (2007) *The Age of Turbulence: Adventures in a New World*, New York: Penguin Press.

Gross, J. (1988) "The New Greed Takes Center Stage," *New York Times*, January 3, p. 2.1.

Guillard, E. (1875) *Les Banques Athéniennes et Romaines, "Trapezites et Argentarii," suivis du Pacte de "Constitut en Droit Romain,"* Paris: Guillaumin.

Guerrera, F. and Beattie, A. (2009) "US Treasury to Take 36% Citi Stake," *Financial Times*, February 27.

Guimberteau, F. (1791) *Institution d'une Caisse nationale Tenant Lieu de Banque Nationale*, Paris: Seligman Collection.

—— (1799) *Réflexions sur le crédit public et sur l'établissement d'une banque*, Paris: Seligman Collection.

Guiral, P. (1976) *La Vie Quotidienne en France a l'Age d'Or du Capitalisme, 1852–1879*, Paris: Hachette.

Gup, B.E. (ed.) (2004) *Too Big to Fail: Policies and Practices in Government Bailouts*, Westport, CT: Praeger.

Haden-Guest, A. (2007) "Hedge Heaven and Hell," *Financial Times*, November 9.

Hagan, J. (2008) "The Perilous Rise and Perhaps Inevitable Fall of Zoe Cruz, Only the Men Survive," *New York Times Magazine*, May 5.

Hailey, A. (1975) *The Moneychangers*, New York: Doubleday.

Hall, B. (2009) "France Steps Up Drive to Sell Morality to Markets," *Financial Times*, January 3.

Hallenstein, I. (trans.) (1985) *Le Mercantilisme et la consolidation de l'économie du monde européen, 1600–1750*, Paris: Flammarion.

Halson, H.V. (1938) *Slump and Recovery, 1929–1937: A Study of World Economic Affairs*, Oxford: Oxford University Press.

Hamilton, W. (1980) *Money Should Be Fun*, Boston: Houghton Mifflin Company.

Hankey, T. (1887) *The Principles of Banking, Its Utility and Economy: With Remarks on the Working and Management of the Bank of England*, 4th edition, London: Effingham.

Hancock, D. (1975) "An Undiscovered Ocean of Commerce Laid Open: India, Wine and the Emerging Atlantic Economy, 1703-1813," in Bowen, H.V., Lincoln, M., Rigby, N. (eds.) *The World's of the East India Company*, Rochester, NY: Boydell Press with the University of Leicester, p 164.

Hansell, S. (2000) "Storied Bank Failed to Move With Times," *New York Times*, September 13.

Hardy, T. (2009) *Tess of the d'Urbervilles*, Oxford: Oxford World Classics.

—— (2009) *Jude the Obscure*, Oxford: Oxford World Classics.

Harsin, P. (1928) *Les doctrines monétaires et financières en France du XVI XVIII siècle*, Paris: Alcan.

—— (1933) *Crédit Public et Banque d'état du 16ieme au 18eme Siècle*, Geneva: Droz.
Harvey, J. (1870) *Usury, the Scourge of Nations*, London: Austin.
Hawley, C. (1955) *Cash McCall*, New York: Houghton Mifflin.
Hayek, F. (1949) *Individualism and Economic Order*, London: Routledge.
Hazera, J.C. (1987) "Privatisations: La Mécanique de la Generale," in *Le Nouvel Economiste*, June 19.
Heilbroner, R. (1989) "The Triumph of Capitalism," *New Yorker*, January 23.
—— (1993) *21st Century Capitalism*, New York: W.W. Norton & Company.
Henry, O. (1994) *The Best Short Stories of O. Henry*, New York: Modern Library.
Herodotus (1960) *Herodotus*, trans. A.D. Godley, vol. 1 London: William Heinemann.
Hincker, F. (1974) *Expériences bancaires sous l'Ancien Régime*, Paris: PUF.
Hofstadter, R. and Hofstadter, B.K. (1982) *Great Issues in American History*, New York: Vintage Books.
Holtfrerich, C.-L. (1989) "The monetary unification process in nineteenth century Germany," in Dececco, M., Giovannini, A. (eds.) *A European Central Bank?*, Cambridge, MA :Cambridge University Press.
Honigman, A.F. (2008) "ArtForum Berlin," November 13. Saatchi Blog, online, available at: www.saatchi-gallery.co.uk/blogon/art_news/ana_finel_honigman_reports_on_artforum_berlin/5083 (accessed April 17, 2009).
Hotchkiss, P. (1892) *Banks and Banking (1171–1892): A Historical Sketch*, New York and London: Knickerbocker Press.
Houellebecq, M. (2001) *Plateforme*, Paris: Flammarion.
Howatson, M.C. (1989) *The Oxford Companion to Classical Literature*, Oxford: Oxford University Press.
"How to Spend It" (2008) *Financial Times Magazine*, December 14.
HSBC History Wall (c.1895) *Image 1578*. Online, available at: www.hsbc.com/1/2/about-hsbc/group/history/hsbc-history-wall.
Hughes, J. and Mac Donald, S. (2002) *International Banking*, New York: Addison Wesley.
Hugo, V. (1967–1970) *Oeuvres Complètes*, Paris: Le Club français du livre.
Hunt, E.S. (1999) *A History of Business in Medieval Europe, 1200–1550*, Cambridge, UK: Cambridge University Press.
Hunt, J. (2008) "Guaranty Trust Morgan's Broadway Baby," *Financial History*, spring 2008.
"ICICI'S Kochhar Joins Elite Female Group" (2008) *Financial Times*, December 20.
"In Praise of Free Markets" (2008) *Financial Times*, September 27.
International Herald Tribune (1992, 1993, 1994, 1995) *French Company Handbook*, Neuilly Cedex: IHT.
"Islamic Banks Urged to Show West the Sharia way Forward" (2008) *Financial Times*, December 27.
Izraelewicz, E. (1983) "Les rescapes de la nationalisation," *L'Expansion*, March 18.
Jackson, K. (ed.) (1995) *The Oxford Book of Money*, Oxford: Oxford University Press.
James, H. (1877) *The American*, Boston: Houghton Mifflin.
Jannet, C. (1892) *Le Capital, la spéculation et la finance au XIXe siècle*, Paris: Plon.
Jeanneney, J.N. (1981) *L'Argent Cache*, Paris: Fayard.
—— (1981) *La Faillite du Cartel 1924–1926*, Paris: Editions du Seuil.
Jellinek, F. (1965) *The Paris Commune of 1871*, New York: Grosset and Dunlap.
Jonson, B. (2004) *Volpone*, New York: Kessinger Publishing.
Joret, D. (1867 [1451]) *Procès de Jacques Coeur, Argentier du Roi Charles VII*, Paris.

Judt, T. (2005) *Post War: A History of Europe since 1945*, New York: Penguin Press.

Juvenal (1958) *The Satires*, trans. R. Humphries, Bloomington: Indiana University Press.

Kafka, F. (1946 [1927]) *Amerika*, trans. E.O. Muir, New York: New Directions Publishing Co.

Kamensky, J. (2008) *The Exchange Artist*, New York: Viking.

Kay, J. (2008) "Bankers, Like Gangs, Just Get Carried Away," *Financial Times*, February 13.

Kennedy, P. (1987) *The Rise and Fall of Great Powers*, New York: Random House.

Keynes, J.M. (2006) *General Theory of Employment, Interest and Money*, New Delhi: Atlantic Publishers and Distributors.

Kindleberger, C. (1993) *A Financial History of Western Europe*, second edition, Oxford: Oxford University Press.

—— (2005) *Manias, Panics and Crashes, A History of Financial Crisis*, New York: John Wiley & Sons.

Kleinfield, N.R. (1984) *The Traders*, New York: Holt, Rinehart & Winston.

Kobrak, C. (2008) *Banking on Global Markets Deutsche Bank and the United States 1870 to the Present*, Cambridge, UK: Cambridge University Press.

Kobrin, R. (2007) "The Almighty Dollar: East European Jews, Money and Speculation in Gilded Age America," University of Pennsylvania Conference.

Kouwe, Z. (2008) "Financier is Found Dead in a Madoff Aftermath," *New York Times*, December 24.

Kramer, J. (1984) "Letter from Europe" *New Yorker*, July 26.

—— (1988a) *Europeans*, New York: Farrar, Strauss and Giroux.

—— (1988b) "Letter from Europe," *New Yorker*, May 30.

—— (1989) "Letter from Europe," *New Yorker*, February 13.

Kreinin, M. (2000) Speech, ITFA Conference.

—— (2006) *International Economics, A Policy Approach*, Ohio: Thomson Southwestern.

Kuisel, R. (1981) *Capitalism and the State in Modern France*, Cambridge, UK: Cambridge University Press.

Labrousse, E. (1933) *Esquisse du mouvement des prix et des revenus en France au XVIIIème siècle*, 2 vols., Paris: Dalloz.

Laclos, P. Choderlos de (1782) *Les Liaisons Dangereuses*, Paris: Flammarion.

Lacouture, J. (1973) *André Malraux*, Paris: Editions du Seuil.

—— (1982) *Leon Blum*, trans. G. Holoch, London: Holmes and Meier.

La Fontaine, J. de (1954) *Oeuvres Completes, Tome I Fables, Contes et Nouvelles*, Paris: Bibliotheque de la Pleiade.

Lancaster, H. (1945) *Sunset: A History of Parisian Drama in the Last Years of Louis XIV (1701–1715)*, Baltimore: Johns Hopkins Press.

Lanchester, J. (2008) "Melting into Air," *New Yorker*, November 10.

Landes, D.S. (1961) "The Old Bank and the New: The Financial Revolution of the Nineteenth Century," in F.M.-J. Crouzet, W.H. Chaloner, and W.M. Stem (eds.) *Essays in European Economic History 1789–1914*, London: Edward Arnold.

—— (1999) *The Wealth and Poverty of Nations*, New York: W.W. Norton & Company.

—— (2003) *The Unbound Prometheus: Technological Change and Industrial Development in Western Europe from 1750 to the Present*, Cambridge, UK: Cambridge University Press.

—— (2006) *Dynasties*, New York: Penguin Books.

Lang Lang (2008) "How To Spend It: Perfect Weekend," *Financial Times*, December 14.

Lapidus, M. (1997) *Understanding Russian Banking*, Kansas City: Mir House International.

Larbaud, V. (1913) *A.O. Barnabooth*, Paris: Gallimard.

Larivey, P. de (1579) *Le Esprits*, Paris.

Latham, E. (1964–1983) *The John Putnam Thatcher Series*, New York: Simon and Schuster.

—— (1971) "The Longer the Thread," New York: Pocket Books.

Law, J. (1934) *Oeuvres complètes*, P. Harsin (ed.) Paris: Editions Sirey.

"Leading Businesswomen in the Arab World" (2008) *Financial Times Special Report*, June 23.

Leahy, J. (2008) "ICICI Kochar Joins Elite Female Group," *Financial Times*, December 19.

Le Carre, J. (1963) *The Spy Who Came in from the Cold*, London: Coward-McCann Inc.

Lehman, H. (1991) *Holocaust and Shilmim, The Policy of Wiedergutmachung in the early 1950s*, occasional paper, no. 2, Washington, DC: German Historical Institute.

Lesage, A.-R. (1973 [1709]) *Turcaret*, Paris: Librairie Larousse.

Lefèvre, A. (1873) *Les Finances Particulières de Napoléon III*, Paris: Sagner.

LeGoff, J. (1956) *Marchands Et Banquiers Au Moyen Age*, Paris: PUF.

Lemaitre, F. (1966) *L'Auberge des Adrets, Robert Macaire*, Grenoble: Boissard.

Le Nouvel Observateur (1988) "Les Candidats de l'Argent," April 22–28.

Leonhardt, D. Rampell (2009) "How the Government Dealt With Past Recessions," *New York Times*, January 26.

Leroy, M. (1954) *Histoire des Idées Sociales en France*, Paris: Gallimard.

"Le Scandal Bancaire du Siecle" (1994) *Le Point*, May 26.

Lessing, G.E. (2004) *Nathan the Wise*, translated, edited and with an introduction by Ronald Schecter, Boston: Bedford-St Martin's.

Levy, J.P. (1967) *The Economic Life of the Ancient World*, Chicago: University of Chicago Press.

Levy-LeBoyer, M. (1964) *Les Banques Européennes et L'Industrialisation Internationale au 19ieme Siècle*, Paris: Presse Universitaire de France.

—— (1985) *L'Economie Française Au XIX Siècle, Analyse Macroéconomique*, Paris: Economica.

Lewis, M. (1989) *Liar's Poker Rising through the Wreckage on Wall Street*, New York: W.W. Norton & Company.

—— (2008–2009) "After the Fall, Greed, Stupidity and Really Bad Luck: How Wall Street Did Itself In," *Portfolio*, December–January.

Lewis, S. (1919) *Babbit*, New York: Grosset & Dunlap.

—— (1920) *Main Street: The Story of Carol Kennicot*, New York: Grosset & Dunlap.

Lex (2000) *Financial Times*, October 25.

Lillo, G. (1731) *The London Merchant or History of Georges Barnwell*, London.

Limbaugh, R. (2009) Conservative Party Convention in Washington, DC, February 28, CNN.

Lindsay, J. (1979) *Hogarth His Art and His World*, New York: Taplinger Publishing Company.

Lissagaray, P. (1886) *Histoire de la Commune de 1871*, trans. E. Aveli, London: Reeves and Turner.

Lo, A.W., MacKinlay, C. (2002) *A Non-Random Walk down Wall Street*, Princeton, NJ: Princeton University Press.

Lockhart, J. (1927) *Le Marche Des Changes De Paris*, Paris: Presses Universitaires de France.

Lowenstein, R. (2000) *When Genius Failed: The Rise and Fall of Long Term Capital Management*, New York: Random House.

—— (2005) "See a Bubble?," *New York Times Sunday Magazine*, June 5.

Lüthy, H. (1959) *La Banque Protestante en France de la Révocation de L'Edit de Nantes a la Révolution*, Paris: SEVPEN.

Luzzatto, G. (1969) "The Italian Economy in the First Decade after Unification", *Essays in European Economic History*, London: Edward Arnold.

McClelland, J.S. (ed.) (1971) *The French Right: From de Maistre to Maurras*, New York: Harper Torch Books.

McCutcheon, G.B. (1903) *Brewster's Millions*, New York: Grosset & Dunlap.

Machlup, F. (1960) *Essais de Sémantique Economique*, New Jersey: Prentice Hall.

Macleod, A. (1984) "In Search of the Belgian Dentist," *Euromoney*, June, p. 55.

Mackay, C. (1852) *Extraordinary Popular Delusions and the Madness of Crowds*, London: Natural Illustrated Library.

Ma, Jian. (2008) *Beijing Coma*, trans. F. Drew, New York: Farrar, Straus and Giroux.

Malkiel, B.G. (2003) *A Random Walk down Wall Street*, New York: W.W. Norton & Company.

Malraux, A. (1933) *La Condition Humaine*, Paris: Gallimard.

—— (1960) *Romans*, Paris: Bibliothèque de la Pléiade.

Mann, T. (1936) Buddenbrooks. Gesammelte werke. Vienna: Bermann Tisher Verlag.

Markham, J. (1988) "Au Revoir to Ideology," *New York Times*, April 10.

Marlowe, C. (1950) *The Alchemist; The Jew of Malta: Plays and Poems of Christopher Marlowe*. New York: E.P. Dutton Co.

Marquand, J.P. (1949) *Point of No Return*, Boston: Little, Brown & Co.

Marsy, C. (1890) *Nicolas Fouquet: Surintendant des Finances*, Paris: LeFebre.

Martin, F. (1865) *Stories of Banks and Bankers*, London: MacMillan.

Martin, P. (1995) "When New Into Old Won't Go," *Financial Times*, March 4/5.

Martinuzzi, E. and Prince, T. (2007) "Moscow Bankers get $7 Million Payday, Double New York Average," *Bloomberg News*, 14 May. Online, available at: www.bloomberg.com/apps/news?pid=20601109&refer=home&sid=arvBIGUV7HIo.

Marx, K. (1971a) *Das Kapital*, ed. Frederich Engel, Chicago: Regnery Gateway.

—— (1971b) *The Paris Commune of 1871*, trans., ed. Christopher Hitchens, London: Sidwich and Jackson.

Marx, K. and Engels, F. (1971) *Writings on the Paris Commune*, H. Draper (ed.), New York and London: Monthly Review Press.

Matthews. K. and Norton, S. (2008) *The EU Single Banking Market Programme: Fit for Purpose?*, London: Global Vision Perspective.

Mauriac, F. (1927) *Thérèse Desqueyroux*, Paris: Grasset.

Maurois, A. (1926) *Bernard Quesnay, Oeuvres complètes*, vol. 5, Paris: Grasset.

Maurras, C. (1933) *Dictionnaire Politique et Critique*, vol. 1, Paris: Cite des Liures.

Mayer, M. (1997) *The Bankers, The Next Generation*, New York: T.T. Dutton.

Mazower, M. (1998) *Dark Continent: Europe's Twentieth Century*, New York: Vantage Books.

"Meddling With European Banks" (1999) *The Economist*, July 10.

Melville, H. (1857) *The Confidence-Man: His Masquerade*, London: Longman, Brown, Green, Longmans and Roberts. Online, available at: http://etext.lib.virginia.edu/toc/modeng/public/MelConf.html.

Merkin, D. (2007) *New York Times*, October 14.

Michel, L. (1989) *La Commune*, Paris: Editions Stock Plus.

Michelet, J. (1965 [1842]) *Le Peuple*, Paris: Juillard.

"Middle East Banking and Finance Survey" (2008) *Financial Times Special Report*, November 25.

Miguard, J. (1795) *La France sauvée par ses impositions et ses finances*, Paris.

Mihm, S. (2007) *A Nation of Counterfeiters: Capitalists, Con Men and the Making of the United States*, Cambridge, MA: Harvard University Press.

—— (2008) *Financial History*, 90, spring 2008.

Miler, R. (1993) *Citicorp, the Story of a Bank in Crisis*, New York: McGraw Hill.

Milne R., Wilson, M. (2009) "Bitter End," *Financial Times*, January 10–11.

Minc, A. (1997) *La mondialisation heureuse*, Paris: Plon.

—— (2000) *WWW. capitalism.fr.* Paris: Bernard Grasset.

Mirabeau (1787) *Dénonciation de L'Agiotage*, Paris.

—— (1792) *Les Finances ou le Pot au Feu Nationale du Grand*, Paris: Seligman Collection.

Mitchell, C. (1933) Stock Exchange Practices Hearings, Pecora Committee, March.

Mitchell, M. (1936) *Gone With the Wind*, New York: Macmillan Publishers.

Mitterrand, F. (1993) *Antenne 2*, interview, October.

Molière (1965) *Œuvres Complètes*, Paris: Garnier-Flammarion.

Montaigne, M. de (1960) *Essais,* 2 vols., Paris: Classiques Garnier.

Montesquieu (1961[1720]), *Oeuvres completes*: *Lettres Persanes*, Paris: Bibliotheque de la Pleaide, letter 24.

Montella, C. (1987) *19, Bd. Des Italiens, Le Crédit Lyonnais: Culture et Fondation*, Paris: Editions Lattes.

Moreau, E. (1954) *Souvenirs d'un gouverneur de la Banque de France*, Paris: Editions Genin.

Morin, J. (1983) *Souvenirs d'un banquier français*, Paris: Denoel.

Morton, F. (1979) *A Nervous Splendor Vienna 1888–1889*, New York: Penguin Books.

—— (2009) "The Armageddon Waltz," *New York Times,* Sunday March 8, p. WK12.

Mosser, F. (1972) *Les Intendants des Finances au 18ieme Siècle (1715–1772)*, Geneva: Droz.

Moussa, P. (1988) "A quoi sert une banque d'affaires," *Banque*, no. 393, April.

Mrs Moneypenny (2008) "Women Bankers: Credit Where It's Due," *Financial Times*, November 1.

Muisit, G. le (1350) *C'est des Marchands.*

Murphy, A.L. (1997) "Investors in London's First Stock Market Boom," University of Leicester paper.

Museum of American Finance (2007) New York.

—— (2009a) Lecture, New York, March 3.

—— (2009b) Buttonwood Agreement document, exhibit, New York, January to March 20.

Myers, M. (1970) *A Financial History of the United States*, New York: Columbia University Press.

Nasar, S. (1991) "The Risks and the Benefits of Letting Sick Banks Die," *New York Times*, February 20, p. A.1.

Nash, N. (1987) "Treasury Now Favors Creation of Huge Banks," *New York Times*, June 7.

Negro, M. del, Kay, S. (2002) "Global Bank, Local Crisis, Bad News from Argentina," *Federal Reserve Bank of Atlanta Economic Review*, Washington, DC: Federal Reserve Bank of Atlants.

Nelson, K. (2008) "Money is in the Air," *New York Times*, April 6.

Nemirovsky, I. (2006) *Suite Française*, trans. S. Smith, New York: Vintage International.

Newsweek (2009) "We are all Socialists Now," *Newsweek,* February 16, cover.

New York Sun (2007) Architecture, July 26.

Niederhoffer, V. (1997) *The Education of a Speculator*, New York: Wiley.

Nignard, J. (1795) *La France sauvée par ses impositions et ses finances*, Paris.

Norris, F. (1928) *The Pit, A Story of Chicago (1902) Complete Works*, New York: Doubleday.

Nouveau compte rendu au Tableau historique des finances d'Angleterre (1784) London: Columbia University Seligman Collection 1779–1930.

Oldham, K. (1975) *Accounting Systems and Practices in Europe*, Farnborough, UK: Gower Press.

"On the Continent, on the Cusp" (2000) *New York Times*, May 14, p. 3:1.

O'Rourke, P.J. (2007) *P.J. O'Rourke on Wealth of Nations*, New York: Atlantic Monthly Press.

*Oxford English Dictionary (OED) Compact Edition (*1971) Oxford: Oxford University Press.

Paine, L.S., Knoop, C.-I. and Sesia. A. Jr. (2008) "Leading Citigroup" *Harvard Business Case Study* 9–308–001, April 18, Cambridge, MA: Harvard University Press.

Pamuk, O. (2005) *Istanbul: Memories and the City*, New York: Knopf.

Pauphilet, A. (ed.) (1952) *Historiens et Chroniqueurs du Moyen Age*, Paris: Bibliotheque de la Pleiade.

Perier, C. (1863) *La Situation Financière en 1863*, Paris: Dentu.

Périers, B. de (1965 [1558]) *Les nouvelles recréations et joyeux devis*, Paris: Bibliothèque de la Pléiade.

Petit-Dutaillis, G. (1964) *Le Crédit et les Banques*, Paris: Editions Sirey.

—— (1982) *Portraits de Banquiers*, Paris: Banque.

Petkanas, C. (2008) "The Hostess With theMostest," *New York Times Style Magazine*, November 9.

Petronius (1924) *Satyricon*, trans. Heseltine, London: William Heinemann.

Peyrefitte, A. (1994) *C'était de Gaulle*, Paris: Editions De Fallois, Fayard.

Philipps, K. (2009) "Financial Inquiries and the Pecora Legacy," The Caucus – The Politica and Government Blog of the *New York Times*, May 6.

Pilling, D. (2009) "Japan Harks Back To an Age of Innocence," *Financial Times*, March 4.

Piquet, J. (1936) *Des Banquiers au Moyen Age: Les Templiers*, Paris: Hachette.

—— (1939) *Les Templiers: Etude de Leurs Operations Financières*, Paris: Hachette.

Pirenne, H. (1963) *Histoire Economique et Sociale du Moyen Age*, Paris: Presse Universitaire de France.

Plender, J. (1994) "The Battling Old Lady," *Financial Times*, July 23/24.

Plessis, A. (1982a) *Régents et Gouverneurs de la Banque de France sous le Second Empire*, Geneva: Droz.

—— (1982b) *La Banque de France Et ses Deux Cents Actionnaires sous le Second Empire*, Geneva: Droz.

—— (1983) "La Bourse et la societe française du Second Empire," *Romantisme-Revue du Dix-neuvième siecle*, no. 40.

Poe, E.A. (1927) *The Business Man: The Works of Edgar Allen Poe in One Volume*, New York: P.F. Collier and Son Co.

Poorvliet, R. (1991) *Daily Life in Holland in the Year 1566 and The Story of My Ancestor's Treasure Chest*, trans. K. Ford Chest, New York: Harry N. Abrams.

Pope, A. (1752) *The Works of Alexander Pope Esq. in Nine Volumes Complete*, London: J. and P. Knapton, Lintot, Tonson and Draper and Bathurn.

Portfolio Business Intelligence (2007–2009) Conde Nast Portfolio.

Potut, G. (1964) *La Banque de France, du franc germinal au crédit contrôle*, Paris: Plon.

Prévost, A. Abbe de. (1965 [1731]) *Histoire du Chevalier des Grieux et de Manon Lescaut*, Paris: Garnier.

"Private Banking" (2007) *Financial Times Special Report*, June 17.

Prost, A. and Vincent, G. (ed.) (1991) *Private Lives*, trans. A. Goldhammer, Harvard: Harvard University Press.

Proust, M. (1989) *A la recherche du temps perdu*, Paris: Bibliothèque de la Pléiade.

Prudhon J (1893) *Manuel des Agents de change, banque, finance et commerce*, Paris: Rousseau.

Quint, Barbara Guilder (1983) *Wall Street Talk*, New York: Walker Books.

Quint, M. (1991) "Big Bank Merger To Join Chemical, Manufacturers," *New York Times*, July 16.

Rambure, D. (1984) "La Compensation des paiements en ecus," *Banque*, no. 443, October.

Rand, A. (1943) *The Fountainhead*, New York: Bobbs Merrill.

—— (1957) *Atlas Shrugged*, New York: Random House.

Rappard, W.E. (1966) *Economistes Genevois du 19ieme Siècle*, Geneva: Droz.

Reich, R. (1991) *The Work of Nations*, New York: Vintage Books.

Reid, E. (1963) "The Role of the Merchant Banks Today,"Address to the Institute of Bankers, London, May 15.

Renouard, Y. (1941) *Les Relations des Papes D'Avignon et des Compagnies Commerciales, 1316–1378*, Paris: Boccard.

Restif de la Bretonne, N. (1960) *Les Nuits de Paris*, Paris: Hachette.

Revel, J.F. (1970) *Ni Marx, ni Jésus*, Paris: Laffont.

—— (2002) *L'Obsession anti-americaine*, Paris: Plon.

Ricard, S. (1686) *Le Nouveau Negociant*, Bordeaux: Infolio.

Rich, F. (1987) "The Stage: 'Serious Money'," *New York Times*, December 4, p. C.3.

"Rich and Famous" (2008) *Financial Times*, March 6.

Richardson, S. (2007) *Clarissa Harlowe or the History of a Young Lady*, London: Bibliobooks.

Ries, P. (1994) "The PM's Friends," *International Economy*.

Rinder, L. (ed.) (2003) *The American Effect*, New York: Whitney Museum of American Art, Harry N. Abrams

"Rising Sun on Wall Street" (1987) *Business Week*, March 16.

Rivoire, J. (1985) *Histoire de la monnaie*, Paris: PUF, Coll. Que Sais-je.

Roosevelt, F. (1933) "On the Bank Crisis," Radio Address. Online, available at: www.fdrlibrary.marist.edu/031233.html.

Roover, R. de (1944) *Early Accounting Problems of Foreign Exchange*, Cambridge, UK: Cambridge University Press.

—— (1948) *Money Banking and Credit in Mediaeval Bruges*, Cambridge, MA: Harvard University Press.

—— (1949) *Gresham on Foreign Exchange*, Cambridge, UK: Cambridge University Press.

—— (1953a) *L'Evolution de la Lettre de Change*, Paris: Colin.

—— (1953b) *The Bruges Money Market Around 1400*, Cambridge, UK: Cambridge University Press.

—— (2005) with Murray, J., *Bruges, Cradle of Capitalism 1280–1390*, Cambridge, UK: Cambridge University Press.

Rosenberg, N. and Birdzell, L.E. (1986) *How the West Grew Rich: The Economic Transformation of the Industrial World*, New York: Basic Books.

Rosenblum, M. (1986) *Mission to Civilize the French Way*, New York: Harcourt, Brace, Jovanovich.

Rossant, M.J. (1987) "Baron Guy de Rothschild, Starting Over in America," *New York Times Magazine*, December 5.

Rotelli, C. (1982) *Le Origini Della Controversia Monetaria (1797–1844)*, Bologne: Il Malino.

Row, J. (2008) "Beijing Coma" Sunday Book Review, *New York Times*, July 13.

Rude, G. (1971) *Hanoverian London 1714–1808*, Berkeley: University of California Press.

Rueff, J. (1933) *La Reforme du Systeme Monétaire Internationale*, Paris: Plon.

Sabouret, A. (1987) *MM Lazard, Frères et Cie, Une Saga de la Fortune*, Paris: Oliver Orbin.

Sade, D.A.F. de (1791) *Justine ou les malheurs de la vertu*, Paris: Giraud.

—— (1968) *Juliette*, trans. A. Wainhouse, New York: Grove Press.

Safire, W. (2007) "On Language," *New York Times Magazine*, December 9.

—— (2008) "Moral Hazard," *Sunday New York Times Magazine*, April 6.

Sage, A. (2008) "SocGen Trader Will Not Be Made a Scapegoat," *New York Times*, February 5.

Saint-Germain, J. (1960) *Samuel Bernard, banquier du roi*, Paris: Hachette.

Saint-Simon, L.de Rouvroy de (1879–1928) *Mémoires de Saint-Simon*, Paris: Hachette.

Sakolski, A.M. (1932) *The Great American Land Bubble:* New York: Harper & Brothers.

Sampson, A. (1981) *The Money Lenders*, London: Hodder and Stoughton.

Sante, L. (2003) *The American Effect, Global Perspectives on the United States 1990–2003*, New York: Whitney Museum of American Art.

Sartre, J.P. (1971) *L'Idiot de la Famille: Gustave Flaubert de 1821–1857*, Paris: Gallimard.

Savary des Bruslons, J. (1741) *Dictionnaire universel de commerce*, Paris: Veuve Estienne.

Savary, T. (1697) *Le Parfait negociant*, Paris: Veuve Estienne.

Say, L. (1882) "Politique financière de la France," *Journal des Economistes*.

Schama, S. (1987) *The Embarrassment of Riches: An Interpretation of Dutch Culture in the Golden Age*, New York: Random House.

Schneider, S.C., Barsoux, J-L. (1997) *Managing Across Cultures*, New Jersey: Prentice Hall College Div.

Schultz, H. (2003) "Economic Nationalism in East Central Europe in the Nineteenth and Twentieth Century," Frankfurt-am-Main: Frankfurt Research Project.

Schwartz, N.D. and Bennhold, K. (2008) "In France, the Heads No Longer Roll," *New York Times*, February 17.

Scott, W.R. (1910–1912) *The Constitution and Finance of English, Scottish and Irish Joint Stock Companies*, 3 vols., Cambridge, UK: Cambridge University Press.

Sedaine M.-J. (1880) *Le Philosophe Sans le Savoir*. Paris, Librairie des Bibliophiles.

Sedillot, R. (1979) *Histoire du franc*, Paris: Editions Sirey.

See, H. (1929) *Esquisse dune histoire économique et sociale de la France*, Paris: Alcan.

Servan-Schreiber, J.J. (1967) *Le Defi Americain*, Paris: Denoel.

"Sex and Money: Wealthy Women" (2007) *The Economist*, June 16.

Shakespeare (1974) *The Riverside Shakespeare, The Complete Plays and Poems of William Shakespeare*, Boston: Houghton Mifflin.

Shaw, G.B. (1958) *Saint Joan, Major Barbara, Androcles the Lion*, New York: Modern Library.

Shell, M. (1982) *Money Language and Thought*, Berkley: University of California Press.

Sherwood, S. (2007) "Where To Go in 2008: Luxury Destination – Moscow: Travel," *New York Times*, December 9.

Shleifer, A. (2000) *Inefficient Markets: An Introduction to Behavioural Finance*, Oxford: Oxford University Press.

Shull, B. (1993) *The Limits of Prudential Supervision: Economic Problems, Institutional Failure and Competence*, intro. Hyman Minsky, New York: Jerome Levy Economics Institute, Bard College, no. 5.

—— (2005) *The Fourth Branch: The Federal Reserve's Unlikely Rise to Power and Influence*, London: Praeger.

Siebert, M. (2002) *Changing the Rules: Adventures of a Wall Street Maverick*, New York: Simon and Schuster.

Siesic, P. (1992) "L'Histoire de la Stabilisation Poincaré," *Banque De France Bulletin Trimestriel*, no. 84.

Silk, L. (1988) "Is Wall Street as Bad as It Is Painted," *New York Times*, January 3, p. 2.20.

Simiand, F. (1934) *La Monnaie, Réalité Sociale*, Paris: Annales Sociologiques.

Simmel, G. (1978 [1900]) *The Philosophy of Money*, Boston: Routledge and Kegan Paul.

Sinclair, U. (1908) *The Money Changers*, New York: John Long.

Singer, M. (1985) *Funny Money*, New York: Knopf.

Smith, A. (1999) *An Inquiry into the Nature and Causes of the Wealth of Nations*, edited by A. Skinner, New York: Penguin Classics.

Smith, J. (1796) "An Examination of Mr. Paine's "Decline and Fall of the English System of Finance," in *A Letter to a Friend*, London: G.G. and J. Robinson.

—— (1990) "Britain's Labour Party Plans a Post Thatcher Government," *International Economy*, June–July.

Smith, T. (1999a) *Topper*, New York: Modern Library.

—— (1999b) *Topper Takes a Trip*, New York: Modern Library.

Soignac, F. (1790) *Nouveau et vrai moyen de rétablir en Finance l'aisance et la félicité ou procès du plan d'une Banque nationale uniquement en espèces qui a pour base la maxime reçue*, Marseille.

Solomon, D. (2005) "Questions for Carl Icahn", *New York Times Magazine*, June 5.

"Special Report Private Banking" (2007) *Financial Times*, June.

Spinelli, F. and Fratianni, M. (1991) *Storia Monetari d'Italia, L'Evoluzione del Sistema Monetario et Bancario*, Milan: Mondardori Editore.

Spooner, F. (1956) *L'Economie Mondiale Et Les Frappes Monétaires En France*, Paris: Colin.

Sraeel, H., and Scott, J. (2006) "The 25 Most Powerful Women In Banking, A Celebration of Excellence" *US Banker*, October 23.

Stead, C. (1966 [1938]) *House of All Nations*, New York: Holt Rinehart, Winston.

Steele Jordan, J. (2000) *The Great Game: The Emergence of Wall Street as a World Power: 1653–2000*, New York: Simon & Schuster.

Steele, R. and Addison, J. (2004) *Spectator: 1711-1712*, vols. 1–3, Project Gutenberg. Online, available at: www.gutenberg.org/etext/1230.

Steinbeck, J. (1936) *In Dubious Battle*, New York: Modern Library.

Stendhal (1960 [1830]) *Le Rouge et le Noir*, Paris: Editions Garnier Frères.

Stern, F. (2006) *Five Germanys I Have Known*, New York: Farrar, Strauss and Giroux.

Sterne, L. (1979) *Tristam Shandy*, New York: W.W. Norton Critical Edition.

Sterngold (1986) "New Rivals Aside, Wall Street Still Calls the Tune," *New York Times*, October 9.

Stevens, M. (1997) "On the Money: Cartoons from the New Yorker," *New Yorker*, May 19.

Stevenson, J. (2008) "Ice King," *New York Times*. Online, available at: www.nytimes.com/2008/12/06/opinion/06opart.html?_r=1 (accessed March 22, 2009).

Stevenson, R. (1998) "Financial Services Heavyweights Try Do-It-Yourself Deregulation," *New York Times*, April 7.

Stewart, J.B. (1991) *Den of Thieves*, New York: Simon & Schuster.

Stiller, J (2008) "The Thrift Movement in America 1909–1920," *Financial History*, 90, spring 2008.

Storey, G. (2002) "Two Centuries of Bulls and Bears," *Seaport Magazine*, fall.

Strouse, J (1998). "The House of Morgan," *New Yorker*, November 23.

Styne, J. (1949) "Diamonds are a Girl's Best Friend."

Sutherland, J. (ed.) (1975) *The Oxford Book of Literary Anecdotes*, London: Oxford University Press.

"Survey of Most Respected Companies" (2007) *Financial Times*, April.

Swarte, V. (1893) *Un banquier du trésor royal au XVIIIème siècle: Samuel Bernard, sa vie, sa correspondance 1651–1739*, Paris: Berger Levravit et Cie.

Swift, J. (1966) *Selected Prose and Poetry*, New York: Holt Rinehart, Winston.

Szramkiewicz, R. (1974) *Les Régents et Censeurs de la Banque de France*, Geneva: Droz.

Tamaki, N. (1995) *Japanese Banking, A History 1859–1959*, Cambridge, UK: Cambridge University Press.

Tawney, R.H. (1953) *Religion and the Rise of Capitalism*, New York: Mentor.

Taylor, M.C. (2004) *Confidence Games, Money and Markets in a World without Redemption*, Chicago: University of Chicago Press.

Taylor, G.and Lavagnino, J. (eds.) (2008) *Thomas Middleton: The Collected Works and Companion Two Volume Set*, Oxford: Oxford University Press.

Teichman, G. (2004) *Sal. Oppenheim jr. & Cie-Geschichte einer Bank und einer Familie*, Koln: Bacht Grafische Betreibe und Verlag.

Tendron, R. (1983) "Les Cowboys de Wall Street," *L'Expansion*, June 19–30.

Tett, G. (2008) "A Lack of Trust Spells Crisis in Every Financial Language," *Financial Times*, March 17.

Thackeray, W.M. (1906) *Vanity Fair, A Novel Without a Hero*, London, Edinburgh: Thomas Nelson and Sons.

"The Bank, the Studio, the Mogul and the Lawyers" (1993) *The Economist*, London, January 23, p. 4.

"The Florin in Your Pocket" (1995) Editorial, *Financial Times*, September 15.

"The Giants Retrench, After Major Losses Banks No Longer Want to Be Money Centers But Regionals" (1989) *Business Week*, April 3.

"The King of Wall Street" (1985) *Business Week*, December 9.

"The Traders Take Charge" (1984) *Business Week*, February 20.

"The Worlds Largest Companies" (2002) *Financial Times*, May 10.

"The Worlds Largest Companies" (2003) *Financial Times*, May 27.

"The Worlds Largest Companies" (2004) *Financial Times*, May 28.

"The Tokyo Summit has Laid the First Cornerstone of a New International Economic Regime" (1986) *L'Expansion*, May 16.

Thiers, A. (1903) *Notes et Souvenirs, 1870–1873*, Paris: Calman-Levy.

Thierry, A. (1961 [1848]) *Recits des Temps Merovingiens*, Paris: Classiques Larousse.

Tilly, R. (2003) *Geld Und Kraft In Der Wirtschaftgeschicgte*, Stuttgart: Steiner.

Tocqueville, A. de (1981) *De la Democracie en Amerique*, vol. 2, Paris: GF-Flammarion.

Todisco, U. (1969) *Le Personnel de la Cour des Comptes, 1807–1830*, Geneva: Droz.

Traub, J. (2007) "The Measures of Wealth," *New York Times*, October 14.

Travers, P.L. (1934) *Mary Poppins*, London: Harper Collins.

Treaty on European Union, The Maastricht Treaty (1993) Office for Official Publications of the European Communities, December.

Trollope, A. (1995) *The Way We Live Now*, New York: Penguin Classics.

Truell, C. (1997) *New York Times*, September 25.

Twain, M. (1905) *One Million Pound Bank Note: Complete Works*, New York: Collier.

Uchitelle, L. (2007) "The Richest of the Rich, Proud of a New Gilded Age," *New York Times*, July 15, p. 1.

Ulrich, L. (1991) *Good Wives: Image and Reality in the Lives of Women in Northern New England, 1650-1750*, New York: Vintage Books, p. 37-38.

Union Prayerbook for Jewish Worship (1960) New York: Central Conference of American Rabbis, part II.

United Nations Interaction Council (1991) *The Role of Central Banking in Globalized Financial Markets*, April.

University of California (1979) *The Dawn of Modern Banking*, ed. Center for Medieval and Renaissance Studies, UCLA, New Haven: Yale University Press.

Usher, A.P. (1943) *The Early History of Deposit Banking in Mediterranean Europe*, Cambridge, MA: Harvard University Press.

Vachon, D. (2007) *Mergers ands Acquisitions*, New York: Riverhead Books.

Valladao, A.G.A. (1993) *Le XXIe siecle sera americain*, Paris: La Decouverte.

Valles, J. (1857) *L'Argent par un homme de lettres, devenu homme de la Bourse, Rentier, Agioteur, Millionnaire*, Paris: Ledoyen.

—— (1938) *Souvenirs D'un Etudiant Pauvre*, Paris: Gallimard.

—— (1985) *Œuvres complets*, R. Bellet (ed.), Paris: Fayard.

—— (1970) *Le Bachelier*, E. Carassus (ed.), Paris: Garnier Flammarion.

Vigne, M. (1981) *Le Banque à Lyon du 15ieme au 18ieme Siècle*, Geneva: Droz.

Vilar, P. (1976) A *History of Gold and Money 1450–1920*, Barcelona: Anel.

Virgil (2006) *The Aeneid*, trans. Robert Fagles, New York: Viking.

Voltaire (1961) *Melanges*, Paris: Bibliotheque de la Pleiade.

Wall Street Journal (1999) "Dow Industrials Shift May Bring Increase in Index-Based Funds: Shuffling of the Blue Chips," *Wall Street Journal*, October 27, p. C15.

"Wall Street's Unreal World" (1998) Editorial, *Financial Times*, April 7.

Walter, I. and Smith, R.C. (2000) *High Finance in the Euro-Zone: Competing in the New European Capital Market*. London and New York: Financial Times and Prentice Hall.

Warburg, P. (1907) "Defects and Needs of Our Banking System,"*New York Times*, January 6.

Warren, R.P. (1943) *At Heaven's Gate*, New York: Random House.

Wasserman D. (2009) "Careful! That Stuff's Tainted with Liberalism," *Boston Globe*, March 2. Online, available at: www.boston.com/bostonglobe/editorial_opinion/outof-line/2009/03/gop_and_jobless.html.

Weber, E. (1991) *My France, Politics, Culture, Myth*, Cambridge, MA: Belknap Press of Harvard University Press.

Weber, M. (1961) *General Economic History*, New York: Charles Scribner.

Weber, N.F. (2007) *The Clarks of Cooperstown*, New York: Knopf.

Werblowsky, Z. and Wigoder, G. eds. (1966) *The Encyclopedia of the Jewish Religion*, New York: Holt, Rinehart and Winston.

Wharton, E. (1985) *Novels: The House of Mirth, the Reef, The Age of Innocence*, New York: Library of America.

Whitney, C. (1993) "Blaming the Bundesbank," *New York Times Magazine*, October 17, p. 6.19.

Wheatcroft, G. (2007) "Capitalism Turns on 'Poor Conrad'," *Financial Times*, July 17.

Wheatly, J. (2009) "Brazil President Blames White People for Crisis," *Financial Times*, March 27.

"Why Free Markets Must Be Defended" (2008) Editorial, *Financial Times*, December 27.

Wilkins, M. (1989) *History of Foreign Investment in the United States*, Cambridge, MA: Harvard University Press.

Wikipedia (n.d.) online, available at: http://en.wikipedia.org/wiki/Scrooge_McDuck#Wealth (accessed July 15, 2009).

Wolf, M. (2003) *Why Globalization Works*, New Haven: Yale University Press.

—— (2007) "Unfettered Finance Is Fast Reshaping the Global Economy," *Financial Times*, June 18.

Wolfe, T. (1987) *Bonfire of the Vanities*, New York: Farrar, Strauss and Giroux.

—— (2007) "The Pirate Pose," *Portfolio*, May. Online, available at: www.portfolio.com/executives/features/2007/04/16/The-Pirate-Pose.

"Work in Progress, A Survey of European Business and the Euro" (2001) *The Economist*, London, December 1.

Wright, R. (2000) "Women and Finance in the Early National U.S.," *Essays in History* vol. 42, Corcoran Department of History at the University of Virginia.

Wroe, A. (1995) *A Fool and His Money, Life in a Partitioned Town in Fourteenth Century France*, New York: Hill and Wang.

Zola, E. (1891) *L'Argent*, Paris: Fasquelle.

—— (1972) *L'Argent*, Paris: Collection Folio, Gallimard.

Index

Printed in the USA/Agawam, MA
July 14, 2015

619198.027